JUDICIAL REVIEW OF
COMMERCIAL REGULATION

Judicial Review Of Commercial Regulation

JAIME ARANCIBIA

OXFORD
UNIVERSITY PRESS

OXFORD
UNIVERSITY PRESS

Great Clarendon Street, Oxford OX2 6DP

Oxford University Press is a department of the University of Oxford.
It furthers the University's objective of excellence in research, scholarship,
and education by publishing worldwide in

Oxford New York

Auckland Cape Town Dar es Salaam Hong Kong Karachi
Kuala Lumpur Madrid Melbourne Mexico City Nairobi
New Delhi Shanghai Taipei Toronto

With offices in

Argentina Austria Brazil Chile Czech Republic France Greece
Guatemala Hungary Italy Japan Poland Portugal Singapore
South Korea Switzerland Thailand Turkey Ukraine Vietnam

Oxford is a registered trade mark of Oxford University Press
in the UK and in certain other countries

Published in the United States
by Oxford University Press Inc., New York

© Jaime Arancibia, 2011

The moral rights of the authors have been asserted

Crown Copyright material reproduced under Class Licence
Number C01P0000148 with the permission of OPSI
and the Queen's Printer for Scotland

Database right Oxford University Press (maker)

First published 2011

British Library Cataloguing in Publication Data
Data available

Library of Congress Control Number
2010941953

Typeset by Newgen Imaging Systems (P) Ltd., Chennai, India
Printed in Great Britain
on acid-free paper by
CPI Antony Rowe, Chippenham, Wiltshire

ISBN 978–0–19–960907–9

1 3 5 7 9 10 8 6 4 2

For Carolina

Foreword

When I began to practise public law in 1980, judicial review cases typically concerned immigration, welfare, and prison law. The defendants were central or local government. And judicial review was seen as a Cinderella subject, a means by which the poor and the needy could be helped to go to the ball, or at least be given a fair opportunity to do so.

In the last thirty years, public law has come of age. Individuals and corporations have recognized that public law is a powerful weapon for challenging the decisions of regulators who are thought to have breached legal requirements, procedural or substantive. Judicial review today is as likely to involve the grievance of a multinational company that a statutory body has refused it a telecommunications licence as a complaint about a failure to provide a housing benefit. The attention paid to Cinderella in the field of regulatory law, and the sums spent on her, have helped her develop into a Princess of the legal system, the subject of a rich body of case-law and academic analysis which has made her into a more mature and interesting legal concept.

But judicial review in the context of the regulation of economic activities has, hitherto, involved less intrusive standards of judicial supervision than can be found in many other contexts. Judges confer a broad margin of discretion on commercial regulators, and are reluctant to find that they have acted unreasonably or disproportionately. This conservatism has, on occasions, even affected the court's approach to complaints about the fairness of the procedure or the regulator's interpretation of the rules conferring its jurisdiction or limiting its powers.

Dr Arancibia criticizes this judicial caution. He argues for more intensive standards of judicial review, at all stages of consideration of the claim, from standing through to remedies. He has chosen his subject well. It is one of the central issues in the development of the next generation of judicial review principles: should judges continue to accord a generous degree of discretion to economic regulators by reason of their expertise and statutory responsibilities, or is this a failure by the judiciary to perform their statutory responsibilities, and apply their expertise, to maintain high legal standards in economic regulation? Dr Arancibia's command of all the relevant legal materials and the lucidity and integrity of his analysis raise the level of the debate to new heights. His arguments cannot be ignored.

I first met Dr Arancibia at a conference on judicial review in Hong Kong in December 2008 organized by the Chinese University of Hong Kong and the University of Cambridge. The proceedings at the conference, and in particular Dr Arancibia's contribution, emphasized the extent to which the problems of judicial review, and progress towards the solutions, are international. Legal ideas do not stop at passport control. Academic and practising lawyers from all jurisdictions will learn much from Dr Arancibia's work.

Lord Pannick QC

Blackstone Chambers,
Temple,
London
28 August 2010

Preface and Acknowledgements

Ubi Emporium ibi iudices. Some markets need regulation to be perfect and judges to be fair. The principle that the exercise of regulatory power must be subject to a proper degree of judicial scrutiny is firmly rooted in the rule of law and the rights of market players. However, UK courts have traditionally adopted a rather different approach to commercial regulation. They say that there are good reasons in this context for taking a non-interventionist stance towards the substantive activities of the regulator. This book delves into the debate on this issue by providing a critical view of the courts' deferential attitude and advocating a more intensive form of review based on the principle of proportionality which is more satisfactory in terms of individual justice.

This task is undertaken in three principal stages. First, the deferential approach of the courts is articulated and substantiated. It is explained that it is particularly based on the regulator's expertise and institutional autonomy, and the demands of administrative efficiency, which would prevent the courts from interfering with the regulator's decision, interpretation of rules and findings of facts. Secondly, it is argued that this doctrine seems to be inconsistent with relevant values of English public law which protect individuals from capricious and arbitrary executive action. In particular, it seriously affects the right of the applicant to obtain an independent assessment of the validity of the impugned decision by a court which acts as ultimate arbiter of law. Finally, it is contended that close supervision over decisions which alter or determine the operation of markets is necessary to reach a level of judicial control that is consistent with the requirements of fairness and reasonableness in this area and with proper respect for the rights of the parties involved. This alternative approach is particularly founded on the principle of proportionality, which entails a greater judicial attenuation of administrative autonomy in order to ensure that actions do not go beyond what it is strictly necessary to achieve the desired outcome.

This book is based on my doctoral thesis submitted to the Faculty of Law at the University of Cambridge. The research was made possible through the support of the Chilean government, the Chevening Programme of the UK Foreign and Commonwealth Office, the Cambridge Overseas Trust and Universidad de los Andes (Chile) to all of whom I am very grateful. I am enormously indebted to Professor Christopher Forsyth for his wise and stimulating supervision of my research work, his insightful comments on the drafts of the manuscript, and his unflagging support of the publication of this book. I would also like to recall my special gratitude to Carolina, my wife, without whose patient support, and great encouragement this project would not have been possible. The book is dedicated to her.

Special thanks are due to Dr. Mark Elliott of Cambridge University for reading the thesis, his very helpful comments on it and his generous sharing of time to discuss some problems with me. I am also grateful to Lord Pannick QC for writing the foreword; to Oxford University Press for their advice and assistance in the publication process, and to the magical town of Cambridge, where academic dreams come true.

                                                                Jaime Arancibia

September 2010

Contents

Table of Cases

UNITED KINGDOM

OTHER JURISDICTIONS

1

Judicial Review of Commercial Regulation

1. Judicial Review and the Administrative State in Context

The basic idea that courts must police the boundaries of administrative power is firmly based on the constitutional principle of the rule of law. The function thus ascribed to the judiciary *vis-à-vis* the limitation of executive actions is crucial to promote the virtues of legality, fairness, and reasonableness which this principle has traditionally embodied.[1]

British courts have long been required to vindicate these norms on review in order that citizens are protected from unlawful decision-making in the public sphere. Of course, this endeavour is not devoid of theoretical and practical issues, as it presents the court with countervailing forces which it must seek to balance. Indeed the legal positions of Parliament, the government, the courts, and private parties in judicial review cases each contribute to the intricate combination of arguments which form the background against which the judge applies the law.

More specifically, it can be argued that differences in the judicial emphasis on these positions have explicitly furnished an intelligible justification for the solution concerning most of the controversial issues in the field, such as those relating to the foundations of judicial review, standing to apply, scope of supervision, effectuation of legislative intention, non-statutory intervention, grounds of review, and intensity.

In considering the relevance and content of these criteria, the courts have also struggled to deal with the manner in which administrative law evolves over time. This development relates, for instance, to the dynamic influence exerted by European law, the heightened status of human rights, more complex statutory regulation, and fluid changes in the structures of government.

---

[1] This proposition is uncontroversial and it has been recognized by many distinguished authors. See, for example, Dicey, Albert V., *An Introduction to the Study of the Law of the Constitution*, (London: Macmillan, 1885) especially chapters I, IV, XII and XIII; Raz, Joseph, *The Authority of Law*, (Oxford: Oxford University Press, 1979) 210–221; Jowell, J., 'The Rule of Law Today', in *The Changing Constitution*, J. Jowell and D. Oliver (eds.), (Oxford: Oxford University Press, 1994) 17–23; Craig, Paul, 'Formal and substantive conceptions of the Rule of Law: An analytical framework' [1997] *Public Law*, 467–487; Allan, Trevor, 'The Rule of Law as the Foundation of Judicial Review', in *Judicial Review and the Constitution*, Christopher Forsyth (ed.), (Oxford: Hart Publishing, 2000) 419; Woolf, Lord H. 'The Rule of Law and a Change in the Constitution' [2004] 63(2) *Cambridge Law Journal*, 317–329; and Bingham, Sir T. 'The Rule of Law' [2007] 66(1) *Cambridge Law Journal*, 67–85.

In light of this sophisticated array of arguments, there is little doubt that, while institutional and legal principles can guide the court's exercise of supervisory supervision, they are not sufficiently exact to allow it to determine the precise approach which should be adopted in every context. The theoretical framework which permits that approach to be justified also requires the judge to evaluate the characteristics of the particular legal environment in which the decision-making process has been conducted. Consequently, it has become a settled principle of British and European law that the application of different standards of judicial scrutiny in a public law case depends upon the subject matter at hand.[2] As Lord Steyn said in *Daly*: 'in law, context is everything'.[3]

Context-sensitive analysis therefore can and should be harnessed to serve a better understanding of the development of any model of supervision. If judicial control is not to be likened to insensitive and inaccurate proceedings in which legal nuances are regrettably overlooked, then it must be rationalized in terms of subject-matter. Although this is still a very general consideration, it is one which crystallizes in the purpose of this book. In particular, by acknowledging the need to give contextual validation to the manner in which oversight powers are exercised, the above-mentioned principle may enhance thematic research and scholarship in the area of judicial review. The present work, therefore, attempts to undertake such an analysis within the specific context of commercial regulation, to which we now turn.

2. Judicial Review in the Commercial Context

There are infinite ways in which economic activities of the individual may be affected by bodies performing public functions. Although a significant number of these decisions are capable of coming before the courts in judicial review proceedings, not all of these challenges can be included within the narrower phenomenon of judicial review in the commercial context. What really makes this subject distinguishable from other aspects of judicial review is that it is essentially and directly concerned with the development and protection of economic activities,[4] that is to say, it deals with applications against public decisions which have a significant impact on the operation of markets through command and control.[5] Thus, it can

---

[2] See generally Laws, Sir John, 'Wednesbury', in *The Golden Metwand and the Crooked Cord*, C.F. Forsyth and I. Hare (eds.), (Oxford: Oxford University Press, 1998) 313; De Búrca, Gráinne, 'The Principle of Proportionality and its Application in EC Law' [1993] 13 *Yearbook of European Law*, 105; Elliott, Mark, 'The Human Rights Act 1998 and the Standard of Substantive Review' [2001] 60(2) *Cambridge Law Journal*, 312–315; and Clayton, Richard, 'Principles for Judicial Deference' [2006] 11(2) *Judicial Review*, 129–130.

[3] *R v. Secretary of State for the Home Department, ex p Daly* [2001] U.K.H.L. 26, [2001] 2 A.C. 532 at [32]. See also the dictum of Sir Thomas Bingham in *R v. Ministry of Defence, ex p Smith* [1996] Q.B. 517, at 554; the dictum of Lord Hope of Craighead in *R v. Secretary of State for the Home Department, ex p Launder* [1997] 3 All E.R. 992; the dictum of Laws LJ in *R v. Secretary of State for the Home Department, ex p Amjad Mahmood* [2001] H.R.L.R. 14; and in *International Transport Roth GmbH v. Secretary of State for the Home Department* [2002] E.W.C.A. Civ 158, paragraph 76.

[4] Engelman, Philip, *Commercial Judicial Review*, (London: Sweet & Maxwell, 2001), 3.

[5] This is Prosser's core conception of market regulation, which is also close to the definitions used by many economists, industries, and in popular debate. Prosser, Tony, *Law and Regulators*, (Oxford: Clarendon Press, 1997) 4.

be differentiated from other areas of judicial review such as immigration, health, education, housing, planning, and prisoner rights which, although they may have a considerable effect on economic activities, are not principally concerned with commercial decisions.

Nevertheless, it has to be emphasized that there is an inevitable overlap in certain cases arising in both commercial and other contexts. For example, there have been instances of decision-making involving both economic interests and international sanctions,[6] safety of life at sea,[7] and the protection of health.[8] For this reason, it seems complex to attempt a definition of the subject which would provide a pristine demarcation between commercial cases and the rest. However, despite this difficulty in accurately identifying the boundaries of judicial review in the market context, secondary sources provide us with a relatively workable criterion based on the authority's function. In this sense, commercial judicial review is concerned with the supervision of those bodies responsible for the regulation of economic activities.[9]

There are, in fact, a remarkable number of governmental departments and independent agencies empowered to oversee the efficient working of different markets such as TV and radio broadcasting,[10] financial services,[11] public utilities,[12]

---

[6] See *R v. The Treasury and The Bank of England, ex p Centro-Com (SRL)* [1994] The Times, 27 May, concerning the implementation of the United Nations Security Council Resolution 757 which prohibits any person from supplying or delivering any goods to a person connected with Serbia or Montenegro, in response to the tragic events which had been taking place in Yugoslavia.

[7] See *R v. Department of Transport, ex p Presvac Engineering Ltd*, [1991] The Times, 10 July. In that case Presvac Engineering, a company which specializes in the manufacture of valves for ship, cargo and bunker tanks, sought to challenge a certificate issued by the Secretary of State for Transport which certified that Martin valves (Presvac's competitor) comply with regulations laid pursuant to the International Convention for the Safety of Life at Sea, 1974. See also *R v. Secretary of State for Social Services, ex p Wellcome Foundation* [1988] 2 All E.R. 684. In 1998, this Department underwent a de-merger, creating freestanding departments for Health and Social Security. The latter merged into the Department for Work and Pensions in 2001.

[8] See *R v. Secretary of State for Health, ex p United States Tobacco International Inc.* [1991] 3 W.L.R. 529. In this case the applicants sought judicial review of the validity of the Oral Snuff (Safety) Regulations 1989, which prohibited persons from supplying 'oral snuff', a substance manufactured from tobacco plants, on the ground of its possible carcinogenic effects.

[9] Gordon, Richard, *Judicial Review: Law and Procedure*, 2nd edn., (London: Sweet & Maxwell, 1996), 246. See also Black, J., Muchlinski, T. and Walker, P. (eds.), *Commercial Regulation and Judicial Review*, (Oxford: Hart Publishing, 1998) 1–17; Engelman, (as above n. 4), 3–46; Lidbetter, Andrew, 'Judicial Review in the Company and Commercial Context' [1995] 10 *Butterworths Journal of International Banking and Financial Law*, 63–70.

[10] The Office of Communications (OFCOM), established by the Office of Communications Act 2002 and empowered under the Communications Act 2003.

[11] a) The Financial Services Authority. This body was created in October 1997 as successor to the Securities and Investments Board, and now exercises statutory powers given to it by the Financial Services and Markets Act 2000; b) the Takeover Panel. This independent body was established in 1968 in order to supervise and regulate takeovers and other matters in accordance with the rules set out in the City Code on Takeovers and Mergers. Its statutory functions are set out in and under Chapter 1 of Part 28 of the Companies Act 2006. It has also been designated as the supervisory authority to carry out certain regulatory functions in relation to takeovers pursuant to the Directive on Takeover Bids (2004/25/EC); c) and the Financial Ombudsman Service. This body was established by the Financial Services and Markets Act 2000 as an independent public body which resolves individual disputes between consumers and financial services firms.

[12] a) The Water Services Regulation Authority (OFWAT), which regulates the privatized water and sewerage industry in England and Wales pursuant to the Water Act 2003; b) The Office of Gas

banking,[13] trade and industry,[14] agriculture,[15] and the gaming industry.[16] These bodies make decisions on a regular basis which may have far reaching consequences on the respective markets. In particular, it must be emphasized that, given the increasing importance of law in commercial regulation and the ever-lengthening agenda of complex regulatory issues, executive decisions adopted by these authorities may not only alter the operation of private business; they may also substantially affect the position of numerous individuals who have become entitled to test their rights and obligations against the legal frameworks of each economic sector.[17]

This factor, in turn, has significantly enhanced the role of the courts as the guardians of law and protectors of individual rights, so that there is no difficulty over the principle that regulatory decisions are subject to judicial review.[18] Rather, applications for judicial review can be brought against the regulator itself if it is considered that it has exceeded its powers. In fact, the increasing number of applications for judicial review brought against these authorities shows clearly that they have no immunity from the rule of law. Specifically, applications for judicial review have been brought against many of their activities including, *inter alia*, licensing, rule-making, interpreting rules, determining prices and conditions of service, deciding disputes, monitoring, and penalizing. It is submitted that these

and Electricity Markets (OFGEM). This body was formed in 1999 by the merger of the Office of Electricity Regulation (OFFER) and Office of Gas Supply (OFGAS). Its main powers derive from the Gas Act 1986, the Electricity Act 1989, the Competition Act 1998, the Utilities Act 2000, the Enterprise Act 2002 and the Energy Act 2004; c) PhonepayPlus (previously known as ICSTIS) is the regulatory body for premium rates services in the UK on Ofcom's behalf; d) The Office of Rail Regulation. This body was established on 5 July 2004 under the Railways and Transport Safety Act 2003; e) OFCOM.

[13] The Bank of England. This body was founded in 1694. Its current goal is to maintain a stable and efficient monetary and financial framework as its contribution to a healthy economy.

[14] a) Department for Business, Innovation and Skills (BIS), which was created on 5 June 2009 by the merger of the Department for Innovation, Universities and Skills (DIUS) and the Department for Business, Enterprise and Regulatory Reform (BERR); b) The Office of Fair Trading. This is a statutory body established by the Fair Trading Act 1973, and then modified by the Enterprise Act 2002, whose main function is to protect consumer interests, while ensuring that businesses are fair and competitive; c) The Competition Commission. This is a non-departmental public body created by the Competition Act of 1998 as successor to the Monopolies and Mergers Commission. Its powers are mainly governed by the Enterprise Act 2002; d) Companies House, an executive agency of the Department of Business, Innovation and Skills which examines and stores company information delivered under the Companies Act 2006 and related legislation; e) The Intellectual Property Office. This is the operating name of 'The Patent Office', a regulatory body which was set up by the Patents Law Amendment Act 1852 as the United Kingdom's office for the granting of patents, and the registration of industrial designs and Trade marks. It is currently an executive agency of the Department for Business, Innovation and Skills.

[15] The Department of Environment, Food and Rural Affairs; The Food Standards Agency. This is an independent government department created by the Food Standards Act 1999 to protect consumer interests in relation to food safety and standards.

[16] The Gambling Commission, created under the Gambling Act 2005 as successor to the Gaming Board for Great Britain.

[17] Scott, Colin, 'The Juridification of Relations in the UK Utilities Sector', in *Commercial Regulation and Judicial Review*, (as above n. 9), 20.

[18] Wade, W. and Forsyth, C.F., *Administrative Law*, 10th edn., (Oxford: Oxford University Press, 2009) 133; Baldwin, R. and Cave, M., *Understanding Regulation*, (Oxford: Oxford University Press, 1999) 299.

are precisely the challenges which fall under the category of commercial judicial review.

Furthermore, this situation of judicial supervision is likely to increase in the near future. Three reasons, in particular, stand out. First, the Legislative and Regulatory Reform Act 2006 imposes several statutory obligations on all regulators which provide further and more specific grounds on which to challenge regulatory action before the courts.[19] Secondly, the recent extension of the powers of regulators to impose sanctions, provided by the Regulatory Enforcement and Sanctions Act 2008 is, at least, a reflection of the increasing tendency of the legislator to deepen and enhance administrative influence over markets, thereby increasing the likelihood of litigation in this field. Thirdly, the recent sub-prime financial crisis originating in the United States is expected to have a major impact on how the issue of market regulation is approached around the world. In particular, it has been argued that legislation has been inadequate to deal with the subsequent credit crunch in the UK and that, therefore, both public oversight of capital and the authorities' responsiveness to risk should be strengthened.[20] This view is most clearly reflected in the Banking Act 2009—which provides regulators with new powers to deal with banks that get into financial problems—and the recently announced Basel III bank rules on capital requirements.[21] This critical scenario, in general, might prompt greater attention to commercial rights and to their vindication against regulators by different means.

Taken together, these considerations also combine to justify the need to address this matter. Once it is accepted that the standards of judicial review depend on the context, and that commercial judicial review is a context which raises particularly sensitive issues concerning governmental intervention with people's activities or liberties, it becomes apparent that embarking upon the study of this subject is a useful and interesting endeavour.

3. The Book: Challenging Judicial Deference

At first glance, questions related to judicial review seem equally pertinent in the commercial context as they are in other areas of governmental activity. As Julia Black and Peter Muchlinski observe, there is nothing special about this specific area of law,

the questions posed by commercial judicial review are posed in the context of judicial review more generally, and there is no aspect of the commercial context which suggests that they should be answered in a particular way.[22]

---

[19] See Black, Julia, 'Tensions in the regulatory state', *Public Law*, 2007, 72–73.

[20] Gieve, John (Deputy Governor, Bank of England), 'The Financial Cycle and the UK Economy', speech given at the London Stock Exchange, 18 July 2008, available at <http://www.bankofengland .co.uk> accessed 26 September 2010, 5. In the area of finance, see Turner, Lord Adair, *The Turner Review: A Regulatory Response to the Global Banking Crisis*, March 2009, 88–91, available at <http://www.fsa .gov.uk/pubs/other/turner_review.pdf> accessed 26 September 2010.

[21] These rules were announced by the Basel Committee on Banking Supervision of the Bank for International Settlements on 12 September 2010.

[22] Black and Muchlinski, (as above n. 9), 15.

A similar point is expressed by Philip Engelman. He observes that 'the trends developing in commercial Judicial Review are simply illustrative of the developing jurisprudence in Judicial Review generally'.[23]

Nevertheless, these authors agree that a 'number of factors which combine in the area of commercial regulation to ensure that it provides a particularly challenging context for judicial review'.[24] In particular, it is observed that,

> ...although many of the principles which are applied in commercial judicial review cases are common to those to be found in judicial review cases generally, there are a number of themes which appear to be developing which require more specialist consideration.[25]

One of these issues concerns the cautious approach that the courts adopt in exercising their supervisory powers over regulatory decisions. Indeed, although English courts have traditionally held a policy of judicial deference towards administrative action,[26] expressed in cases like *GCHQ*,[27] this approach has been particularly light in the field of market regulation. As Colin Scott points out, 'there is a view that the courts take a more restrictive attitude to judicial review in cases involving commercial regulation'.[28] In fact, there have been numerous cases in which the courts state that the issue is judicially cognizable but there are good reasons for taking a non-interventionist approach to the substantive activities of the public body. Prominent among these considerations are the need to pay deference to the regulator's expertise and institutional autonomy, and the demands of administrative efficiency, which prevent the courts from interfering with the development of regulatory policies. Thus, it appears that, in this specific context, the attitude of the judiciary relies heavily on the qualities and interests of the decision-maker rather than on the position of the private litigant, who normally seeks effective review of the contended decision.

However, it is worth noting that this policy of judicial deference seems to be inconsistent with relevant values of English public law which protect individuals from capricious and arbitrary executive action. Specifically, it may be argued that such restraint may adversely affect the right of the applicant to obtain an independent assessment of the validity of the impugned order. Indeed, by relying upon the decision-maker's criteria to provide a definitive answer to the legal issues presented, the courts have implicitly declined to act impartially, independently forming its own opinion on the legal merits of the case. In practice, this situation gives executive measures a prodigious binding effect, since affected private parties have almost no realistic chance of persuading the court that their complaints are well founded.

---

[23] Engelman, (as above n. 4), 5.   [24] Black, Muchlinski and Walker, (as above n. 9), 15.
[25] Engelman, (as above n. 4), 4.
[26] Elliott, Mark, 'The Human Rights Act 1998 and the Standard of Substantive Review', (as above, n. 2), 301–308.
[27] *Council of Civil Service Unions v. Minister for the Civil Service* [1985] A.C. 374 at 410. Lord Diplock said that a decision may be irrational and so liable to be quashed only if it 'is so outrageous in its defiance of logic or of accepted moral standard that no sensible person who had applied his mind to the question could have arrived at it'.
[28] Scott, (as above n. 17), 24. See also Prosser, Tony, 'The Powers and Accountability of Agencies and Regulators', in *English Public Law*, David Feldman (eds.), (Oxford: Oxford University Press, 2004) 296.

Thus, it may create a dangerous opportunity for economic authorities to impose decisions upon citizens without meaningful judicial control. In this sense, the current approach to commercial regulation appears to entail a serious abdication of the court's role as ultimate arbiters of law. This abdication, which has received relatively little attention, ought to worry those who are concerned with securing individual justice in the field.

It is the purpose of this book to contribute to the debate on this issue by advocating a more intensive form of judicial review. It will be argued that only by adopting a close supervision over decisions which alter or determine the operation of markets is it possible to reach a level of judicial control that is consistent with the requirements of fairness and reasonableness in this area and with proper respect for the rights of the parties involved. This approach is particularly founded on the idea that a good system of public regulation over private business necessarily requires the court to play a more interventionist role which ensures impartial protection of market players. In this sense, it expresses a particular mode of relation between judges and decision-makers which leaves little room for executive immunity.

In light of this, it becomes clear that the present work challenges the much more deferential attitude which has traditionally been exhibited by the domestic courts *vis-à-vis* decisions of economic authorities. Indeed, by suggesting that a relatively intrusive form of review should be adopted, this view provides an approach which is in sharp contrast with the current jurisprudence on the matter. In this way, it also represents an invitation to the judges to move beyond their actual perception of their limited role within the regulatory framework and recognize the need to engage in a stricter model of substantive review which reflects the importance of securing effective judicial protection of private interests.

In developing this alternative doctrine, it is worth emphasizing that the framework within which it should apply is a complex construct made up of many factors and reasons. They all combine to constitute the basis upon which the more rigorous approach is founded: they supply the mechanism through which judicial review can be applied to executive decisions which impact upon private business in a manner which is consistent with the concrete protection of individual rights. These important ideas are explored in detail in different parts of the book. However, it is important, at the outset, to be clear about the basic content of the principal arguments in favour of intensive review which the book develops. Four, in particular, should be mentioned.

First, it will be argued that the necessity of adopting such an approach derives, in part, from the argument of lack of ministerial accountability, which indicates that diminution in the power and effectiveness of political control over independent regulators necessarily requires the courts to strengthen oversight of their decisions in order to maintain the constitutional balance of power. Secondly, it will be noted that the current context of open and competitive markets clearly purports to advocate a less deferential judicial attitude which ensures that decision-makers do not hamper liberal economic policies. The third idea relates to the fundamental right to a fair hearing which, in accordance with the jurisprudence of the European Court of Human Rights (ECtHR), entitles individuals to access to a court of 'full jurisdiction' in regard to regulatory decisions made in the absence of procedural safeguards which are 'decisive' of private rights and obligations. The fourth argument concerns the principle of legal certainty. As seen below, this doctrine presupposes a level of judicial intervention which goes beyond the orthodox approach in that it further constrains the discretionary freedom of the decision-maker to make frequent changes of law or policy which may undermine the rights of those induced to rely upon them.

Nevertheless, once these factors are appreciated, it becomes necessary to address a more specific point. The development of a more intensive form of review raises important issues regarding the constitutional relationship between the judiciary and the executive. Independently of the substantive merits of such a shift in the commercial context, it is relatively clear that it entails a reduction in agency autonomy which appears to be inconsistent with precisely the courts' perception of their position within the fundamental order. In particular, the judges have recognized that it is inappropriate for them acting on their own motion to try to change the constitutional distribution of judicial and administrative functions.[29] In light of this, it is possible to argue that a fully satisfactory justification for the proposed view must necessarily be based on legal principles which accord a lower margin of freedom to the decision-maker, thereby permitting greater judicial intervention. In other words, it is necessary to draw upon a doctrine which expresses a rather different conception of the separation of powers in the sense that it leaves it to the court, rather than to the executive, to determine how the balance between rights and competing regulatory claims ought to be struck. It will be argued below that such doctrine is forthcoming once the principle of proportionality to which public authorities and judges are progressively being subjected is taken into account within the particular field.

As Mark Elliott correctly explains, the doctrine of proportionality entails a greater judicial attenuation of administrative autonomy than does the traditional approach to substantive review.[30] In particular, it holds that the mere existence of public policy considerations is not sufficient in itself to establish the reasonableness and legality of the decision. In order to determine whether the challenged decision is justified in law, the court must also be satisfied that the qualification placed on the applicant's rights is proportionate to the competing policy aim being pursued. On this view, therefore, the balance between individual rights and public interest is primarily for the courts; they become entitled to set aside most of the executive actions which go beyond what they consider is strictly necessary to achieve the desired outcome. In this manner, the proportionality-based approach clearly narrows the range of options which are available to the decision-maker at the substantive level.

Questions therefore arise concerning precisely whether this intensive mode of judicial review should apply in the context of commercial regulation. The following sections demonstrate that the answer to this question is firmly in the positive. This

---

[29] See Elliott, 'The Human Rights Act 1998 and the Standard of Substantive Review' (as above n. 2), 310–311.

[30] Ibid., 302–315.

follows mainly from the requirement, in section 2 of the Human Rights Act 1998 (HRA), that domestic courts should take into account the jurisprudence of the European Court of Human Rights in Strasbourg (ECtHR) which indicates that the principle of proportionality occupies a pivotal role in assessing executive action which impacts upon private business. In addition, proportionality is a general principle of EC law and therefore national courts are obliged to apply it in economic regulation cases which have a Community law element. Thus, it becomes clear that there are at least two significant types of case in which judicial supervision based on the proportionality standard constitutes an adequate remedy for the purpose of protecting private interests against the abuse of regulatory power.

This conclusion has important consequences for judicial review in the commercial context. In approaching the control exercised over market authorities under the principle of proportionality, it is crucial to understand that the court becomes the primary judge of where the balance lies between the interests of the community and the interests of the litigants. More specifically, the judges must be alert to the importance of ensuring that interference by the decision-maker with the rights of market players is justified in that it cannot go beyond what is strictly necessary to secure the regulatory objective. Once this is recognized, it becomes apparent that English courts, in relation to decisions which determine the operation of private business, should refuse to adopt the cautious approach which is predominant in the present case law. Rather, they should go on to ask whether the magnitude of the qualification placed on the private interest was proportionate to the regulatory aim sought to be achieved.

This question thus lies at the core of the effort to provide an approach to regulatory decisions which is both satisfactory, in the sense that it conforms to the relevant requirements of individual justice, and constitutionally valid, in that it entails a shift in the balance between the judicial and executive branches of government which has been authorized by parliament, rather than by judges, through human rights and EU legislation. In particular, by acknowledging that the proportionality test underlies the courts' supervisory endeavour, significant shortcomings of the traditional deferential approach can be avoided: as it involves a fair balance between individual rights and competing public policy considerations, the alternative approach facilitates a more independent and impartial assessment of the merits of the case; moreover, since this mode of analysis requires a compelling justification for qualifying individual rights, it reduces the risk of the decision-maker imposing arbitrary decisions upon citizens without effective supervision. These ideas are explained in more detail below, when considering the benefits of the proportionality test for the applicant's position in regard to the different aspects of the impugned decision. However, it is helpful to set them out briefly at the outset. Six points, in particular, fall to be considered.

The first one relates to the application of Article 6 of the European Convention on Human Rights and Fundamental Freedoms ('the European Convention'). It will be argued that only by adopting a proportionality-based reasoning the English courts will be able to ensure that their jurisdiction is sufficiently full in order to 'cure' the lack of impartiality and independence of economic authorities which determine civil rights and obligations. Secondly, it will be noted that, by requiring the courts to apply a criterion of substantive review which is narrower than the traditional test, the principle of proportionality has the advantage of reducing the zone of immunity within which regulatory decision-making is free from judicial scrutiny, thereby securing a higher level of protection against the abuse of executive power. Thirdly, it will be argued that this reasoning is central to the interpretation of vague terms, because it requires the courts to determine whether the meaning chosen by the decision-maker is proportionate to the competing policy and aim being pursued. The fourth context concerns factual review. As seen below, it appears that the question posed by the proportionality test increases pressure for a wider jurisdiction over facts, since it strongly relies on the detailed factual context in which the decision is adopted. The fifth point which will be made relates to the protection of legitimate expectations. It is submitted that this more rigorous approach to regulatory decisions, which the proportionality doctrine institutionalizes, also reduces the freedom of the executive to depart from its prior interpretations and policies, so that it may be reconciled with the need to protect the interests of those parties who reasonably relied on their application.

Finally, the adoption of the doctrine of proportionality will be considered in relation to the exercise of the court's remedial discretion. In this context, its importance is two-fold. On the one hand, it might require the payment of compensation to the innocent parties against whom the remedy is either refused or granted in order to ensure that interference with their rights is proportionate to the aim sought to be realized, namely, the protection of the competing private and public interests. On the other hand, it suggests that, in such circumstances, the court should exercise its discretion against the party who would be subsequently entitled to the lowest amount of damages from the public authority. In this manner, a reasonable relationship of proportionality can be established between the need to protect the individual's rights and the demands of the general interest of the community in protecting societal resources.

Thus the principle of proportionality operates, in the present context, to ensure that, so far as possible, the courts' supervisory jurisdiction is exercised in a manner which is consistent with both the requirements of public policy and the rights of the applicant in relation to administrative justice. Specifically, this mode of analysis directs attention towards the reasoning process adopted by the decision-maker, rather than towards its qualities, and it can therefore be usefully applied to facilitate a more effective and impartial review of the contended decision. Moreover, by requiring a balance to be struck between the different interests at stake, it has the advantage of allowing the courts to provide an equitable solution to the problem of competing, but equally legitimate, claims at a remedial level. Hence the need for the proportionality standard as the mechanism by which intensive judicial control is exercised in the commercial context.

At this point, however, it might be noted that the influence of this form of review is relatively limited because it does not extend to cases which fall outside the scope of the HRA or EU law. It is not, therefore, inconceivable that the court may adhere to a less rigorous approach in relation to regulatory decisions which involve elements of general administrative law only. However, as seen below, it is this book's contention that such conclusion would be inconsistent with a series of normative and pragmatic reasons which indicate that the proportionality test will have a broader influence on English law, thereby requiring the courts to adopt a more intensive standard of review even in areas where it is not currently used. In other words, it seems likely that this principle of review will be recognized as an independent ground of review that can be applied to any type of executive intervention on the rights and interests of market players.

4. The Structure of the Book

The foregoing analysis indicates that the focus of this book is on what the appropriate intensity of judicial review should be in the commercial context. As seen above, the answer to this question is revealed upon consideration of several factors related to the balance of power in the public sphere. However, given that these conditions might entail the application of polar-opposite approaches to the contested order, it appears that the mere preference for a particular set of arguments does not suffice to justify the judgement of the court because it would fail to furnish a complete account of the views at stake. Evaluative analysis of the legitimacy of the competing arguments is therefore necessitated in order to provide a more complete framework within which the courts may determine the intensity of their supervision. In particular, it is necessary, in articulating a more intrusive form of review, to first provide an explanation of the content and implications of the factors which induce the courts to adopt the deferential approach. By doing so, it will be possible to understand better the need to change the *status quo* and inspire judges to get familiar with interventions that aim at increasing the protection of market players.

In light of this, the reading of the present book is loosely arranged in accordance with the structure of a legal disputation. This means that presentation of arguments will be structured according to the headings that mark the arguments for and against the orthodox approach, which are followed by the reasons for preferring a stricter scrutiny which attempts to avoid the shortcomings of the doctrine identified in the previous chapters.

Thus the analysis begins, in the following chapter, by examining that approach which may be regarded as orthodoxy. Specifically, this part is divided into two sections. The first one explains the main arguments upon which the cautious approach is founded. In particular, they point towards two important features of modern administration such as expertise and institutional autonomy which indicate that regulators are far better equipped than the courts to deal fairly and impartially with technical issues arising from the relevant context. Moreover, it is argued that a less strict standard of review would be consistent with the notion of regulatory effectiveness, which demands decisiveness and certainty on the part of executive bodies. The second section of this chapter provides an account of the cases in which the courts have traditionally shown reluctance to review regulatory decisions in the commercial context. It is worth noting that this view is not confined to a particular stage of the judicial review process but it has been expressed in relation to different aspects of the contended order which may require the supervision of the courts. Thus the authorities indicate that deference should be accorded to the decision-maker's criteria in regard to factual findings, substantive choices, and interpretation of vague or self-regulatory rules. It will be observed that, in most of the cases, the justification given by the courts for showing deference to the decision-maker is rooted in the *Wednesbury* principle, which allows the courts to strike down administrative decisions only in rather extreme circumstances. An interesting form of judicial restraint can also be found in the field of remedies, where the courts have sometimes refused to grant relief to the successful applicant in order to protect the interest of the administration and the position of third parties who may have reasonably relied on the validity of the impugned decision.

The book then moves on to consider, in the next chapter, the arguments against the orthodox approach. It will be noted that this doctrine has kept the focus away from the position of the applicant—who is seeking effective review of the administrative order—and has, instead, prompted greater concentration on the criteria and interests of the decision-maker, thereby severely undermining judicial protection of individual rights against the abuse of executive power. This situation entails an inevitable clash with relevant principles of English public law which advocate a more equitable analysis of the claims of the competing parties. Two principal matters require consideration. First, it will be argued in section 2 that the present doctrine—which justifies judicial caution on the basis of the regulator's special qualities and the need for administrative efficiency and certainty—is inconsistent with the position which postulates the courts' role as ultimate and impartial guardians of law. Indeed, by deferring to the regulator's own criteria for applying the law to particular factual situations the courts are implicitly declining to make an independent assessment of the merits of the case. On this view, therefore, it is the administrative authority, rather than the judge, which ultimately provides the reasons upon which the case is decided. It is argued below that this outcome must be rejected as both unsatisfactory, in the sense that it eschews the rights-based conception of public law adjudication which inheres in the context of liberalized markets, and unconvincing, in that it relies on an erroneous account of parliament's intention.

Secondly, it will be shown, in section 3, that there exist specific sets of reasons which militate against the application of the orthodox doctrine in the fields of factual findings and remedial discretion. As regard the latter, it is suggested that leaving *ultra vires* decisions unaffected in order to protect decisiveness and certainty in volatile markets is seriously flawed because it fails to provide an adequate protection of the rights of the successful applicant. In particular, it is argued that this view is inconsistent with the principles of legality and fair competition in the market economy, which provide inspiration for the exercise of the court's remedial discretion in favour of those directly affected by the unlawful order. In addition, it will be demonstrated that it is not at all clear that this approach is correct, as a matter of justice, to assert that the applicant's interests should be trumped or outweighed by reference to the protection of administrative convenience and third-party rights.

In light of the significant shortcomings of the traditional doctrine, Chapter 3 then goes on to suggest the adoption of a more satisfactory and convincing approach to regulatory measures which may render judicial oversight workable in terms of individual justice. The better view, it is argued, is that a stricter form of scrutiny should be adopted which allows the courts to conduct a careful and independent inquiry into the challenged order, so that citizens may be effectively protected from capricious and arbitrary governmental action. The difficulty, however, is that such a doctrine reveals a related shift in constitutional and institutional competence from the regulator to the judge which cannot be achieved without legislative warrant. Thus, some explanation is still required of the normative considerations which may motivate the courts in engaging in high-intensity substantive rights adjudication.

This task is undertaken in Chapter 4, where it will be argued that there appears to be a natural relationship between, on the one hand, the adoption of a more rigorous judicial attitude towards market regulation and, on the other hand, the ethos of European law. It is contended below that effect must be given to the legislation and decisions of European courts which, by virtue of the Acts of Parliament, have become part of the English legal order with the direct and indirect effect of rendering the domestic court's supervision ever more intrusive. In this sense, the European content of regulatory law acts as a legal warrant that furnishes an adequate explanation for the change of approach in commercial judicial review. This idea will be developed in three principal stages. First, in section 2, it is explained that these norms rest on the foundational values of liberal-market democracies which clearly demand that judges should act in a strict and neutral way in order to avoid undue interference with economic rights and freedoms. Secondly, section 3 shows that one relevant legal expression of this doctrine is the right to a court of 'full jurisdiction', which reasserts meaningful judicial oversight of regulators in accordance with Article 6(1) of the European Convention. Thirdly, in section 4, the principle of proportionality is presented as an attempt to articulate a more structured form of inquiry which postulates a balanced approach to market regulation under the explicit influence of European law, and which therefore satisfies the dual imperatives of impartiality and constitutional legitimacy.

Thus, Chapter 5 goes on to consider the implications and advantages of proportionality in relation to the different aspects of the challenged decision which may require the supervision of the courts. Specifically, it is argued in sections 1 to 3 that, by adhering to a robust judicial attitude based on this doctrine, it is possible to begin to deal with the difficulties which prevent the orthodox approach from providing an adequate control of the decision-maker's criteria on the reasonableness of the decision, interpretation of rules, and factual considerations. In addition, section 4 seeks to articulate a 'proportional' approach to the problem of remedial discretion which accurately captures the idea that the court's primary role is to protect citizens against executive abuse, as it takes into account the interests of third parties and public administration without going so far as to deny effective relief to the applicant.

Finally, Chapter 6 supplies a particular explanation concerning the scope of the principle of proportionality. It observes that there are justified reasons to think that this doctrine will be recognized as an independent ground of review within domestic law. As seen below, this has important implications for the intensity of judicial review in the relevant context: in particular, the courts are entitled to adopt a more rigorous test to deal with claims arising not only under the Human Rights Act or EC law, but also under other areas of national law that have direct impact upon the operation of private businesses.

In Chapter 7, in addition to the specific conclusions reached in each chapter, three broader and integrated themes are analysed which further illuminate the response to the question of the intensity of judicial review in the commercial context which the present book seeks to supply. The first thematic point which emerges relates to the existence of contextual factors which specifically support the adoption of a more intensive form of review in the field. Secondly, it will be argued that it is necessary to appreciate that the proposed approach supplies alternative means to deal with the problem of judicial intervention without seriously affecting the applicant's interest in seeking review and protection. The final point which emerges concerns the need to bear in mind that market regulation through technical rules is a relatively new phenomenon in the United Kingdom, and therefore, susceptible of being grasped gradually, but surely, by the judges.

2

The Orthodox Deferential Approach

1. Introduction

It has already been noted that the English courts traditionally adopt a deferential approach towards executive decisions in the commercial context. The reasons which underlie this attitude are closely associated with the notion that market regulation is primarily a matter for the government and not a matter in relation to which the courts should exercise control. Thus, faced with the task of determining issues in this field, the judges have given considerable weight to the views of the executive, which is particularly well-placed to deal with the subject in pragmatic terms. Hence Engelman comments that,

unless one can show a plain case for interference, the courts are reluctant to substitute their own views of what should have been the right decision in the market place for those of the regulatory bodies who where charged with making that decision'.[1]

In light of this, an explanation of the orthodox approach must form the logical starting point of any discussion of the intensity of judicial review in the commercial context.

This task is undertaken in two principal stages. Section 2 of this chapter will endeavour to give an overview of the main arguments which support this doctrine and the goals which it claims to secure. In essence, it will be showed that a great emphasis has been placed on the decision-maker's special qualities and the need to ensure regulatory effectiveness. The third section concentrates on the cases in which the courts, acting in their supervisory function, have adopted a deferential approach in relation to the exercise of power by regulatory bodies. Specific references will be made to the judicial cautious attitude towards different aspects of the matter of judgement.

2. The Rationale Behind the Orthodox Approach

In general terms, it is claimed that the great strength of the deferential approach to regulatory decisions is its capacity to reconcile judicial review with the principles which govern executive intervention in the economic sphere. Supporters of

[1] Engelman, Philip, *Commercial Judicial Review*, (London: Sweet & Maxwell, 2001) 139.

the orthodox view explain that effective implementation of public policies in the market context necessarily requires the courts to be especially cautious in reviewing administrative decisions in order to avoid unnecessary disruptions in ordinary business relationships and the imposition of poorly considered criteria. Moreover, the court's decision to leave the body's decision relatively untouched clearly facilitates the incorporation of technical rules into the regulatory framework, thereby ensuring administrative efficiency and the successful achievement of regulatory goals. Hence the present doctrine might be characterized as a context-sensitive approach which enjoys systemic coherence, by requiring the courts to review impugned decisions in a manner which is consistent with, rather an affront to, the principles of good administration and market performance.

This reasoning envisions a broader role for the judges in the commercial sphere, which allows them to act 'as a regulatory force in government'[2] that gives further effect to the judgements of the decision-maker. Under the deferential approach, the courts are seen to act as public policy instruments which collaborate with the executive more than arbiters of justice, facilitating the task of the agencies. As Martin Loughlin observes,

today it seems that the courts are critically involved in the management of public business; '*fiat justicia...*' plays no significant role in the modern world of judicial review.[3]

In this sense, the present doctrine appears to shift the focus away from the somewhat strictly legal questions of individual rights with which the courts have traditionally been preoccupied in the private context and, instead, prompts greater concentration on public policy considerations. Once this change of perspective is appreciated, it becomes unsurprising that judges favour regulators' criteria and that, as Black and Muchlinski explain, the commercial aims of regulation are given 'a wide margin of appreciation so that the regulator can freely achieve control over the market, often in ways that the participants may find disagreeable'.[4]

It is therefore possible to argue that the reluctance of the courts to exercise a more intensive supervision over regulators also reflects a conception of judicial review which is more directed towards the achievement of social objectives than simple adjudication of two competing views on a limited and defined issue. In particular, it points towards a model of dispute resolution that is relatively based on public policy considerations and which thereby fully acknowledges the imperatives of commercial authorities, rooted in the needs and competing interests of individuals participating in complex markets, which apparently underpin the need for judicial restraint. On this view, therefore, the courts are encouraged to look at the broader impact of reviewing and invalidating administrative decisions and take into account not only the interests of the applicant, but also the legitimate

---

[2] Le Sueur, Andrew, 'Justifying Judicial Caution: Jurisdiction, Justiciability and Policy' in *Judicial Review: A Thematic Approach*, Brigid Hadfield (ed.), (Dublin: Gill & Macmillan, 1995) 250.

[3] Loughlin, Martin, 'Courts and Governance' in *The Frontiers of Liability*, Peter Birks (ed.), Vol. 1, (Oxford: Oxford University Press, 1994) 108.

[4] Black, J., Muchlinski, P. and Walker, P. (eds.), *Commercial Regulation and Judicial Review*, (Oxford: Hart Publishing, 1998) 13.

regulatory goals. In other words, the court's reasoning should rest not on legal argument and precedent but on the practical repercussions of intervening so as to ease the tension identified by John Alder between 'protecting the victim of an abuse of power and protecting third parties who rely upon official action, avoiding disruption to the administrative process, and safeguarding the autonomy and responsiveness of decision-makers'.[5]

Thus, the conceptual defence of the orthodox approach is ultimately based upon the need to consider the position of the different actors involved in the regulatory decision-making process, especially that of the public authority. If this premise is accepted, it necessarily follows that the court's role must be confined to the identification and protection of their interests in a way which is compatible with the requirements of economic policy as seen by the decision-maker. In light of this, the following sub-sections consider two specific sets of reasons which have been given for elevating administrative views and goals above the court's independent judgement of what is reasonable and lawful. The first one relates to the special features of commercial regulators which, it is submitted, allow them to make well-informed and autonomous decisions. The second set is relatively pragmatic in nature, in that it indicates that adoption of a more intensive form of judicial review would pose severe problems to regulatory effectiveness, since it necessarily inhibits the efficient resolution of complex issues and undermines the authority of the decision-maker in a manner which creates great uncertainty in the market community.

2.1 The regulator

The orthodox approach holds that administrative authorities are in a far better position than the judges to resolve regulatory issues. In their opinion, this would be precisely the feature of commercial judicial review which allows the courts to show a high level of deference to the views, interpretations and decisions of public bodies consistently across the board. The current attitude of the judiciary thus appears to constitute the legal expression of the greater ability of the executive branch to deal with complex problems. The writing of Professor Christopher Edley furnishes a helpful starting point in this regard.[6] The core of his argument is that doctrines shaping judicial deference to administrative decisions reflect perfectly an underlying reliance on the positive attributes of the executive's decision-making paradigm (scientific expertise) and a clear response to the negative norms of the decision-making method naturally associated with the judiciary (adjudicatory fairness). His thesis therefore forms a useful focus for identifying the set of normative associations used by the courts to define and police institutional roles and domain, usually in the context of calibrating the degree of judicial restraint to bear in deciding administrative law cases. The essence of Edley's view is captured in the following

---

[5] Alder, John, 'Obsolescence and Renewal: Judicial Review in the Private Sector' in *Administrative Law Facing the Future: Old Constraints and New Horizons*, P. Leyland and T. Woods (eds.), (Oxford: Oxford University Press, 1997) 180.

[6] Edley, Christopher, *Administrative Law: Rethinking Judicial Control of Bureaucracy*, (New Haven: Yale University Press, 1990).

table, which summarizes Edley's table on the reasons underlying the advantages of the executive branch over the judiciary in decision making:[7]

Attributes associated to decision-making methods of the Executive and the Judiciary

Primary *situs*	Executive	Judiciary
Paradigm or method	Scientific expertise	Adjudicatory fairness
Attributes	*Positive.* Specialized knowledge, rationality, objectivity, managerial efficiency, empiricism, verifiable evidence, and deductive reasoning.	*Negative.* proceduralistic; stylized; arcane; conservative and past-focused; stultifying; paralysing.

It follows from this list that, when the court insists that it must defer to administrative decisions, it is basically articulating and giving effect to those bureaucratic values and features which are presumptively alien to the judiciary. Deference therefore lies on the sole ground that public law issues which are more appropriate for the expert method are likelier game for intervention by the administration. Understood thus, judicial restraint seems constitutionally legitimate because it rests on 'propositions about comparative institutional competence, about desirable institutional roles, and about the problem-solving qualities called for by the tasks of government'.[8]

For instance, it may be argued that self-denial postures in the judicial sphere are worthwhile because they serve the principle of good government, enabling the executive to apply its method of reasoning, so safeguarding expert adjudication of highly complex issues; that managerial efficiency is promoted if administrative decisions are conclusive and binding on the court (and undermined if they are not); and that a limited approach to review involves no risk of the courts imposing poor technical criteria or frustrating the ability of government to meet urgent public needs.

It is noteworthy that the foregoing set of reasons accords with the explanation which is traditionally furnished by the judicial deference doctrine in the context of economic regulation. Indeed the concerns underpinning such respect for administrative decisions are eminently consistent with the arguments advanced by legal scholars who advocate a more interventionist role for the regulator in public litigation *vis-à-vis* the courts. In particular, four principal factors help to explain the privileged position of market authorities.

The first factor concerns the highly technical knowledge and experience of the decision-maker. It is widely recognized that, in an age of technological advances and increased commercialization, regulators have become enclaves of expertise. The need to deal with complex issues in the economic sphere has fundamentally changed the context within which regulatory decisions are made, requiring

---

[7] Ibid., 21.   [8] Ibid., 16–17.

administrators to be especially skilled to analyse market trends and developments. Later on, administrative expertise has also been gained through self-tuition and cumulative years of experience. The point is expressed well by Daniel Solove. He observes that the increase of the quantity of complex information and detail regarding numerous realms of regulated activity has greatly improved agencies' ability to 'sift through all the information, to weed out the good data from the bad, and to understand the field'.[9] Thus the expertise of the regulator is now viewed as deriving from the fact that it is collecting and analysing data to assess the market's operation on a permanent basis. In addition, it is argued that administrative bodies tend to have an expert knowledge as to how the particular statute is to be applied, because of the close relationship that may have existed between them and Parliament during the legislative process. As Stephen Breyer, distinguished law professor and American Supreme Court Justice, observes, the regulator that enforces the statute,

may have had a hand in drafting the provisions. It may posses an internal history in the form of documents or handed-down oral tradition that casts light on the meaning of a difficult phrase or provision.[10]

In addition, the agency staff,

in close contact with relevant legislators and staffs, likely understands the *current* congressional view, which, in turn, may, through institutional history, reflect prior understandings.[11]

In light of this special knowledge, it becomes apparent that regulatory views and opinions will necessarily be better than those of the court. Accordingly, it is suggested that it would not be absurd, nor contrary to the rule of law, for the court to prefer the criteria adopted by the expert regulator to its own, since they are those which best meet market technical needs and the intention of Parliament. As Black and Muchlinski explain, it may be emphasized that an expert body is best placed to make the best decision, and that 'such expertise confers legitimacy on the regulator's decision, reducing if not eliminating the need for judicial intervention'.[12]

The second factor, which is closely related to the first, focuses on the lack of expertise in the judiciary to deal with such multifaceted technical matters. It has been argued that the courts are not well prepared to determine technical issues and that any intervention in this sphere would be detrimental to good public administration and the effective operation of the market. As is apparent from the comments of Genevra Richardson and Maurice Sunkin, it would be wrong to encourage a

---

[9] Solove, Daniel, 'The Darkest Domain: Deference, Judicial Review, and the Bill of Rights' [1999] 84 *Iowa Law Review*, 969.
[10] Breyer, Stephen, 'Judicial Review of Questions of Law and Policy' [1986] 38 *Administrative Law Review*, 368.   [11] Ibid.
[12] Black, Muchlinski and Walker, (as above n. 4), 9. Baldwin, R. and McCrudden, C., *Regulation and Public Law*, Law in Context, (London: Weidenfeld & Nicholson, 1987) 48. See also the model of deference based on 'epistemic' considerations which has been proposed by Young, Alison, 'In Defence of Due Deference' [2009] 72(4) *The Modern Law Review*, 554–580.

generalist judge to become involved in the process of dispute resolution in highly specialized and complex areas. They say that,

if the judiciary is without the expertise, experience and information appropriate to the task of identifying, and then imposing, standards of rationality, judicial review cannot be expected to perform at anything other than a symbolic level.[13]

Similarly, Loughlin doubts that the judges have the cognitive, conceptual and material resources to enable them to perform the functions expected.[14] In the American context, it was difficulties of this sort which resulted in Stephen Breyer setting the stage for a discussion of the following compelling questions:

how could anyone expect a non-technical panel of judges to do anything but accept the agency's decision as rational where the subject matter is so complex? How could a judge lacking a technical background (even if filled with doubt) do anything but hesitate to affix the label 'irrational' and overturn an expert agency's judgement in such a case...?[15]

This situation appears to raise a particular problem for the interpretation of technical rules. It is argued that, given that the courts do not have sufficient expertise or knowledge to understand technical provisions, it is likely that they will end up giving a meaning to words which the market context does not warrant. As Black observes, the most noted implication of the lack of expertise among judges is that it can raise the prospect of the courts,

imposing decisions which do not make sense in the regulatory context in which they have to apply, and which either ignore the purpose of the legislation or rules, or are based on inaccurate or inconsistent ideas of them.[16]

In practice, she notes, a close judicial involvement in the rule application process could also be 'a source of uncertainty if the judicial interpretation of regulatory terms is not one which the regulator and regulated would share'.[17] Consequently, it is suggested that the judges should be unwilling to intervene in cases involving the construction of substantive rules which may be technical, so that the meaning of the terms which is ultimately imposed to the parties does not entail concern about disruption of markets. In US law, for example, it is this imperative of securing deference to agency technical interpretations which dictates the necessity for the court not only to uphold any 'reasonable' interpretation of ambiguous terms made by it,[18] but also to overcome the doctrine of *stare decisis*, by allowing it to reverse a statutory interpretation that had previously been construed by the court.[19]

---

[13] Richardson, G. and Sunkin, M., 'Judicial Review: Questions of Impact' [1996] *Public Law*, 80.
[14] Loughlin, Martin, 'Innovation Financing in Local Government: The limits of Legal Instrumentalism—Part 2' [1991] *Public Law*, 590.
[15] Breyer, Stephen, *Economic Reasoning and Judicial Review*, AEI-Brookings Joint Center 2003 Distinguished Lecture, (Washington D.C.: The AEI Press, 2004) 11.
[16] Black, Julia, 'Reviewing Regulatory Rules: Responding to Hybridisation' in Black, Muchlinski and Walker, *Commercial Regulation and Judicial Review*, (as above n. 4), 133.
[17] Ibid., 134.
[18] See the Supreme Court's leading judgment in *Chevron U.S.A. Inc. v. Natural Res. Def. Council*, 467 U.S. 837 [1984].
[19] See the judgment of the Supreme Court in *National Cable & Telecommunications Association v. Brand X Internet Services*, 125 S. Ct. 2688 [2005].

The third factor which assists in explaining why it is satisfactory to accord deference to market authorities, concerns the fact that duties and procedures of the regulators are much more suited for dealing with technical economic issues than those of the courts. These matters are thought likely to be better analysed and decided by following procedures such as those already used in administrative law which are still efficient and short when compared with that normally used by the courts to resolve legal disputes. In particular, Robert Baldwin and Christopher McCrudden explain that these decision-making methods are particularly designed to guarantee 'economy, speed in decision-making, ability to adapt quickly to changing conditions, and freedom from technicalities in procedures'.[20] The ability of the regulators to 'relax the formal rules of evidence when appropriate, to avoid an over-reliance on adversarial techniques, and to avoid strict adherence to their own precedents'[21] is another common cited advantage. In addition, executive bodies are also thought to be the only ones which can expend the time and energy necessary to properly address complex issues in the relevant field. All this suggests that it would be difficult for the courts to reach the correct decision with regard to the technical matter in dispute without giving a high level of deference to the regulator which apply purpose-designed procedures.

It has already been argued that the advantages regulatory procedures and duties are said to have over traditional court proceedings—which in turn may justify the cautious approach of the judges in dealing with claims in the market sphere—can be observed nowhere more clearly than in the context of decisions which involve the interpretation of substantive rules which may be difficult to implement or modify. There are two practical reasons underlying this conclusion.

First, it is noted that commercial authorities are often charged with implementing numerous provisions so as to deal with problems closely entangled. If these problems are treated separately, they will not be treated well. Thus, the regulator appears to be in a far better position than the judiciary, reacting as it must to single cases, to respond to interpretive issues which demand complex interactions among various cleanup strategies.[22] For example, Aileen McHarg explains that the interpretation of rules concerning costs issues in telecommunication services impacts not only on other operators,

it also has implications for other aspects of the regulatory regime, including the price caps and the financing of universal service obligations, which temper the Director's obligation to promote competition.

Thus, the regulator's task is to balance conflicting interests within the context of statutory objectives. Accordingly, she continues,

his more comprehensive and consultative approach to interpreting technical provisions seems likely to produce more satisfactory results than an abstract process of interpretation by the courts.[23]

---

[20] Baldwin and McCrudden, (as above n. 12), 5.   [21] Ibid.
[22] Sunstein, Cass, 'Law and Administration after Chevron' [1990] 90 *Columbia Law Review*, 2088.
[23] McHarg, Aileen, 'Regulation as a Private Law Function?' [1995] *Public Law*, 549.

Secondly, it must be considered that parliaments are unable to amend every statute to account for new developments which may affect regulatory performance, such of those involving technological capacity, economics, the international situation, or even law.[24] In the light of these fast changes, the role played by the agencies in being forward-looking, alert to trends that might impact markets, and well focused on the daily issues clearly indicates that they are more suitable than courts to interpret ambiguous statutes in a way that responds efficiently to the new conditions. Hence, it would be improper for the courts to impose strict limits on that interpretive power since, logically, this may cause the ossification of policy. For example, it is argued that the judicially-imposed duty to act in a consistent manner is, in effect, undermining the regulators' ability to depart from previous meanings in the light of contemporary changes. It is for this reason that McHarg holds that 'it may be wiser in the context of the complex and fast-moving world of utility regulation to avoid the rigidities that such obligation might create'.[25]

The fourth factor which, it is submitted, contributes to the importance of leaving to the regulator the primary judgement on the points raised in commercial judicial review, has to do with the need to give effect to the will of Parliament. Those who locate administrative authority within a normative framework which establishes a clear demarcation between the provinces of executive and judicial power argue that the court cannot intervene in the affairs of the regulator because it would be itself taking the place of the body to which Parliament has entrusted the decision. As Black and Muchlinski observe, it may be argued that the constitutional principle of parliamentary sovereignty underlies the idea that,

Parliament has given certain powers to those bodies to perform certain functions; those powers were not given to the courts, and it is not for the courts to exercise powers of which they are not the donee.[26]

Thus, it appears that the exercise of statutory powers by the regulator urges a certain form of judicial restraint in that stringent substantive review of their decisions would expose the courts to the charge that they are undertaking functions exclusively vested in the executive by the legislator.

Professor Paul Craig points out that a similar criterion comes from the old case law in the United Kingdom. He explains that the collateral fact doctrine or the commencement theory of limited review was adopted because the courts believed that these best captured the appropriate balance *between judicial control and agency autonomy*. Accordingly, they did not believe that they should be substituting judgement on every issue of law and fact, since this would 'emasculate autonomy over issues which have been assigned to the agency by Parliament'.[27]

---

[24] Sunstein, (as above n. 22), 2088.
[25] McHarg, Aileen, 'A Duty to be Consistent? *R v. Director General of Electricity Supply, ex p Scottish Power plc*' [1998] 61 *The Modern Law Review*, 100.
[26] Black, Muchlinski and Walker, (as above n. 4), 10.
[27] Craig, Paul, *Administrative Law*, 6th edn. (London: Sweet & Maxwell, 2008) 465.

Viewed in a contemporary setting, the legitimacy of this view also derives from the fact that the Parliament has established several independent agencies which undertake important regulatory functions in the market field at arm's length from central government.[28] These bodies, which were mainly created after the privatization process took place in the eighties, constitute a significant institutional innovation in the British legal order, as they have a substantial amount of autonomy to exercise their powers and duties. For example, they are given directions from government only in limited circumstances and there is no legal duty on them to respond to Select Committee reports. In this sense, the independence afforded to agencies as non-ministerial government departments is said to represent a deliberate choice of the legislator to ensure a much lower degree of accountability which may result in more room for manoeuvre and flexibility to meet regulatory commitments. Accordingly, it has been suggested that judicial review in this context should be especially limited, in order to avoid engaging in matters exclusively entrusted by Parliament to autonomous bodies.[29]

The implications of this doctrine for the intensity of judicial review would also become apparent once the distinction between appeal and review is taken into account.[30] In the British legal system, judicial control of the merits of the administrative decision, that is to say, the exercise of the court's power to determine whether the impugned decision is right or wrong, necessarily requires express statutory authorization. Thus, only if the relevant statute makes provision for 'appeal' against the offending order can the court substitute its own view on the matters in issue for that of the body. Otherwise, the court cannot intervene. In contrast, the system of judicial review, which is concerned only with the question whether the act under attack is lawful or unlawful, does not require express provision because it is based on Parliament's intention to leave it to the judges to set the precise limits of administrative competence in light of the rule of law.[31] In light of this distinction, it is argued that the deferential approach adopted by the courts in judicial review proceedings is a fundamental mechanism for upholding the will of Parliament. In particular, it prevents the judiciary from passing judgement on the merits of the decision in a way which would cause review on the legality to become very like appeal in cases where this proceeding may not be provided by the legislature.

The discussion on this point has been particularly related to the judicial assessment of the reasonableness of the administrative decision and the executive interpretation of law. Thus, Elliott explains that the *Wednesbury* approach,[32] which

---

[28] For these bodies see Graham, Cosmo, *Regulating Public Utilities*, (Oxford: Hart Publishing, 2000); Harlow, C. and Rawlings, R., *Law and Administration*, 3rd edn., Law in Context, (Cambridge: Cambridge University Press, 2009) 141–144, 295–339; Baldwin and McCrudden, (as above n. 12), 3–31.

[29] See Harlow and Rawlings, (as above n. 28), 330–332.

[30] For this distinction see Wade, W. and Forsyth, C.F., *Administrative Law*, 10th edn., (Oxford: Oxford University Press, 2009) 28–29; Cane, Peter, *Administrative Law*, 4th ed., Clarendon Law Series, (Oxford: Oxford University Press, 2004) 29–32.

[31] See Elliott, Mark, *The Constitutional Foundations of Judicial Review*, (Oxford: Hart Publishing, 2001) 97–163.

[32] See below, Section 3.2.2.

postulates an unreasonable decision as something extreme and rare, is seen to reflect the 'self-denying ordinance which reviewing courts have long accepted in pursuit of the 'appeal-review' (or 'merits-legality') distinction which the constitutional separation of powers has traditionally been thought to demand'.[33] It follows from this that the courts should be prevented from recognizing proportionality, a more rigorous standard of reasonableness, as an independent head of review since this would involve an improper willingness on its part to go to the merits rather than to the legality of the decision.

In addition, it is a primary concern for advocates of the orthodox view to hold that the 'correctness' approach to interpretation, according to which all legal rules have a correct meaning which has to be determined by the courts, must be rejected because it eradicates the line between review and appeal. In particular, it is argued that in adopting this approach the court would be in danger of reviewing the merits of the decision without statutory authorization. As Black points out, if the court is concerned with the rightness of the impugned construction, it would be opening the judicial doors to those aggrieved by a regulator's decision on the application of a rule, 'effectively allowing for each an avenue for appeal where statute may not in fact provide one'.[34] In regard of this criticism, it has been suggested that the judges should confine themselves to review the 'reasonableness' rather than the 'correctness' of the executive interpretation, as this would keep the decision of the merits for the regulator itself, and controlled only by an statutory appeal proceeding.

Finally, it is worth noting that the argument based on the need to respect the will of the legislator has also been used to advocate the application of the deferential approach to decisions of self-regulatory organizations which oversee specific markets. Given that these bodies make and apply their own rules, they have been properly regarded as both legislators and administrators. Consequently, it is suggested that a high level of deference should be accorded to their views and interpretations of terms, since they perfectly reflect the will of the rule-maker itself. In this sense, as Black points out, the present approach appears to buttress a more pluralistic conception of law which requires the courts to recognize the existence of others spheres of legal relations—in which mini-legal systems are operated by bodies that are able formulate and apply their own rules—and 'not seek to cast the net of legal logic over them'.[35]

2.2 Regulatory effectiveness

The second set of reasons for preferring an approach to regulatory decisions which places significant reliance on the views and opinions of public bodies relates to the potentially negative implications that a more intensive form of

---

[33] Elliott, Mark, 'The HRA 1998 and the Standard of Substantive Review' [2002] 7(2) *Judicial Review*, 100.

[34] Black, Julia, 'Reviewing Regulatory Rules: Responding to Hybridisation' (as above n. 16), 135.

[35] Black, Julia, 'Constitutionalising Self-regulation' [1996] 59(1) *Modern Law Review*, 31.

review may have for the exercise of administrative functions and the operation of markets. Proponents of the orthodox doctrine say that it can hardly be argued that a regulator is acting efficiently when its decisions are often altered or its policies distorted by the constant and direct intervention of the courts in commercial disputes. It is for this reason that they suggest that it is more satisfactory to embrace a deferential standard of review which may render judicial oversight more acceptable in terms of regulatory effectiveness. On this view, therefore, any attempt to adopt a very robust attitude towards the contended decision is rejected as untenably disruptive because it would seriously undermine the implementation of policies and certainty among businesses. In particular, it is necessary to mention four specific problems which the more rigorous approach encounters.

The first difficulty may be characterized as the deterrent effect on the decision-making process, relating to the way in which judicial review may produce timidity and feebleness of action on the part of regulators, because of the fear that their decisions will be modified or invalidated by the court. It is argued that public bodies are more likely to be excessively cautious and slow in responding to the needs of the markets—even if such slowness is detrimental to good administration—when the individuals have ample opportunity to question the validity of their decisions by judicial means, since, in these situations, there is a substantial risk of invalidation and liability. As Black and Muchlinski point out, an excessive subjection of commercial authorities to judicial review would severely limit their capacity to intervene in the economic process that they are charged with overseeing, because it 'may render regulators more cautious and as a result less efficient in using their expertise to protect workable market relations'.[36] For example, it has been suggested that the decision-maker's apprehension with regard to the action of the courts creates 'ossification' of rule-making.[37]

This issue has been frequently considered in relation to financial services regulation. It is explained that, given that authorities in this field are required to make many difficult judgments which may affect a wide range of regulated businesses or individuals, it is likely they will be inhibited in the performance of their functions by the threat of judicial supervision. This much is clear from the view expressed by Lord Burns during the parliamentary debate on the Financial Services and Markets Bill. He said that 'if everything that the organisation did was subject to legal action, I am persuaded that that could lead only to over-regulation and excessive caution on behalf of the regulators'.[38] To similar effect Alan Page writes that 'the quality and effectiveness of supervision will suffer, it is argued, if regulators

---

[36] Black, Muchlinski and Walker (as above n. 4), 13. See also Walden, Ian, 'Telecommunications Law and Regulation: An Introduction' in *Telecommunications Law*, I. Walden and J. Angel (eds.), 1st edn., (Oxford: Blackstone Press, 2001) 9.

[37] Prosser, Tony, *Law and Regulators*, (Oxford: Clarendon Press, 1997) 279–280; McGarity, Thomas, 'Some Thoughts on "Deossifying" the Rulemaking Process' [1992] 41 *Duke Law Journal*, 1400; Pierce, Richard, 'Seven Ways to Deossify Agency Rulemaking' [1995] 47 *Administrative Law Review*, 59–95.

[38] HL Debs., col. 29, 21 February 2000.

have the threat of legal actions for damages hanging over their heads when taking difficult decisions'.[39]

Thus it becomes apparent that the behaviour and the judgement of bodies which regulate the operation of complex markets such as financial services might be affected by the knowledge that their decisions will be subject to enhanced judicial review in the High Court. In particular, it is argued that such situation may discourage the public authority from adopting the real decision which it considers to be important for the market. Lord Alexander of Weedon Q.C., former Chairman of the City Panel on Takeovers and Mergers, captures this point when he remarks that,

there is some danger at present that regulators may be reluctant to take the right course in what they believe is the substance of an issue because of a concern that they may not be able to establish the point in court.[40]

In fact, he refers to the finding in Sir Godfray Le Quesne's report on Barlow Clowes that the Department of Trade and Industry had on occasions been reluctant to follow what it thought to be the best course because of the risk of challenge.[41]

In light of this it has already been argued that regulatory decisions should be subject to a less intense scrutiny which may render the authority more confident in its powers and as a result more effective in deciding regulatory issues; only where the courts show themselves to be deferential towards the decision-maker will the problem of excessive cautiousness on his part be solved. Thus, the relative immunity of regulators from the jurisdiction of the courts also appears to be premised on the proposition that they should not be inhibited in the exercise of their functions by fear of expansive judicial interference and liability. This much is apparent from the cited article of Lord Alexander of Weedon which advocates the use of the deferential doctrine as a mechanism by which the executive body is placed in a strong position to implement its policies and decisions with no fear of any consequence in the judicial sphere. He said that,

whilst it is up to regulators to ensure that they do not 'aim off' out of caution it is also up to the law to show them clearly that judicial review requires of them fair procedures but leaves the substantive decisions to them.[42]

The second problem that intensive judicial review is said to raise relates to the apparent slowness of the court system. Basically, it is thought that judge-based adjudication undermines the effectiveness of commercial regulation because it is not well suited to the quick resolution of complex issues. As Solove explains, the classic disadvantages of the adversarial process such as 'slow slugging along, overburdened judges, lack of specialised knowledge and absence of efficient facilities

---

[39] Page, Alan, 'Regulating the Regulator—A Lawyer's Perspective on Accountability and Control' in *Regulating Financial Services and Markets in the 21st Century*, E. Ferran and C.A.E. Goodhart (eds.), (Oxford: Hart Publishing, 2001) 145.

[40] Alexander of Weedon, Lord Robert, 'Judicial Review and City Regulators' [1989] 52 *The Modern Law Review*, 648.

[41] Ibid.   [42] Ibid.

for digesting and evaluating facts' make it seem like 'a weary dinosaur when contrasted with increasingly detailed technological data, vast quantities of complex and conflicting empirical studies'.[43] In view of these shortcomings, supporters of the orthodox doctrine argue that judicial review is not an adequate method for dealing with market issues which may require rapid resolution and adjudication. Consequently, they conclude that intense scrutiny by the courts is a failure because it risks seriously interfering with the regulator's ability to put new strategies into place in order to address contemporary changes. The better approach, it is suggested, is that the judiciary should exercise its supervisory function with great caution, in a way which may allow the decision-making process to become faster and more efficient.

The third difficulty concerns the risk of tactical litigation which accompanies the constant intervention of the courts in the field of commercial regulation. This may broadly be described as legal actions brought against public authorities with a view to obstructing or hampering their functions. As Anthony Ogus observes, if the gates of judicial review are open too widely, the private interests will have 'an incentive to exploit the process for tactical purposes, thereby frustrating the implementation of public interest goals'.[44] For example, it has already been noted that 'a general admission of error of fact as a ground for judicial review would invite a flood of challenges, drowning the courts with work and sweeping the administrative system into a chaos'.[45] Moreover, this problem is exacerbated because economic decisions are more likely to be challenged in judicial review proceedings by the regulated than by consumers.[46] These actors 'rarely have the same self-limiting financial restraints as individual litigants',[47] therefore they may well be able to afford the cost of tactical litigation for their own commercial ends. Thus it becomes apparent that the courts' more rigorous approach to regulatory decisions may encourage individuals to bring frivolous, unreasonable, or groundless suits which could easily interfere with competitive market processes and decisions. It is precisely this problem of unmeritorious disputes which, it is argued, dictates the necessity of adopting a deferential, rather than a robust, attitude towards decision-makers that may contribute to maintaining regulatory effectiveness.

This philosophy is evident, for example, in the British contribution to the debate on the European Directive on Takeover Bids which came into force on 20 May 2004, after almost twenty years of negotiation. The government's main concern was that this measure would necessarily provide new opportunities to challenge the decisions of the Panel on Takeovers and Mergers, a self-regulatory organization, in a way which might 'hinder the effectiveness of the takeover regulation in

---

[43] Solove, (as above n. 9), 1007.

[44] Ogus, Anthony, *Regulation: Legal Form and Economic Theory*, (Oxford: Clarendon Press, 1994) 117.

[45] This stance is described by Demetriou and Houseman in 'Review for Error of Fact—A Brief Guide' [1997] 2(1) *Judicial Review*, 28.

[46] Cane, Peter, 'Mapping the Frontiers' in *The Frontiers of Liability*, (as above n. 3), 153.

[47] Black, Muchlinski and Walker, (as above n. 4), 14.

the United Kingdom'.[48] Under the new regime, it was argued, the function of the Panel will have full statutory backing. Consequently, a new statutory head of illegality for breach of the Directive will be created, which, because it gives a wider scope to individuals to challenge regulatory rules and decisions, it could certainly give rise to vexatious litigation. In view of this, during discussions in Brussels the delegates' primary negotiation aim was 'to ensure that any change to the legal basis of the regulation of takeovers in the UK does not make it easier for parties to a bid to challenge decisions through the courts and to engage in tactical litigation'.[49] In particular, they sought the inclusion of a provision in the Directive which allowed national courts to minimize the risks associated with increased judicial scrutiny of regulatory decisions such as slowness and lack of flexibility in the takeover regime. This was partially achieved through Article 4.6 of the Directive, which expressly provides that national courts can still 'decline to hear legal proceedings and to decide whether or not such proceedings affect the outcome of a bid'.

Subsequently, in January 2005, the Department of Trade and Industry published a Consultation Paper for the implementation of the Directive.[50] In this document, the government strongly argued that the legislation should be designed to eliminate the threat of tactical litigation posed by the new legal framework, which could undermine the 'important benefits of the current system' of takeover regulation in Great Britain in terms of 'speed, flexibility and certainty'. This intention was welcomed by the regulatory authority. Peter Scott QC, Chairman of The Takeover Panel, said that the proposals set out by the government to avoid tactical litigation will, if finally adopted, 'secure the flexibility of approach and the speed and certainty of decision-making that has been the hallmark of the Panel's takeover regulation'.[51] Thus it becomes clear that the view of executive bodies in relation to judicial review in takeover cases is entirely of a piece with the argument advanced in this section—that the courts should refrain from interfering in the legal affairs of the business community in order to ensure regulatory efficiency and effectiveness.

Finally, this ascription to the prevention of tactical litigation of the status of key principle within the takeover statutory regulation in the UK was echoed by Part 28 of the Companies Act 2006, which implemented the Directive. When introducing the Bill in Parliament, Lord Sainsbury of Turville said that 'the Bill's provisions aim to ensure that tactical litigation seeking to delay or frustrate a takeover bid will not become a feature of our takeover markets'.[52] Indeed, this Act makes

---

[48] Explanatory Memorandum of the Ministry of Trade and Industry, Lord Simon, 24 May 1999. See also Andenas, Mads, 'European Take-over Regulation and the City Code' [1996] 17(5) *Company Lawyer*, 150–152.

[49] Ibid.

[50] Department of Trade and Industry, *Company Law Implementation of the European Directive on Takeovers Bids. A Consultative Document*, (London: DTI, 2005).

[51] Explanatory Paper of The Takeover Panel, January 2005, 1.

[52] The Parliamentary Under-Secretary of State, Department of Trade and Industry, 'Company Law Reform Bill', HL Col 186, 11 January 2006.

explicit reference to limits relating to reviews of and appeals from Takeover Panel decisions.[53]

The fourth difficulty arising from a more rigorous approach to regulatory decisions concerns the risk of uncertainty in the market. It has already been argued that limitation of the agency's authority entailed by intensive review produces an environment of pervasive unpredictability which has substantial adverse effects upon the implementation of regulatory decisions. This is particularly problematic in the case of self-regulatory organizations which oversee the operation of specific markets. As Richard Gordon observes,

the effectiveness of a self-regulatory body in this sensitive field depends in the main on the perception by the market and by City institutions that the regulator in question is an authoritative decision-maker. The quashing or doubting of its decisions by the court can undermine its authority, with possibly severe consequences in a volatile market.[54]

For example, counsel for the Panel of Takeovers and Mergers in the *Datafin* case[55] contended that applications brought in the middle of a bid clearly may affect the operation of the market, and even short-term dislocation could be very harmful in terms of reliance on the validity of regulatory decisions. In this scenario, the only real conclusion that the potential investor can reach is that a certain rule or decision may or may not be lawful in the future depending upon the outcome of an unpredictable game.

More recently—and, interestingly, within the specific context of takeovers regulation—the government has expressed equally negative views on this matter. It has said in its Consultative Document on the implementation of the Directive on Takeovers Bids that,

the certainty afforded by the current system for regulating takeover activity would be seriously undermined if transactions could be unravelled following a legal challenge against a Panel decision or as a result of a breach of the Code. Bid parties would be unable to rely on the certainty offered by the Code and the decisions of the Panel.[56]

Accordingly, it is proposed that, in order not to undermine certainty in the stockmarket, individuals should be precluded from taking legal proceedings which may frustrate or hamper the bid or the defence of a bid. In particular, it would be

---

[53] Section 951 provides for a number of layers to go through before bringing judicial proceedings (the 'Hearings Committee' and the 'Takeover Appeal Board'); Section 956 provides that (1) contravention of rule-based requirements does not give rise to any right of action for breach of statutory duty, and that (2) contravention of a rule-based requirement does not make any transaction void or unenforceable or (subject to any provision made by rules) affect the validity of any other thing; Section 961 provides that the Panel is not to be liable in damages for anything done (or omitted to be done) in, or in connection with, the discharge or purported discharge of the Panel's functions. See Section 4.7

[54] Gordon, Richard, *Judicial Review: Law and Procedure*, 2nd ed., (London: Sweet & Maxwell Ltd. 1996), 253–254.

[55] *R v. Panel on Takeovers and Mergers, ex p Datafin plc.* [1987] 1 All E.R. 564. See Section 3 below for further details.

[56] Department of Trade and Industry, (as above n. 50), 17.

preferable for the courts to refuse to set aside transactions or decisions by reason of breach of the Code.[57]

Furthermore, it has been argued that this element of uncertainty is perpetuated by the court's inability to predict how its decision will affect the economic and social context within which the dispute arises. Given that the adjudicative model of decision-making applied by the judiciary usually confronts a static and precisely defined issue, it appears that the courts cannot really encompass and take into account the complex repercussions that may result from any change in the economic scene which cannot be addressed by the parties to the dispute.[58] This situation is likely to cause great uncertainty among large sections of the business community as to whether their position will be considered by the court in deciding the case, which might in turn be inconsistent with the regulatory objective of providing predictability in the market by implementing policies and decisions that pay due regard to the concerns of all the participants. In particular, it is argued that this environment of instability can have two negative effects.

First, those who view certainty in terms of a condition of market regulation which facilitates trade and management decisions have resorted to the notion that judicial intervention has an adverse effect on the economy on the whole. They point out that economists and students of finance long have observed a strong negative correlation between regulatory uncertainty created, *inter alia*, by judicial intervention and the general level of business investment. For example, Richard Pierce explains that,

> to the extent that uncertainty in the decision-making process causes uncertainty over the future price at which various forms of energy can be obtained, investment in a wide variety of industries will be retarded.[59]

Thus it appears that the sense of uneasiness for the future which the intervention of the courts fosters can have negative consequences not only for the operation of specific markets but also for the functioning of the complex modern economy due to network effect. All this suggests that the judiciary should abstain from intruding into multifaceted questions whose importance transcends the result in the case then at bar, favouring instead adherence to the criteria of the regulator which has been specifically entrusted with the task of establishing a coherent policy with respect to matters of substantial public concern.

Secondly, it is submitted that the incapacity of the courts to get involved in wider issues of impact can affect the past on legal relationships established by third parties in good faith. Given that the scope of litigation is defined by the grounds argued by the parties, it must follow that it is almost impossible for the courts, when deciding whether to grant relief to the applicant, to take into account the position of third parties who have reasonably relied on the validity of the impugned decision. Consequently, when an attempt is made to resolve the dispute at hand by

[57] Ibid.

[58] Fuller, Lon L., 'The Forms and Limits of Adjudication' [1978] 92 *Harvard Law Review*, 394.

[59] Pierce, Richard, 'The Choice between Adjudicating and Rulemaking for Formulating and Implementing Energy Policy' [1979–80] 31 *The Hastings Law Journal*, 24.

quashing that order, there is a clear risk of serious breach of the principle of legal certainty, since such invalidation would entail, as a matter of law, the frustration of legitimate expectations of innocent individuals. In light of this, it is argued that the courts need to look at the broader impact of invalidating administrative decisions and take into account not only the interests of the applicant and the defendant, but also the position of third parties.

In practice, these are the competing interests that should weigh with the court particularly in deciding whether to grant or withhold relief in the context of volatile markets, should it determine that there is a legal flaw in the exercise of a particular power. On this view, the court might well withhold from making a formal order, if it considers that to do so would have a detrimental impact either on the position of the administration or on interest of *bona fides* parties who have been misled by the unlawful order. Thus, in such cases, rather than automatically quashing the particular decision in question, the judiciary could, it is said,

refrain from granting retrospective relief to the applicant as a way to avoid wide scale injustice to third parties and administrative chaos which is not merited by the type or degree of illegality involved.[60]

Sir Thomas Bingham appears to advocate such an approach only to a very limited extent. In his well-known article on public law remedies,[61] he points out that, although the discretion to refuse relief in commercial cases should remain subject to significant limits, it becomes apparent that, when faced with 'a clash' between the rights of the individual and the wider interest of society, the courts ought to tip the balance in favour of the latter. In particular, this writer suggests that the maxim *fiat justitia ruat coelum* may be most firmly insisted upon when 'the administrative heavens are not expected to fall', so that regulatory chaos can be avoided:

it would seem to me wise for the courts to venture into this uncharted minefield with considerable circumspection lest the cure be more damaging to the wider investing public than the disease.

On this view, therefore, a more pragmatic, utilitarian approach which leads to qualified declarations of judicial abstinence in this area must be preferred to 'the high ground of purist principle'.

Finally, it is worth noting that this philosophy is also evident in section 31(6) of the Supreme Court Act, which entitles the High Court to refuse the relief sought on delayed applications if it considers that it 'would be likely to cause substantial hardship to, or substantially prejudice the rights of, any person or would be detrimental to good administration'.[62] Thus, the principle of legal certainty as to the validity of governmental actions finds a particular place within the context of time

---

[60] Lewis, Clive, 'Retrospective and Prospective Rulings in Administrative Law' [1988] *Public Law*, 104.

[61] Bingham, Sir Thomas, 'Should Public Law Remedies be Discretionary?' [1991] *Public Law*, 64–75.

[62] For discussion, see Beloff, Michael, 'Time, Time, Time It's on my Side, Yes It is' in *The Golden Metwand and the Crooked Cord*, C.F. Forsyth and I. Hare (eds.), (Oxford: Oxford University Press, 1998), 267–295. See also Craig, (as above n. 27), 903–908; Sunkin, Maurice, 'Remedies Available in

limits: the requirement that important decisions should not be able to be set aside long after the event in order to prevent adverse impact on third parties and administrative efficiency is recognized by the legislator as essential for the correct exercise of remedial discretion.

3. Case Law

We have seen that the argument for less intensive judicial review is especially forceful in the commercial context, where it is considered to be the better reaction to the problems that beset supervision of regulatory decisions. It is now necessary to consider the case law in which this doctrine has been applied. In particular, it may be helpful to provide an account of the different aspects of the contended decision in respect of which deference is claimed. The analysis will begin with the situations where the courts have refused to review the factual evidence supporting the administrative decision. This will be followed by a consideration of the cases in which substantive choices made by the regulators are held to be immune from judicial scrutiny. It will be seen that this policy of judicial deference is based on the notion that the courts may only set aside the conclusion reached by the decision-maker in extreme circumstances. We shall then explore the application of the doctrine in relation to the authority's reasoning process. The focus will then shift to the deferential attitude exhibited by the courts *vis-à-vis* the executive interpretation of vague rules. Finally, this section will consider situations where the courts have refused to quash unlawful decisions on the ground that the granting of relief would be detrimental to the interests of the administration and the position of third parties.

3.1 Questions of fact

The cases show that there is a great unwillingness on the part of the judges to review the regulator's findings of fact. The general assertion is made that the existence or non-existence of a fact should be left to the judgement and discretion of the decision-maker. In particular, it is the role of the court not to substitute its decision of that fact for that of the executive body to whom Parliament has entrusted the decision-making power and which, as a primary and experienced fact-finder, has had the benefit of actually weighing the evidence in a way that better deals with the technically complex subject matter. In practice, this approach signifies that if the regulator's decision was made on the basis of a mistake of fact, the court could intervene and possibly quash the order only if it is obvious that it is perverse. Outside this category, it is not accepted that

Judicial Review Proceedings' in *English Public Law*, D. Feldman (ed.), (Oxford: Oxford University Press, 2004), 943–945; and the *Caswell* case, below at n. 155, 63–64.

a decision can be flawed on the ground that it is based on an erroneous finding of fact.

It may be helpful, for the purpose of analysing the case law on this subject, to consider the different reasons which have led the judiciary to apply such a deferential approach in the last century. Indeed, it worth noting that, although the court's traditional refusal to review findings of fact reflects the underlying notion that decision-makers are better placed to deal with evidential issues, the justification for this attitude has evolved from a very rigid analysis of the scope of administrative jurisdiction to the consideration of factors related to regulatory effectiveness such as agency expertise and the desire for speedy decisions on public law matters.

Thus, earlier cases of judicial cautiousness in this field concerned the distinction between errors of fact which relate to the kind of case into which an authority could inquire and those which relate to the truth or detail of the findings that it made.[63] The first ones were regarded as jurisdictional, which means that the court could intervene because the authority was outside the 'scope' which had been assigned to it by the legislature. In contrast, the second type of errors were categorized as non-jurisdictional, which implies that the judge could not intervene, for the agency had simply made an error within its assigned area. Nevertheless, it is worth pointing out that, in practice, this contrast became blurred in light of the courts' decision to consider orders reached on 'no evidence' as non-jurisdictional. Consequently, most of the disputed questions of fact were in general exempt from review by the judiciary.

An early example of this can be seen in *R v. Nat Bell Liquors Ltd.*[64] The respondents were a large business of liquor exporters, based in Edmonton. In 1920, they were convicted before a magistrate of that town, for unlawfully keeping a quantity of liquor contrary to the Liquor Act and the amendments thereto. By a subsequent order, the magistrate declared the whole of the liquor, and the vessels in which it was contained, to be forfeited to the Crown. Thereupon the respondents moved, by way of certiorari, to quash the order on the ground, *inter alia*, that there was no evidence to convict. However, Lord Sumner adopted a limited form of review and concluded that 'no evidence' was not a jurisdictional defect.[65] Commenting this

---

[63] Craig, *Administrative Law*, (as above n. 27), 438–439.

[64] [1922] 2 A.C. 128, 151–154.

[65] A justice who convicts without evidence is doing something that he ought not to do, but he is doing it as a judge, and if his jurisdiction to entertain the charge is not open to impeachment, his subsequent error, however grave, is a wrong exercise of a jurisdiction which he has, and not a usurpation of a jurisdiction which he has not. How a magistrate, who has acted within his jurisdiction up to the point at which the missing evidence should have been, but was not, given, can, thereafter, be said by a kind of relation back to have had no jurisdiction over the charge at all, it is hard to see. It cannot be said that his conviction is void, and may be disregarded as a nullity, or that the whole proceeding was *coram non judice*. To say that there is no jurisdiction to convict without evidence is the same thing as saying that there is jurisdiction if the decision is right, and none if it is wrong; or that jurisdiction at the outset of a case continues so long as the decision stands, but that, if it is set aside, the real conclusion is that there never was any jurisdiction at all.

criterion, Craig says that,

thus, a conviction, regular in its face, was conclusive of all the facts stated in it, including those necessary to give the justices jurisdiction. On this hypothesis, there was clearly no place for review of finding of facts, in the sense of determining whether the evidence justified the application of a statutory term to particular facts.[66]

In more recent cases, however, the arguments underlying judicial reluctance to review the factual basis of decisions have been closely related to the regulator's technical knowledge and institutional autonomy as well as to the effectiveness of the decision-making process.

General Electric Co. Ltd. (G.E.C.) v. Price Commission[67] is one of the leading authorities on the issue. The regulator had been empowered under section 6 of the Counter-Inflation Act 1973 to ensure control over prices by means of a code set out in the Schedule to the Counter-Inflation (Price and Pay Code) (No 2) Order 1973 made under section 2 of the Act of 1973. In January 1974, G.E.C, the principal manufacturer of electrical goods in Britain, gave notice to the commission of its proposals to increase several of its prices to customers. But the agency refused to authorize these increases on the ground that, if permitted, the company would be exceeding the level of profit allowable. G.E.C. sought declarations as to the correct method of determining their 'reference level' under the Price Code, but failed before the Court of Appeal. Lord Denning MR recognized that there were no statutory terms which excluded the right of the company to have recourse to the courts to determine its rights, but stressed that reading the legislation, it seemed clearly to be implied that the original findings of fact were for the commission, and not for the courts of law. He said this firstly on the ground of expertise.[68] His Lordship also stressed that the determination of issues of fact needs a speedy decision which is necessarily inconsistent with the judicial process.[69]

---

[66] Craig, (as above n. 27) 503.

[67] [1975] I.C.R. 1.

[68] [T]he matters to be decided are so technical and so complex that they can only be well determined by a body of experts such as the Price Commission. For one thing, the commission have to interpret the code. It is expressed in words and phrases of technical import. Accountants may understand them, but very few others do so. Next, the commission have to apply the code to the affairs of the company. This means analysing the accounts of the company and putting each item into its proper place. Calculations must be made so as to find the 'total cost per unit of output', the 'net profit margin', and the 'reference level'. This may be child's play for accountants, but it is hard going for others. Then the commission have to determine the amount of 'any allowable cost increase' which is permissible on account of increased costs: and whether it should be abated or not so as to keep the profit within bounds. All this may be within the skills of accountants, but it would be unwise for anyone else to attempt it.

[69] Many of the matters have to be decided very quickly. When costs are rising rapidly, the manufacturer must be able to pass them on in a short time to his buyers. Otherwise he will soon bankrupt. But he cannot increase his prices unless they are first approved of by the commission. He will, therefore, be alert to give notice to the commission of any proposed increase: and he will have every right to expect a decision within a few weeks. He cannot wait for a long investigation comparable to a trial in court—with pleadings, witnesses, arguments and so forth.

   Finally it must be borne in mind that inflation is a great and urgent problem. It requires drastic remedies to be immediately applied. Parliament has prescribed a remedy. It has

Finally, Lord Denning based his arguments on the ground of autonomy and lack of appeal proceedings.[70]

A similar view was expressed by Lord Justice Roskill. Although he accepted that the courts were well capable of determining some issues of fact and of doing it speedily,[71] he stressed that in the instant case such a task had been clearly entrusted by Parliament to the Price Commission and not to the courts.[72]

In financial services regulation this approach can be seen in *R v. Panel on Takeovers and Mergers, ex p Datafin plc.*[73] The applicants had complained to the panel that two companies had acted 'in concert', contrary to the code of conduct prescribed by the regulator, in the course of a contested take-over for a company. The Panel rejected the complaint and the applicants sought to impugn the decision before the court. On the hearing, the respondent contended that the supervisory jurisdiction of the court was confined to bodies whose power derived solely from legislation or the exercise of the prerogative, and that therefore judicial review did not extend to a body such as the panel. Although the court rejected this allegation,[74] it argued that a deferential approach should be adopted to reviewing the regulator's findings of fact.[75] Furthermore, this verdict demonstrates clearly that

---

established the Price Commission. If this remedy is to be effective, the decisions under the code must be taken by the commission quickly and implemented at once. They must be final in this sense, that they are not subject to appeal or to any stay pending an appeal. They cannot wait to be determined by the courts.

[70] I think the Price Commission stand in a position similar to other bodies we have had. Parliament often entrusts the decision of a matter to a specified person or body, without providing for any appeal. It may be a judicial decision, or a quasi-judicial decision, or and administrative decision. Sometimes Parliament says its decision is to be final. At other it says nothing about it. In all these cases the courts will not themselves take the place of the body to whom Parliament has entrusted the decision. The courts will not themselves make the original findings of fact. The courts will not themselves embark on a rehearing of the matter.

[71] That task may sometimes be speedily discharged by such judges if the parties ask for a speedy decision and waive some of the formalities of the judicial process [page 18, D].

[72] One has only to read the statute and the code to see that the duty is given to and only to the Price Commission . . . it is against all principle as well as against the clear intention of the Act of 1973 and the code that whenever a difference of opinion on fact is likely to arise or has arisen between a manufacturer and the commission, the manufacturer seeking to assert a particular view as to what (for example) are the generally accepted accounting principles applicable to a particular subject matter, can rush to the courts and say, 'Please say that it is our view of the facts which is correct'; and then claim that the commission are bound by that decision of the court upon such a question of fact.

[73] As above n. 55.   [74] See especially the judgment of Lloyd LJ.

[75] Sir John Donaldson stated:

In a case, such as the present, where the complaint is that the panel should have found a breach of the rules, but did not do so, I would expect the court to be even more reluctant to move in the absence of any credible allegation of lack of bona fides. It is not for a court exercising a judicial review jurisdiction to substitute itself for the fact-finding tribunal.

There was some failure on the part of the applicants to appreciate, or at least to act in recognition of the fact, that an application for judicial review is not an appeal. The panel and not the court is the body charged with the duty of evaluating the evidence and finding the facts. The role of the court is wholly different.

deference to the factual part of the Panel's decision was based in the expertise of the regulator.[76]

A similar line of reasoning was applied in *R v. Securities and Futures Authority (SFA), ex p Panton*.[77] The case concerned the refusal of the authority, a self-regulatory organization set up under the Financial Services Act (1986), to investigate Mr. Panton's complaints about the conduct of a company, unless new facts or evidence came to light. Sir Thomas Bingham MR held in the Court of Appeal that although financial regulators are bodies over whom the court can, in appropriate circumstances, and will, exercise a supervisory jurisdiction, it must be also be recognized that the clear intention of the Act is that factual matters should be exclusively decided by these organizations. Therefore, it is not the functions of the court in anything other than a clear case to second guess their decisions or, as it was, to look over their shoulder.[78]

This reticence has also been expressed in regulated public utilities according to the judgment of the High Court in *R v. Independent Television Commission (ITC), ex p Virgin Television Ltd*.[79] In this case, the applicant sought to challenge the decision of the regulator which awarded the Channel 5 licence to another bidder. However, Henry LJ dismissed the application on the ground that a cautious approach over facts should be adopted.[80]

---

[76] [T]he chairman's long, detailed and helpful affidavit well illustrates the need for the court to avoid underestimating the extent to which expert knowledge can negative inferences which might otherwise be drawn from a partial knowledge of the facts and the extent to which a greater knowledge of the facts can make a decision which at first might seem faintly surprising, not only explicable, but plainly right. Thus the panel from its expertise knew that no significance should be attached to the bare fact that KIO used Greenwell Montagu as their brokers.

[77] 20 June 1994 (unreported Lexis). All regulatory functions of this body were taken over by the Financial Services Authority as of December 2001.

[78] Accordingly, he concluded that:

Thus, the position that I think we end up with is that these bodies are amenable to judicial review but are, in anything other than very clear circumstances, to be left to get on with it. It is for them to decide on the facts whether it is, or is not, appropriate to proceed against a member as not being a fit and proper person and it is essentially a matter for their judgment as to the extent to which a complaint is investigated. That being so, I am not for my part persuaded that either of the major decisions which Mr Panton wishes to challenge are ones which this court could properly hold to be unlawful. They may involve factual error. There may even be disputable questions of law which arise. But it appears to me that these decisions that Mr Panton seeks to attack fall well within the jurisdiction accorded to the SFA and I am quite satisfied that the court would be exceeding its proper role on the facts disclosed by this application if it were to grant leave to move for judicial review and seek in effect to interfere with what the SFA has done.

[79] [1996] E.M.L.R. 318. The ITC ceased to exist from 18 December 2003 and its duties were assumed by OFCOM. See also *R v. Director General of Gas Supply, ex p Smith*, CRO/1398/88, QBD, 31 July 1989: 'Parliament has conferred a broad discretion upon the Director and it is for him to exercise judgment on questions of fact'. This post was replaced by OFGEM.

[80] The ITC's decision under section 16(1)(a) involved matters of judgment which had been entrusted by Parliament to an expert body which was also responsible for finding the facts on which the judgment was to be based. The exercise was not simply a quantitative exercise but involved qualitative analysis and judgment...The factual part of the

A similar criterion was applied by the Queen's Bench Division in *R. v. Director General of Telecommunications, ex p Cellcom Ltd and others*.[81] In that case, a group of independent service providers to end-users in the field of mobile telephony sought judicial review of decisions of the regulatory body that, in order to promote competition between network operators, the conditions of the licences of the new and loss-making entrants into the market (Mercury and Orange) which placed constraints on their freedom to trade should be relaxed. The applicants perceived the proposed relaxation as having severe adverse effect on their ability to retail airtime profitably. In deciding the case, Lightman LJ expressed a strong refusal of the courts' intervention on the ground of factual basis. He explained that the court should be 'very slow to impugn decisions of fact made by an expert and experienced decision-maker', and that it must surely be 'even slower to impugn his educated prophesies and predictions for the future'. In practice, this means that the judge could only interfere if the Director's resolution of disputed questions of fact is 'perverse eg. if his reasoning is logically unsound'.

Another example can be seen in *R v. Radio Authority, ex p Bull and another*.[82] Here, the respondent authority prohibited the advertising of Amnesty International British Section (AIBS) on commercial radio to publicize the plight of people in Rwanda and Burundi. The regulator argued that the applicant was a body whose objects were 'mainly of a political nature' which was accordingly prohibited from advertising on the radio (Broadcasting Act 1990, s 92(2)(a)(i)). In deciding the conflict, the Court of Appeal accorded a high degree of deference to the respondent's findings of fact on the basis of legislative will.[83] This case is also interesting because judges considered in *obiter dicta* that the regulator had taken a decision based on a wrong assessment of facts, but it was their duty to accept it in the name

Commission's decision necessarily involved consideration of evidence presented to it. It was for the Commission to evaluate that evidence, and no one else...There must accordingly be a natural, as well as a judicial, reluctance to conclude that the decision was flawed. This is not a consequence of judicial conservatism or intellectual disinclination. It is a logical consequence of the perceived care and meticulous approach which the Commission brought to bear on its task of assessment and evaluation in accordance with what Parliament has entrusted to it. It is also a consequence of the limits which the court is required to observe in determining whether or not the decision maker has arrived at a decision which has a sufficient factual basis.

Moreover, the judge wanted to go further by sending a clear message to the claimants:
It followed that a very heavy burden fell on a party seeking to challenge such a decision.

[81] *The Times*, 7 December, 1998. CO/2088/98. The post of Director General of Telecommunications was abolished in 2003, and replaced by OFCOM.

[82] *The Times*, 21 January, 1997. [1996] E.M.L.R. 68. The Radio Authority ceased to exist on 29 December 2003 and its duties were assumed by OFCOM.

[83] Parliament having entrusted a specialist body with the duty to determine (i) whether a body's objects are wholly or mainly political and (ii) whether individual advertisements are directed towards political ends, the court would, in any event, be slow to interfere with that authority's evaluation of the facts.

of autonomy and expertise.[84] In addition, the court expressed its surprise about the way in which the authority found itself able to reach its final conclusion that Amnesty International British Section's objects were mainly political.[85]

3.2 Substantive review

The doctrine of judicial self-restraint has also been reflected in substantive review matters. There are cases where the courts have shown a marked reluctance to control the outcome of the decision-making process. The basic assumption is that the administration of public affairs ought to be conducted by the government rather than by the courts. To ensure this, the judiciary should interfere with the content of executive decisions only when it is very far beyond the rational as the judiciary sees it. This means that, so long as it does not act in a totally absurd way, the public body might make any decision it wishes. In this sense, the deferential attitude of the English courts is seen to express a particular conception of the separation of powers according to which the primary judgement concerning the reasonableness of the decision is for the regulator. Nevertheless, while the argument of institutional competence is perhaps the most tangible explanation for the cautious approach to substance-oriented review, it is possible to identify additional catalysts which have motivated the judiciary to play a limited role in the commercial context. Two, in particular, stand out.

3.2.1 *The war and the law prior to Wednesbury*

The courts in some early cases kept regulatory decisions relatively immune from scrutiny partly due to the second world war, and because the statutes contained criteria which were considered to be less amenable to judicial review. That is the case, for example, in *R v. Comptroller General of Patents, ex p Bayer Products, Ltd.*[86] The Emergency Powers (Defence) Act, 1939 had provided that His Majesty may by Order in Council make regulations,

as appear to him to be necessary or expedient for securing the public safety, the defence of the realm, the maintenance of public order and the efficient prosecution of any war in which His Majesty may be engaged, and for maintaining supplies and services essential to the life of the community.

---

[84] Lord Justice Brooke stated:

Like Lord Woolf M.R., I can find no fault in the Radio Authority's interpretation of the law. It is, however, unclear to me, as it is to him, whether they did properly take into account every material consideration when reaching their decision in this case. But since they are a lay body charged with a difficult task on whom Parliament has imposed the unusual obligation of having 'to do all that they can to secure' the statutory objectives, I consider that it would be wrong for a court to interfere with the decision they made.

[85] If half of A.I.B.S.'s campaigning aims were non-political, and the educational and research objects of A.I.B.S.C.T. in the field of education and research were not mainly political, what was it that persuaded the authority to decide this case in the way they did?

[86] [1941] 2 K.B. 306.

Under this provision, His Majesty in Council empowered the Comptroller of Patents to suspend the trade mark rights of an enemy or an enemy subject, which included certain trade marks owned by British subjects operating enemy-owned patents. Bayer Products applied to the King's Bench Division for an order of prohibition to be directed to the Comptroller to restrain him from exercising any jurisdiction or making any orders under the Order in Council. The company argued, *inter alia*, that the defence regulation was *ultra vires* because it was not necessary nor expedient for any purpose laid down by the Emergency Powers (Defence) Act, 1939. Thus, the question raised in the court was whether or not such rule was within the powers conferred by the Act to His Majesty in Council. The Court of Appeal adopted a less intensive form of substantive review and refused to judge the necessity or reasonableness of the contended order.[87]

Historically, time of war has also been a factor which induces courts to exhibit a deferential attitude towards the reasons which underlie the administrative decision. In the present case, for example, Clauson LJ held that it was not within the power of the court to review His Majesty's reasoning process when he has stated that a regulation appeared to him to be necessary or expedient for certain purpose.[88]

3.2.2 *The Wednesbury Approach*

It was the crucial and much quoted decision of the Court of Appeal in *Associated Provincial Picture Houses Ltd. v. Wednesbury Corporation*,[89] however, that consolidated the courts' doctrine of self-restraint and the clear demarcation between the respective provinces of executive and judicial power within the constitutional

---

[87] Scott LJ stated:

Be that as it may, in my opinion, the effect of the words 'as appear to him to be necessary or expedient' is to give to His Majesty in Council a complete discretion to decide what regulations are necessary for the purposes named in the sub-section. That being so, it is not open to His Majesty's courts to investigate the question whether or not the making of any particular regulation was in fact necessary or expedient for the specified purposes. The principle on which delegated legislation must rest under our constitution is that legislative discretion which is left in plain language by Parliament is to be final and not subject to control by the courts. In my view, the sub-section clearly conferred on His Majesty in Council that ultimate discretion. It is easy to see why that discretion must be a very wide one. The history of this war has shown all kinds of ways in which, for instance, the maintenance of supplies and services are essential to the life of the community. I cannot imagine a case where that is more obviously true than that of the supply of the many modern medicaments which are necessary for the medical profession and for the maintenance of our medical services.

[88] In my view, this court has no right or jurisdiction to investigate the reasons which moved His Majesty to reach the conclusion that it was necessary or expedient to make the regulation. The legislature has left the matter to His Majesty, and this court has no control over it. This court, in my view, has no duty and no right to investigate the advice given to His Majesty which moved him to the view that it was necessary or expedient for the purposes in question to make this regulation, and I know of no authority which would justify the court in questioning the decision which His Majesty, as I understand it, has stated that he has come to—namely, that this regulation is necessary or expedient. If His Majesty has once reached that conclusion, that regulation is the law of the land, subject to the fact that the Act specially provides machinery by which, if either House of Parliament is disposed to take a view differing from that upon which His Majesty has been pleased to act, the order can be annulled.

[89] [1948] 1 K.B. 223 at 234.

order. This leading authority represents the second and more fundamental catalyst for the development of the deferential approach to decisions in the sphere of
market-regulation. The claimants, who were the proprietors of a cinematograph
theatre in Wednesbury, sought a declaration from the court that the condition
imposed by the licensing authority, which prohibited the admission of children
to Sunday performances to be held in that cinema, was unreasonable and *ultra
vires* the decision-maker. In dismissing the appeal of the petitioners, Lord Greene
held that when the executive authority is entrusted by Parliament with discretion on a matter in which the knowledge and experience of the authority can be
trusted to be of value, what purports to be an exercise of that discretion can only
be challenged in the courts in a very limited class of case. In such circumstances,
he said, the decision of the public authority may only be set aside if it is wholly
absurd.[90]

This dictum highlights the central characteristic of substantive review in the
present context: the fact that the judiciary must apply a policy of judicial deference to the outcome of the decision-making process. The rationale underlying this doctrine, which is collectively described as the *Wednesbury* approach,
has been developed in the foregoing section. It is sufficient, for the present,
to note that the issue reduces to one of expertise and institutional autonomy.
Judges generally feel that they are not well-placed to resolve issues of technical regulation and that, for this reason, discretion on these matters has been
entrusted by Parliament to executive bodies with the knowledge and experience which can best be trusted to deal with. Consequently, in judging whether
the administrative decision is rational, and hence lawful, the courts should
necessarily rely upon the standard of substantive fairness adopted by the well-
equipped and qualified body; only if its conclusion is totally absurd may the
court intervene. The relevant implications of this approach for the relationship
between the judiciary and the executive are well explained by Elliott in his
article on human rights and substantive review.[91] Two, in particular, should be
mentioned.

First, since the court can interfere only with executive action which is outwith
the range of substantive options which are open to the decision-maker, it follows
that the impugned decision made within that scope must be held to be lawful even

---

[90] [I]f it is proved to be unreasonable in the sense, not that it is what the court considers
unreasonable, but that it is what the court considers is a decision that *no reasonable body
could have come to*. It is not what the court considers unreasonable, a different thing
altogether. If it is what the court considers unreasonable, the court may very well have
different views to that of a local authority on matters of high public policy of this kind.
Some courts might think that no children ought to be admitted on Sundays at all, some
courts might think the reverse, and all over the country I have no doubt on a thing of that
sort honest and sincere people hold different views. The effect of the legislation is not to
set up the court as an arbiter of the correctness of one view over another. It is the local
authority that are set in that position and, provided they act, as they have acted, within
the four corners of their jurisdiction, this court, in my opinion, cannot interfere.

[91] Elliott, 'The Human Rights Act 1998 and the Standard of Substantive Review' [2001] 60(2)
Cambridge Law Journal, 301–336.

though the judge finds that it is incoherent and lacking in adequate justification. Elliott explains that,

the factor which permits the co-existence of what seem, intuitively, to be two mutually inconsistent conclusions is the secondary nature of the role which the court is confined when it applies the reasonableness test.[92]

Indeed, under the *Wednesbury* approach, the judgement as to whether the administrative discretion has been exercised reasonably is primarily for the executive. Only if the decision is beyond the range of substantive responses which are available to the reasonable decision-maker can the court, exercising its secondary judgement, properly interfere. In light of this, it is not surprising that the court may uphold an executive order made within that margin of appreciation which it considers to be unjustified and mistaken. Hence this writer comments that *Wednesbury* review 'erects a substantial zone of immunity within which administrative decision-making is protected from judicial scrutiny'.[93]

The second important point to note is that, in cases concerned with rights, this approach is seen to leave it to the executive to determine how the balance ought to be struck between the interests of the individual and competing public policy claims; in Elliott's words, 'only if its evaluation of the relative importance of the two factors is so untenable as to be absurd may the court intervene'.[94] In particular, he notes that the existence of an apparent justification for the restriction of rights is almost sufficient in itself to establish the validity of the decision. Provided that a public policy consideration exists, and can be placed in the balance against the rights-based arguments of the claimants, the courts are reluctant to require a greater justification from the decision-maker, 'subject to the proviso that a wholly absurd decision could be set aside as being manifestly unreasonable'.[95] Thus, there is practically no discussion as to whether the administrative interference with the applicant's rights is justified by a sufficiently important public interest.

At this point, it is worth emphasizing that the present doctrine is the most important tool used by English courts to control discretionary decisions in the commercial context. The test which the seminal *Wednesbury* decision institutionalized in 1948 has been applied on a number of occasions. Thus, in *R v. Trade and Industry Secretary, ex p. Lonrho plc*,[96] the application of this deferential approach was accepted even by the applicant. What had happened was that the authority decided to defer publication of the report of the inspectors appointed by him to investigate the affairs of the House of Fraser Holdings plc (Fraser), and not to refer to the Monopolies and Mergers Commission the merger relating to the acquisition by Al Fayed Investment and Trust (UK) plc of that company. Counsel for the applicant recognized that the discretion of the Secretary of State must be exercised by

---

[92] Ibid., 305.   [93] Ibid., 306.
[94] Ibid. See the dictum of Simon Brown LJ in *ex p Smith*, (as above, n. 79), at 540.
[95] Ibid., 307.
[96] [1989] 2 All E.R. 609, [1989] 1 W.L.R. 525, [1989] B.C.C. 633. See also *Cityhook Ltd. and another, R (on the application of) v. Office of Fair Trading and others* [2009] E.W.H.C. (Admin) 57 at para 136 and 165.

him in a manner which was not unreasonable, in the *Wednesbury* sense. However, it submitted that the decision-maker had failed to meet that standard of reasonableness in the particular case. The court found for the defendant. Nevertheless, in deciding the case, it confirmed the doctrine that judges should be reticent about intruding into the regulator's decision. Lord Keith of Kinkel held that the decision-maker alone was charged and authorized by parliament to exercise that discretion. Consequently, the courts must be careful 'not to invade the political field and substitute their own judgment for that of the minister'.

In *Brind and others v. Secretary of State for the Home Department*,[97] the House of Lords defended the ordinary *Wednesbury* test from criticism and declined to recognize proportionality as an independent head of review. The case concerned directives issued by the Home Secretary to the Independent Broadcasting Authority and to the British Broadcasting Corporation, prohibiting the broadcasting of direct statements by representatives of proscribed organisations in Northern Ireland. The applicants, who were journalists, sought judicial review of the decisions on the ground, *inter alia*, that the authority had acted without necessity, disproportionately, and perversely. Lord Ackner advocated *Wednesbury* as the right approach to avoid the courts deciding upon the merits.[98] Furthermore, Lord Lowry provided a complete list of classical reasons to justify the court's reluctance to apply a more searching scrutiny in cases not involving a Community law element.[99]

---

[97] [1991] 1 A.C. 696.

[98] This standard of unreasonableness (*Wednesbury*), often referred to as 'the irrationality test', has been criticised as being too high. But it has to be expressed in terms that confine the jurisdiction exercised by the judiciary to a supervisory, as opposed to an appellate, jurisdiction. Where Parliament has given to a minister or other person or body a discretion, the court's jurisdiction is limited, in the absence of a statutory right of appeal, to the supervision of the exercise of that discretionary power, so as to ensure that it has been exercised lawfully. It would be a wrongful usurpation of power by the judiciary to substitute its view, the judicial view, on the merits and on that basis to quash the decision ... To seek the court's intervention on the basis that the correct or objectively reasonable decision is other than the decision which the minister has made, is to invite the court to adjudicate as if Parliament had provided a right of appeal against the decision, that is to invite an abuse of power by the judiciary.

[99] (1) The decision-makers, very often elected, are those to whom Parliament has entrusted the discretion and to interfere with that discretion beyond the limits as hitherto defined would itself be an abuse of the judges' supervisory jurisdiction. (2) The judges are not, generally speaking, equipped by training or experience, or furnished with the requisite knowledge and advice, to decide the answer to an administrative problem where the scales are evenly balanced, but they have a much better chance of reaching the right answer where the question is put in a *Wednesbury* form. The same applies if the judges' decision is appealed. (3) Stability and relative certainty would be jeopardised if the new doctrine held sway, because there is nearly always something to be said against any administrative decision and parties who felt aggrieved would be even more likely than at present to try their luck with a judicial review application both at first instance and on appeal. (4) The increase in applications for judicial review of administrative action (inevitable if the threshold of unreasonableness is lowered) will lead to the expenditure of time and money by litigants, not to speak of the prolongation of uncertainty for all concerned with the decisions in question, and the taking up of court time which could otherwise be devoted to other matters. The losers in this respect will be members of the public, for whom the courts provide a service.

A similar doctrine was applied by the House of Lords in *R v. Independent Television Commission, ex p TSW Broadcasting Limited*.[100] Here, the agency had rejected the application of the highest bidder for a Channel 3 licence without giving reasons for its conclusion. Lord Templeman said that a challenge on unreasonableness under the Broadcasting Act 1990 cannot be based on the wider proportionality or human rights ground of review but has a narrow scope often referred to as *Wednesbury*.[101] The judgment in *Wildman v. Ofcom*[102] also made clear that telecoms licensing is an area in which the court should allow the regulator 'a wide measure of discretion and width of decision'.[103]

This deferential approach was also adopted in *Appollo Ltd. v. Independent Television Companies Association Ltd. and another*.[104] The case concerns the regulator's refusal to grant to that company advertising time on television and radio for a Sunday publication known as 'Sunday Sport'. The authority argued that it was a 'girlie magazine' more than a conventional newspaper. In his verdict at the Queen's Bench Division, Taylor LJ held that the grounds of judicial review do not permit the court to consider the merits of the original decision, though the substance of the decision may be impugned insofar as it is obviously perverse or absurd.[105]

---

[100] *The Times*, 13 March 1992. The same criterion was followed by Henry LJ in *R v. Independent Television Commission, ex p Virgin Television Ltd.*, (as above n. 79).

[101] Only if the reasons given by the ITC for the decision to reject the application of TSW disclosed illegality, irrationality or procedural impropriety, then, in accordance with the speech of Lord Diplock in *Council of Civil Service Unions v the Minister of Civil Service*, and the judgment of Lord Greene MR in *Associated Provincial Picturehouses Ltd v Wednesbury Corporation*, could the decision be open to judicial review. This is not a case in which TSW can rely on any breach of the principle of proportionality or can require a close scrutiny of possible threats to human rights or fundamental freedoms... Where a decision is made in good faith following a proper procedure and as a result of conscientious consideration, an applicant for judicial review is not entitled to relief save on the grounds... [Wednesbury].

[102] [2005] E.W.H.C. (Admin) 1573.

[103] At para. 67. Here the claim for judicial review was dismissed on the ground, *inter alia*, that,

Ofcom is an expert body, and it, and not the Court, has been given the responsibility for making the evaluations and exercising the discretions inherent in a licensing process that involves the selection of only one of a number of applicants to be awarded a licence [at para. 14]. See also the judgment of Silber J in *R v. Secretary of State for Trade and Industry, ex p BT3G Ltd and One 2 One*, a case concerning licences for the so-called third generation of mobile phones ('Universal Mobile Telecommunications System') [2001] Eu L.R. 326 at para. 183–187.

[104] 5 September 1986. CO/1140/86.

[105] I emphasise at the outset of this part of the case that it is clear and trite law, in exercising its judicial review jurisdiction, the Court is not empowered to substitute its own opinion for that of the body entrusted with responsibility under the statute. It is not whether I consider that this mock-up is in like case with the other exhibits from other newspapers which have been provided. The question is all to do with the decision-making process. All I am here to do is to consider whether that process has been properly conducted or whether the result to which it came was one which no reasonable committee or authority could have reached... it seems to me that on any view of this matter, the material which is before me is such that I could not possibly say the decision reached here was irrational in the sense that it defied logic or was outrageous or that no reasonable committee could have come to that conclusion.

A comparable attitude was shown by the Court of Justice in *R v. Director General of Telecommunications, ex p Cellcom Ltd and others*,[106] where Lightman LJ said that the deferential approach inherent in the *Wednesbury* principle should also operate to direct judicial supervision over the authority's reasoning process.[107] In this sense, two particular points must be made. The first one relates to the weight to be given to the 'relevant' consideration taken into account by the regulator. His Lordship held that so long as the decision-maker takes that consideration into account, the weight to be given to it and indeed 'whether any weight at all should be given to that consideration is a matter for the Director alone, so long as his decision is not perverse'.[108] Secondly, it is argued that the courts must be particularly careful in their review of written reasons of the regulator for his decision. Lightman LJ illustrated this approach by reference to the judgment of Lord Wilberforce in *Secretary of State for Education and Science v. Tameside Borough Council*.[109]

The application of the *Wednesbury* test in the law relating to public utilities was recently reaffirmed in *R (London and Continental Stations and Property Ltd) v. The Rail Regulator*.[110] The claimant, a train operating company, sought judicial review to challenge the legality of the regulator's decision as to the appropriate method of calculating compensation for damage to its business flowing from disruption and alteration to the station during construction work. However, the Administrative Court dismissed the application on the ground, *inter alia*, that such damage could

---

[106] As above, n. 81.

[107] His Lordship expressed that,

> where the Act has conferred the decision-making function on the Director, it is for him, and him alone, to consider the economic arguments, weigh the compelling considerations and arrive at a judgment. The applicants have no right of appeal: in these judicial review proceedings so long as he (regulator) directs himself correctly in law, his decision can only be challenged on *Wednesbury* grounds…The Court must be astute to avoid the danger of substituting its views for the decision-maker and of contradicting (as in this case) a conscientious decision-maker acting in good faith with knowledge of all the facts.

[108] Similarly, in *Mabanaft Ltd., R (on the application of) v. Secretary of State for Trade and Industry* [2008] E.W.H.C. (Admin) 1052, regarding a new system of oil stocking obligations, Mr. Justice Beatson held that,

> while the balancing of relevant considerations is primarily for the public authority, the court may intervene if manifestly excessive or manifestly inadequate weight is given to a relevant consideration [at para. 74].

[109] [1976] A.C. 1014 [1976] 3 All ER 665. In this case he stated,

> These documents are to be read fairly and in *bonam partem*. If reasons are given in general terms, the court should not exclude reasons which fairly fall within them: allowance must be fairly made for difficulties in expression. The Secretary of State must be given credit for having the background to this situation well in mind, and must be taken to be properly and professionally…His opinion, based, as it must be, upon that of a strong and expert department, is not to be lightly overridden.

A similar approach was adopted in *Nicholds and others v. Security Industry Authority* [2006] E.W.H.C. (Admin) 1792 paras. 64 and 87, regarding licensing criteria under s. 7 of the Private Security Industry Act 2001.

[110] [2003] E.W.C.A. Civ 2607. This body was replaced with the Board Office of Rail Regulation in 2004. See also *AES Kilroot Power Ltd., Re Application for Judicial Review*, a case concerning electricity generation licensing, [2008] N.I.Q.B. 62 at para 40.

only be measured with precision by the regulator. It was held that the courts were technically unable to determine exactly, even after the event, what the true cost to the company's business would have been. There was therefore a clear reason for deferring to the Director's expert and informed judgement on the matter.[111] In particular, his Lordship stated that, in the light of the *Wednesbury* principle, the courts should accord great deference to the expertise of the regulator and his advisors.[112]

Finally, there has also been a *Wednesbury* standard of deference by the court to the regulator in environmental cases. In *Levy v. Environmental Agency*,[113] which concerned the authority's decision to permit Blue Circle to use scrap tyres as substitute fuel, Silber J characterized the regulator's expertise and the will of parliament as key features of judicial supervision in this context, and the court's role therefore was confined to 'review with a built in latitude'.[114]

---

[111] Moses LJ held that:

The nature of the subject matter with which the Regulator had to deal reinforces the reluctance a court must feel in intervening... It must be borne in mind that the Regulator was concerned with issues of economic policy and of economic theory and practice. Whilst references to deference may now be regarded as 'vieux jeux' after the observations of Lord Hoffman in *R (ProLife Alliance) v. BBC* [2003] 2 W.L.R. 1403 at paragraphs 74 to 77 the context of this case demonstrates that the role of the courts to constrain the Regulator's exercise of his decision making power is small. See also the dictum of Mr Justice Sullivan in *Great North Eastern Railway Ltd. v. Office of Rail Regulation and others* [2006] E.W.H.C. (Admin) 1942 at paras. 39 and 44; and that of Mr. Justice Beatson in *Centro, R (on the application of) v. Secretary of State for Transport and another* [2007] E.W.H.C. (Admin) 2729, para. 36.

[112] It must also be borne in mind that the Regulator obtained expert advice from MVA (a firm of consultants on transport economics)... It was the adoption of that advice which formed the focus of LCSP's (claimant) challenge. In *R v. Council of Legal Education, ex parte Edess* [1995] Admin LR 357 the court ruled that when a decision maker has instructed suitable experts and used them in a sensible way, that effectively discharged his duties under *Wednesbury*.

In considering the various challenges advanced to the Regulator's directions I must, accordingly, bear in mind that he was reaching his conclusions in a field in which he was both expert and experienced. He was advised by experts... Further, he was concerned with predictions for the future incapable of any exact measurement. All these factors demonstrate that what Simon Brown LJ described as 'the constraining role of the courts' (see *Carson and Reynolds v. The Secretary of State for Work and Pensions* [2003] E.W.C.A. Civ 797 at para 73) is indeed modest.

[113] [2002] E.W.H.C. 1663.

[114] It (the margin of appreciation) is substantially wider than the average or conventional margin for two different but overlapping reasons. First, when producing the Decision Document, the Agency was performing a function, which Parliament had entrusted to it as being within its particular expertise... the Agency is one of the more specialised bodies, which when considering the June 2000 application had to use very sophisticated specialised scientific and environmental knowledge and expertise... [at para. 77].

Second, as De Smith, Woolf and Jowell have explained with my emphasis added in Judicial Review of Administrative Actions (5th Edition) at paragraph 13-015 that when reviewing a decision, the courts are 'careful not readily to interfere with the balancing of considerations which are relevant to the power that is exercised by the authority'. As I have explained in paragraph 43 above, the Agency was required to carry out a balancing operation in evaluating Blue Circle's application and so these words are relevant and apposite [at para. 78].

See, further, Fordham, Michael, *Judicial Review Handbook*, 3rd edn., (Oxford: Hart Publishing, 2001) 222.

3.2.3 Self-regulation

It is interesting to note that the *Wednesbury* approach has also been applied to decisions of self-regulatory bodies empowered to oversee the operation of private businesses.[115] In this situation, however, it is contended that the standard of substantive review should be even more deferential than that imposed on public authorities who exercise statutory powers. The rationale underlying this assertion is that, where discretion is exercised without legal authorization, review is no longer rooted in the principle of parliament sovereignty, which requires the judiciary to keep bodies within the boundaries imposed by statute. Rather, the courts intervene in the context of an alleged misapplication of the regulators' own rules, which could properly be altered by them at any time. In light of this, there is a greater need to consider and be sensitive to the criteria supplied by self-regulatory organizations, which may best represent the will and spirit of the rule-maker.

This approach can readily be seen in the field of financial services regulation. Thus, in the *Datafin*[116] case, Sir John Donaldson adopted the *Wednesbury* test in determining the situations in which the court would interfere with the decisions of the City Panel on Takeovers and Mergers, a self-regulatory body wielding considerable *de facto* power.[117]

A similar reticence is evidenced by the Court of Appeal in *R v. Panel on Takeovers and Mergers, ex p Guinness*.[118] The plaintiffs had applied to the Panel on Take-overs to postpone a hearing concerned with one aspect of their take-over bid for Distillers Co. plc., either until after the publication of the inspectors' report and the determination of the criminal proceedings or until after the inspectors had concluded their investigations when full evidence would have become available. The Panel refused to adjourn, and after a hearing, concluded that Guiness plc. had acted contrary to the code. In reviewing the impugned order, Lord Donaldson MR employed a restrictive reading of the rationality test as a mechanism through

---

[115] For the amenability of these bodies to judicial review see Cane, Peter, 'Self-Regulation and Judicial Review' [1987] 6 *Civil Justice Quarterly*, 324–347; Forsyth, Christopher, 'The Scope of Judicial Review: Public Duty not Source of Power' [1987] *Public Law*, 356–367; Tridimas, Takis, 'Self-regulation and Investor Protection in the United Kingdom: The Take-over Panel and the Market for Corporate Control' [1991] 10 *Civil Justice Quarterly*, January, 38–42; Lidbetter, Andrew, 'Judicial Review in the Company and Commercial Context' [1995] 10 *Butterworths Journal of International Banking and Financial Law*, 62–70; Black, Julia, 'Constitutionalising Self-regulation' (as above n. 35), 24–55; Elliott, *The Constitutional Foundations of Judicial Review*, (Oxford: Hart Publishing, 2001), 165–196; Wade and Forsyth, (as above n. 30), 540–548.

[116] (As above, n. 55). See also the judgment of Lord Lloyd of Berwick in *R. v. Investors Compensation Scheme ex p Bowden*, [1996] A.C. 261, and the case comment written by Andrew Lidbetter, 'Judicial Control of Financial Services Legislation' [1995] *Journal of Business Law*, 590–596.

[117] The role of the court is wholly different. It is, in an appropriate case, to review the decision of the panel and to consider whether there has been 'illegality', i e whether the panel has misdirected itself in law, 'irrationality', i e whether the panel's decision is so outrageous in its defiance of logic or of accepted moral standards that no sensible person who had applied his mind to the question to be decided could have arrived at it.

[118] [1990] 1 Q.B. 146 at 159.

which deference towards a self-regulatory body may be secured.[119] In addition, Lord Woolf went on to explain that such an approach is particularly based on the lack of statutory guidelines for task performance.[120]

The adoption of a very cautious approach to self-regulatory orders is also evident in *R v. International Stock Exchange, ex p Else Ltd.*[121] The case concerned a decision of the Committee on Quotations of the Stock Exchange that cancelled the official listing of shares in a company in which the applicants were shareholders. The company sought to impugn the decision on the ground, *inter alia*, that they were entitled under article 15 of Council Directive (79/279/E.E.C.) n1 to be notified and given an opportunity to make representations to the committee prior to the making of any decision to cancel. Sir Thomas Bingham said that the principle that self-regulatory substantive questions are ultimately for the decision-maker flows basically from its higher level of expertise in the field.[122] He also applied this criterion two years later in *R v. SFA, ex p Panton*,[123] adding that it is also founded an accurate understanding of legislative will.[124]

More recently, such deference on expertise grounds can be seen in *Albatros Warehousing BV, R (on the application of) v London Metal Exchange Ltd.*,[125] a case concerning a sanction imposed by the defendant, a self-regulatory body, on the operator of a warehousing business. The Court held that although the decision was

---

[119] Irrationality, at least in the sense of failing to take account of relevant factors or taking account of irrelevant factors, is a difficult concept in the context of a body which is itself charged with the duty of making a judgment on what is and what is not relevant, although clearly a theoretical scenario could be constructed in which the panel acted on the basis of considerations which on any view must have been irrelevant or ignored something which on any view must have been relevant.

[120] [I]n the case of a statutory body it is possible to identify considerations which it is under a statutory obligation to take into account or to ignore. Failure to comply with this statutory obligation can invalidate a decision. However, there is no equivalent obligation in the case of the panel ... In the normal case a body such as the panel will retain a very wide discretion how it performs the task it sets itself and the court will regard its role as being one of last resort reserved for plain and obvious cases.

[121] 16 October 1992. [1993] Q.B. 534.

[122] I would simply observe that the problems facing any shareholder seeking to mount such a challenge are formidable in the extreme. In a highly sensitive and potentially fluid financial market, the factors listed in section 31(6) of the Act of 1981 have a special significance. And the courts will not second-guess the informed judgment of responsible regulators steeped in knowledge of their particular market.

A similar approach has been applied to self-regulation in the pharmaceutical market. See *R v. Code of Practice Committee of the Association of the British Pharmaceutical Industry, ex p Professional Counselling Aids Ltd.* [1990] 10 B.M.L.R. 21.

[123] As above n. 77.

[124] It seems to me quite plain that they are bodies over whom the court can, in appropriate circumstances, and will, exercise a supervisory jurisdiction, but recognition of that jurisdiction must in my judgment be combined with a recognition that the clear intention of the Act is that the bodies established under the Act should be the regulatory bodies and that it is not the function of the court in anything other than a clear case to second guess their decisions or, as it were, to look over their shoulder.

[125] [2000] E.W.H.C. (Admin) 314.

amenable to judicial review, it was correct to defer to the regulator's view on the ground that,

It was an expert body which was well placed to assess the needs of the market, the impact of a breach of the rules and what was required in order to deter future breaches and secure confidence in the market. The court does not have the same expertise in such matters, [at para 57.]

3.3 Interpretation of rules

The results of applications for judicial review in the commercial context also demonstrate that courts have been particularly circumspect in matters concerning the construction of regulatory norms. Interestingly, the judicial approach to executive interpretations of vague terms appears to recognize the logic of *Wednesbury* as the formula to determine whether the specific meaning adopted by the authority is permissible within a range of possible meanings which such a term could bear. The point is explained well by Lord Irvine of Lairg,

the general rule is that if, on its true construction, a concept is a flexible and evaluative one, whose rational application to the same facts may produce conflicting conclusions, it is the view of the rational decision-maker and not the view of the court, which governs.[126]

Thus, in cases where the judge decides that the rule-maker has not directly addressed the point of rule interpretation, he should,

take care to abstain, under the mantle of construction, from elevating what is, in truth, a mere relevant consideration into a or the purpose of a statutory provision, thus curbing a valuable and legitimate facet of administrative autonomy.[127]

In practice, as Craig correctly observes, this means that the courts must uphold the agency's reasonable finding,

even though it was not the interpretation which the court itself would have adopted, and even though it was only one of a range of permissible such findings that could made.[128]

It therefore becomes clear that regulatory constructions of wide terms are immune from judicial scrutiny as long as they remain within the bounds of mere rationality: a court may only set aside the interpretation adopted by the regulator if it is so untenable as to be manifestly unreasonable.

The decision of the House of Lords in *R v. Monopolies and Mergers Commission (MMC), ex p South Yorkshire Transport Ltd.*[129] goes precisely in this direction. What had happened was that two companies which operated bus services within

---

[126] Lord Irvine of Lairg, 'Judges and Decision-Makers: The Theory and Practice of *Wednesbury* Review' [1996] *Public Law*, 69.
[127] Ibid.   [128] Craig, (as above n. 27), 468.
[129] [1993] 1 All E.R. 289, [1993] 1 W.L.R. 23, [1993] B.C.C. 111. The MMC was replaced with the Competition Commission on 1 April 1999. See also the more recent judgment of Mr. Justice Moses in *T-Mobile (UK) Ltd. and Ors, R (on the application of) v. Competition Commission and Anor* [2003] E.W.H.C. (Admin) 1555, at 118; and the judgment of Mr. Justice Davis in *R (BBC) v. Information Commissioner* [2007] 1 W.L.R. 2593, where he coins the term 'South Yorkshire principle'.

a certain area of the United Kingdom area claimed that the Commission had no jurisdiction to investigate their merger, because the reference area was not 'a substantial part of the United Kingdom', as it was required by s 64(3) of the Fair Trading Act 1973. The court was, therefore, called upon to decide whether the interpretation of the public body in relation to the phrase in question was consistent with purposes of the Act. Lord Mustill gave judgment for the MMC and adopted an approach to executive interpretation of rules which is very reminiscent of the *Wednesbury* test. He held that this is one of those cases where the criterion established by the statute for an administrative judgement is 'so imprecise that different decision-makers, each acting rationally, might reach differing conclusions when applying it to the facts of a given case'. In particular, it was recognized that,

even after eliminating inappropriate senses of 'substantial' one is still left with a meaning broad enough to call for the exercise of judgement rather than an exact quantitative measurement.

In light of this, Lord Mustill concluded that,

the court is entitled to substitute its own opinion for that of the person to whom the decision has been entrusted *only if the decision is so aberrant that it cannot be classed as rational'*.

Approaching the matter in this way, His Lordship was quite satisfied that 'there was no ground for interference by the court, since the conclusion at which the Commission arrived was well within the permissible field of judgement'.

A similar result was reached in *R v. Medicines Control Agency (MCA), ex p Pharma Nord (UK) Ltd*,[130] where the Court of Appeal held that the interpretation of the term 'medicinal products' within the meaning of Article 1.2 of Directive 65/65[131] was an issue 'not ideally suited to the adversarial processes', and 'in relation to which the court should be wary of becoming involved'. It was recognized that the main reason underlying this deferential attitude was that the regulatory agency was in a better position to evaluate the evidence than a judge. In Lord Woolf's words, 'it has accumulated experience in relation to other products which a court lacks. It is an expert body. The MCA has to develop a consistent policy between similar products'. In practice, it was precisely this premise which led his Lordship to apply the *Wednesbury* test:

if the case was one where the MCA could not reasonably have come to the decision which it did so that the outcome was one which is conventionally determined on applications for judicial review, the position would be different.

In *R v. Radio Authority, ex p Bull and another*,[132] a comparable reticence to the construction of the rules was exhibited. Again, the point is captured well by Lord Woolf MR. He said that such kind of judicial deference is consistent with the most natural

---

[130] [1998] 44 B.M.L.R. 41.
[131] 'On the approximation of provisions laid down by Law, Regulation or Administrative Action relating to proprietary medicinal products'.
[132] (As above, n. 82). See also *R (Hunt) v. Independent Television Commission* [2003] E.W.C.A. Civ 81.

reading of the broad statutory term, which calls for the fact-finding and interpretive skills of the regulator rather than the abilities most familiar to courts.[133]

This approach has also been evidenced with respect to the Financial Ombudsman Service. The dicta in *R. (on the application of Norwich and Peterborough Building Society) v. Financial Ombudsman Service Ltd.*[134] provides a good example. In this case, the independent authority had ordered the applicant, a building society, to pay compensation to an account holder on the ground that it had been 'unfair' in not paying the correct interest rate. The company claimed that the finding of 'unfairness' involved a misconstruction of the banking code. The court, however, found for the respondent. In his judgment, Ouseley LJ appeared reluctant to quash the Ombudsman's construction of that term on the basis of its wide meaning.[135] It was therefore held that the interpretation of the respondent is immune from judicial scrutiny provided that it remains within the bounds of reasonableness.[136]

3.3.1 Self-regulation

The courts have also applied the mode of analysis supplied by the *Wednesbury* test to review the interpretation of self-regulatory rules. This current trend in the jurisprudence is especially noteworthy in the context of financial services regulation, where decision-makers have been accorded an even higher level of deference than that given to public bodies constructing statutory terms. The reason is as follows. If a regulator is responsible for setting its own framework, then it has to be given considerable latitude for interpreting rules because it is the legislator and could lawfully change them at any time.[137] In general terms, it is explained, judicial supervision over the construction of rules is based on the need to enforce the will of the rule-maker, especially the parliament. Consequently, where the authority applying the specific provision is both legislator and interpreter, the courts should exhibit a sensitivity towards its construction of the norm which they would not show to some

---

[133] From an examination of the different elements of s. 92(2)(a)(i) it is apparent that it is difficult to identify with precision the parameters of the paragraph. The language of the provision therefore allows the authority a reasonable degree of tolerance in its application...Because of its lay nature and the terms of s. 92(1) the court should be prepared in this situation to allow the authority a margin of appreciation and *only interfere with its decisions when there is a manifest breach of the principles applied on application for judicial review.*

[134] [2002] E.W.H.C. (Admin) 2379, [2003] 1 All E.R. (Comm) 65.

[135] The Ombudsman is entitled, and consistency in decision-making probably obliges him, to develop criteria as to what constitutes unfairness. Those criteria are a matter for him. The very concept of 'unfairness' is very wide, and permits reasonable people to disagree. But its very width serves as a caution against over-active judicial intervention in the approach adopted by the Ombudsman, in the criteria which he develops or in the application of those criteria or of the concept of unfairness to the circumstances of the case.

[136] It is only if the Ombudsman has committed *such errors of reasoning as to deprive his decision of logic that it can be said to be legally irrational.* The court should be very wary of reaching such a conclusion. Its own views as to what would be fair are not to be substituted for the Ombudsman's views when what is at issue is a question of the substantive merits of a decision as to unfairness.

[137] See Black, 'Reviewing Regulatory Rules: Responding to Hybridisation' (as above n. 16), 142–146.

other regulators, because it may best represent the spirit of the lawgiver. In practice, this means that a judge may only set aside the interpretation placed by the self-regulatory organization on its own rules if it is patently unreasonable.

The leading case on this point is considered to be *R v. Panel on Takeovers and Mergers, ex p. Datafin plc.*[138] Lord Donaldson was of the view that the Panel had to be given considerable leeway in interpreting its own self-regulatory code. His approach clearly accords with the logic inherent in *Wednesbury*, which recommends judicial assessment of administrative decisions on the basis of rationality.[139] He reiterated this opinion in *ex p Guinness*.[140] It was held that self-regulatory agencies such as the Panel should be subject to a lesser degree of review on the basis that it is more difficult, in the established grounds of review, to scrutinize decisions of a body interpreting its own rules.[141]

A more strict approach to the interpretation of self-regulatory rules, however, was that adopted in *R v. Independent Committee for the Supervision of Telephone Information Services (ICSTIS) Ltd., ex p Telephone Entertainment Service and Others.*[142] In this case, the applicant sought to challenge the body's interpretation of its own Code of Practice, concerning the content of advertisements. The court found for the defendant. Interestingly, it did not even pause to consider the issue. Kennedy LJ refused leave to apply for judicial review on the ground that it is difficult to find any legal flaw in the misconstruction of the rules a body who is both legislator and interpreter.[143]

---

[138] As above n. 55. See also *R v. SIB and PIA, ex p Sun Life Assurance Society plc.* [1996] 2 B.C.L.C. 150.

[139] When it comes to interpreting its own rules, it must clearly be given considerable latitude both because, as legislator, it could properly alter them at any time and because of the form which the rules take, ie laying down principles to be applied in spirit as much as in letter in specific situations. Where there might be a legitimate cause for complaint and for the intervention of the court would be *if the interpretation were so far removed from the natural and ordinary meaning of the words of the rules that an ordinary user of the market could reasonably be misled*. Even then it by no means follows that the court would think it appropriate to quash an interpretative decision of the panel. It might well take the view that a more appropriate course would be to declare the true meaning of the rule, leaving it to the panel to promulgate a new rule accurately expressing its intentions.

[140] As above, n. 118.

[141] Illegality would certainly apply if the Panel acted in breach of the general law but it is more difficult to apply in the context of an alleged misinterpretation of its own rules by a body which under the scheme is both legislator and interpreter...And similar problems arise with procedural impropriety in the narrow sense of failing to follow accepted procedures, given the nature of the panel and of its functions and the lack of any statutory or other guidance as to its procedures which are intended to be of its own devising.

[142] 6 February 1992. CO/2439/91. See also *R v. ICSTIS ex p Firstcode*, CA, [1993] C.O.D. 325.

[143] Mr Robertson (for the applicant) is still faced with the difficulty that what was being done at this stage of the body's determination was to interpret its own provisions. Admittedly ICSTIS is not precisely the same body as the body which formulated the Code which it was seeking to apply, but it is useful to remind myself, as suggested by Mr. Pannick (for the respondent) in the submissions which he put before me in writing, of what was said by Lord Donaldson in *R v. Panel on Takeovers and Mergers, ex parte Guinness*, namely, that illegality would certainly apply if the Panel acted in breach of the general law but it is more difficult to apply in the context of an alleged misinterpretation of its own rules

3.4 Remedies

The last form of judicial deference which must be addressed relates to the exercise of discretion in regard to the relief claimed by the applicant. In the law relating to volatile markets there are situations in which the courts have refused to grant a remedy against the unlawful decision in order to avoid substantial hardship to the interests of the administration and the rights of innocent parties who have relied on the validity of the decision-making process. As a consequence, the particular decision in question is left unaffected notwithstanding the fact that it is legally flawed. Importantly, this reasoning appears to ascribe to the values of legal certainty and administrative convenience a greater relevance than that ascribed to the principle of legality, by conceding that the operation of the *ultra vires* doctrine is legitimate so long as it is not detrimental to the position of third parties or good administration.

A straightforward example of this approach is provided by the case of *R v. Monopolies and Mergers Commission, ex p Argyll plc*.[144] The appeal arose in the context of a contested take-over bid in which the Argyll group of companies and Guinness were rival suitors for the hand of Distillers Co. The Secretary of Trade and Industry referred Guinness' bid to the Monopolies and Mergers Commission for an inquiry and report. The effect of this reference was supposedly to take Guinness out of the competition to acquire the share of capital of Distillers. However, Guinness told the chairman of the commission that it intended to abandon its proposal and submit a revised bid. Based on the foregoing, the chairman, with the consent of the Secretary of State, decided to lay aside and not proceed with the reference on the ground that the proposal had been abandoned. Guinness then made a new offer. Argyll sought judicial review of the chairman's decision contending, *inter alia*, that Guinness Ltd had merely retained its original proposal in a modified form, and that the chairman had no jurisdiction to act alone in deciding not to proceed with the reference.

The court, however, found for the defendant. Sir John Donaldson first held that the courts should approach their duties with a proper awareness of the needs of public administration. In particular, he drew attention to a few which are relevant in the financial field for the purpose of certainty on the issue at stake.[145] These

---

by a body which under the scheme is both legislator and interpreter. It may be that those words are not entirely apposite to this situation, but it seems to me that the same general approach would have to be adopted here even if there was not the difficulty to which I have already alluded to make this an inappropriate case in which to grant leave. I do not grant leave.

[144] [1986] 1 W.L.R. 763.

[145] Good public administration is concerned with substance rather than form ... with the speed of decision ... Good public administration requires a proper consideration of the public interest ... of the legitimate interests of individual citizens, however rich and powerful they may be and whether they are natural or juridical persons. But in judging the relevance of an interest, however legitimate, regard has to be had to the purpose of the administrative process concerned ... Lastly, good public administration requires decisiveness and finality, unless there are compelling reasons to the contrary.

considerations thus led the learned judge to conclude that the particular decision in question should be left untouched on the ground that public reliance has been placed on them.[146]

Similar suggestions had appeared in the dicta of Macpherson J in *R v. Monopolies and Mergers Commission, ex p Air Europe Limited*.[147] Here the applicant sought an order of certiorari to quash the report of the Monopolies and Mergers Commission into the proposed merger of British Airways and British Caledonian Group Plc. His Lordship's view was that judicial intervention should be avoided where the work has been done, the expense incurred, and the steps taken in reliance upon the regulator's decision.[148] This criterion was reaffirmed in *Wildman v. Ofcom*.[149]

A further clarification of this approach can be found in the judgment of Lord Donaldson MR in *R v. Panel on Takeovers and Mergers, ex p Datafin plc*.[150] In commenting the decision of the court in *Argyll*, he insisted on the importance of refusing relief in order to enhance efficiency and predictability in the stock-market.[151] However, what is most noteworthy about this dictum is the important proviso that

---

[146] The financial public has been entitled to rely on the finality of the announced decision to set aside the reference and on the consequence that, subject to any further reference, Guinness were back in the ring, from 20 February until at least 25 February when leave to apply for judicial review was granted, and possibly longer in the light of the judge's decision. This is a very long time in terms of a volatile market and account must be taken of the probability that deals have been done in reliance on the validity of the decisions now impugned. Taking account of all these factors, I do not consider that this is a case in which judicial review should be granted. Accordingly, I would dismiss the appeal.

[147] [1988] 4 B.C.C. 182.

[148] This court has of course to look at the situation as it has developed; and the weight of the additional evidence put before us, and the chance of it altering the Commission's views is in my judgment far outweighed by the prejudice which British Airways would suffer by being put out of the competition again after much activity since the Commission allowed it back into the arena.

Six weeks is a long period in the timetable of interlocking takeover bids in the financial climate of the 1980s. I am convinced that I would in any event in all the circumstances have been against the grant of relief, both because of the problem of formulating any relief which would be workable and in the exercise of the court's general discretion in the light of all that has happened commercially since the report was made. I too would dismiss this application.

[149] As above n. 102. Mr Justice Stanley Burnton said at para. 14:

Ofcom's decisions may have substantial financial consequences, as may any decision of the Court to set aside a decision of Ofcom to award a licence to a particular applicant. In the exercise of its judicial review jurisdiction, the Court may set aside a decision of Ofcom if it is shown that it made a material error of law, but the power to do so is discretionary. In my judgment, the Court must exercise a high degree of caution before interfering with a decision such as the present, and do so only if it is shown that there has been real unfairness to a candidate or a significant error of law or other error giving rise to the power, on judicial review, to quash the decision.

[150] As above n. 55. See also the dicta of Carnwath J in *R v. British Advertising Clearance Centre, ex p Swiftcall*. Div. Ct., 16 November 1995, Lexis Transcript.

[151] That case also illustrates the awareness of the court of the special needs of the financial markets for speed on the part of decision-makers and for being able to rely on those decisions as a sure basis for dealing in the market. It further illustrates an awareness that such decisions affect a very wide public which will not be parties to the dispute and that their interests have to be taken into account as much as those of the immediate disputants.

in such circumstances the court might also made a declaration that applies only to unlawful decisions in the future. This doctrine, which is known as 'prospective overruling', is essentially designed to offer legal guidance for the future without invalidating the particular decision in question, thereby paying regard to most of the competing interests at stake.[152]

This approach was supported by the judgment of the Court in *ex p Guinness*.[153] In this case Lord Donaldson MR complained that his passage in *Datafin* had been misunderstood, at least by academic writers. For this reason, he went on to clarify the doctrine of prospective relief by emphasizing a conception of judicial review which is concerned not only with third party rights but also with public interest considerations regarding regulatory effectiveness.[154]

One example of judicial refusal to grant relief simply in order to avoid adverse impact on administration is provided by *Caswell v. Dairy Produce Quota Tribunal for England and Wales*.[155] The applicants, dairy farmers in South Wales, sought to challenge the Dairy Produce Quota Tribunal's refusal to change their milk produce quota two years after the impugned decision was made. The judge held that the Tribunal had erred in construing pertinent regulations but declined to grant both certiorari and mandamus, in the exercise of the discretion conferred by section 31(6) of the Supreme Court Act 1981, on the ground that there had been undue delay in making the application and that the grant of the substantive relief would likely be detrimental to good administration.[156]

---

[152] Nevertheless, I wish to make it clear beyond a peradventure that in the light of the special nature of the panel, its functions, the market in which it is operating, the time scales which are inherent in that market and the need to safeguard the position of third parties, who may be numbered in thousands, all of whom are entitled to continue to trade on an assumption of the validity of the panel's rules and decisions, unless and until they are quashed by the court, I should expect the relationship between the panel and the court to be historic rather than contemporaneous. I should expect the court to allow contemporary decisions to take their course, considering the complaint and intervening, if at all, later and in retrospect by declaratory orders which would enable the panel not to repeat any error and would relieve individuals of the disciplinary consequences of any erroneous finding of breach of the rules. This would provide a workable and valuable partnership between the courts and the panel in the public interest and would avoid all of the perils to which counsel for the panel alluded.

[153] As above n. 118.

[154] When the take-over is in progress the time scales involved are so short and the need of the markets and those dealing in them to be able to rely on the rulings of the panel so great that contemporary intervention by the court will usually either be impossible or contrary to the public interest. Furthermore, it is important that this should be known, as otherwise attempts would undoubtedly be made to undermine the authority of the panel by tactical applications for judicial review. On the other hand, once the immediate problem has been dealt with by the panel, no similar objections would apply to a retrospective review of its actions designed to avoid the repetition of error, if error there has been.

[155] [1990] 2 A.C. 738.

[156] The appeal was dismissed both by the Court of Appeal and the House of Lords. In the latter, Lord Goff stated:

In the present context, that interest (in good administration) lies essentially in a regular flow of consistent decisions, made and published with reasonable dispatch; in citizens knowing where they stand, and how they can order their affairs in the light of the relevant decision. Matters of particular importance, apart from the length of time itself, will

In *Levy*,[157] the court held that even if the claimant had succeeded on any of his complaints, it would not have quashed the contested authorization on the basis, *inter alia*, that such refusal would protect both the environment from pollution and the investments made by the authorized company from the date of the decision until the time when the application was made by the claimant.

Finally, it is interesting to note that the foregoing criterion based on good administration and the rights of innocent parties has been used even to refuse the grant of permission to apply for judicial review, especially in licensing and tendering processes. In *R v. Independent Television Commission, ex p TV NI Ltd and Another*,[158] such grant was refused to the disappointed bidders of regional TV channel licences on the ground that it would adversely affect good administration and market dealings undertaken by the prospective licence holders 'in good faith and in ignorance that apparent certainties were in fact not certain at all'. Similarly, in *Mass Energy Ltd v. Birmingham City Council*,[159] the court refused leave to move to the unsuccessful tenderer of a waste disposal contract in order to avoid consequent disruption and delay in the operation of that contract. Also, in *Grierson, R (on the application of) v. Atlantic Broadcasting Ltd and Others*,[160] a legal action was brought against Ofcom's decision to award a licence to a commercial radio station. The court refused permission on the ground, *inter alia*, that the grant of leave would have caused considerable financial loss to the licensee.

4. Conclusion

The purpose of this chapter has been to outline the principal characteristics of the deferential approach to regulatory decisions in the business context. It is possible to acknowledge that this doctrine has emerged largely as a preferred mechanism for protecting decisions made by executive bodies which are especially qualified and competent in their field of practice. It is argued that regulators are expert decision-makers to which parliament has provided specific duties and procedures to deal with complex issues in a manner which is more sensitive to the difficulties that can arise in the commercial system. It is for this reason that they are able to react quickly to new circumstances, to provide accurate and consistent interpretations of technical terms, and to take into account the impact of market intervention on all

---

be the extent of the effect of the relevant decision, and the impact which would be felt if it were to be re-opened. In the present case, the court was concerned with a decision to allocate part of a finite amount of quota, and with circumstances in which a re-opening of the decision would lead to other applications to re-open similar decisions which, if successful, would lead to re-opening the allocation of quota over a number of years. To me it is plain, as it was to the judge and to the Court of Appeal, that to grant the appellants the relief they sought in the present case, after such a lapse of time had occurred, would be detrimental to good administration...I can perceive no error here which would justify interference with the judge's conclusion...For these reasons, I would dismiss the appeal.

[157] As above n. 113.   [158] *The Times*, 30 December, 1991.
[159] [1994] Env L.R. 298.   [160] [2005] E.W.H.C. (Admin) 1899.

the subjects involved. In addition, these bodies are thought not to be as restricted in time to analyse detailed data and information as are the courts. Hence it is recognized that the adoption of a deferential standard of review would be the best way in which the operation of the supervisory jurisdiction may be reconciled with the needs of fast-moving markets, since it readily captures the benefits of leaving skilled, flexible, and responsive authorities to perform their tasks undisturbed.

Such a mode of review has also emerged as a reaction to the apparent inability and incapacity of the courts to deal with complex economic matters and to look at the whole of the problem. The judiciary has been accused, *inter alia*, of being inexpert, ill-equipped, overburdened, slow, and structurally inefficient to exercise control over the implementation of decisions and policies in today's dynamic markets. It therefore appears that judicial review in this area would necessarily involve the imposition of decisions which ignore the realities and responses of the relevant actors and would fail to provide a quick and efficient solution to legal issues. Moreover, the intervention of the courts is thought likely to have serious implications for the effectiveness of regulation. In particular, it is argued that judicial oversight may create an atmosphere of hostility towards the regulatory body which renders it excessively cautious and as a result less efficient in performing its duties; that such environment makes easy for parties to engage in tactical litigation designed to hinder or thwart the achievement of regulatory goals; and that it undermines the finality and decisiveness of administrative orders in a way which causes great uncertainty among market players. Taken together, these factors combine to question the appropriateness of judicial supervision of economic authorities and to weigh in favour of adopting a 'light touch' approach which leaves impugned decisions relatively unaffected, thereby ensuring speed, efficiency and certainty in the regulation of markets.

As is clear from the analysis above, English courts have already adopted this less rigorous scrutiny in cases dealing with market regulation. They appear readily to accept that judicial reluctance in this area is presently a feature of the legal system which greatly enhances the authority conferred by parliament to specialized bodies which are in a far better position to address highly technical questions. In light of this, there is a relevant list of instances in which the judiciary has regarded it as acceptable to defer to the decision-maker's findings and views. Thus, it is possible to identify examples which illustrate the application of the doctrine of deference in relation to questions of facts, standards of reasonableness, interpretation of rules, and the exercise of remedial discretion. In all these cases, one discerns a line of reasoning to the effect that the courts recognize and respect the regulatory decision. In this sense, it is tolerably clear that the postulated attenuation of judicial supervision over commercial authorities applies to most of the elements of their decision.

At this point, however, it is necessary to assert that arguing that judicial deference expresses a mode of relation between judges and decision-makers which ensures the imposition of informed decisions and safeguards the interests of good administration does not, on its own, establish the legitimacy of the orthodox approach within the legal framework. In spite of its claimed importance for the market regulation system, this doctrine is unduly simplistic because it manifestly overlooks the need to afford adequate protection to the interests of the applicant, who is seeking to avoid the consequences of an act which may be in excess of power. It must be recalled that the notion of individual justice is essential to a proper model of judicial review, in order that citizens may be effectively protected from arbitrary administrative decisions. More specifically, this means that judicial power must be exercised in a manner which is neutral and independent so that parties may be entitled to an impartial and full hearing on the issue and to be granted effective relief, should the judge come to the conclusion that the contended decision is unlawful. In this sense, the importance of taking into account the position of the plaintiff certainly embodies a set of principles and practices for ensuring a fair trial which is substantially broader than the bare notion of societal interest. Consequently, it is possible to argue that the application of the orthodox approach—which postulates regulatory expertise and effectiveness almost as the comprehensive criterion to determine the intensity of judicial review in the commercial context—clearly renders the supervisory jurisdiction of the courts unworkable in terms of legal theory, because it wrongly neglects the normative basis that justifies judicial review in a form that pays due regard to the submissions of the litigant.

The next chapter seeks to substantiate this claim by showing that the traditional attachment of domestic courts to the deferential approach is inconsistent with specific principles which centrally underpin the development of equitable judicial review, and thus it is also incompatible with the core contention of the individual justice concept enshrined in English law. In addition, it will be argued that some of the arguments advanced for judicial restraint are not capable of providing a convincing explanation of this attitude, either because they are based upon inaccurate ideas of administrative autonomy and public law adjudication or simply because they fail to consider alternative means to overcome the problem of market disruption and uncertainty without going so far as to affect the applicant's right to effective scrutiny of the challenged decision.

3

Objections to the Orthodox Approach

1. Introduction

It was explained in the previous chapter that the courts have asserted that, in order to develop a satisfactory system of judicial review in the commercial context, they must necessarily adopt a deferential attitude towards the regulator which facilitates the implementation of expert decisions in complex markets. For this reason, it is suggested that judicial supervision over the different aspects of the contended order can be justified only if it is consistent with the terms expressed in the *Wednesbury* case, according to which the authority's judgement should be set aside only in rather extreme circumstances. On this view, the existence of a decision which is not wholly absurd is sufficient condition for meeting the judicially-determined standard of fairness. Moreover, since the exercise of the courts' remedial discretion cannot severely undermine the principle of administrative convenience and the position of third parties, it follows (once the existence of these interests is established) that judicial review of regulatory power, if it is to be legitimate, must ultimately be confined to the identification of legal flaws, thus leaving impugned decisions unaffected.

However, notwithstanding the reasons of the judiciary and supporters of the orthodox doctrine, it is possible to argue, with great respect, that this approach is in many ways unsatisfactory. In particular, it seriously undermines the position of the applicant who is seeking effective consideration of his claim and adequate protection from unlawful administrative action. Indeed, if the court decides not to review the particular decision in question and to rely instead upon the opinion of the regulator, it is implicitly declining to make an independent assessment of the merits of the case. Thus, in practice, the applicant is denied the neutral review of the contended order that he is entitled to expect from the judiciary, to the extent that it is the decision-maker, rather than the judge, which ultimately provides the reasons upon which the case is decided. Similarly, if the court is reluctant to interfere with the ordinary course of market regulation by granting a remedy, it necessarily follows that the plaintiff will suffer the consequences of an unlawful decision which is harmful to his interests. In such circumstances, the judiciary, far from adopting an equitable choice regarding the interests of competing parties, actively says something which benefits some individuals at the expense of the legitimate interests of others.

The principal purpose of this chapter is to underscore the significance of this point in terms of legal principles. It will be argued that the doctrine of judicial deference (at least that expressed in the market context) does not fit comfortably with the current model of judicial review, particularly in light of the notion of individual justice, which requires the judiciary to take into consideration the interests and welfare of the individual litigant. Under this approach, it may be that the court's supervisory capacity would be limited such that it would fail to give effect to the basic principles which safeguard the interests of private parties in their relations with public authorities. An explanation therefore will be provided of these norms and the specific manner in which they have been disregarded by the courts in dealing with challenges to regulatory decisions. This idea will be developed in two principal stages. The first one identifies the general shortcomings that beset the orthodox doctrine: that is, they can be seen in most of the cases in which deference has been accorded to the executive. The second stage concerns the particular problems which this approach encounters when applied in the context of factual mistakes and remedial discretion.

2. General Shortcomings of the Deferential Approach

The present section seeks to demonstrate that the traditional reluctance of the courts to draw into question the conduct of commercial regulators—which may severely undermine the position of the applicant—is legally unworkable because it often runs counter to the relevant principles of English public law which demand that judicial review must be exercised in a manner which is effective and equitable. In addition, it will be argued that some of the contentions advanced in support of such an approach are unconvincing, because they are based on mistaken assumptions about how administrative autonomy and convenience should be balanced against judicial control. For the purposes of clarity, this analysis will be structured around the main rationales for the deferential attitude developed in Chapter 2 section 2. Thus it is necessary to consider the specific problems which the arguments based on the characteristics of the decision-maker and the requirement of regulatory effectiveness pose for individual justice.

2.1 The regulator

It was explained in the previous chapter that the orthodox view holds that it is inappropriate for the courts to demand justifications for decisions adopted by expert bodies entrusted by Parliament with powers and duties to deal with complex economic issues. In this sense, the higher level of deference accorded to market regulators appears to derive ultimately from their special abilities and functions. This sub-section argues that there are substantial problems with this influential discourse. In order to do so, the three main points which collectively form the relevant proposition must be distinguished and analysed in turn.

2.1.1 Regulatory expertise

In several senses, reaching the conclusion that the courts should defer to the regulator's technical knowledge would be dissatisfying. Three principal reasons must be mentioned.

First, it can be argued that this approach breaches the principle of judicial impartiality, because it leads the judge to act pre-disposed or prejudiced against one party's position for reasons unconnected with the merits of the case. We have seen above that the judiciary is willing to uphold regulatory decisions for the mere fact that they come from a very skilful and experienced decision-maker. If the court finds that the respondent is an expert authority, it will almost automatically decline to make its own independent judgement on a particular issue. It therefore becomes apparent that, in such circumstances, the case is resolved on the basis of the level of knowledge of the parties rather than on the strength of their arguments. As a consequence, there is virtually no room for the applicant to disagree about the substantial content of the impugned order. It is submitted that this situation is clearly contrary to the notion of equal justice under the law which, in this particular field, guides the courts to focus more appropriately and directly on the decision-making process and outcome, and not to be influenced by any extrinsic consideration such as the parties' ability to understand technical subjects.

This claim is consistent with traditional conceptions of adversarial proceedings, which place the official at an equal level along with other citizens, and the dynamic which they dictate *vis-à-vis* the manner in which the court should analyse the submissions of the parties. The point is well captured by Trevor Allan. He says that the complaint of both parties 'must elicit an appropriately pertinent response for the consideration of an arbitrator who is entirely, and visibly, independent of the executive'.[1] In the light of this scheme, a person, who presents even an

erroneous complaint of unlawful or unconstitutional action, which has affected him adversely, is entitled to proper reasons for its rejection; and these reasons should address the relevant points of law, not dismiss them on extraneous grounds of political expediency or extraordinary deference.[2]

More specifically, the negative implications of the deferential approach based on the expertise of the regulator can be rationalized against the background of the rule against the bias, which has been lucidly described by Lord Phillips MR in *Director General of Fair Trading v. Proprietary Association of Great Britain*.[3] In this case, concerning restrictive trade practices, he explained that a breach of this principle can be expressed in several ways,

Bias is an attitude of mind which prevents the judge from making an objective determination of the issues that he has to resolve. A judge may be biased because he has reason to prefer

---

[1] Allan, Trevor, *Constitutional Justice*, (Oxford: Oxford University Press, 2001) 192.

[2] Ibid., 163. See also his 'Human Rights and Judicial Review: A Critique of Due Deference' [2006] 65(3) *Cambridge Law Journal*, 676, 683, 688–689, 694–695; and 'Common Law Reason and the Limits of Judicial Deference' in *The Unity of Public Law*, David Dyzenhaus (ed.), (Oxford: Hart Publishing) 2893–06.

[3] [2000] 1 W.L.R. 700.

one outcome of the case to another. He may be biased because he has reason to favour one party rather than another. He may be biased not in favour of one outcome of the dispute but because of a prejudice in favour or against a particular witness which prevents an impartial assessment of the evidence of that witness. Bias can come in many forms. It may consist of irrational prejudice or it may arise from particular circumstances which, for logical reasons, predispose a Judge towards a particular view of the evidence or issues before him.

This dictum highlights the defining feature of the notion of impartiality inherent in the judicial function; that no special importance ought to be attached to the position of one of the parties due to reasons which are unrelated to their arguments and submissions. There is therefore a strong case for concluding that adopting a verdict or 'final say' in a conflict between equal parties (before the law and the court),[4] but relying ultimately in the criterion of one of them just for being an expert, renders the judgement biased because it would be unfairly influenced by elements extrinsic to the contentions of the case. It would be a kind of predetermination which makes the court to take the effective decision in advance, with a measure of respect that is distinct from the inherent persuasiveness of the regulator's arguments,[5] thus 'rendering the hearing futile and the result a foregone conclusion'.[6]

Once we move to a position in which the issues appear just too difficult to be justiciable we are in danger of losing lawful decision-making to the equivalent of 'the man from Whitehall knows best'.

Moreover, it is necessary to note that the difficulty raised by the deferential approach in terms of bias is even greater when one considers the application of statutes that place a duty on the public body. For example, section 7(1) of the Environmental Protection Act 1990 imposes a duty on the Agency to include such conditions in an authorization as it 'considers appropriate'. In these cases, the statutory provision directly concerns the regulator's own jurisdiction rather than the rights and duties of others. Accordingly, if the court decided to defer to the agency's 'expert' interpretation of that rule, it would be effectively making a party the judge of its own case with regard to the nature and scope of its powers.[7] This outcome is clearly contrary to the principle *nemo iudex in re sua* which normatively disqualifies a subject 'from determining any case in which he may be, or may fairly be suspected to be, biased'.[8] It is therefore possible to assert that judicial restraint in this context is particularly improper, because it runs directly against the core values of natural justice which ensure that any hearing is conducted by a neutral and independent judge.

---

[4] Wade, W. and Forsyth, C.T., *Administrative Law*, 10th edn., (Oxford: Oxford University Press, 2009) 27.

[5] Woodward, D.R. and Levin, R.M., 'In Defense of Deference: Judicial Review of Agency Action' [1979] 31 *Administrative Law Review*, 332.

[6] Wade and Forsyth, (as above n. 4), 399. A critical view has also been expressed by John Swift in competition law. See his article, 'Judicial Control of Competition Decisions in the UK and EU', Competition Commission Autumn Lecture, September 2004, available at <http://www.competition-commission.org.uk/our_role/cc_lectures/judicial_control_210904_swift.pdf>, 13.

[7] Saunders, Kevin, 'Agency Interpretations and Judicial Review: A Search for Limitations on the Controlling Effect given Agency Statutory Constructions' [1988] 30 *Arizona Law Review*, 788. See also Wald, Patricia, 'Judicial Review of Economic Analyses' [1983–84] 1 *Yale Journal on Regulation*, 49.

[8] Wade and Forsyth, (as above n. 4), 380.

Secondly, the need to overcome traditional inhibitions against entering the 'expertise' arena stems from the very problem of accountability which, as Ogus points out, is no different from those frequently encountered by principals who employ expert agents to carry out certain profit-making tasks.[9] He explains that,

> given the greater knowledge and expertise possessed by agents, principals have to confer on them discretion as to how to perform the tasks and, unless constrained, agents may exploit the discretion to advance *their own interests*, rather than those of their principals.[10]

It follows from this that if the courts defer to the superior ability of agencies, they might be paying deference not only to the primary decision makers' expertise and strategic advantages. As Aronson observes, they may also be deferring to some extent to the primary decision makers' *values*.[11] In that way, he says, those values would be co-opted by the court itself; specifically judicial decisions would be infiltrated by the economic and managerial values of the primary decision-makers instead of those of the legislator. Thus, judicial review's values may have, over time, 'the chameleon quality of reflecting their subjects' values'.[12] This situation would clearly pose an undue threat to the basic principle of parliamentary supremacy in lawmaking, increasing as it would the risk of bias and self-dealing on the agency's part.

In addition to the regulator's own interests which may affect the view of a deferential court, a significant external influence is revealed when attempts are made by regulated industries to dominate the agency. It is equally clear, therefore, that if the courts approached the decision of the 'captured' body on the basis of expertise, they would be paying deference neither to the principals nor the agents, but to the values of well-organized pressure groups which constrain regulators' vision and makes them unenthusiastic about their mandates.[13]

Thirdly, it must be noted that the argument focused on expertise is relatively unconvincing, because it is essentially rooted in the mistaken assumption that the regulator is the only one who possesses the technical knowledge and experience to deal with the issues arising under the market legislation. This position overlooks the fact that private companies which operate in a particular market are normally managed and advised by economic and legal experts. These people are obviously capable of providing 'technical' alternative views to those of the agency. Consequently, it is highly unlikely that legal disputes in this field will arise between wise and inexperienced parties, as advocates of the deferential approach tend to present it. Rather, empirical evidence suggests that commercial judicial review often occurs

---

[9] Ogus, Anthony, *Regulation: Legal Form and Economic Theory*, (Oxford: Clarendon Press, 1994), 111.

[10] Ibid., 111–112 (emphasis added).

[11] Aronson, Mark, 'A Public Lawyer's Response to Privatisation and Outsourcing', in *The Province of Administrative Law*, Michael Taggart (ed.), (Oxford: Hart Publishing, 1997) 51.

[12] Ibid.

[13] It is precisely for this reason that some American courts have refused to apply the doctrine of deference on the basis of administrative expertise. As Foster explains, they have actually become more constructing, imposing more-stringent requirements on regulators, such as the duty to document their actions carefully and reveal the reasons for their decision-making in a way that opens them to challenge and eliminates conflict of interest. See Foster, Christopher, *Privatization, Public Ownership and the Regulation of Natural Monopoly*, (Oxford: Blackwell, 1992) 263.

between informed and skilled players of the same game who are seeking to test their rights and duties against the legal order. Once this feature of the system is appreciated, it becomes clear that the expertise rationale is questionable, because it fails to capture the private party's equal ability to deal with complex economic issues. In the light of this symmetry, says Elliott, 'it is surely incumbent upon the court to ascribe weight to that view (of the party) just as it would ascribe weight to the view of an expert public authority defendant'.[14]

At this point, however, it may be counter-argued that the deferential approach is, in truth, based on the greater expertise of regulators as compared to the traditional courts rather than to private parties. It is precisely this advantage that decision-makers are said to have over judges which, it may be suggested, dictates the necessity of adopting a less intensive supervision over administrative activities. Perhaps it is true that sometimes it is difficult for the courts to develop the different kinds of expertise needed to deal with technical matters. However, although it is acknowledged that this rationale is more persuasive than the former, it is still open to criticism. Three points must be made.

First, once the courts come to accept the regulatory decision on the basis of its own lack of knowledge, a significant problem of logic arises. It is very difficult for the court to support both the proposition that it lacks knowledge on the issue and the conclusion that the adopted decision is lawful. If the judge does not feel qualified to properly understand the conflict, it cannot legitimately make a judgement which is detrimental to the interests of one of the parties. Such an attitude would clearly involve a *reductio ad absurdum* argument, ('if it is too complicated for me to understand, the agency must be right')[15] which renders the rationale of the court dubious and weak. The court is either able to deal with the issue, in which case it is entitled to resolve the dispute at hand, or it is not, in which case it should refrain from determining that there is no legal flaw in the exercise of a particular power. The judiciary cannot simultaneously be unable to consider technical decisions at stake and able to reach a definitive judgement on their validity.

Similarly, and relying upon a sort of temporal version of this argument, Lord Steyn has suggested extra-curially that the courts could not make a judgement on a complex issue 'on *a priori* grounds without scrutiny of the challenged decision since nobody can know in advance whether it has been infected by manifested illegality'.[16]

Secondly, it may be argued that the problem of lack of expertise on the part of the judges has been exaggerated by the proponents of the orthodox view. This is clear when one considers that market issues the courts have been faced with are far from being a highly complex, arcane field of technical knowledge. There are numerous examples in the case law cited in the previous chapter which substantiate this claim. For instance, it may be difficult to maintain that the courts are substantially unable to review administrative decisions which refuse to investigate complaints

[14] Elliott, Mark, 'Proportionality and Deference: The importance of a Structured Approach' in C.F. Forsyth, M. Elliott, S. Jhaveri, A. Scully-Hill and M. Ramsden (eds.), *Effective Judicial Review: A Cornerstone of Good Governance*, (Oxford: Oxford University Press, 2010) 274.

[15] Wald, (as above n. 7), 48.

[16] Steyn, Lord J., 'Deference: A Tangled Story' [2005] *Public Law*, 351.

about commercial activities; impose restrictions on advertising on radio and television; relax licence conditions which restrict free trade; award a licence to the lowest bidder; prohibit the admission of children to a cinema on Sundays; interpret expressions such as 'acting in concert', 'substantial part of the United Kingdom', or 'unfairness' in relation to the payment of interest rates; defer the publication of reports relating to the affairs of a company; and cancel the official listing of shares in a company without notice. Importantly, these are to be regarded as *ad hoc* examples of regulatory orders which have been challenged in courts. It appears that their content is, in many senses, understandable. In particular, their central rationale and legal implications are clear or, at least, no more complex than those in other areas of judicial review. Consequently, it is possible to assert that although some knowledge of the industry would be helpful, it is not absolutely necessary in order to deal with these cases in a comprehensive and fair manner.

This point is usefully illustrated by the litigation in the European Court of Justice in Luxembourg (ECJ). Although it is staffed primarily by generalist judges, once we peer into its inner workings, it is difficult to find that they have severe difficulties for understanding the reasons and choices of the decision-makers. As Garreth Wong points out,[17] over half of the past and present judges of the court have been former academics or members of national courts without any extensive political or administrative experience. However, this has not stopped the court from developing a detailed doctrine of stringent scrutiny, namely proportionality. Most significantly, he says, much of the criticism against the court is aimed at its perceived political activism in the way it applies the test, and not towards its ability to rule competently on complex matters. These specific considerations lead him to conclude that though a background in practical administration is an added bonus in judges using a more rigorous standard of review, it is by no means a necessary one. As far as the domestic experience is concerned, a similar development can be seen in planning matters, where the relatively detailed and technical prescription of the context for individual decisions has not prevented the courts from establishing, where appropriate, complex criteria to which authorities must adhere, thereby evidencing specialized knowledge of this area of law.[18]

Thirdly, it is necessary to stress that the court's primary role in the legal system is not based on the need to make expert judgments about regulatory functions, but on the importance of ensuring a fair and just adjudication of disputes. As Owen Fiss observes, the special competency of the courts lies not in the domain of instrumentalism, of mere expertise rationality, but in the domain of constitutional values, 'a special kind of substantive rationality, and that expertise is derived from the special quality of the judicial process—dialogue and independence'.[19] Consequently, although the courts may be viewed as in one

---

[17] Wong, Garreth, 'Towards the Nutcracker Principle: Reconsidering the Objections to Proportionality' [2000] *Public Law*, 105–107.

[18] Supperstone, M. and Goudie, J., *Judicial Review*, 2nd edn., (London: Butterworth & Co, 1997) 5.38.

[19] Fiss, Owen, 'Foreword: The Forms of Justice' [1979] 93 *Harvard Law Review*, 34. See also, Plemming, Nigel, 'Judicial Review of Regulators', in *Effective Judicial Review: A Cornerstone of Good Governance*, (as above n. 14), 342, 355–356.

sense the less experienced bodies in dealing with complex matters, they still have a crucial role to play in difficult cases, by providing an appropriately detached and impartial view of the matter in dispute. It is precisely this duty to act fairly and objectively which, as seen above, prevents them from deferring to the executive branch's criteria. All this suggests that, in such cases the judges, far from abdicating that responsibility on the basis of ignorance, should endeavour to use all the means available to understand the conflict in a more accurate way.[20] In this manner, they would be able to provide an approach to regulatory decisions which is both impartial, in the sense that it denotes absence of bias in favour of the decision-maker, and technically accurate, in that it demonstrates a greater awareness of complex issues in market regulation.

In practice, this relates to mechanisms by which a non-expert court would be able to take due account of scientific expert testimony in the course of deciding whether a regulatory decision or interpretation is lawful. Specifically, it is argued that a structured reasoning process must be used in order to perform in a technical non-arbitrary manner. The point is expressed well by Professor Scott Brewer.[21] He observes that there are crucial steps that a general court must take to satisfy the conditions of the emerging rule of law norm of *intellectual due process*, which is also a necessary condition of *epistemic legitimacy* that legal systems demand when operating to grant or deprive people of rights. These guidelines are designed to ascertain the truth of complex issues by, for example, requiring the judicial use of formal tools of scientific method and analysis, providing a satisfactory account of the cognitive aims of science, and supplying the conceptual basis for judicial review which enjoys factual, methodological, and axiological coherence.

Britain has recently begun to move in this direction, by introducing concrete correctives to adversarial procedures rules which facilitate the judicial resolution of significantly complex disputes. In particular, the Civil Procedure Rules which came into force in 1999, as part of the governmental response to the findings of Lord Woolf's report on access to justice (1996), focus, *inter alia*, on the basic premise that the expert's function is to 'educate' the judge to enable him to reach a properly informed and impartial decision.[22] Consequently, under Part 35 of the Act, the courts were empowered to control expert evidence in order to develop a better understanding of highly technical subject areas.[23] Thus, for instance, judges have power to direct a discussion between experts for the purpose of requiring them to identify matters agreed and outstanding areas of difference (Rule 35.12); to direct that evidence is to be given by a single joint

---

[20] Allison, John, 'The Procedural Reason for Judicial Restraint' [1994] *Public Law*, 452–473; Cane, Peter, *Administrative Law*, 4th edn., Clarendon Law Series, (Oxford: Oxford University Press, 2004), 58.

[21] Brewer, Scott, 'Scientific Expert Testimony and Intellectual Due Process' [1997–98] 107 *Yale Law Journal*, 1535–1681.

[22] Wolf, Lord Harry, *Access to Justice*, (London: HMSO, 1996) Chapter 13. See generally, Blom-Cooper, Sir Louis QC (ed.), *Experts in the Civil Courts*, (Oxford: Oxford University Press, 2006).

[23] See also the 'Practice Direction' that supplements Part 35, and the *Code of Guidance on Expert Evidence*, whose publication was authorized by the Master of the Rolls in December 2001.

expert (Rule 35.7);[24] and to appoint expert assessors to assist them in complex litigation (Rule 35.15). In this sense, the reform is likely to effect a significant reorientation, in practical terms, of the relationship between courts and complex litigation. The prospect of procedures which assure that judges are adequately informed when they make rights effective in administrative disputes is likely to ensure some form of judicial review of regulatory decisions that implicate sophisticated economic reasoning.

It is worth noting that solutions of this sort are also apparent in some American jurisdictions. Federal courts, for example, have adapted their procedures in a number of ways such as permitting wide discovery of evidence, reliance on legislative facts,[25] and allowing arguments by experts and those interested in the outcome of a case but with no legal standing (*'amicus curiae* arguments').[26] Judges have also been called to enrich their knowledge through lived experiences, such as visiting the institutions that they review in order to study them and actually learn from them.[27] Importantly, this positive and supportive attitude—which involves taking measures to improve the adjudication process—is far more helpful to the individual than a list of justifications for deference heavily focused upon the current limitations of the judiciary rather than on its potential for reform and change.[28]

The foregoing analysis thus demonstrates that the claim to acceptability on the basis of expertise suffers considerable shortcomings in the light of the principles of natural justice, and the potential ability of private parties and the courts to provide technical views on the subject-matter. Specifically, by applying a deferential approach to decisions made by those who apparently 'know best', the court fails to conduct the impartial assessment of the merits of the case that private parties—particularly those which are as skilled and experienced as the regulator— are entitled to expect in accordance with the rule against the bias. The importance of ensuring that the courts cannot be predisposed to ruling a particular way on an issue thus supplies the principal basis on which the expertise rationale must be rejected.

We thus reach the position that, in order to apply a more satisfactory approach to regulatory decisions, the court should necessarily analyse the points of fact or law presented to it by the parties without considering the level of expertise or experience that they exhibit, but the substantial merit of their allegations. This means

---

[24] The exercise of this power has been positively evaluated by the Lord Chancellor's Department in its consultation papers. See, for example, *Emerging Findings; An Early Evaluation of the Civil Justice Reforms,* March 2001; and *Further Findings: A Continuing Evaluation of the Civil Justice Reforms,* August 2002.   [25] See also section 3 of chapter 5.

[26] Baldwin, R. and McCrudden, C., *Regulation and Public Law,* Law in Context, (London: Weidenfeld & Nicholson, 1987), 67.

[27] Solove, Daniel, 'The Darkest Domain: Deference, Judicial Review, and the Bill of Rights' [1999] 84 *Iowa Law Review,* 1022.

[28] Ibid., 1011. He observes that 'deference assumes a static model of adjudication, viewing its current difficulties as the inevitable consequences of an unchanging process'. According to this Burkean vision of the judiciary, material conditions regarding adjudication are rigid and unchanging.

that their judgment should proceed objectively from the proofs and arguments advanced at the hearing.[29] In practice, as Allan suggests,

it is for the public authority to persuade the court, on the basis of its own argument, that the citizen's complaint is unfounded, and for the court to determine the balance of argument between the litigants on the materials supplied.[30]

More specifically, he stresses that,

the soundness of any conclusion, even on a matter involving specialist expertise, must be capable of demonstration by argument; there is otherwise no opportunity for the litigant to challenge the government's course of action.[31]

Nevertheless, the argument of this sub-section should not be misunderstood. Regulatory expertise is a great resource in the commercial context because it allows agencies to be 'enmeshed in the actual practical difficulties of institutions, steeped in the facts, and constantly aware of the needs and concerns of practice'.[32] It surely is true therefore that in discharging their responsibility to determine the validity of a commercial decision, courts should consider the agency's views. However, the question is not whether the agency's justification or the quality of the decision-making process shall be accorded respect.[33] The precise problem is the extent to which the agency's criterion shall necessarily affect or control the court's judgement. Here the argument has been that the special expertise of the agency is not so strong claim as to altogether oust the judges, to justify deference to the executive, leaving the courts to do nothing more than confirm the *ipse dixit* of the regulator. In other words, it is not for the judges to adopt a 'light touch' over regulatory decisions in virtue of their comparative weakness or lack of special knowledge. Courts must still remain critical of official expertise, assessing its cogency in the light of the arguments presented. As Solove suggests, they should,

prevent experts and institutions from cloistering themselves from the rest of the world, keeping their fields insular and impenetrable. Courts should force experts to engage in a dialogue with the non-experts. Judges must remain wary of blind acceptance of authority and subject everything to constant critical inquiry.[34]

It is noteworthy that this idea of appreciating the expertise of the regulator in light of the evolution of complex and dynamic markets, while recognizing that the specific requirements of validity and reasonableness can most appropriately be determined by the courts through the forensic process is already apparent in some cases. In particular, there have been interesting attempts to craft a proper reconciliation

---

[29] See, for example, Romero, Alejandro, 'La Fundamentación de la sentencia como elemento del debido proceso' [2006] in *Sentencias destacadas 2005: una mirada desde la perspectiva de las políticas públicas*, A.F. Vöringer, (Santiago: Instituto Libertad y Desarollo, 2006), 15.

[30] Allan, *Constitutional Justice*, (as above n. 1), 191.

[31] Allan, 'Human Rights and Judicial Review: A Critique of Due Deference' (as above n. 2), 692.

[32] Solove, (as above n. 27), 1020.

[33] See Knight, Christopher, 'Proportionality, the Decision-Maker and the House of Lords' [2007] 12(4) *Judicial Review*, 221–227.

[34] Solove, (as above n. 27), 1020.

of the competing desiderata: on the one hand, the advantages of using administrative technical knowledge and, on the other, the recognition that in the British
system it is the judiciary's responsibility to decide independently the questions of
fact and law brought within the jurisdiction of the courts.

The formulation in *H.T.V. Ltd. v. Price Commission*,[35] a case concerning the
interpretation of technical terms by the agency charged with the task of restrain-
ing the prices of goods and services, provides a good example. Lord Scarman first
held that although the interpretation of statutory language (including the language of delegated legislation) is a matter of law, the meaning of technical words
is a matter of fact to be determined by the opinion of those experts in the appropriate technique. Nevertheless, he then went on to state that, at the end of the
process of fact finding, which includes the evidence of experts to ascertain the
meaning of technical words, the interpretation of legislative language remains a
question of law:

It is, therefore, a matter for the courts, unless their jurisdiction has been expressly excluded.
And it takes very clear language indeed to exclude the supervisory jurisdiction of the High
Court when what is challenged is the determination of a governmental agency exercising
statutory functions which contain a significant judicial element.

... technical terms should not deter the courts from exercising their powers of supervision. Their meaning will be elucidated, with the help of an expert, by the commission. But
when this has been done the legislative language is for the courts to construe. However
obscure the jargon, it is the language used or approved by Parliament, itself a representa-
tive non-technical institution. If Parliament uses it, the courts must be prepared to give it
meaning: and this in the ultimate is a legal, not a technical, process.

A similar view was expressed by Pennycuick V-C in *Odeon Associated Theatres
Ltd v. Jones (Inspector of Taxes)*.[36] Although this case involves the assessment of
private expertise for the determination of principles of commercial accountancy
rather than, as in the instant subject, one of regulators' expertise, the analogy is
nevertheless useful. The court expressly held that no matter how valuable the criteria provided by the specialists, there are convincing reasons to entrust the final
decision to the court,

In so ascertaining the true profit of a trade the court applies the correct principles of the
prevailing system of commercial accountancy. I use the word 'correct' deliberately. In order
to ascertain what are the correct principles it has recourse to the evidence of accountants.
That evidence is conclusive on the practice of accountants in the sense of the principles on
which accountants act in practice. That is a question of pure fact, but the court itself has
to make a final decision as to whether that practice corresponds to the correct principles
of commercial accountancy. No doubt in the vast proportion of cases the court will agree
with the accountants but it will not necessarily do so. Again there may be a divergency of
view between the accountants, or there may be alternative principles, none of which can be
said to be incorrect, or, of course, there may be no accountancy evidence at all. The cases
illustrate these various points. At the end of the day the court must determine what is the
correct principle of commercial accountancy to be applied.

[35] [1976] I.C.R. 170.   [36] [1971] 2 All E.R. 407, [1971] 1 W.L.R. 442.

The same theme is apparent in the jurisprudence of the ECJ. In the *Miro* case[37] the German government contended that national authorities were in the best position to make decisions which depended on the commercial view prevailing in the country concerned. Accordingly, it was for those expert decision-makers and not for the court to determine whether a prohibition on using the appellation 'jenever' can be necessary for products which do not satisfy certain requirements. However, their Lordships dismissed the argument on the ground that a proper allocation of powers enables the court to review expert judgements on a full jurisdiction basis:

As regards the latter argument, it must be stated that neither article 30 of the treaty nor indeed article 36 reserves certain matters to the exclusive jurisdiction of the member states. When in order to satisfy mandatory requirements recognized by community law national legislation creates obstacles to the fundamental principle of the free movement of goods, it must observe the limits laid down by community law. It is for the court, which interprets community law in the final instance, and for the national courts, which reach their decisions on the basis of that interpretation, to ensure that those limits are observed. In the final analysis the German government's argument amounts to a repudiation of review by the court and therefore runs counter to the uniformity and effectiveness of community law. It must therefore be rejected.

Furthermore, in recent years, a growing emphasis on procedural guarantees in respect of complex and scientific assessments made by regulators is increasingly apparent in the jurisprudence of the ECJ. This, in turn, has been widely perceived as judicial review operating in a form which secures respect for both law and science. The point is illustrated with particular clarity by the dicta of the court in *Pfizer*[38] and *Artegodan*,[39] concerning the application of the precautionary principle to regulations on possibly harmful food or medicinal products respectively.[40] In particular, although it continues to be persuaded of the importance of not substituting its assessments and judgement for that of the expert institution, the court no longer views this as sufficient means by which to reach a lawful decision. Instead, it adopts as its starting point the premise that such scientific assessment must be carried out in accord with relevant procedural principles. For instance, these principles have explicitly influenced the court to justify the regulator's obligation to provide specific reasons of a scientific level,[41] to obtain expert opinion based on the principles of excellence, independence and transparency,[42] to disregard the technical judgement of politically dependent bodies,[43] and to require new scientific data in order to justify the withdrawal of an authorization.[44]

The application of these criteria, as Craig rightly points out, exemplify an important shift in the approach to judicial review in EU law in that it entails a careful examination of the regulator's reasoning process in the context of substantive

---

[37] *Criminal proceedings against Miro BV*, Case 182/84 [1985] E.C.R. 03731.
[38] *Pfizer Animal Health SA v. Council*, Case T-13/99 [2002] E.C.R. II-3303.
[39] *Commission v. Artegodan GmH*, Case C-39/03 P [2003] E.C.R. I-7885.
[40] For a general analysis of this principle, see Craig, Paul, *EU Administrative Law*, (Oxford: Oxford University Press, 2006) 717–748.
[41] *Pfizer*, (as above, n. 38), at para. 199.   [42] Ibid., at paras. 268–270.
[43] Ibid., 283.   [44] *Artegodan*, (as above, n. 39), at paras. 187–195.

review as a means of preventing arbitrary decision-making.[45] Thus, the court guides the regulator's exercise of expert discretion in a manner which both provides a convincing consideration of technical *auctoritas* and reconciles it with the rule of law framework.

2.1.2 *The will of Parliament*

It was suggested in the previous chapter that, in adopting a deferential attitude towards regulatory choices in the commercial context, the court is observing the will of Parliament, in the sense that it respects the degree of autonomy granted to the decision-maker by the legislator. The present sub-section argues that this assertion, although theoretically possible, cannot be reasonably made to justify the current approach of the courts. Indeed, it is widely recognized that Parliament is able to limit the supervisory jurisdiction of the judiciary in order to provide a certain degree of independence to executive bodies. In particular, it may 'at any stage legislate so as to change, curtail, or qualify' the grounds of review[46] or modify 'the intensity, nature or availability of review in a particular area'.[47] However, it is submitted that, in general, this is not the case with market regulators. Three principal matters require consideration.

2.1.2.1 The expression of legislative will

The first problem with this argument is closely related to the rules of manner that determine how legislative will is to be expressed. It can be argued that the courts' deferential approach to regulatory decisions cannot satisfactorily be explained in terms of the implementation of legislative policy because no such intention has been expressed by Parliament in accordance with those requirements. This is clear when one considers the implications which follow from the initial ascription to the legislator of the purpose to provide effective and equitable judicial review.

As Elliott explains, the exercise of judicial review jurisdiction occurs within a constitutional setting that leads the courts to impute to Parliament an intention to legislate consistently with the rule of law.[48] There is therefore a strong presumption that the legislator intends the rule of law to be upheld, so that only very clear language is capable of rebutting that presumption.[49] In particular, it is argued that principles such as access to courts, natural justice,[50] and good administration— which are vindicated through judicial review, and which are based firmly on the rule of law doctrine—could only be interfered with or suspended by using clear

[45] Craig, (as above, n. 40), 479.

[46] See Laws, Sir John, 'Illegality: The Problem of Jurisdiction' in Supperstone and Goudie, *Judicial Review*, (as above n. 18), 4.18.

[47] Elliott, Mark, *The Constitutional Foundations of Judicial Review*, (Oxford: Hart Publishing, 2001) 78.

[48] Elliott, Mark, 'The Ultra Vires Doctrine in a Constitutional Setting: Still the Central Principle of Administrative Law' in *Judicial Review and the Constitution*, Christopher Forsyth (ed.), (Oxford: Hart Publishing, 2000) 103.

[49] Elliott, (as above n. 47), 148.

[50] See Wade and Forsyth for evidence that 'any departure from the universally acknowledge principle of natural justice required clear words of enactment' (as above n. 18), 394.

language.[51] Understood thus, the courts cannot assume that, in the absence of very clear countervailing evidence, Parliament intends to curtail their supervisory jurisdiction.

Consequently, Le Sueur points out that any decision of the court about the contraction of its jurisdictional powers 'ought to be justified primarily on the basis of legal argument, rather than merely by a general appeal to the desirability of changing or keeping the current confines of judicial review'.[52] It is interesting to note that a similar approach has been suggested in the United States. For instance, Cass Sunstein points out that the best reconciliation between the goal of limiting administrative discretion and the desire to ensure that courts defer to the agency's specialised fact-finding and decision-making competence would call for a principle requiring a clear legislative displacement of judicial review.[53] Similarly, Professor Edley has argued that when Congress has not 'deliberately and clearly confined the scope of judicial review ... it is inappropriate for the Court to refrain from exercising its traditional responsibility to say what the law is'.[54] Otherwise, it can be added, the deferential approach would entail an unauthorized delegation of a constitutional power vested in the judiciary to the administrative decision-maker, which contravenes the principle *delegatus non potest delegare*.

It is worth emphasizing that this requirement is particularly important in policy environments in which it is suggested that the operation of these principles should be not only qualified or limited but also suspended. In these cases, it is said, a very clear 'ouster clause' or 'preclusive provision' must be inserted in the legislative act in order to explicitly prevent review of a specific discretion. Thus, for example, section 4(4) of the Foreign Compensation Act 1950 is in these terms: 'the determination by the Commission of any application made to them under this Act shall not be called in question in any court of law'. Similarly, section 25 of the Acquisition of Land Act 1981 provides that compulsory purchase orders 'shall not ... be questioned in any legal proceeding whatsoever'.

Thus it becomes apparent that, in order to justify a policy of judicial restraint in the commercial context by reference to the intention of Parliament, the court must necessarily refer to a specific statutory provision that permits the reduction or exclusion of review by using very clear language. In particular, it is submitted that given the high level of deference accorded to executive decisions in this field, which practically amounts to judicial abdication or avoidance, an express 'ouster clause' to that effect should be invoked.

Indeed the current doctrine of the judges may be characterized as the most damaging form of deference. In Richard Edwards' words, this kind of attitude

[51] Elliott, (as above n. 47), 78, 138–157. See also Cross, Thomas, 'When To Star is To Continue: Statutory Interpretation in the *Brian Haw* Case' [2007] 12(2) *Judicial Review*, 126.

[52] Le Sueur, Andrew, 'Justifying Judicial Caution: Jurisdiction, Justiciability and Policy' in *Judicial Review: A Thematic Approach*, Brigid Hadfield (ed.), (Dublin: Gill & Macmillan, 1995) 236.

[53] Sunstein, Cass, 'Interpreting Statutes in the Regulatory State' [1989] 103 *Harvard Law Review*, 475–476.

[54] Edley, Christopher, *Administrative Law: Rethinking Judicial Control of Bureaucracy*, (New Haven: Yale University Press, 1990), 144.

sometimes entails that an application is simply dismissed before the court has considered whether the limitation is lawful, as the context of the case at bar is of such a nature (i.e., technical, serious, complex, exclusive) to warrant the courts deferring to the executive.[55] In this sense, the present judicial attitude towards market regulators may also be characterized as result-oriented. When the court chooses to accord an agency such deference, it appears that the decision to defer compels the court to uphold the decision-maker's conclusion.[56] Importantly, the expression of a high level of cautiousness at this stage of the review process may well lead us to conclude, as Beatty does, that this approach, 'like the principle of minimal scrutiny in American constitutional law, has, more often than not meant no review at all'.[57] Self-evidently, it is difficult to simply 'assume' that Parliament intends the principles of judicial review to be abrogated to that extent. It is for this reason that, if the orthodox approach is to be legitimate, it must be based upon a very clear 'ouster clause'.

However, it must be noted, at this point, that most of the statutes governing regulatory decision-making in the business sphere do not provide legislative regulation of the court's supervisory jurisdiction: that is, there are no statutory modifications of the intensity of judicial review in this particular area. Interestingly, although some dissatisfaction has been expressed with the judiciary during the legislative process of specific bills, the critiques which the drafters advanced are not reflected in the statute. The Telecommunications Act 1984 provides a good example. Christopher Foster explains that the government and its civil service advisers who drafted the bill were determined to keep the law and the courts out of the new system. It was to be regulation 'with a light rein', so as to avoid 'creating a legalistic system which would employ lawyers to present cases and which could lead to endless delays in hearings and on appeal'.[58] However, finally, no provision was made to reduce the intervention of the courts into the regulatory process.

Based on the foregoing analysis, it is possible to assert that the doctrine which justifies judicial deference to market regulators by recourse to Parliament's will is unconvincing, because it often fails to identify the specific provisions which adequately convey the legislative purpose of significantly reducing the availability of review in this field. The use of very clear language is the only way in which the legislator may limit the jurisdiction of the courts in a way that rebuts the presumption that it intends the principles of review to be upheld. Thus, so long as Parliament remains silent and inactive on this matter in relation to commercial authorities, it is not open to judges to rationalize high levels of restraint in terms of following its sovereign will. Hence the orthodox approach to regulation, which actually buys into this line of reasoning, appears to be an unpersuasive dogma

---

[55] Edwards, Richard, 'Judicial Deference under the Human Rights Act' [2002] 65 *The Modern Law Review*, 868.

[56] Gerwin, Leslie, 'The Deference Dilemma: Judicial Responses to the Great Legislative Power Giveaway' [1987] 14 *Hastings Constitutional Law Quarterly*, 292.

[57] Cited by Edwards, (as above n. 55), 868.

[58] Foster, (as above n. 13), 125, 267.

which restricts citizen's access to justice where no such restriction was intended by the legislator, thereby introducing a rather artificial ouster clause in the legal system.

2.1.2.2 The limits of legislative competence

The focus has, thus far, been on stressing that the use of clear language is central to any legislative attempt to reduce the availability of judicial review. Nevertheless, it is necessary to note that Parliament's competence in this context is subject to an important limitation: even if it actually decided to preclude judicial review in explicit terms, such alteration may never, whatever the circumstances, deny access to justice altogether. Briefly, as Elliott explains, the wholesale abolition of judicial review may be categorized as 'constitutionally anathema', because it is manifestly inconsistent with one of the most fundamental values which enjoys constitutional status in Britain, namely, the citizen's right of access to a court of general jurisdiction.[59] Such an idea is also favoured by Allan, when he says that express rebuttal of Parliament's presumed intention regarding principles of constitutional importance may not be sufficient to outweigh it.[60] Thus, no matter how strong the need to interfere with the court's jurisdiction may be, it lies beyond the powers of Parliament to curtail the grounds of review in a manner which might completely abrogate this basic tenet of the constitutional order and the rule of law. This prompts two particular remarks.

First, it becomes apparent that commercial legislation cannot contain preclusive provisions which attempt to abolish the courts' entire power of control of regulatory decisions. The idea is that ouster clauses in this field can be constitutionally legitimate only if they can be reconciled with the right of access to justice. Where this is not possible, such norm must be excluded from the particular bill. To leave market authorities at liberty to exceed their powers without any check by the judiciary is therefore improper, irrespective of whether the language of the provision is clear, as it raises the prospect of Parliament displacing a deeply embedded constitutional principle. Hence government and legislators should be particularly careful in choosing interference with the rules of review as a mechanism for effective regulation.

Secondly, and more significantly for the present purposes, it follows that the courts should be reluctant to give literal effect to provisions which appear entirely to preclude supervision of the regulatory discretion in question. Since such an ouster of jurisdiction over the decision-maker constitutes a legislative excess which is contrary to the constitutional imperative of access to justice, the courts would certainly be justified in refusing to recognize it as law. This point is well captured by Lord Woolf. He explicitly acknowledges that the removal or substantial impairment of the entire reviewing role of the High Court on judicial review undermines in a fundamental way the rule of law principle that the courts are the final arbiters

---

[59] Elliott, (as above n. 47), 78, 121. For the developing common law right of access to the courts, see *R v. Chancellor, ex parte Witham* [1998] Q.B. 575.

[60] Allan, Trevor, 'Legislative Supremacy and Legislative Intention: Interpretation, Meaning and Authority' [2004] 63 *Cambridge Law Journal*, 689.

as to the interpretation and application of the law. In these cases, therefore, he suggests that the courts should refuse to accept that the legislation means what it appears to say, so that this core value on which the British unwritten constitution depends may be preserved.[61]

This approach derives support from the judgment of the House of Lords in *Anisminic Ltd v. Foreign Compensation Commission.*[62] The applicants, a British company, sought to challenge the decision of the Foreign Compensation Commission which dismissed their claim to compensation for the loss suffered as a result of the sequestration and expropriation of their mining property in Egypt. The respondent argued that, by reason of the ouster clause contained in section 4(4) of the Foreign Compensation Act of 1950 ('the determination by the Commission of any application made to them under this Act shall not be called in question in any court of law'), the courts were completely precluded from reviewing the lawfulness of that decision. The applicants, however, said that 'determination' meant a real determination which does not include an apparent or purported decision which in the eyes of the law has no existence because it is a nullity. The court found for the applicant. It was held, *inter alia*, that it is the duty of the court to take the meaning which best accords with the principle of access to justice. Lord Reid stated,

> It is a well established principle that a provision ousting the ordinary jurisdiction of the court must be construed strictly—meaning, I think, that, if such a provision is reasonably capable of having two meanings, that meaning shall be taken which preserves the ordinary jurisdiction of the court.

It is important to emphasize that this approach to ouster clauses is not necessarily inconsistent with the principle of supremacy of Parliament in its legislative capacity. Rather, it may be argued that it tends to provide a more accurate interpretation of the legislative will which takes into account not only the plain and natural meaning of the provision but also the constitutional context within which it is applied. This interpretive method has been articulated with particular clarity by Elliott in relation to the modified *ultra vires* doctrine.[63] He explains that, when Parliament enacts such clauses, the courts are constitutionally entitled to assume that it was *its* intention to legislate also in conformity with the rule of law principle, which favours access to courts. This means that the legislature is properly to be regarded as having accepted that the judges can ascribe to the particular text a meaning which differs from that which it may at first appear to bear, in order to ensure the fair resolution of legal disputes. Thus, through a process of statutory interpretation which considers Parliament's commitment to certain fundamental norms, it is perfectly possible to explain the courts' treatment of preclusive clauses 'in a way which accommodates both the theory of parliamentary sovereignty and the constitutional duty of the judges to uphold the rule of law'.[64]

---

[61] Woolf, Lord Harry, 'Droit Public—English Style' [1995] *Public Law*, 67–69.
[62] [1969] 2 A.C. 147.
[63] Elliott, (as above n. 47), Chapters 3 and 4.
[64] Ibid., 123.

It might be useful at this point to summarize the position presented in the last sub-sections by saying that it consists of two central propositions, each of which has implications for the practice of judicial review in the market field. First, that Parliament must use very clear language in order to reduce the intensity of review, thereby rebutting the presumption that it intends the principles of review to be upheld. This means, in turn, that the court's great reluctance to scrutinize commercial regulatory decisions could only be justified by reference to parliamentary intention if legislation in this field contained explicit provisions in this regard. As this is not the case in the present law, it is possible to hold that most of the attempts which have been made in this direction are unconvincing. Secondly, that, in any event, there can not be and ought not to be preclusive provisions which completely abolish review of administrative decisions, because they are fundamentally inconsistent with the rule of law, which favours access to a court of general jurisdiction. Consequently, in approaching clauses which appear to grant market authorities absolute immunity from judicial scrutiny, the courts, far from giving literal effect to them, should strive to apply a rule of construction which protects access to justice by preserving some role for review.

2.1.2.3 The content of legislative will in relation to autonomous agencies

There is, however, a third response to the argument that judicial deference to the regulator is based on the need to give effect to the will of Parliament. It must be recalled that one of the variants of this discourse relates to the establishment of independent agencies. In particular, it is argued that the courts cannot intervene in the affairs of these bodies because the legislator has entrusted them with autonomous powers to perform regulatory tasks without disruptions. However, it is contended here that this explanation is flawed, because it fails to capture Parliament's true intention behind the employment of these organizations. Two particular reasons can be given.

First, it must be stressed that the mentioned independence has been exclusively granted to operate in a governmental sphere of relations in order to reduce control from the central power and Parliament only. It was by no means designed to alter the intensity of judicial review upon regulatory decisions. This conclusion arises plainly from the analysis of secondary sources which elucidate the legislative reasons underlying the creation of autonomous agencies. The explanation provided is commonplace,[65] but it has been articulated with particular clarity by Sir William Wade and Professor Christopher Forsyth.

It is observed in the tenth edition of their distinguished work *Administrative Law* (Chapter 5) that public corporations set up at arm's length from central

---

[65] See Hague, D.C., Mackenzie, W.J.M. and Barker, A.P (eds.), *Public Policy and Private Interests: 'The Institutions of Compromise'*, (London: Macmillan Press, 1975) 362; Feldman, David, 'Convention Rights and Substantive Ultra Vires' in *Judicial Review and the Constitution*, D. Feldman (ed.), (Oxford: Oxford University Press, 2004) 261–262; Graham, Cosmo, *Is there a Crisis in Regulatory Accountability?*, Discussion Paper, (London: Charted Institute of Public Finance and Accountancy, 1995); Harlow, C. and Rawlings, R., *Law and Administration*, 3rd ed., Law in Context, (Cambridge: Cambridge University Press, 2009) 329. For a discussion of this issue in American Law, see Peters, A., 'Independent Agencies: Government's Scourge or Salvation?' [1988] 2/3 *Duke Law Journal*, 1988, 286–296.

government have been used to carry out specific administrative functions which need to be taken out of politics.[66] Specifically, this means that these bodies are expected to work free from partisan politics and party political influence. In the most obvious case of agencies established to monitor the operation of the privatized companies, it is noted that the legislator has intended 'to shift power from the hands of a minister, accountable to Parliament, into the hands of an independent regulator'. Indeed, it is explained that the only common element throughout the different acts concerning utilities such as telecommunications, gas, electricity, and water was 'the sharply reduced role of government policy...Regulation was to be done by regulators, not by ministers'.[67] In this manner, 'ministerial interference, often politically motivated, which frustrates the operation of the market forces', may be prevented.[68] In addition, these writers observe that, under this new constitutional experiment, accountability to Parliament for the regulation of the activity in question 'has generally been confined to appearances before Select Committees'.[69] Thus, it becomes clear that, as far as the issue of accountability is concerned, the legislative reasons for resort to agencies are exclusively related to the need to depart from the principles of ministerial and parliamentary accountability. It is precisely for this reason that the vacuum of control in which regulators operate has been regarded as an 'improvement on the highly politicised environment which made such difficulties for the old nationalised industries'.[70]

A similar situation can be found in the field of financial services regulation, where Parliament has been creating autonomous bodies in order to remove the exercise of powers, duties and functions from traditional ministerial responsibility and parliamentary accountability.[71] The current authority in this context is the Financial Service Authority (FSA), an independent non-governmental organization which is given statutory powers by the Financial Services and Markets Act 2000 and is funded entirely by the firms it regulates. Page points out that the lack of ministerial controls exercisable over this body should not cause surprise. He invites us to recall that the Act's intention is precisely to entrust regulatory functions to a separated body as opposed to ministers. In fact, he reports that the government resisted attempts made at the pre-legislative stage to take a reserve power over the board on the basis that it would lead it 'back again in the situation we wanted to avoid by having an independent regulator in the first place'.[72]

Approaching the issue from this perspective, it is possible to reach the conclusion that, since the legislator has decided to use agencies in the market field only to reduce interference from government and Parliament, it must follow that any attempt to attribute to it, in making this change in the style of public organization,

---

[66] Wade and Forsyth, (as above, n. 4), 125.

[67] Ibid., 147.   [68] Ibid.   [69] Ibid., 156.   [70] Ibid., 158.

[71] See Hopper, Martyn, 'Financial Services Regulation and Judicial Review: The Fault Lines' in *Commercial Regulation and Judicial Review*, J. Black, P. Muchlinski and P. Walker (eds.), (Oxford: Hart Publishing, 1998) 66.

[72] Third Report from the Treasury Committee, HC (1998–199) 73. Cited by Page, Alan, 'Regulating the Regulator—A Lawyer's Perspective on Accountability and Control' in *Regulating Financial Services and Markets in the 21st Century*, E. Ferran and C.A.E. Goodhart (eds.), (Oxford: Hart Publishing, 2001) 133.

an intention that there should be less judicial control of regulatory decisions is artificial. The legislative history makes it clear that these bodies are independent only
in respect of those they regulate and of governmental pressure to be over-intrusive.
No mention is made of the possibility of decrease in judicial accountability as a
necessary effect of the placing of administrative burdens on autonomous agencies.
The *ratio legis* underlying this relatively new process of transferring powers cannot, therefore, be persuasively invoked to justify the court's deferential approach
towards regulatory decisions.

Secondly, the idea that Parliament has intended that the intensity of judicial
review must remain untouched, while ministerial and parliamentary accountability are dramatically reduced to ensure the independence of market regulators,
should not seem strange or startling when one considers the appropriate balance
of powers within the constitutional order. Indeed it is a well-established principle
of the British constitution that the democratic deficit caused by the decline in the
governmental ability to scrutinize administrative decisions must be filled by the
courts through effective judicial review.[73] In particular, it is argued that recourse
to judicial scrutiny appears to be the most appropriate means to avoid the risk of
bias and self-dealing on the part of the decision-maker, which naturally follows
from the absence of other channels of review. Thus, the less effective the political
mechanisms of accountability with respect to administrative decisions, the more
the case for exercising legal control over them. Actually, it is possible to observe
that the decline in the effectiveness of political checks against the executive has
strongly influenced the late twentieth century expansion of judicial review.[74] In
this sense, Michael Beloff points out that judges have lost faith in Parliament's ability as scrutineer and have seen an increasing need to take on the task themselves as
a necessary part of maintaining the constitutional balance of power.[75] Elliott comments that these developments are to be welcomed: 'it is one of the strengths of the
unwritten constitution that such informal evolution is possible'.[76]

Furthermore, contemporary judgments in the public law sphere demonstrate
that this doctrine is also applicable to the balance between European and British
judicial power in human rights cases, as domestic courts have taken to heart the
contention that the absence of willingness to scrutinize administrative discretion
on the part of foreign institutions operates to influence the courts in the adoption

---

[73] Oliver, Dawn, 'Law and Politics and Public Accountability. The Search for a New Equilibrium'
[1994] *Public Law*, 246; Sedley, Stephen, 'The Moral Economy of Judicial Review' in *Frontiers of
Legal Scholarship*, Geoffrey P. Wilson (ed.), (Chichester: Chancery Law Publishing, 1995) 160; Wolf,
Lord H., 'Judicial Review—The Tensions between the Executive and the Judiciary' [1998] 114 *Law
Quarterly Review*, 591.

[74] See the judgment of Lord Mustill in *R v. Secretary of State for the Home Department, ex p Fire
Brigades* [1995] 2 A.C. 513 at 567. See also Brennan, Gerard, 'The Purpose and Scope of Judicial
review' in *Judicial Review of Administrative Action in the 1980s*, Michael Taggart (ed.), (New York:
Oxford University Press, 1986) 19.

[75] Beloff, Michael, 'Judicial Review—2001: A Prophetic Odyssey' [1995] 58 *Modern Law
Review*, 143; Radford, Mike, 'Mitigating the Democratic Deficit? Judicial Review and Ministerial
Accountability' in *Administrative Law Facing the Future: Old Constraints & New Horizons*, P. Leyland
and T. Woods (eds.), (Oxford: Oxford University Press, 1997).

[76] Elliott, (as above n. 47), 69.

of a stricter standard of review. This point is captured well by two judges in *A v. Secretary of State for Home Department*,[77] a case concerning legal challenges to the detention regime under the Anti-terrorism, Crime and Security Act 2001. Lord Hope of Craighead held that 'when the European Court of Human Rights talks about affording a margin of appreciation to the assessment of the British Government it assumes that its assessment will at the national level receive closer scrutiny'.[78] Similarly, Lord Rodger of Earlsferry stressed that 'the considerable deference which the European Court of Human Rights shows to the views of the national authorities in such matters really presupposes that the national courts will police those limits'.[79] Understood thus, the judicial attitude to executive measures which are immune from political supervision and those which have been accorded some leeway by the European Court of Human Rights are of a piece with one another: in each case, the function of the judiciary is to ensure that, so far as possible, such accountability vacuum is filled.

Against this background it is unsurprising that the legislator has decided not to insulate market regulators from judicial review. Only by preserving the role of the courts in determining the lawfulness of impugned decisions is it possible to reconcile the use of independent agencies—that entails a diminution in the ability of the central government and Parliament to hold the executive to account—with the fundamental principle of balance of powers, which is essential to prevent or correct abuses of public power in democratic societies. There are therefore good reasons to think that it was Parliament's view that the greater measure of autonomy enjoyed by economic agencies, far from robbing the courts of their supervisory jurisdiction, leaves no option but to ensure the exercise of judicial scrutiny in a manner which counteracts the dead ground left by lack of traditional lines of accountability. In light of this, it appears that the existing justification for judicial deference to autonomous bodies on the basis of legislative intent is not only unconvincing, but even contrary to the social imperative of checks and balances between the branches of power.

Thus it is possible to establish the constitutional necessity of connecting the existence of public corporations in the market field with the imposition of more stringent standards of fairness on decision-makers by the courts. This conclusion is bolstered when the reaction of leading writers to the creation of these bodies is considered. Michael Taggart, for example, has welcomed this approach, noting that 'the courts retain a potentially important role, all the more so due to the accountability vacuum' created by the process of privatization.[80] Similarly, Martyn Hopper has said that judicial supervision 'ought to be of particular relevance to bodies such as the financial service regulators, whose activities are (for good reason) insulated from legal control by government'.[81] In particular, he argues that the courts have a fundamental constitutional role to play in complementing the processes of

---

[77] [2004] U.K.H.L. 56 at 29, [2005] 2 W.L.R. 87.
[78] Elliott, (as above n. 47), 131.
[79] Ibid., at 176.
[80] Taggart, Michael, 'Corporatisation, Privatisation and Public Law' [1991] 2 *Public Law Review*, 107.
[81] Hopper, (as above n. 71), 68.

government's and Parliament's oversight, by ensuring that the regulator effectively implements the regulatory scheme set out in the legislation and do not abuse the powers put at their disposal.[82]

As regards self-regulation, this point has been well captured by the dicta of Lloyd LJ in the *Datafin* case.[83] He had this to say about judicial supervision of the Panel on Takeovers and Mergers:

The fact that it is self-regulating, which means, presumably, that it is not subject to regulation by others, and in particular the Department of Trade and Industry, makes it not less but more appropriate that it should be subject to judicial review by the courts. It has been said that it is excellent to have a giant's strength, but it is tyrannous to use it like a giant.[84]

In light of this, it appears that the effective judicial response to the creation of independent regulators operates as a natural and 'healthy' adjustment of functions within a dynamic model of separation of powers. As Cynthia Farina observes,

as power flows among the power centres in government, new patterns of counterbalance emerge to provide restraint. This movement of power can be accepted so long as equilibrium can then be re-established.[85]

This model of flexible balance of powers is very helpful to understand the increasing importance of judicial review in the context of market regulation. Specifically, it acknowledges that although the constitution allows enormous power to be funnelled into independent regulatory agencies, this acceptance is not to be mistaken for unconditional licence: 'innovation in one area may call for a responsive shift in other areas'.[86] It follows from this that the concentration of powers in this new species of decision-makers can be reconciled with the principle of separation of powers only if it is offset by correlative stronger checks, particularly judicial checks.

A similar adjustment of powers can be found in other jurisdictions. Professor David Mullen, for instance, has suggested that as political accountability in Canada is not working in conventional ways, 'there should be much room for courts to provide surrogate accountability vehicles'.[87] Similarly, Giandomenico Majone points out that the American experience shows that,

a highly complex and specialised activity like regulation can be monitored and kept politically accountable only by a combination of control instruments: legislative and executive oversight, strict procedural requirements, public participation and, most importantly, substantive judicial review.[88]

---

[82] Ibid., 86.

[83] *R v. Panel on Takeovers and Mergers, ex p Datafin plc.* [1987] 1 All E.R. 564.

[84] The adoption of a more intensive form of judicial review of non-statutory powers is also based on democratic principles. See Cohn, Margit, 'Judicial review of non-statutory executive powers after Bancoult: a unified anxious model' [2009] *Public Law*, 2009, 282–284.

[85] Farina, Cynthia, 'Statutory Interpretation and the Balance of Power in the Administrative State' [1989] 89 *Columbia Law Review*, 497.   [86] Ibid.

[87] Mullen, David, 'Judicial Deference to Executive Decision-Making: Evolving Concepts of Responsibility' [1993–94] 19 *Queen's Law Journal*, 159.

[88] Majone, Giandomenico, 'The Rise of the Regulatory State in Europe' [1994] 17 *West European Politics*, 93. Cited by Page, (as above n. 72), 127.

In particular, he argues that the greater importance of judicial oversight in the regulatory state derives largely from the lack of fully effective alternative mechanisms of accountability.

Actually, Carl McGowan observes that the United States Congress has 'neither the resources nor the inclination to exercise more than occasional oversight of independent agencies proceedings'.[89] Since its attention is focused only on widespread problems or truly egregious disputes, it is incapable of treating unfairness and overreaching in the ordinary case.[90] In addition, Merrill explains that presidential oversight over regulators has inherent limitations. He notes that, given the vastness of the federal bureaucracy, it is simply unrealistic to expect that the president or his principal lieutenants can effectively monitor the policymaking activities of all federal agencies. In his opinion, therefore, the only effective institutional mechanism for protecting citizens against arbitrary or aggrandizing action by agencies is judicial review.[91]

For the present purposes, it is also significant that the American legislature appears to recognize the exercise of judicial supervision as a basic condition for transferring rule-making functions to non-departmental public bodies. As Judge Leventhal stated,

> Congress has been willing to delegate its legislative powers broadly—and the courts have upheld such delegation—because there is court review to assure that the agency exercises the delegated power within statutory limits.[92]

Accordingly, it is observed that the administrative state in the United States has become constitutionally tenable mainly because of the Supreme Court's requirement that rule-making power may be transferred to independent agencies *so long as* it will be adequately judicially controlled.[93] These statements, therefore, provide further refutation of the notion, present in some judicial and academic circles, that it is the intention of Parliament that the substantial measure of autonomy enjoyed by regulatory agencies calls for a drastic reduction in the availability of judicial review.

The Anglo-American constitutional experience thus clearly suggests that, in Parliament's view, the more limited the ability of government and the legislature to stop clear abuses of the power conferred on regulators, the more important the courts' constitutional role of checking the abuse of public, regulatory power. It is for this reason that the creation of autonomous regulators seems to involve a double legislative intention. On the one hand, it expresses a need to transfer powers to the independent regulator in order to put the activity out of political pressure. On the other hand, at the same time, it indicates an implicit plea to the judiciary to control some topics which are going to be immune from governmental supervision. In this

---

[89] McGowan, Carl, 'A Reply to Judicialization' [1986] 2 *Duke Law Journal*, 224.
[90] Ibid.
[91] Merrill, Thomas, 'Judicial Deference to Executive Precedent' [1991–92] 101 *Yale Law Journal*, 997.
[92] *Ethyl Corp. v. EPA*, 541 F.2d 1, 68 (D.C. Cir. 1976).
[93] Farina, (as above n. 85), 487.

sense, a highly politicized control is replaced by another which is supposed to be impartial and technical.

2.1.3 Legality and merits

As seen above, proponents of the orthodox approach argue that it is also based on the recognition of the distinction between legality and merits. Since the judicial review procedure is never, or only exceptionally, concerned with the latter, the cautious attitude towards the decision-maker, it is said, emerges as a useful tool to avoid precisely an impermissible intrusion into the executive realm. In this sense, the deference shown to the regulator appears to be really little more than the distinction between legality and merits in the context of market regulation.

However, this view must be challenged. Although it is true, at root, that such distinction precludes the determination—by way of judicial review—of whether the action is 'right or wrong', it must be stressed that, in the commercial sphere, this is secured by the adoption of the most damaging approach which falls within the range of choices (not necessarily legitimate) open to the court. In particular, the judicial scrutiny in this field is so deferential that it amounts in effect to the denial of the judicial review jurisdiction altogether. Indeed, by simply dismissing the particular application on the ground that the decision has been made by an expert, efficient, and duly empowered regulator, the court is not only refusing to substitute its own view of the merits for that of the decision-maker, it is actively opposing any form of judicial review, including that of legality. In other words, the present response to the problem of regulatory autonomy seeks to avoid the test of correctness at one end of the review continuum by applying a test of reasonableness which precludes control in all its sections or points. Some companies actually have described the current approach, namely *Wednesbury*, as a 'sledgehammer, it creates an uphill struggle on the part of the regulated body to prove that the regulator was completely unreasonable or stark raving mad'.[94]

Such a doctrine is fundamentally inconsistent with the constitutional role of the courts as guardians of law. Judicial control of lawfulness is a fundamental mechanism for upholding the rule of law, as it ensures that powers are exercised only within their true limits. Specifically, by passing judgement on whether the administrative decision was made arbitrarily, for an improper motive or by the wrong procedure, the judicial review process clearly favours the protection of the citizen's rights against the abuse of authority. As Wade and Forsyth remark, 'all power is capable of abuse, and that the power to prevent abuse is the acid test of effective judicial review'.[95] In light of this, it becomes apparent that the current lack of legality control in the business field represents a form of deference which severely weakens administrative law's capacity to protect private interests at stake. In spite of its apparent consistency with the distinction between appeal

---

[94] See the statement of Robert Armour, Secretary of British Energy, to the Select Committee on Constitution of the House of Lords, 6th Report of Session 2003–2004, *The Regulatory State: Ensuring its accountability*, Volume II (HC 68-II), Oral Evidence, Wednesday 9 April 2003, question 256.
[95] Wade and Forsyth, (as above n. 4), 30.

and review, the particular approach in question abrogates the fundamental principles of fairness and reasonableness which the rule of law doctrine embodies, thereby risking the creation of a totalitarian state that successfully nullifies basic economic freedoms.

It is precisely this type of reasoning that underlies the criticism levelled at the high degree of deference accorded to commercial authorities, and emphasizes the need to adopt an alternative form of inquiry which is both jurisdictionally satisfying and pragmatically workable. In particular, it is necessary to articulate a judicial approach which deals with the issue of merits without taking the constitutionally unacceptable step of granting generous immunity to potentially capricious or oppressive regulatory decisions by also denying review on the ground of illegality. The idea is to adopt a more intensive test of legality which, in Richard Edward's words, may avoid the present 'danger' of indiscriminate judicial deference and judicial abdication.[96] This task is undertaken in Chapter 5, where it is argued that a solution to this problem is forthcoming once the principle of proportionality is taken into account.

For the present purposes, however, it is important to acknowledge that the application of a more searching scrutiny than that required under the current jurisprudence would not be necessarily conducive to a transgression of the bounds of the courts' allotted constitutional province. Alternatively, it may signify the adoption of an intermediate position which leads the judge to take some effective view of the lawfulness of the particular decision in question without going so far as to use the test of correctness. Thus, for Craig, when the court exercises a heightened *Wednesbury* or proportionality review, it is certainly not imposing what it believes to be the 'correct' answer to the issue. Rather, it is exclusively concerned with the legality of the contested action, but in a manner which requires the decision-maker to provide a fully reasoned case so as to secure the repudiation of arbitrary power.[97] This doctrine is to be welcomed, to the extent that it accommodates both the theory of jurisdiction and the constitutional duty of the judges to uphold the rule of law by paying due regard to the relative weight accorded to relevant interests.

2.2 Regulatory effectiveness

It will be recalled from Chapter 2 that the exercise of judicial review in the commercial field might seriously undermine the effectiveness of the regulatory system. In particular, the court's intervention in the affairs of public authorities is thought likely to cause discouragement and fear to officials, ossification of rule-making, excessive slowness in the decision-making process, tactical litigation, and uncertainty among individuals. This has led the courts and some writers to argue that the judges should refrain from reviewing regulatory decisions in order to ensure the

---

[96] Edwards, Richard, 'Judicial Deference under the Human Rights Act' [2002] 65 *The Modern Law Review*, 65, 872.

[97] Craig, Paul, *Administrative Law*, 6th edn., (London: Sweet & Maxwell, 2008) 636–639.

quick and efficient implementation of market policies. The concern of the present sub-section is to evaluate this doctrine in legal terms, by considering whether it is compatible with the notion of individual justice enshrined in the system of judicial review. The following paragraphs, therefore, do not purport to contradict the fact that the court's supervision over economic authorities may affect public policy interests. This may be so to some extent.[98] They do, however, point towards the conclusion that the existence of this difficulty is not a sufficient condition for advocating a high degree of judicial restraint. Within a constitutional framework which primarily requires the courts to protect individuals against the abuses of executive power, the intensity of judicial review cannot be severely reduced for the sake of political expediency. A more appropriate response to the problem of regulatory effectiveness might therefore be to suggest that it can be overcome without going so far as to interfere with the right of innocent applicants to an effective assessment of their claim. The alternative solutions to the risk of tactical litigation provide a good example in this regard.

2.2.1 Public Policy Considerations

Indeed the most compelling argument which can be made against the effectiveness rationale is that it is not capable of providing a fair mechanism of supervision that takes into account the right-based arguments of the claimants. The very fact that judges are guided—and, hence, apparently shaped—by administrative efficiency makes it very difficult for citizens to obtain a thorough review of the impugned decision that acts as a check on the abuse of executive power. In practice, the courts will refuse to make such a careful evaluation in order to avoid the inconveniences this may cause to the market regulation system. Thus, on this view, the rights of the aggrieved individual are significantly trumped or outweighed by the public interest in hard and fast reactions to changing conditions on the part of economic authorities.

It is worth noting that the application of this doctrine also furnishes evidence of the demise of the juridification process in the United Kingdom business sector. The increasing importance of law and rights in liberalized markets has indeed encouraged the judiciary to exercise self-restraint a as way to ensure that the incidences of litigation—which typically accompany this tendency[99]—do not interfere with the efficiency of expert administration. Viewed in this manner, it may be argued that the requirement of regulatory effectiveness, from which the practice of judicial deference is said to spring, appears to be incompatible not only with the court's supervisory role in this field but also with the entire process by which relations

---

[98] It is worth noting that not all applications for judicial review in themselves threaten undesirable delay to regulatory decisions. Indeed, there have been cases where recourse to judicial review has been deployed speedily. Even in the context of financial services, where there is a great need for the speedy resolution of disputes in order to avoid uncertainty in the market, the use of judicial review has proved to be an efficient procedure; the *Argyll* case ([1986] 1 W.L.R. 763), for example, took less than a month from the challenged decision to judgment in the Court of Appeal. See Beatson, Jack, 'Financial Services: Who will Regulate the Regulators' [1987] 8(1) *Company Lawyer*, 1987, 34.

[99] Scott, Colin, 'The Juridification of Relations in the UK Utilities Sector' in Black, Muchlinski and Walker, (as above n. 71), 20.

between decision-makers and market players come to be subjected to legal values and rules. As Black and Muchlinski point out, complaints about judicial intervention are often just complaints about law; 'what is often really wanted is a law free zone'.[100] In particular, they explain that 'the plea for non interventionist judicial review is often at root a plea to remove law from the field altogether. Judicial review is simply one manifestation of the increasing role played by law and legal values in regulation, a role which some would resist'.[101]

These statements expose in especially clear terms the most substantial shortcoming of the argument in question: if it were accepted, then the court would risk abdicating its ultimate responsibility to protect individual rights in particular and the legal order as a whole by reviewing the lawfulness of executive decisions. This view is apparent from the comments of writers who, for reasons of legal principle, contend that a model of judicial review which is dependant on the demands of public policy would be fundamentally repugnant to the notion of individual justice. Thus, for example, Allan says that a political question doctrine that required 'extraordinary' deference to the executive would undermine judicial protection of the rule of law entirely.[102] In effect, he says, proposals to alter the judicial role in public law proceedings, adapting it to the needs of policy formulation and scrutiny, invite us 'to replace courts by executive agencies, with doubtful consequences both for the security of constitutional rights and the health of democracy'.[103] Andrew Le Sueur captures the same point when he remarks that the increasing importance of legal rights and the court's role in protecting them may be lost 'if the judges assert power to trump rights for reasons of public policy such as administrative convenience'.[104]

In light of this—and, in particular, given the way in which the waves of juridification in the economic sectors appear to turn organisational and supply questions into specific legal rights enforceable within the British legal system—it is strongly arguable that effective judicial review ought to take place irrespective of whether it may affect the interests of the administration. The formalisation of regulatory relations in juridical terms should operate, in the present field, as a catalyst which prompts the courts to provide a meaningful scrutiny of challenged decisions in order to secure the interests of market players. In this way it becomes apparent that the judiciary should adhere to a form of adjudication that is primarily committed to checking and preventing unauthorized agency encroachments on individual rights, rather than to the policy of ensuring that governmental actions are not disrupted. As Le Sueur remarks in a more general context, an alternative route must be taken, and that is,

to assert that 'law' *is* distinct from policy and politics and that at the core of the court's work should be the protection of legal rights of individuals (including group rights) rather than evaluating what is the collective interest.[105]

---

[100] Black, Muchlinski and Walker, (as above n. 71), 16.
[101] Ibid.   [102] Allan, (as above n. 1), 164.   [103] Ibid., 198.
[104] Le Sueur, (as above n. 22), 248–249.   [105] Ibid., 250.

In particular, the idea is to have, as Anthony explains,

judges who will faithfully apply the law that limits the agencies, rather than judges who reflexively approve restrictive agency actions regardless of their basic legality in order to support results they find politically congenial.[106]

It follows that, whenever there is a plausible claim that a regulatory decision has affected established rights, there cannot properly be a form of deference to it that precludes ordinary legal analysis on the basis of public policy considerations.[107] In particular, as Allan points out, 'it would clearly be mistaken to think that legal principles are inapplicable merely because an administrative decision has wide-ranging consequences for the public interest'.[108] The preferred response to this cause of action would therefore be to hold that a proper model of adjudication—which, in practical terms, determines whether the court may legitimately exercise its supervisory jurisdiction—ought to 'maintain a genuine distinction between law and politics'[109] that allows judges to intervene in cases where governmental actions may have infringed existing legal rights even though this would be contrary to administrative convenience. Thus, appropriate weight may be attached to the interests of private parties within a particular normative environment. It is worth mentioning two matters which provide at least some indication that, in the specific context of market regulation, the courts should apply this rights-based doctrine.

First, Lon Fuller's often quoted account of adjudication on 'polycentric' questions may be considered. Briefly, these involve decisions which are so complex and multi-faceted in their effects that it is probable that the judgement of the court upon them will have far-reaching implications that go beyond the interests of the parties to the dispute.[110] Under the effectiveness rationale, this type of case would certainly call into question the court's decision to intervene, since it would be incapable of affording each affected and interested party a meaningful participation through proofs and arguments. Fuller contends, however, that mere presence of polycentric elements does not necessarily preclude the courts from properly handling the problem by adjudication as usually conducted: 'the fact that an adjudicative decision affects and enters into a polycentric relationship does not of itself mean that the adjudicative tribunal is moving out of its proper sphere'.[111] Rather, this is often a matter of degree, 'a question of knowing when the polycentric elements have become so significant and predominant that

---

[106] Anthony, Robert, *Unlegislated Compulsion: How Federal Agency Guidelines Threaten Your Liberty*, Cato Policy Analysis No. 312, (Washington,D.C.: The Cato Institute, 1998), available at <http://www.publications.parliament.uk/pa/Id200304/Idselect/Idconst/68/68.pdf>.

[107] Allan, (as above n. 1), 162–163.   [108] Ibid., 189.

[109] Ibid., 198.

[110] For example, he says that the court's decision to raise the price of aluminium,

'may effect in varying degrees the demand for, and therefore the proper price of, thirty kinds of steel, twenty kinds of plastics, and infinitude of woods, other metals, etc. Each of these separate effects may have its own complex repercussions in the economy'. Lon L. Fuller, 'The Forms and Limits of Adjudication' [1978] 92 *Harvard Law Review*, 394.

[111] Ibid., 403.

the proper limits of adjudication have been reached'.[112] In particular, he argues that, so far as market cases are concerned, judicial adjudication is not in fact unsuited to absorb polycentric issues: 'there is no better illustration of a polycentric relationship than an economic market, and yet the laying down of rules that will make a market function properly is one for which adjudication is generally well suited'.[113]

Fuller has attempted to justify this conclusion by explaining that the field of commercial relations, which is penetrated by rights, especially allows the court to reformulate polycentric issues so as to make them amenable to solution through adjudicative procedures.[114] He argues that the transformation by which economic relations tend to crystallize into 'rights' simplifies the problem to the point where it can be arbitrated in the form of arguments supporting competing interests. Thus, by structuring the relations of individuals to one another in terms of rights and duties, the juridification process in the economic sphere appears to provide a common principle which appropriately controls these relations from a single angle, thereby facilitating the conversion of every managerial problem into something suitable for decision by adjudication. In this sense, what seems to be a situation of interacting points of influence is in fact a case of competing legal demands that the courts must balance and measure. Prima facie, this approach directly challenges the orthodox doctrine that the courts should refrain from deciding polycentric problems and it appears that, if accepted, it would effectively accommodate the form of adjudication to the specific nature of the problem.

In practice, this point has a significant consequence for restrictive measures by which the regulator seeks to pursue not only a primary legitimate objective but also wider public policy considerations such as, for example, the protection of health, environment or employability. The logic here is that the broader the range of secondary policy aims that are pursued the more severe the measure. Mark Elliott explains that the court may be tempted to allow polycentric decisions which are more restrictive of rights than is strictly necessary to achieve the statutorily described objective in order to protect other public interests which are valuable to the decision-maker. The question for the court would therefore be whether those measures are 'reasonably', rather than 'strictly', necessary to facilitate the achievement of different objectives.[115]

However, Elliott lucidly argues that this judicial technique is problematic since it ultimately frees the decision-maker to choose not only the means but also the objectives of public policy, thereby circumventing the terms of the enabling legislation and 'subjugating rights to considerations of expediency to an unacceptable degree'.[116] Interestingly, the central solution which he advances to the problem is consistent with Fuller's conception of policy considerations as competing interests that must be equally subject to the court's primary judgement. It follows that, in

---

[112] Ibid., 398.   [113] Ibid., 403.   [114] Ibid., 405.
[115] Elliott, Mark, 'Proportionality and Deference: The importance of a Structured Approach' (as above, n. 14), 278.
[116] Ibid., 280.

such cases, secondary aims should also be scrutinized at the three relevant stages of the proportionality analysis: legitimacy, necessity and, most importantly, balancing. Specifically, a judicial decision must be taken about whether the human rights loss which the impugned measure entails is justified or outweighed by the public policy gains it purchases.[117]

Secondly, it is particularly instructive to consider that, as far as market-regulation is concerned, the proposed rights-based approach has been endorsed by the jurisprudence of the ECtHR in licensing cases. In *Tre Traktörer Aktiebolag*,[118] for example, the Swedish government contended that reasons existed for not submitting to civil or administrative courts questions relating to the revocation of licences to serve alcoholic beverages. In their opinion, such matters formed part of the implementation of the national policy concerning alcoholic beverages. Thus, by invoking the existence of policy considerations as the juridical basis of judicial restraint, the government implicitly acknowledged that public interest must take precedence over that of the applicant. However, the Strasbourg Court did not share this contention. It was of the view that despite the features of public policy mentioned by the respondent, the dispute in question did concern a 'right' of the company whose violation might be claimed before the judiciary. In this manner, the court reaffirmed the notion that, so long as the challenged decision is said to have affected the interests of the applicant, the necessity of exercising effective judicial review arises irrespective of whether the dispute touches on questions of political expediency.

Importantly, therefore, the requirement that the courts must undertake a meaningful review of regulatory decisions—even within a context where complex and political repercussions may result from their intervention—can be rationalized by reference to the need to provide adequate protection to the rights of private individuals, which have become a central feature of regulatory law in liberalised markets. On this view, it does not lie outside the judiciary's role to interfere with and supervise the implementation of economic decisions that may have infringed such legitimate interests. Thus, although it is possible that the exercise of judicial review in this sphere leads to some disruptions in regulatory activities, the juridified context within which they are performed provides that such prospect cannot be a sufficient condition for the court to adopt a policy of restraint or deference towards the decision-maker. In other words, the judge must still conduct a neutral and thorough assessment of the validity of the decision, in order to ensure that the limits the regulator imposes on guaranteed rights are reasonable and justifiable.

Having set out a model of adjudication within which regulatory action is in effect constrained and reviewed as a consequence of the growing emphasis on economic rights as legally enforceable constructs, it is necessary, however, to enter two caveats concerning the specific role which the courts should play in this area.

First, it is trite, but nevertheless worth emphasizing, that this form of review can be reconciled with the constitutional order only if it is conceptualized in a

---

[117] Ibid., 279–280.   [118] 4/1988/148/202.

rights-oriented manner. This means that the judiciary is properly to be regarded as exercising supervision over regulatory policy choices in so far as they are claimed to have caused harm to identifiable persons. It follows from this that, in the absence of such complaint, the court should refrain from determining the lawfulness of the particular decision in question, in order to avoid illegitimate interference with matters of general public interest. Thus, once the exercise of regulatory discretion is located within its proper normative context, it becomes clear that the focus on rights must operate to limit the exercise of judicial power. Since the seepage of law and rights into market regulation is a process which shapes the environment within which decisions are subject to judicial scrutiny, it is not open to the courts to resolve issues that cannot be reduced to questions of individual interest.

This much is apparent from Allan's text on justiciability and jurisdiction, which maintains that the legitimacy of the court's decision depends on scrupulous adherence to a relatively narrow focus of inquiry.[119] In particular, he says that the legitimacy of the court's constitutional role as interpreter of statues derives mainly from the protection thereby afforded to individual rights and expectations against the abuse of executive power. Where no threat to such interests can be shown to exist, the interpretive function is less readily defensible: 'there are often no settled principles by which the court can justify a reading of the statute that other public agencies reject'.[120] It is for this reason that the prospect of too expansive a doctrine of standing or too intrusive a style of review where no citizen's rights are affected may pose a serious problem to the constitutional allocation of powers, since they reflect an abstract-public concern for vindicating the bare words of statutes which practically abolishes the distinction between questions of legal principle and those of public policy entrusted to the executive branch of government.[121] This misreading of the model of adjudication in public law matters also becomes apparent upon consideration of the potential conflict identified by Cane between 'the willingness of most judges to interpret the standing requirement widely, and the continuing uneasiness of English courts at the prospect of becoming too involved in matters which are politically sensitive'.[122]

Interestingly, the abandonment of the doctrine of adjudication based on individual rights, in favour of a wider interest-representation model, thus suggests that 'public interest' arguments may be characterized not only as advocating judicial restraint and deference to government, but also as urging judicial activism. Indeed, there is reason to fear that judicial consideration of desirable social goals might precipitate excessive interference in administrative decision-making, as the court might be more willing to extend their jurisdiction to hear anyone who is concerned about relevant issues. Understood thus, the expanded view on justiciability does not constitute any advance on the path to maintain a genuine distinction between

---

[119] Allan, (as above n. 1), 161–99.   [120] Ibid., 196.
[121] Ibid., 196–197.
[122] Cane, Peter, 'Mapping the Frontiers' in *The Frontiers of Liability*, Peter Birks (ed.), Vol. 1, (Oxford: Oxford University Press, 1994) 153.

law and politics, because it leads the judges to wrongly usurp the role of executive bodies in meeting community needs. In the American context, for example, such criterion has been lucidly described by Richard Stewart as tending 'to make the court a planning agency rather than a forum where relief can be obtained by persons asserting violations by officials of duties imposed by law'.[123]

In the light of these dangerous developments, derived either from judicial restraint or activism on the basis of public interest, it is crucial therefore to remark that the legitimacy of the courts' supervisory function is heavily dependant on the need to respond to the claims of affected parties; and that the limited nature of the judicial review proceedings is an essential requirement of the constitutional order, precluding them from fulfilling a legislative or policy-making role for which they are largely unauthorized.

It is worth noting that this is actually a well established criterion in section 31(3) of the Supreme Court Act 1981 and RSC Ord. 53(7), now CPR Part 54 ('sufficient interest in the matter to which the application relates'); and in the Enterprise Act 2002 ('person aggrieved'). It has also been recognized in relation to challenges to measures under Article 230(4) of the EU Treaty ('direct and individual concern'),[124] and section 7 of the Human Rights Act 1998 ('victim').[125]

Such a model of adjudication thus expresses a conception of the separation of powers which provides a proper balance between the regulator's legitimate function to make judgements concerning the public interest and the court's duty to resolve issues of legal principle.

A good illustration of this political equilibrium in the domestic context can be seen early in *H.T.V. Ltd. v. Price Commission*,[126] where Lord Scarman usefully

---

[123] Stewart, Richard, 'The Reformation of Administrative Law' [1975] 88 *Harvard Law Review*, 1734.

[124] For the market regulation context, see *Unión de Pequeños Agricultores*, C-50/00P [2002] 3 C.M.L.R. 1. A Spanish trade association which represents the interests of small agricultural businesses brought an action, pursuant to the fourth paragraph of Article 173 of the EC Treaty (now Article 230 EC), for annulment of a Council regulation which reformed the common organization of the olive oil markets. The ECJ held that the appellant did not have standing to bring such action, on the ground that the question did not affect 'specific natural or legal persons by reason of certain attributes peculiar to them, or by reason of a factual situation which differentiates them from all other persons and distinguishes them individually in the same way as the addressee'. See also *Confederation Nationale des Producteurs de Fruits et Legumes v. Council*, Case 16/62 [1962] ECR 471 (fruits and vegetables market); *Codorniu v Council*, Case C-309/89 [1994] ECR I-1853, paras 17–20 (regulation of the sparkling wine market); *Sadam Zuccherifici and Others v. Council*, Case 41/99 [2001] ECR I-4239, para 27 (market in the sugar sector); *Nederlandse Antillen v. Council*, Case 452/98 [2001] ECR I-8973, para 60 (rice market); and *Jégo-Quéré & Cie SA v. Commission of the European Communities*, Case 177/01 [2002] E.C.R. II-02365. For a detailed analysis of the European case law, see Ward, Angela, *Individual Rights and Private Party Judicial Review in the EU*, Oxford European Community Law Library Series (Oxford: Oxford University Press, 2007) 284–290.

[125] For the difference between these standing tests, see Legere, Edite, '*Locus Standi* and the Public Interest: A Hotchpotch of Legal Principles' [2005] *Judicial Review*, 128–134. For the consideration of companies as victims under the HRA, see Emberland, Marius, *The Human Rights of Companies*, (Oxford: Oxford University Press, 2006) 65–109.

[126] *H.T.V. Ltd. v. Price Commission* [1976] I.C.R. 170. For a more recent account of this doctrine, see the judgment of Lord Hoffmann in *R (on the application of Prolife Alliance) v. BBC* [2003] 2 W.L.R. 1403 at 75–76; and the judgment of Lord Bingham of Cornhill in *A v. Secretary of State for Home Department* (as above, n. 77).

outlined the specific conditions under which the courts can interfere with decisions of an economic authority. He stated that,

> I would, therefore, agree with the Price Commission that questions of fact and policy in
> the implementation of the code are for them to determine: and that their determination
> is not subject to review by the courts unless it can be shown that they have fallen into an
> error of law in the construction of statutory language or have acted unfairly. Though they
> are a policy body fighting inflation, they are also and agency implementing a code. It is a
> code which directly affects the rights of commercial and industrial enterprises. It is not
> really surprising that a code must be implemented fairly, and that the courts have power to
> redress unfairness.

The second caveat stems from the observation that judicial review in the business
field might have negative implications for regulatory effectiveness and the operation of markets. It has already been argued in the foregoing paragraphs that such
difficulties cannot be resolved by exercising judicial restraint. However, it is necessary to assert that this restriction does not exclude the use by the court of alternative mechanisms by which the potential adverse effects of its intervention can be
reduced or even eliminated without altering the proposed rights-based model of
adjudication. Indeed, it should be primarily a concern for the judiciary to perform
its necessary function in a manner which least constrains the ability of regulators
to implement market policies. Within this framework, therefore, judicial or legislative measures which contribute to lessen the delaying or harassing effects of review,
provide effective redress to innocent third parties,[127] and avoid vexatious litigation seem to be of particular relevance. Detailed evaluation of these instruments
lies beyond the scope of the present work.[128] Nevertheless, for the purposes of
the present argument, it may be useful to mention that the last solution is already
available in the British legal order.

   Indeed, the procedural restrictions of Ord. 53 are essentially aimed at minimizing the frustrating effect which the threat of challenge might cause on the implementation of public interest goals. Specifically, the requirement of leave to apply for
judicial review is designed, *inter alia*, to relieve respondents of the need to defend
groundless challenges to their decisions and actions. As Loughlin says,

> the primary justifications for the leave filter are those of promoting the efficient use of court
> time and protecting public administration by ensuring the expeditious determination of
> unmeritorious claims which could, through uncertainty engendered by delay, otherwise
> frustrate the efficient conduct of public business.[129]

To similar effect, and more pertinently, Jeffrey Jowell writes that obstructive litigation is unlikely to succeed in the context of market regulation, as the filtering
system made in the form of the leave stage of the application for judicial review

---

[127] See Chapter 5, Section 4.5.
[128] For a general list of 'filtering' mechanisms, see Woehrling, Jean-Marie, 'Judicial Control of
Public Authorities in Europe: Progressive Construction of a Common Model' [2005] 10(4) *Judicial
Review*, 322–323.
[129] Loughlin, Martin, 'Courts and Governance' in *The Frontiers of Liability*, Peter Birks (ed.),
Vol. 1, (Oxford: Oxford University Press, 1994) 102.

is custom-built to halt unmeritorious tactical litigation in its tracks.[130] These considerations were particularly instrumental in persuading Sir John Donaldson MR in the *Datafin*[131] case to hold that:

> it is clearly better, as a matter of policy, that legal proceedings should be in the realm of public law rather than private law, not only because they are quicker, but also because the requirement of leave under Ord 53 will exclude claims which are clearly unmeritorious.

Thus, it becomes clear that, by enabling judges summarily to analyse the merits of applications for judicial review, it is possible to arrive at a satisfactory solution to the problem of strategic or frivolous actions. In fact, the latest research on the subject shows that there has been a striking decline in the permission grant rate due to failure to satisfy judges that claims are sufficiently arguable.[132] This requirement is therefore to be welcomed to the extent that it provides an alternative to the unconvincing orthodox approach, which seeks to circumvent the impact of tactical litigation by postulating a dramatic decline in the intensity of judicial review that fails to take into account the position of the applicant. In particular, it can be argued that the leave filter constitute a valuable attempt to articulate a mechanism which operates as a prerequisite for the review process itself, and which therefore satisfies the dual imperative of avoiding the use of applications simply as a ploy and facilitating subsequent in-depth examination of really arguable cases. Actually, there is strong evidence that despite the decline in leave grant rates, access to justice has improved in terms that viable claimants are more likely to achieve satisfactory outcomes.[133] In light of such interesting statistics, it appears that the challenge faced by the courts nowadays is to find additional mechanisms which may equally succeed where the deferential approach fails by contributing to ensure regulatory effectiveness without undermining the system of protection against unlawful performance of governmental activities.

3. Particular Difficulties of the Orthodox Approach

The charge most frequently levelled against the traditional judicial approach to market regulation is its inability to provide an impartial view of controversial issues which fits comfortably with legal principles that safeguard the interests of private parties in their relations with public authorities. It has already been argued that such a mode of review fails to give effect, for instance, to the rule against the bias, the right of access to a court, and the doctrine of balance of powers within the constitutional order. However, this is certainly not the only criticism which can be made of the orthodox view. It is the purpose of the remainder of this chapter to set out other significant shortcomings of the deferential doctrine in relation to specific

---

[130] Jowell, Jeffrey, 'The Takeover Panel: Autonomy, Flexibility and Legality' [1991] *Public Law*, 158.
[131] As above n. 83.
[132] Bondy, Varda and Sunkin, Maurice, *The Dynamics of Judicial Review Litigation: The resolution of public law challenges before final hearing*, The Public Law Project, London, 2009, 49–69.
[133] Ibid., 69.

aspects of the court's decision, namely review of factual determinations and discretionary remedies.

3.1 Questions of facts

The challenge to the core orthodoxy—that the regulator has been accorded a high degree of autonomy over questions of fact—is mainly based on the increasing emphasis on the rule of law as a legally enforceable concept that places the doctrine of judicial deference under growing strain. In recent years, distinguished scholars and judges have shifted the focus away from the somewhat political questions— such as whether the courts may alter the constitutional allocation of powers— which prevented heightened scrutiny and have, instead, concentrated on turning the general principles embodied in the rule of law into specific mandates which greatly reduce executive margins of freedom. On this view, the court's traditional reluctance to review factual evidence is increasingly perceived as a rather anomalous situation.

The driving force behind this change of approach is the conviction that a policy of judicial indulgence towards executive decisions on matters of fact may amount to a serious abuse of discretionary power. In particular, it greatly increases the risk of administrative decisions which are based on no satisfactory evidence, as the mere existence of the power to act is almost sufficient in itself to establish the validity of the decision, regardless of the factual merits of the case. The point is expressed well by Ian Yeats.[134] His contention is that the judicial role in evidentiary matters is to secure that the administrative system is likely to produce results which are correct or at least satisfying to the system. Accordingly, if a court is less inclined to interfere in this field, then a significant incentive to poor administration would be created: in a practical sense, the public body would be under no enforceable obligation to base its decisions on all relevant information, or make reasonable findings. This approach is, in turn, fundamentally repugnant to the notion of rule of law, which indicates that effective judicial control is needed which ensures fairness in public decision-making.

Yeats's analysis of this matter is also based on considerations of logic and legal certainty.[135] He observes that where the court refuses to review because, as it is said, the alleged error involves a question ultimately entrusted to the decision-maker, this means that findings of fact are valid not because they are correct, but because 'there was no one with authority to say that it was wrong'. By definition, therefore, the judicial analysis fastens on the characterization of the question to be decided rather than on the quality of the answer. In practice, this gives 'the undesirable impression that the decision was wrong but unreviewable, that officials were getting away with blunders'. Consequently, it appears that, if the court defers to the agency's conclusions on facts, not only it is likely that the latter will remain at large

---

[134] Yeats, Ian, 'Findings of Fact: The Role of the Courts' in *Administrative Law & Government Action*, G. Richardson and H. Genn (eds.), (Oxford: Oxford University Press, 1994) 153.
[135] Ibid., 132.

to potentially make insupportable findings, but the damage that can be done in terms of fomenting a climate of impunity which undermines the sense of trust and security in the individuals is significant.

Against this background it becomes apparent that, in order to build a satisfactory approach to administrative findings of fact, the judges should move to a tighter form of supervision which secures respect for the principles of good administration.[136] In short, the idea is to prevent abuse of discretionary power by requiring some proof that the decision is indeed justified by the evidence on the facts of the particular case. It is worth noting that the recent case law has advocated just such an approach, which urges abandonment of the limited theory of jurisdiction in favour of further intervention.

Thus, writers such as Wade, Forsyth[137] and Craig[138] remark that in the recent years there has been a significant change in the jurisprudence concerning the approach to findings of evidence. The conceptual basis which underlies judicial restraint in this field has increasingly been called into question, as the courts began to reassess the constituent elements of jurisdiction and regard 'no evidence' as a ground for review.[139] Within this framework, therefore, the power of review is seen to extend to any case where the evidence, taken as a whole, is not reasonably capable of supporting the finding. Furthermore, in tune with the new approach, the rules of court have made express provision for cross-examination, interrogatories and discovery of documents, and for the trial of issues of fact.[140] According to Forsyth and Dring, this development certainly represents the 'conquest of the final frontier' in classical administrative law, since it finally holds decision-makers to be accountable to the established law over all matters for which they should be accountable.[141]

There is, moreover, authority for the proposition that the courts will review where the relevant fact was a matter which expressly or impliedly had to be taken into account.[142] In the case of abuse of power, for example, one of the expanding grounds of challenge is relevancy, by which the taking into account of irrelevant considerations or the failure to consider relevant justifications can be an error of law. Such a charge may be sustained by examination of the formal record of the decision but in many cases may require detailed evidence of the context of the

---

[136] See Purdue, Michael, 'The Scope for Fact Finding in Judicial Review' in *Droit Sans Frontières*, G.J. Hand and J. McBride (eds.), (Holdsworth Club, Birmingham, 1991) 201.

[137] Wade and Forsyth, (as above n. 4), 229–236.

[138] Craig, (as above n. 97), 475–499.

[139] See e.g. *Coolen Properties v. Minister of Housing and Local Government* [1971] 1 W.L.R. 433; the judgment of Lord Diplock in *R v. Deputy Industrial Injuries Commissioner, ex p Moore* [1965] 1 Q.B. 456; *R v. Bedwellty JJ, ex p Williams* [1997] A.C. 225.

[140] Rules of the Supreme Court, Ord. 33 r. 3; Ord. 53 r. 8, in Crown Proceedings Act, 1998, Sch 1.

[141] Forsyth, C.F. and Dring, E., 'The Final Frontier: The Emergence of Material Error of Fact as a Ground for Judicial Review' in Forsyth et al., (as above, n. 14), 263.

[142] See e.g. the judgment of Watkins LJ in *R v. London Residuary Body, ex p Inner London Education Authority, The Times*, 24 July 1987, CO/8/87; and *South Oxfordshire District Council v. Secretary of State for the Environment* [1981] 1 W.L.R. 1092. See Jones, Timothy H., 'Mistake of Fact in Administrative Law' [1990] *Public Law*, 1990, 507–526. This Secretary of State was succeeded by the office of Secretary of State for the Environment, Transport and the Regions and then Secretary of State for the Environment, Food and Rural Affairs.

decision-making.[143] In addition, it seems most probable that wrongful refusal to receive evidence, and also wrongful admission of evidence, will be within the scope of inquiry under the new doctrine.[144]

In relation to mere factual mistakes, it is suggested that they have also become a ground of judicial review.[145] This view was expressed with particular clarity by the Court of Appeal in *E v Home Secretary*,[146] an immigration case. It observed that the taking into account of a mistaken fact may well be a new branch of the *ultra vires* doctrine, as it could not be easily absorbed into traditional legal grounds of review. For example, in the Court's view, it may be at least artificial to say that there was a failure to base the decision on 'any evidence', or even that it had 'no justifiable basis' in cases where there is actually *some* evidential basis for the decision. It would also be difficult to give the status of 'failure to provide reasons that are adequate or intelligible' to cases where the reasoning actually reveals that the decision-maker fell into error. Such situations, says the Court, point the way to a separate ground of review, based on unfairness, which arises from the combination of key factors: a mistake as to a relevant and established (uncontentious and objectively verifiable) fact, and the creation of an erroneous impression which plays a material (not necessarily decisive) part in the reasoning, and for which the claimant could not be fairly responsible. It is against this background that the court's control over administrative findings of fact would be still further tightened and, as Wade and Forsyth say, 'would consign much of the old law about jurisdictional fact, etc., to well-deserved oblivion'.[147]

In light of these developments, there is a strong case for concluding that, when faced with the question of whether a finding of fact is reviewable or of regulatory concern only, the court should give greater weight to considerations of justice and fairness, rather than striking out in a rigid deferential direction which coheres less well with the rule of law and the recent jurisprudence. Specifically, in determining the control which the courts should exercise in the commercial context, it is crucial to be aware of the wider theory of jurisdiction on which the new authorities against executive immunity are based. The judges must therefore be alert to the importance of ensuring that errors of fact can be dragged forth into the glaring day for judicial scrutiny, as the following dictum of Lord Denning in *Laker Airways v. Department of Trade*[148] states,

when discretionary powers are entrusted to the executive by statute, the courts can examine the exercise of those powers to see that they are used properly, and not improperly or mistakenly. By 'mistakenly' I mean under the influence of a misdirection in fact or in law.

---

[143] Purdue, (as above n. 136), 193.   [144] Wade and Forsyth, (as above n. 4), 235.
[145] For the general application of this doctrine see the judgments of Lord Scarman and Lord Wilberforce in *Secretary of State for Education and Science v. Tameside Borough Council* [1976] 3 All E.R. 665; the judgment of Lord Denning MR in *Secretary of State for Employment v. ASLEF* (No. 2) [1972] 2 Q.B. 455 at 493; *Smith v. Inner London Education Authority* [1978] 1 All E.R. 411. More recently, *R (Marsh) v. Lincoln District Magistrates' Court* [2003] E.W.H.C (Admin) 956; and the opinions of Phillips MR, Mantell and Carnwath LJ in *E v. Home Secretary* [2004] E.W.C.A. Civ 49 (2 February). See also Wade and Forsyth, (as above n. 4), 234; and Forsyth and Dring, (as above n. 14), 245–263.   [146] As above, n. 145.
[147] Wade and Forsyth, (as above n. 4), 234.   [148] [1977] Q.B. 643.

A second noteworthy judgment in the context of market regulation is that in *Office of Fair Trading ('OFT') and Others v. IBA Healthcare Ltd.*[149] The appellants, two companies engaged in the supply of software and systems to the healthcare applications market, sought to challenge the judgment of the Competition Appeal Tribunal ('CAT') which quashed the decision of the OFT no to refer their proposed merger to the Competition Commission for detailed investigation. They argued, *inter alia*, that, by carrying out a fact-intensive review of the regulatory decision which went beyond the *Wednesbury* standard, the CAT had failed to apply 'the same principles as would be applied by a court on an application for judicial review', as required by section 120(4) of the Enterprise Act 2002. In this sense, the present appeal seemed to rely on the traditional notion that *Wednesbury* reasonableness should be the universally-applicable doctrine in the context of conventional judicial review in the United Kingdom. Lord Carnwath, however, said that in cases concerned with questions of factual judgement rather than with policy or discretion—which, in his opinion, are the normal subject-matter of the *Wednesbury* test—'there is no doubt that the court is entitled to enquire whether there was adequate material to support that conclusion'. The question whether the evidentiary material relied on by the OFT could reasonably be regarded as dispelling the uncertainties highlighted by its decision was therefore 'wholly suitable for evaluation by a court'. Thus, his Lordship considered that the requirement of applying ordinary principles of judicial review in competition cases could be policed by the court by means more intrusive than the *Wednesbury* test, namely a relatively detailed examination of factual findings.

The CAT subsequently applied this guidance in *UniChem v OFT*,[150] regarding another refusal of the OFT to refer a merger to the Competition Commission. In particular, it held that:

In the present context (competition), the Tribunal's review may properly be more intense than it would be if issues of policy or politics were involved. Indeed, it appears to be common ground that the Tribunal has jurisdiction, acting in a supervisory rather than appellate capacity, to determine whether the OFT's conclusions are adequately supported by evidence, that the facts have been properly found, that all material factual considerations have been taken into account, and that material facts have not been omitted [para. 174].

3.2 Judicial restraint in the remedial context

As we saw earlier, the judiciary has been relatively circumspect about granting remedies in the context of volatile markets such as financial services. In particular, there is authority for the proposition that a court may, in the interest of regulatory efficiency, and taking into account the situation of third parties who have relied on the integrity of the decision-making process, be moved either to withhold relief or simply make a declaration that applies only to decisions in the future. However, it

---

[149] [2004] E.W.C.A. Civ 142. See Kennelly, Brian, 'Judicial Review and the Competition Appeal Tribunal' [2006] 11(2) *Judicial Review*, 160–170.
[150] [2005] C.A.T. 8.

is worth noting that the exercise of such a broad discretion may well be a source of injustice for the applicant and other parties affected by the executive action. That problem forms the focus of the remainder of this chapter, which is divided into two parts. First, sub-section 3.2.1 will consider the particular difficulties which the court's cautious approach encounters when adopted in regard to the exercise of remedial discretion. Secondly, in sub-sections 3.2.2 to 3.2.4, an assessment is made of the main principles underlying this doctrine which demonstrates that it is not at all clear that they must take precedence over competing claims of legality and fair competition. A better view, it is suggested in sub-section 3.2.5, is that the courts should articulate a more moderate response to this problem which may provide a balanced protection of the different interests at stake.

3.2.1 *The shortcomings of the current approach*

In truth, the principal difficulty which lies at the core of this doctrine is not that the court accords some relevance to the needs of the administration and third parties. The real problem is that it implicitly postulates the mere existence of these interests as a sufficient condition to withhold relief. Indeed the present attitude of the courts towards remedial discretion shows clearly that any *ultra vires* decision which, in any sense, undermines administrative efficiency or gives rise to legitimate expectations in complex markets must be allowed to stand.

This stance becomes immediately apparent by observing the inescapable language used by the judges in refusing to grant effective remedies. As seen above, a number of leading authorities have left flawed decisions unaffected simply on the basis that deals may have been done in reliance on the validity of the decision impugned.[151] In this sense, reasonable reliance appears to be a sufficient condition which requires the court to be 'in any event in all the circumstances...against the grant of relief'.[152] Consequently, the judiciary is expected to allow contemporary decisions in the commercial context to take their course, intervening, 'if at all, later and in retrospect by declaratory orders'.[153] Moreover, the fact that, in most of the cases, judicial statements are unaccompanied by any consideration of the need to protect the beneficiaries of the *ultra vires* doctrine, confirms that the courts are willing to adopt the detriment to the executive and third parties as the only determinant of the final choice in regard to remedies in the context of volatile markets.

Once this starting point is accepted, it becomes necessary to unpack its implications. In particular, there are three significant difficulties which the present doctrine inevitably raises.

The first important point to note is that it leads to the collapse of the principle of legality, with the courts being enabled to preclude its application for the sake of expediency and legal certainty. Indeed it is clear from the foregoing description of the approach that its objective is to supply a mechanism through which an executive decision can be applied even though the court has determined that it is *ultra vires*. It is therefore self-evident that, in such cases, there is a serious breach of the

---

[151] See, for example, the *Argyll* case, (as above n. 98).   [152] Ibid.
[153] *Datafin*, (as above n. 83).

doctrine according to which invalid decisions should be incapable of having any legal effect.

It must be emphasized that this development is manifestly inconsistent with the traditional recognition of the logical connection between unlawfulness and invalidity by the courts. The *Hoffmann-La Roche*[154] case exemplifies the acknowledgement of this relationship in the commercial context. In that case, a group of companies which manufactured pharmaceutical products sought a declaration that the decision of the Secretary of State for Trade and Industry, the effect of which was to reduce the price of tranquillizing drugs known as 'Librium' and 'Valium', was *ultra vires* and invalid. The House of Lords, however, found for the respondent; therefore it did not have to decide how to exercise its discretion in regard to the relief claimed. Nevertheless, Lord Diplock did say *obiter* that it is a natural consequence of the *ultra vires* doctrine that illegal decisions should not have any effect upon the rights of the applicant. His Lordship stated:

> It would, however, be inconsistent with the doctrine of *ultra vires* as it has been developed in English law as a means of controlling abuse of power by the executive arm of government if the judgment of a court in proceedings properly constituted that a statutory instrument was *ultra vires* were to have any lesser consequence in law than to render the instrument incapable of ever having had any legal effect on the rights or duties of the parties to the proceedings.

It is, moreover, clear from this judgment that there is a logical connection between the *ultra vires* doctrine, which is the embodiment of the principle of legality, and the rights of parties affected by the unlawful decision. Thus if an administrative decision is legally flawed it must, logically, be prevented from causing hardship to these individuals. Consequently, it appears that the present approach to remedies may also substantially prejudice the rights of the successful applicant. By providing that the courts should refuse a remedy in order to protect the interests of the administration and third parties, this view appears readily to accept that the interests of the individual seeking relief are not, in any way, a good reason to consider invalidating the particular decision in question. Therefore, in such circumstances, it is likely that his rights will be affected by the illegal decision without the possibility of getting effective relief in accordance to the classic principle *ubi jus, ibi remedium*.

In light of this, it may also be argued that the doctrine in question appears readily to accept that innocent parties should suffer the consequences for wrongful decisions they did not take. Indeed, at this stage of the process, the court has already come to the conclusion that the decision in question is legally flawed. In other words, there is clear evidence that the decision-maker has made a mistake which may have far reaching implications for different individuals. The question therefore arises as to who should bear the loss for such error. It appears that if the approach only takes into account the interests of the administration and the

---

[154] *Hoffmann-La Roche v. Secretary of State for Trade and Industry* [1975] A.C. 295, [1974] 2 All E.R. 1128, [1974] 3 W.L.R. 104.

position of third parties, it necessarily follows that the loss would be imposed upon the innocent applicant who claims to be affected by the *ultra vires* decision. In other words, the immediate effect of withholding relief in such circumstances is therefore a detriment to the party who has successfully demonstrated that the decision was made in excess of jurisdiction. Thus, the burden of ensuring efficiency and respect for third-party rights is entirely left with the innocent party rather than with the authority whose unlawful decision is the cause of the loss.

Secondly, it appears that the court's present approach might pose serious problems to fair competition in the market economy. Two particular points must be made. In the first place, it must be emphasized that this doctrine undermines the application of the principle of equal treatment between commercial actors. In general terms, the existence of a relationship of 'potential contention and rivalry'[155] between undertakings which sell goods or services of the same kind requires authorities to be impartial and to avoid making any decision which may affect fair competition between them. This prohibition also implies the notion that like market players should be treated alike, in the sense that they should not be afforded special privileges which entail differential treatment. On this view, therefore, the court's decision to withhold relief in relation to an *ultra vires* decision which improves the position of some undertakings on the relevant market would clearly harm the competitive process, because it would give them an advantageous treatment to achieve their goals. In other words, the immediate effect of allowing the unlawful decision to stand in such circumstances is to cause other *bona fide* undertakings to suffer permanently the consequences of a benefit illegally granted to their competitors, thereby posing a substantive impediment to effective competition.

The second principle of fair competition which is likely to be trumped by the judge's refusal to grant relief relates to the need to prevent public aid that distorts competition within the European Union. It may well be argued that, if the British State through its courts allowed the continuance of an *ultra vires* decision which advantages some competitors at the expense of others, this would constitute a national aid measure which the affected parties would be justified in refusing to recognize as law, provided that it has not been yet approved by the European Commission as compatible with the Common Market in accordance with Articles 92 and 93 of the EEC Treaty.

This is clear from the judgment of the Court of Appeal in *R. v. Attorney General ex p Imperial Chemical Industries (ICI) Plc*.[156] In this case, the applicant, a petrochemical company employing naphtha as feedstock for the production of ethylene, challenged the approach of the Inland Revenue to the valuation of ethane gas, a different feedstock for the ethylene production used by its competitors. ICI contended that the authority accepted a price for ethane which was substantially below the true market price and that, as a consequence, its competitors were treated as earning lower profits on sales and therefore would benefit from lower taxes. This

---

[155] Goyder, Joanna and Albers-Llevens, Albertarian, *Goyder's EC Competition Law*, 5th edn., (Oxford: Oxford University Press, 2009) 8.
[156] [1987] 1 C.M.L.R. 72, [1986] 1 F.T.L.R. 569.

would be detrimental to ICI, which did not use ethane in its ethylene producing plant and so did not enjoy comparable favourable treatment. The Queen's Bench Division held that the approach adopted by the Revenue was contrary to the relevant legislation and *Wednesbury* unreasonable. However, it refused to grant retrospective relief to the applicant and confined itself to making a declaration which related only to the future in order to protect the interest of third parties. In particular, the judgment of the court was based on the assumption that companies which had already relied on the unlawful price might be prejudiced if the authority's particular decision were struck down and the process of valuation restarted.

ICI appealed against this doctrine which effectively deprived it of the fruits of the litigation, seeking declarations which would have retrospective effect as regards its competitors. The Court of Appeal found for the applicant and granted effective relief. It was held, *inter alia*, that a deliberate continuance in the *ultra vires* application of the statutory provisions constitutes a State aid which, in accordance with the EEC Treaty, cannot be put into effect until the European Commission decides whether it is compatible with the Common Market. The rationale for these provisions is to prevent competition being distorted by 'any aid granted by a Member State or through State resources in any form whatsoever' which 'favours certain undertakings or the production of certain goods'. In the court's opinion it seems inescapable that the persistence, with knowledge, in the misapplication of statutory provisions which produces an advantage distorting competition in favour of a certain undertaking, is an aid. Therefore, the government is under a duty to notify the Commission of such benefit and not to implement it until this authority has approved the same.

Thirdly, in addition to these normative issues, more practical difficulties are revealed when we consider the implications of the judicial refusal to grant relief in the long term. Indeed it is possible to identify two ways in which the possibility of this doctrine being applied, far from protecting market actors, may cause detrimental effects on their behaviour and interests.

First, the prospect of winning the argument that the challenged decision is legally flawed but failing to secure a remedy through the exercise of judicial discretion might well have a deterrent effect on the applicants.[157] As Jowell says, the fact that regulators may be enjoying such blanket immunity from a remedy, which should normally accompany a right, 'in practice removes the incentive to litigation, thus making the opportunity of judicial review in effect a dead letter'.[158] By the same token, the adoption of the doctrine of prospective overruling would not really make a substantial difference to the purpose of supporting access to justice: the incentive to apply for judicial review will still be extremely small if the only remedy in many cases will be a declaration of purely prospective effect.[159] In this sense, Sir Patrick Neill explains that, when companies go to court, 'they are not

---

[157] Lee, Simon, 'Judicial Discretion in Controlling Administrative Discretion' [1987] 104 *Law Quarterly Review*, 167.

[158] Jowell, J. 'The Takeover Panel: Autonomy, Flexibility and Legality', (as above n. 130), 158.

[159] Cane, P. 'Self-Regulation and Judicial Review' [1987] 6 *Civil Justice Quarterly*, 343.

driven by altruism to reform the law for the benefit of other companies in possible future cases. So restricting the remedy could kill off the applications'.[160]

Indeed, it is unlikely that in cases such as *Argyll*, *Air Europe*, *ICI* or *Datafin* the affected companies bother to seek declarations that take effect only in the future as guidance to the authorities in making future decisions. Moreover, as Clive Lewis observes, it is even less likely that their shareholders would approve of such philanthropic gesture on the part of the management.[161] Rather, these claimants only seek to quash an unlawful decision which they see as adverse to their own commercial interests. Viewed in this individual perspective, it is self-evident that any attempt to refuse the granting of relief might dramatically reduce the incentives to apply for judicial review, as this proceeding would no longer be seen as an effective mechanism to obtain redress against the abuse of executive power.

Secondly, there is always the risk that, if this approach is taken too far, with the result that regulatory bodies feel exempted from remedial action, there may be more and more *ultra vires* interference with individual rights. To permanently divorce the declaration of unlawfulness from judicial remedy in a particular regulatory context law would probably raise the prospect of the rights and obligations of citizens being dependant on 'the whims, prejudices or predilections of the individual decision-maker',[162] as he may come to believe that it is a no-go area for judicial constraints, and that he can get away with a breach of the principles of administrative action.[163] The judges would therefore be involved in creating an environment of impunity which leads to further breaches of the law. This is a strong objection, and it is one which has not been satisfactorily answered by the supporters of the orthodox approach.

3.2.2 *The balancing test*

Having set out the adverse effects of the courts' current approach in regard to remedies in the context of volatile markets, it is important, at this point, to evaluate the strength of its rationale. This necessarily requires recourse to all the principles which are relevant to the position of the parties involved. It is clear from the foregoing sub-section that the mere reference to the protection of administrative convenience and third-party rights cannot, on its own, provide a satisfactory justification for withholding relief. If accepted, such reasoning would clearly fail to furnish a complete account of the fundamental legal principles which the courts are empowered to uphold by way of judicial review. Thus, it becomes apparent that any attempt to properly advocate the orthodox doctrine must also address the relevance and implications of the principles which provide inspiration for the protection of the applicant's interests. As Lewis correctly observes in relation to the

---

[160] Neill, Sir Patrick, 'The Case Load and Other Pressures', in *The Frontiers of Liability*, Vol. 1, Peter Birks (ed.), Vol. 1, (Oxford: Oxford University Press, 1994) 89.

[161] Lewis, Clive, 'Retrospective and Prospective Rulings in Administrative Law' [1988] *Public Law*, 83.

[162] Bingham, Sir Thomas 'Should Public Law Remedies be Discretionary?' [1991] *Public Law*, 64.

[163] Lee, Simon, 'Judicial discretion in controlling administrative discretion' [1987] 104 *Law Quarterly Review*, 167.

doctrine of prospective relief, it is necessary to look at the broader impact of the judicial decision and to consider the competing interests of the various groups and the legitimate interests of the administration.[164] It follows from this that, in order to assess the plausibility of the same doctrine, the reasons which justify its application must be contrasted with those upon which the applicant's claim is based. The question therefore becomes whether the interests of the administration and third parties in having the decision treated as legally effective do really outweigh the injustice to those who wish to have it invalidated.

It is worth noting that this balancing test is allowed in various areas in which the principle of legality is compromised and balancing is accepted as legitimate or inevitable.[165] This can be seen, for example, in the law relating to estoppel, invalidity, waiver, and delay, where the need to countenance the balancing derives from the fact that detrimental reliance upon an illegal decision might be a good reason to mitigate the effects of the principle of legality. This view has been expressed with particular clarity by Craig in his comments on *ultra vires* representation.[166] He observes that the existence of a legitimate expectation can certainly be a condition for the courts to allow the deliberate application of a decision that is legally flawed. However, it is also acknowledged that, given that this doctrine can clash with other important legal values, it should only be applied after a comparative analysis—which focuses on the potential effects of the application of each principle to the particular case— demonstrates that it is the least harmful choice. Craig thus concludes that, rather than automatically impeding the application of the jurisdictional principle, *bona fide* reliance upon a decision should operate 'as a trigger to alert a court that a balance between the principle of legality and legal certainty may be required'.[167]

In light of this, the concern of the following sub-sections is to evaluate the orthodox approach to remedies by considering the extent to which the principles of regulatory efficiency and legal certainty must take precedence over those of legality and fair competition. For the purposes of clarity, the analysis will be structured around the two main rationales which support the doctrine in question, each of which raises different issues concerning the court's capacity to protect individual citizens against maladministration.

The argument advanced is that it is not at all clear that the courts are correct, as a matter of justice, to assert that the need to protect administrative interest or legitimate expectations created by *ultra vires* decisions logically requires them to trump the applicant's commercial rights. It is argued below that this view is mainly based upon a fundamental misunderstanding of the role of the court in judicial review proceedings, and of the way in which the rule of law operates to equally protect competing interests in the business field.

3.2.3 *Administrative convenience*

As seen above, this argument holds that the special needs of volatile markets for decisiveness and finality on the part of regulators would likely encourage the courts

---

[164] Lewis, (as above n. 161), 104.   [165] Craig, (as above n. 97), 689.
[166] Ibid., 685–690.   [167] Ibid., 686.

to leave contemporary decisions unaffected in order to improve administrative efficiency and effectiveness. The absence of remedy for what is an *ultra vires* decision would thus serve to eliminate delays in the decision-making process and to increase the regulator's influence on the market performance in the light of strategic goals.

The principal difficulty which this reasoning raises relates to the role that the judiciary should play in deciding public law cases. It appears that the present view demonstrates a clear commitment to the idea that judicial review should be focused on the achievement of public objectives rather than simple adjudication on matters involving limited rights issues. Indeed it is self-apparent that an approach which subordinates the rights of the successful applicant to the interests of the administration is embedded in the doctrine which ascribes to the courts a primary role as public policy instruments which collaborate with the adequate implementation of the regulatory scheme. Thus, rather than exercise their remedial discretion on the basis of legal argument and precedent, that discretion, the present doctrine holds, should take into account administrative convenience.

The implication and conceptual foundations of this orthodoxy have been lucidly explained by Allan. He asserts that the use of the language of 'administrative convenience' clearly signals that, for the court, such criterion would involve a discontinuity: one model of adjudication in which there is an interdependence of legal right and judicial remedy is replaced by 'new forms of relief, which may have wide-ranging effects beyond those of concern to the immediate parties'.[168] In practice, this means that,

the characteristically retrospective nature a judicial opinion, concerning legal relations of the parties in the light of completed events, is displaced by the prospective implementation of arrangements for achieving desirable social goals.[169]

However, as sub-section 2.2 demonstrates, this model of dispute resolution is open to criticism on the ground that it seriously undermines judicial protection of the rule of law. It has already been argued that the 'public interest' rationale poses a great danger to the very idea of juridification in the commercial context and that any attempt to prejudice the rights of the parties for the sake of political expediency would entail abandonment by the judiciary of its traditional role as guardian of law. Further arguments which support this contention are well rehearsed above, and it is unnecessary to repeat them here. It is, however, useful to note that Cane has advocated just such critical view in relation to the exercise of judicial restraint at the remedial stage. In particular, he asserts that the court's reference in the *Datafin* case to a 'workable and valuable partnership between the courts and the Panel in the public interest'—which allows contemporary unlawful decisions to take their course due to the absence of remedy—might express a rather different mode of relation between the branches of power, in which judges should see themselves not as external constraints on the regulatory bodies but as serving essentially the same purposes as the decision-maker. Thus, the use of the term 'public interest' would convey the impression that it is the only relevant interest in play, and that private

[168] Allan, (as above n. 1), 197.   [169] Ibid.

interests which may differ from the court's version of it will be ignored. If this view is accepted, Cane concludes, then,

> it betokens an abdication by the courts of their traditional function of protecting such interests which renders identification of the courts with the ruling elite even more plausible than it already is.[170]

Thus, it becomes clear that the disadvantages to regulatory effectiveness cannot outweigh injustice to the applicant. The fact that the courts must properly consider the legitimate interests of individual citizens and corporations within a juridified scheme of relations necessarily requires the subordination of administrative convenience to the interests of individual justice. By simply justifying the refusal to grant a remedy in terms of efficiency, the first rationale of the present doctrine therefore fails to provide a satisfactory basis for the exercise of this discretion, because it does not accurately capture the primacy of individual rights over public policy considerations within the context of market regulation.

3.2.4 Legal certainty

The difficulty encountered by the argument of administrative convenience, however, is partially avoided by the second rationale behind the current approach, which is predominant in the case law.[171] It does not seek to explain the need to refuse a remedy by reference to efficiency. Rather, it holds that it must be rationalized in terms of legal certainty. In particular, it is argued that remedial discretion must take into account the position of third parties who have detrimentally relied on the validity of the *ultra vires* decision: for example, those who made investments and carried out commercial activities on the reasonable assumption that the particular exercise of administrative power conformed to the law. It seems to follow that, in such circumstances, the courts should abstain from granting relief against the misleading order, as this would undermine certainty in the market. On this view, therefore, the unlawful decision is allowed to stand not for reasons of regulatory effectiveness, but because it has given rise to expectations of substantive benefits on the part of *bona fide* undertakings.

Once this distinction is appreciated, it becomes clear that the latter formula cannot be criticized on the ground that it sacrifices rights merely for the sake of effectiveness. Within this approach, it is third party *rights*, not public policy considerations, which ultimately allow the court to trump the *rights* of the applicant. By the same token, it is *innocent* third parties, not the body who has made the unlawful order, who are the final beneficiaries of the court's reluctance to invalidate the decision which harms the *innocent* applicant. Thus, by allowing the court to refuse a remedy on the basis of legal certainty, the present formula seems to circumvent the difficulties raised by the former argument which is purely based on regulatory efficiency. In this manner, it can be regarded as consistent with the

---

[170] Cane, 'Self-Regulation and Judicial Review', (as above n. 159), 346.
[171] See *Argyll*, [1986] 1 W.L.R. 76; *Air Europe*, [1988] 4 B.C.C. 182; *Datafin* [1987] 1 All E.R. 564; and *Guinness*, [1990] 1 QB 146 at 159.

traditional model of adjudication which promotes a rights-centred approach to the problem of remedies.

However, it is worth noting that when attempts are made to leave *ultra vires* decisions unaffected on the ground of legal certainty, a different type of tension is revealed. Naturally, once the court comes to withhold relief in order to protect those who have been misled by the offending order, the clash of interests between beneficiaries and affected parties is inevitable. Consequently, for the purposes of assessing the correctness and implications of the latter formula, it will be necessary to phrase the problem in terms of competing private rights rather than enhancement of executive efficiency. The question therefore arises whether the interests of third parties, which the principle of legal certainty is said to protect, ought to take precedence over those of the applicant.

In the main, it is the contention of this work that the requirement of legal certainty is not sufficient to outweigh the principles underlying the position of those individuals seeking effective relief against the abuse of power. In particular, it is submitted that the rule of law, which favours access to the courts in order to protect citizens against the abuse of power, requires respect for the rights of the applicant even in cases where there is a need to safeguard the position of third parties. This conclusion becomes apparent when one considers the operation of this constitutional imperative within the public domain.

The rule of law comprehends in a broad sense the fundamental values on which the legal system is based in order to protect individuals from the negative effects of executive abuse.[172] Importantly, it is clear that unlawful decisions may have serious consequences not only for those who have reasonable relied on their validity but also for those who have been directly harmed by their effects, namely, the applicants. The rule of law thus provides that, in order to avoid the adverse consequences of the contended action on the latter, regard has to be had, *inter alia*, to the principle of legality and the principle of equal treatment between parties. In practice, given that the rule of law is regarded as a central principle which shapes the decisions of the courts,[173] it is clear that the specific norms which it embodies will operate, in the present context, as a juristic basis which guides the judges' exercise of remedial discretion. Consequently, if administrative action is in excess of power, the court should necessarily endeavour to ensure substantial justice to the plaintiffs in accordance with the *ultra vires* doctrine and the proscription of discrimination. Ultimately, they are also innocent parties and, therefore, entitled by law to receive adequate protection of their rights.

It is interesting to note that these considerations have inspired some authors to advocate the effective protection of the applicant even at the expense of legal certainty. For example, Lewis explicitly acknowledges that if we desire to control the abuse of power by the mechanism of judicial review, it may be that 'the price to be paid for that is the uncertainty generated by allowing the successful litigant the

---

[172] Elliott, (as above n. 47), 100–104.   [173] Ibid., 102.

incentive of retrospective relief'.[174] To similar effect, Jowell writes that the much-vaunted 'certainty' of the regulator's decisions 'would, in such a case, be perhaps temporarily violated, but in exchange for a greater attention to lawful and fair behaviour in the future. That might seem a fair exchange'.[175]

Thus, it becomes clear that an approach—such as that outlined by the courts—which merely identifies and gives effect to the principle of legal certainty in a straightforward sense, would be inconsistent with the constitutional imperative that requires the courts to apply all the aspects of the rule of law that protect individuals from the consequences of administrative wrongdoing. Indeed the rationale underlying this choice fails to fully acknowledge the importance of the principles which entitle parties directly affected by an *ultra vires* decision to 'reasonably expect' that it will be invalidated.

It is important to note that this view, according to which the court should give effect to the principles of legality and equal treatment even in cases where there has been third-party reliance on the unlawful decision, has already been expressed in the context of commercial judicial review. For example, indications that the principle of legality might well require the courts to protect the applicant in such circumstances are to be found in the ICI case.[176] The Court of Appeal held, *inter alia*, that it must be wrong in principle, when a litigant has succeeded in making good his case and has done nothing to disentitle himself to relief, to deny him any remedy on the basis of third party reliance. Specifically, Lord Oliver of Aylmerton said that such development seems an odd result and one which, at any rate, is very difficult to justify as being fair or reasonable, unless there were extremely strong reasons in public policy for doing so.

This stance also derives support from the Luxembourg jurisprudence. In *SNUPAT*,[177] the applicant, a French undertaking engaged in production in the steel industry, challenged a decision of the High Authority of the European Coal and Steel Community which exempted its competitors from the payment of contributions towards an equalization scheme. The ECJ annulled the decision on the ground, *inter alia*, that such privilege was capable of distorting the competitive relationship existing between the exempted companies and other undertakings. As regards the relief to be granted, the competitor companies claimed that the contested decision could not be quashed with retroactive effect because any alteration of the amounts they had paid in the past would run counter to the principle that the withdrawal of acquired rights is unacceptable. The court, however, held that that allegation disregards the fact that the principle of respect for legal certainty, important as it may be, cannot be applied in an absolute manner, but that its application must be combined with that of the principle of legality.

A similar result has been reached in relation to the principle of equal treatment between commercial undertakings. It is argued the court must grant the relief

---

[174] Lewis, (as above n. 161), 83.
[175] Jowell, J. 'The Takeover Panel: Autonomy, Flexibility and Legality' [1991] *Public Law*, 159.
[176] As above. n. 156.
[177] *Société nouvelle des usines de Pontlieue – Aciéries du Temple (S.N.U.P.A.T.) v. High Authority of the European Coal and Steel Community*, 42, Case 49/59 [1961] E.C.R. 53.

sought even in cases where the unlawful decision has created legitimate expectations on the part of third parties, if it considers that the effects of such an action on the competitive market are regarded as unacceptable. This approach can transparently be seen in the reasoning of the ECJ. Again, in the *SNUPAT* case,[178] the court regarded the equal treatment of commercial competitors as an interest which cannot be outweighed by the hardship to individuals who had detrimentally relied on the exemption from the payment of contributions. It stated that, when applying the balancing approach, it is important to ensure that the following factors are taken into account:

on the one hand, the interest of the beneficiaries and especially the fact that they might assume in good faith that they did not have to pay contributions on the ferrous scrap in question, and might arrange their affairs in reliance on the continuance of this position... on the other hand, the interest of the community in ensuring the proper working of the equalization scheme, which depends on the joint liability of all undertakings consuming ferrous scrap; this interest makes it necessary to ensure that other contributors do not permanently suffer the financial consequences of an exemption illegally granted to their competitors.

Nevertheless, the court made clear that, in this case, the making of the decision whether or not to withdraw the irregular exemptions with retroactive effect on the basis of the different factors set out in the judgment is, in the first place, the duty of the executive. Hence, the ECJ refused to 'put itself in the place of the High Authority' and confined itself to referring the matter back to it. Accordingly, this executive body did make the relevant appraisal and decided to withdraw the exemptions with retrospective effect, which means that competitors' companies were subjected to a levy. This decision was challenged by one of the exempted undertakings in the *Hoogovens* case.[179] The applicant argued that the High Authority did not take proper account of the conflicting interests in question. In its judgment, the Luxembourg Court accepted that it has jurisdiction to review the legality of the administrative decision concerning relief,[180] but it refused to find for the applicant. In particular, it was confirmed that the withdrawal of the disputed exemptions with retroactive effect quite rightly takes account of the interest in the equal treatment of undertakings. The court went on to hold that such principle cannot be outweighed by that of legal certainty. The essence of the argument is contained in the following extract:

the interest of the community, as the SNUPAT judgment had already laid down, requires that the other contributing undertakings shall not be made to suffer the effect of an exemption illegally granted to their competitors.

---

[178] Ibid.

[179] *Koninklijke Nederlandsche Hoogovens en Staalfabrieken N.V. v. High Authority of the European Coal and Steel Community*, Case 14/61, [1962] E.C.R. 253.

[180] It was said that

to recognize the high authority's power of appraisal is not to deny the jurisdiction of the court of justice to see whether the decision of the high authority rests on a correct application of the treaty, of the basic decisions and of the rules recognized by the SNUPAT judgment and whether it is accordingly justified in law.

In addition, the court held that, in appraising the competing interest involved, the decision-maker must not underestimate the importance of the typical aspect of the financial arrangement covering undertakings which are to a large extent in a situation of mutual competition, actual or potential, direct or indirect, total or partial, temporary or permanent. For the court it was reasonable to assume that exempted companies have the advantage over its competitors of either, on the one hand, making a larger profit on the sale of its products or selling them at lower prices and so being assured of a wider market; or, on the other hand, using the economies thus affected for investments which increased its productive capacity. Actually, it was demonstrated during the hearings that exemptions had already afforded the applicant an advantage of five to six million Dutch guilders over each of the other undertakings in the community. It follows from this that a mere withdrawal *ex nunc* would have allowed the continuance of a considerably greater difference in treatment between the applicant and the other contributing undertakings. In the court's opinion, this is obviously an argument which militates in favour of withdrawal *ex tunc*. Indeed retrospective overruling may well constitute a legitimate choice which is necessary, under the particular circumstances of the case, to prevent the consequences of illegal actions which give unfair advantages.

In *Lemmerz-Werke*,[181] the ECJ also confirmed that it is a central principle of financial schemes which target commercial competitors that the responsible bodies must eliminate any possible discrimination between them. Thus, in the present case, the High Authority could not exempt the particular company from the equalization levy for the use of ferrous scrap, because it would be placing it in a privileged position which is unacceptable discrimination against other undertakings that are normally in competition with the exempted company. Importantly, this ascription to the equal treatment between chargeable undertakings of the status of organising principle within the equalization scheme also precludes attempts to benefit companies which have planned their action on the basis that the particular decision was legal:

> in such a financial scheme as the one in question, based on a close interdependence between the contributions of each of the participants, it is above all necessary to ensure equality of treatment between those subject thereto, by eliminating all possibility of discrimination between them. In these circumstances the continuance of rules which would have the effect of conferring unjustified benefits on certain undertakings compared with others, on the pretext that they established legal situations or vested rights, would jeopardize the objectives of the said scheme. It is therefore necessary within the framework of such a scheme to acknowledge that the responsible bodies have the power to make the necessary amendments to such rules in order to eliminate any possible discrimination.

3.2.5 *Avoiding the problem of legitimate competing interests*

In light of the foregoing analysis, it becomes clear that the current doctrine to the problem of competing interests in complex markets is not able to provide a

---

[181] *Lemmerz-Werke GmbH v. High Authority of the ECSC*, Case 111/63 [1965] E.C.R. 677.

satisfactory guidance *vis à vis* the exercise of discretion on whether to grant or withhold relief. A more sensible solution to the problem obviously entails much more than the consideration of the detriment to public administration and third parties. It therefore becomes necessary to articulate an alternative approach that effectively addresses the different interests at stake and attempts to provide a solution that is compatible with the role which the rule of law plays in this area. The question at this point, therefore, is not so much whether the court should grant or withhold relief, but what approach should be applied to ensure that the exercise of the court's remedial discretion does not itself become detrimental to the innocent parties involved. The answer to this problem is provided in sub-section 4.5 of Chapter 5.

4. Conclusion

It follows that there are two main problems which afflict the orthodox approach. The first one is that it is unsatisfactory, in the sense that it has a number of adverse consequences. Properly understood, it purports to give great deference to the regulator as an expert and efficient decision-maker who takes into account wider interests in the market arena, but does so at the expense of the interests of the applicant. This last contention is based on the fact that the notion of judicial restraint relegates the judiciary to the role of 'rubber stamp' which cannot be regarded as providing a real degree of protection against the abuse of executive power.

In particular, by accepting the public body's contention simply on the basis of its special features, the court fails to take an appropriately detached and impartial view of the matter in dispute, for the case is ultimately decided upon elements extrinsic to the arguments of the parties. Consequently, the applicant is clearly deprived of his right to equal justice under the law and to obtain an unbiased judgment. When applied to factual matters, the questioned approach also appears to undermine incentives for good administration and security in the market, as it gives the general impression that the regulator can get away with insupportable findings.

Moreover, it can be argued that the administrative convenience rationale, which leads the courts to be very cautious in commercial cases for the sake of regulatory efficiency, entails a serious abdication of the judge's primary responsibility to protect individual rights in particular and the legal order as a whole through effective review of the lawfulness of impugned decisions. Indeed, it is very difficult to maintain that an applicant has a proper access to a court for redress of grievances when his claim is not given any consideration or priority over those of public interest. A similar problem can be seen in the remedial context, where the court's refusal to grant relief in order to achieve wider interests constitutes a substantial breach of the principles of legality and fair competition, upon which the applicant's claim is based.

Secondly, the present doctrine is unconvincing, in that it is rooted in mistaken assumptions about the ability of private parties and the judges to deal with complex issues. Indeed, by founding judicial restraint on the 'unique' expertise of the decision-maker, the court overlooks the fact that individuals operating in the business field are normally advised by economic and legal experts and, consequently, equally capable of providing 'highly technical' views on the matter in dispute. The discussion above also demonstrates that the apparent lack of expertise in the judiciary to deal with market cases is not a good reason to be deferential to executive power. Such an argument is not only somewhat exaggerated and preclusive of any definitive judgement, but also unduly simplistic, in the sense that it fails to capture the precise role of the courts in the legal system. Crucially, this is grounded in the need to ensure a neutral and just adjudication of disputes rather than in the provision of expert opinion about regulatory functions. It therefore follows that, even in the lack of specialized knowledge, judicial bodies should conduct a thorough and independent review of decisions which secures administrative respect for the rule of law. This task may be facilitated, for example, by the use of expert witnesses or consultants.

In addition, it must be appreciated that the proposition that judicial restraint springs from unwritten legislative will is in many respects unpersuasive. In the first place, it is inconsistent with the presumption that Parliament intends rule of law principles which favour effective judicial review to be upheld. Secondly, it fails to make reference to clear normative language or explicit provisions necessary to signal Parliament's intention to greatly reduce the availability of judicial review in a particular area. Thirdly, the present argument is flawed even with respect to autonomous regulatory agencies. In truth, the creation of these bodies reflects a legislative intent to reduce ministerial and parliamentary accountability only, thereby characterizing heightened judicial scrutiny as a necessary—rather than objectionable—mechanism which fills the democratic deficit caused by the relative lack of political control within the constitutional system.

In light of the significant difficulties that beset the orthodox doctrine, it appears that a more interventionist stance is to be preferred over judicial restraint as the adequate approach to decisions in the context of market regulation. Indeed, as seen above, such a model of review seems to be both more satisfactory and convincing. It allows the court to effectively address the points of law and fact involved in the case; it provides an objective judgement on the issue which better embraces the notion of equality under the law; it precisely captures the parties' similar ability to advance technical arguments; it is consistent with the court's primary task to protect citizens' rights against executive abuse, particularly in the light of the juridification of market regulation; it avoids the risk of arbitrariness which naturally follows from granting too much deference to the decision-maker; it openly acknowledges Parliament's intention to favour access to courts unless otherwise clearly specified; and it vouchsafes the judges' capacity to maintain the constitutional balance of power in the absence of traditional lines of accountability. In short, adherence to a more intensive form of judicial review answers the criticisms which can be levelled at the court's current attitude towards commercial regulators.

In the following chapter, a more detailed explanation of this approach is provided. It will be argued that the adoption of a more robust attitude towards regulatory decisions can be justified not only under the traditional principles of judicial review, but also on the need to pay due regard to the expanded discourse on liberal economy and private rights within the European context. These values—which have long been applied by the ECtHR and the ECJ—confer an important right to citizens to obtain a thorough review of administrative decisions in the commercial context. In particular, they form the basis for the application of the doctrine of proportionality, which requires economic authorities to provide further justification for decisions which affect fundamental rights. The influence of this principle in the United Kingdom has grown dramatically as a result of the activation, in October 2000, of the HRA 1998, which gives greater effect in domestic law to interests set out in the European Convention. Thus, national courts now find themselves under an explicit obligation to adopt a more stringent scrutiny of regulatory performance. In this sense, the European law background appears to fulfil a crucial role by cloaking such rigorous assessment with constitutional legitimacy, notwithstanding that it appears to be incompatible with precisely the traditional demarcation of limits between the executive and the judiciary. The particular effects of this standard of review are explored below.

4

A More Intensive Review Based on European Liberal Influences

1. Introduction

In Chapter 3 the book concentrated on the shortcomings of the deferential judicial attitude towards regulatory decisions, the emphasis being on its failure to supply a standard of review which is consistent with specific principles of English public law concerning, *inter alia*, legality and natural justice. It was found too that, in order to build a more satisfactory and convincing approach, a greater degree of control should be exercised which provides an effective protection against the abuse of regulatory power. For this reason it was contended, in general terms, that the court's decision should proceed objectively from the proofs and arguments advanced at the hearing, and that the interests of the applicant should be taken into account even when they compete with other private or public priorities at stake. The purpose of this chapter is to look more closely into the legal foundations on which this robust, rights-oriented mode of commercial judicial review rests. In particular, it will be argued that the incorporation of large and important areas of European law has brought about significant changes to administrative decision-making and adjudication, often in favour of a comprehensive review jurisdiction which safeguards economic freedoms and liberties against encroachment by the decision-maker. It is within this liberal context that the principles of access to a court of 'full jurisdiction', and, specifically, proportionality, have assumed a heightened prominence in commercial regulation. Each of these contentions will be substantiated below, with particular reference to the beneficial consequences—in terms of balance of powers and interests—that the application of these principles may have on the judicial supervision of the different aspects of the contended order.

2. Courts and Liberal Economy in the European Context

In the last twenty years, commercial judicial review at a European level has been exercised within a context of market liberalization which purports to advocate for a more stringent scrutiny that prevents regulators from hampering free market policies. The basis of this form of review is to be found from a consideration of the European Convention and the EU law, which mark out the limits that the judges impose on the regulator's competence to qualify citizens' economic rights. The influence of this doctrine in the British law has grown significantly, as the judgments of international courts that recognize it have become more and more preponderant.[1] Moreover, it coincides with the domestic need to provide a more intensive form of review which represents constitutional and legal principles with which the notion of individual justice has long been associated. It thus seems to fit well with the contention that the orthodox doctrine to regulatory decisions must be rejected, and that it is more satisfactory to adopt an approach that provides effective protection against unlawful interference with commercial interests. In the following paragraphs, a brief view of the postulated connection between open markets and strict judicial oversight is advanced. Thus, sub-section 2.1 will describe it as a feature of systems which further the values of liberalism. Sub-section 2.2 then goes on to give some indication of its effects in national law.

2.1 Courts and liberal economy

A relevant tension can be appreciated between the political values underlying the legitimacy of administrative government. On the one hand, 'liberal' principles are seen to buttress the notion of balance of power and restrictions to executive action that affects private interests. However, on the other hand, 'progressive' values tend to support extensive governmental intervention into private activities which relieves social problems by recourse to expert and independent decision-makers. Importantly, it appears that each set of political values is closely associated with a different form of commercial judicial review. It is argued that, in order to preserve individual freedoms, the courts ought to apply more rigorous scrutiny to regulatory decisions in the context of *laissez faire* economic policy than to activities inspired by functionalist ideas of social solidarity and development.

This point is illustrated with particular clarity by the work of Professor Carol Harlow and Richard Rawlings.[2] They explain that the views of administrative law may be grouped under two general headings. On *red light* theories the emphasis is on courts rather than on government, since they are conceived as key instruments for the control of power and for the protection of individual liberty against unlawful intrusions of the state. In contrast, the alternative tradition, which they have called *green light*, favours a more deferential attitude of the judiciary which pins its hopes on the political process. This view experiences the control of arbitrary power as another brake on progress which must be avoided by having a corpus of 'realist' and 'functionalist' jurisprudence that considers the law in its social context.

---

[1] See Wade, W. and Forsyth, C.F., *Administrative Law*, 10th edn., (Oxford: Oxford University Press, 2009) 176; Elliott, Mark, *The Constitutional Foundations of Judicial Review*, (Oxford: Hart Publishing, 2001) 198.
[2] Harlow and Rawlings' distinction between red light and green light theories in Harlow and Rawlings, *Law and Administration*, 3rd edn., Law in Context, (Cambridge: Cambridge University Press, 2009), 1–44, 29–90. See also Dyzenhaus, David, 'Form and Substance in the Rule of Law: A Democratic Justification for Judicial Review?' in *Judicial Review and the Constitution*, Christopher Forsyth (ed.), (Oxford: Hart Publishing, 2000) 144.

A similar distinction is advanced by Sydney Shapiro and Richard Levy,[3] who explain that adherence to 'liberal' values requires meaningful judicial review which is consistent with the constitutional framework designed to implement the principle of separation of powers and to protect individual rights. In contrast, 'progressive' values provide the basis for judicial deference that contributes to social and economic improvements made by efficient agencies. These two strains of political values are summarized by the writers in the following table:[4]

Political values and the intensity of judicial review

Political Values	Basis	Implications for Judicial Review
Liberal	Separation of powers and due process	Requires meaningful review
Progressive	Practical necessity, expertise and efficiency	Requires deferential review

In light of this, it becomes apparent that a successful model of judicial review in the context of liberal economies must provide for an effective control on administrative error and abuse which ensures that liberties are not sacrificed to accommodate arbitrary decisions. Heightened scrutiny of the executive branch thus serves as an institution that promotes private ordering, that is to say, freedom to go about one's business without unauthorized regulatory intrusion.[5] It is to the recognition of this doctrine in the English law that we now turn.

2.2 European influences

To this purpose, particular attention must be paid to the process of European liberalization, which has increased the importance of a hard-edged approach to domestic determinations regarding commercial issues. Indeed it can be argued that the normative foundations on which the operation of open and competitive markets—within the old continent—rests suggest that national courts ought to exhibit a more rigorous attitude *vis-à-vis* the outcome of regulatory processes that circumscribe such an autonomy and freedom. Importantly, it appears that the incorporation of these norms into English law goes some way towards accounting for the placement of market regulators inside the scope of more searching judicial inquiry which furthers liberal values. Thus, a new weapon can be included in the armoury for exercising effective judicial review of their decisions. In particular, there are two elements from which this contention derives its legal authority.

---

[3] Shapiro, S.A and Levy, R.E, 'Heightened Scrutiny and the Fourth Branch: Separation of Powers and the Requirement of Adequate Reasons for Agency Decisions' [1987] 2 *Duke Law Journal*, 391. See also Solove, Daniel, 'The Darkest Domain: Deference, Judicial Review, and the Bill of Rights' [1999] 84 *Iowa Law Review*, 966. For a more recent account of this doctrine in American Law, see Bolick, Clint, *David's Hammer: the Case for an Activist Judiciary*, (Washington D.C.: Cato Institute, 2007), Chapter 7.   [4] Shapiro and Levy, (as above n. 3), 391.
[5] Sunstein, Cass, 'In Defense of the Hard Look: Judicial Activism and Administrative Law' 7(1) *Harvard Journal of Law and Public Policy*, 53.

First, the history of the European Convention, particularly in the origins of the right to property, may be considered. Michael Smyth has usefully described how the movement to establish a continental rights regime in the early 1950s was perceived by British political masters at that time as 'the standpoint of a *laissez faire* economy' in an age which paid great attention to planned economy.[6] The statement made by Sir Stafford Cripps, then Chancellor of the Exchequer, at a cabinet meeting held on 1 August 1950 is particularly illuminating. He warned that 'a government committed to the policy of a planned economy' could not ratify the proposed convention because its terms 'would be acceptable only to those who believed in a free economy and a minimum amount of State intervention in economic affairs'.[7] In particular, Cripps was worried that the protection of Convention's rights by the Court of Human Rights would, for example, limit the power of Inland Revenue inspectors to enter private premises and impede the Cabinet plans for nationalization of certain industries.

Thus, there appeared to be a natural relationship between, on the one hand, the idea of economic guarantees disclosed by the draft convention and, on the other hand, the specific powers which the court would exercise by way of judicial review. Briefly, it was understood that the further the recognition of liberal principles, the more stringent the scrutiny of decisions affecting private industry. Hence it is not surprising that Smyth has paraphrased Hersch Lauterpacht to say that the signing of the Convention transformed the legal entity known as the company from 'an object of international compassion into a subject of international right'.[8]

This point perhaps is even more apparent in the controversy about British incorporation of the European Convention throughout the 1970s and 1980s. It is noted that the motivation of many of those advocating for a domestic Bill of Rights was the hope that 'it would restore this country to its former place as an international standard–bearer of liberty and justice',[9] all this when decisions of the European Convention institutions had already made significant changes to regulations and administrative practices affecting individual rights.[10] In particular, it was argued that the introduction of the Convention would lead to enhanced judicial protection from governmental intervention in the property sphere.[11] In 1975, the Rt. Hon. Sir Keith Joseph MP, widely regarded as a significant influence in the creation of what came to be known as 'Thatcherism', said that such a change would, for example, prevent an untrammelled executive from issuing compulsory purchase orders without restraint.[12] In contrast, the incorporation of the Convention was viewed with suspicion by the British left and some academic lawyers on the basis that it represented 'the triumph of liberalism over socialism and

---

[6] Lord Jowitt, then Lord Chancellor. See Marston, Geoffrey, 'The United Kingdom's Part in the Preparation of the European Convention on Human Rights' [1993] 42 *International and Comparative Law Quarterly*, 812. Smyth, Michael, *Business and the Human Rights Act 1998*, (Bristol: Jordan Publishing, 2000) 10.   [7] Smyth, (as above n. 6).

[8] Ibid., 11.

[9] Lord Bingham of Cornhill LCJ, in his Denning Lecture on 2 March 1993. Cited by Smyth, ibid., 14.

[10] Ibid.   [11] Ibid., 297.   [12] Ibid., 13.

as such fixes that triumph irrevocably into the constitution'.[13] As far as the right to property was concerned, they feared that the introduction of such a safeguard would greatly enhance the authority of the Bench to favour vested private interests particularly and *laissez faire* capitalism generally.[14] There is thus a strong case for concluding that, however contentious in political terms, the right to property adopted in Article 1 of the Convention's First Protocol was almost unanimously seen as widening judicial powers in the light of economic liberalism.[15]

The second element relates to the United Kingdom's membership of the European Union. In general terms, the chief impetus for this institution has been the desire to construct an internal market among member states which provides greater protection for the fundamental social and economic rights. In this sense, its importance is two-fold. On the one hand, EC law has played a major role in implementing social policies concerning dialogue between trade union and employers' organizations, opportunities on ageing, and the promotion of equal opportunities and diversity through anti-discrimination provisions. On the other hand, it is undeniable that it has contributed to create an integrated continental economy along liberal market lines such as free movement of capital, maximization of economic competition, and the privatization of public services. It is precisely this second element which, in turn, has placed the practice of judicial deference in the business field under growing strain, given the reasonable perception that the values of free market can be furthered only by means of heightened judicial review that prevents arbitrary interference with private rights.

Tony Prosser has identified one relevant implication of this trend for commercial judicial review in England.[16] He says that the process of European liberalization is likely to increase the importance of law in relation to domestic market regulation by rendering it 'more litigious, with a greater role for the courts'. In particular, the incorporation of Community liberal law into the English legal system may effect a significant change in the broader context within which judicial review of regulatory decisions occurs, as its principles 'are considerably more sophisticated and more far reaching in their implications than are those of the domestic administrative law'. Consequently, it is entirely possible that national courts will have to adopt a more intensive form of review which reflects the direct, as well as indirect, influences exerted by the potentially demanding EU law.

This doctrine, according to which the court's supervisory role becomes more effective in light of EU law liberal values, is usefully illustrated by the Queen's Bench Division's decision in *R (on the application of Orange Personal Communications Ltd) v. Secretary of State for Trade and Industry.*[17] The case concerned Directive 97/13 of the European Parliament and the Council of the European Union on

---

[13] Ewing, K. and Gearty, C., 'Rocky Foundations for Labour's New Rights' [1997] 2 *European Human Rights Law Review*, 150.

[14] Smyth, (as above n. 6), 297.

[15] See also Emberland, Marius, *The Human Rights of Companies*, (Oxford: Oxford University Press, 2006) 48–50.

[16] Prosser, Tony, *Law and Regulators*, (Oxford: Clarendon Press, 1997), 56.

[17] *The Times* 15 November 2000, CO/4231/1999.

a common framework for general authorizations and individual licences in the field of telecommunication services. This Directive, which has been regarded as a 'key part' of the EU-wide liberalization of telecommunications, was designed to produce a system of licensing which is transparent, objective, proportionate, and non-discriminatory.

The United Kingdom was therefore required to adjust the conditions attaching to some 420 licences in order to bring them into line with the Directive. The regime for modifying the conditions of licences was specifically regulated by sections 12 to 15 of the United Kingdom's Telecommunications Act 1984, which provide that this amendment can only be made in one of two ways: either with the licencee's consent or unilaterally by the Director General of Telecommunications following a reference to the Competition Commission requesting them to investigate and report on the questions (a) whether there are matters that operate, or may be expected to operate, against the public interest; and (b) if so, whether the effects adverse to the public interest could be remedied or prevented by modifications of the conditions of that licence.

However, in light of the great difficulties of implementing the amendments in respect of each individual licence, the Director concluded that the necessary modifications could not practically be achieved under the 1984 Act and opted instead for the procedure laid down in section 2(2) of the European Communities Act 1972. In short, this section confers powers to make subordinate legislation for the purpose of implementing any Community obligation of the United Kingdom. By using this category of regulations, the authority was able to insert a raft of new conditions into the 400 or so existing licences. In practice, the new conditions stood alongside the existing licence conditions, which were not amended.

The problem was that the applicants objected to the modification of their licences by the specific inclusion of conditions 56 (market influence) and 56A (service provider) on the ground that they were not justified for the purposes of implementing the Directive. Thus, an issue arose with respect to the proper procedure for the resolution of the dispute as to the appropriateness of the conditions. The applicants argued that the question should be determined under sections 12 to 15 of the Telecommunications Act 1984, which confers jurisdiction on an independent expert body, the Competition Commission, to decide whether the objectives of the Directive require the imposition of such conditions. In particular, they relied on the argument that provisions of the 1984 Act could only be lawfully repealed or amended by subordinate legislation made under section 2(2) of the European Communities Act 1972, provided those regulations explicitly and unambiguously did it. As the implementing regulations did not even mention sections 12 to 15, it was contended that there was no provision for their disapplication. Consequently, the relevant sections of the 1984 Act were still in effect to provide the machinery for the resolution of disputes concerning modification of licence conditions.

The applicants also submitted that the need for explicit disapplication of sections 12 to 15 is reinforced by Article 9(6) in the Directive which requires Member States to lay down 'an appropriate procedure for appealing against such refusals, withdrawals, amendments or suspensions to an institution independent of the national regulatory authority'. As the particular regulations in question made no provision for any appeal, and the limited grounds of challenge available on judicial review did not make adequate provision for an appeal on the merits, it was clear that the United Kingdom had in fact provided such a procedure under sections 12 to 15 of the Telecommunications Act. Consequently, to use section 2(2) of the 1972 Act to evade this procedure would be to breach, rather than secure the implementation of the Directive.

Thus, the Court was called upon to decide, *inter alia*, whether judicial review constitutes an appropriate procedure for 'appealing' against licence amendments in the context of Article 9(6) of the Directive, to the extent it may be used as an alternative and legitimate mechanism for dispute resolution. For the present purpose, it is sufficient to characterise the judgment of Sullivan J as one which emphasises a very close connection between market liberalization and intensive scrutiny of regulatory decisions:

What is an 'appropriate procedure for appealing', and in particular, whether the availability of judicial review makes adequate provision for an appeal, as submitted on behalf of the respondent, must depend upon the context, and especially upon the objectives of the Directive in question. Given that the objective of this Directive is the liberalisation of telecommunications throughout the EU, with 'the lightest possible regulation', it may well have been intended that there should be an appeal on the merits, not confined simply to questions of legality, to an independent body, so that the natural tendency of national regulatory agencies to regulate was kept in check, consistent with this liberalising objective.

On this approach, the specific appeal proceeding laid down in the Telecommunications Act 1984 was plainly consistent with the liberal economic policy underlying the Directive, for it provided in substance (although not in form) an appeal to an institution, the Commission, which has very broad powers to examine the merits of the proposed modification and to decide whether it would be in the public interest. By the same token, the court stressed that:

Regulations which dispense with this appeal on the merits and substitute (by default) the less extensive remedy of judicial review, even if not in breach of the Directive, are at the very least not implementing its requirements in as full-hearted a manner as possible. This underlines the importance of Parliament being told clearly that ss 12 to 15 were being disapplied when modifications to the licence conditions were being made by the regulations.

The foregoing analysis thus reveals that the judicial practice of accepting, without much questioning or inquiring, decisions made by market regulators in England may pose a serious threat to liberal values embedded in European law: it represents a failure to impose rights-based limits which provide for more rigorous requirements of fairness upon the administrator in accordance with international obligations. Conversely, a stricter judicial scrutiny which extends pervasively throughout the regulatory state may be characterized as a potentially positive instrument to protect liberties consistently with European influences on domestic law. It is the specific legal expressions of this doctrine which now fall to be considered.

3. The Right to a Court of Full Jurisdiction in the Human Rights Convention

The first element which may be considered—as part of the European principles of administrative law that reassert meaningful judicial oversight of government—relates to the application of Article 6(1) of the European Convention, which reads, in pertinent part:

In the determination of his civil rights and obligations or of any criminal charge against him, everyone is entitled to a fair and public hearing within a reasonable time by an independent and impartial tribunal established by law.

Prima facie, this provision places administrative bodies which determine civil rights under great strain, as they are often unable to comply with the specific requirements of independence and impartiality. For instance, many of these authorities are open to influences from central government, they lack security of tenure, and their decisions can be revoked by the Minister. However, it is worth emphasizing that the jurisprudence of the ECtHR has said that, even where Article 6(1) does apply, it is not necessary that the primary decision-maker complies with every aspect of it. What the court does insist upon is that, in such circumstances, the dispute must be brought before a judicial body that has 'full jurisdiction', so that the decision-making process as a whole is compliant and the defect in first instance is 'cured'.[18] Thus, it appears that, in the case of insufficiently impartial decisions, the important question will not be whether the administrative decision-maker complies with the duty imposed by Article 6(1), but whether it is subject to the control of a judicial body that does so by exercising 'full jurisdiction' in the sense contemplated by the European authorities.

This requirement of the Strasbourg Court to provide procedural guarantees for executive decisions affecting rights ostensibly fosters judicial engagement in high intensity review. It is clear that national courts are now required to exercise an exhaustive and comprehensive scrutiny of impugned measures that have been made in the absence of procedural safeguards in order to ensure that the decision-making process can accommodate the Convention. It is precisely this imperative of securing compliance with European influences which, it is argued, provides further evidence of the necessity of adopting a robust, rather than deferential, attitude towards commercial regulators. Since their decisions can certainly determine or affect civil rights and obligations, it follows that judicial review of them, if it is to be consistent with human rights principles, must ultimately be about exercising full powers that remedy any falling short of the standards of independence and impartiality by the initial decision-maker. This contention forms the focus of the following three sub-sections.

---

[18] See *Zumtobel v. Austria* [1994] 17 E.H.R.R. 116. This approach, which is principally based on a democratic model of decision-making, was upheld by the House of Lords in the *Alconbury* case, (*R v. Secretary of State for the Environment, Transport and the Regions, ex p Alconbury Developments Ltd.* [2001] 2 W.L.R. 1389).

3.1 Applicability of Article 6(1) to the commercial context

The line of Strasbourg authority makes clear that Article 6(1) extends to administrative proceedings which can be considered 'decisive' of private rights and obligations.[19] For the present purposes, it is important to note that this provision may be generally applied to matters directly regulating property rights[20] and commercial activity through the grant of licences or similar devices.[21] In particular, the ECtHR has stressed that a commercial licence confers a 'right' which is clearly within the scope of Article 6(1).

The decision in *Kaplan v. United Kingdom*[22] is particularly illuminating. On the 13 February 1976 the Secretary of State for Trade served a notice on an insurance company under section 29 of the Insurance Companies Act 1974 imposing restrictions on its ability to enter into a variety of insurance contracts. The ground was that it appeared that the applicant, the comptroller of the company, was not a fit and proper person to carry on insurance business because he had misrepresented the value of some property in the company's accounts. Mr. Kaplan claimed that this was a breach of Article 6(1), arguing, *inter alia*, that the civil rights and obligations of himself and the company were determined without a public hearing before a court. The respondent government, however, submitted that no right to establish or carry on such business was vested in the applicant or the company and that no such 'right' was thus affected. In particular, they argued that under the relevant domestic law a company authorized to conduct insurance business does so by virtue of a privilege granted by the Secretary of State and not as a matter of right. Secondly, they maintained that even if any rights or obligations were affected, they were not 'civil' in character.

The European Commission, however, found for the applicant and declared that, notwithstanding the Minister's power to regulate commercial activities, a 'right' for the purposes of Article 6(1) was involved.[23] In particular, it was held that the direct legal effect of the Secretary of State's action was that the existing 'right' of the

---

[19] *Ringeisen v. Austria* (No. 1) [1971] 1 E.H.R.R. 455 at 490, para. 94; *König*, 1978, A27, p. 30, para. 90. See also *Kaplan v. United Kingdom* [1980] 4 E.H.R.R. 64 at 85, *Jacobsson v. Sweden* [1989] 12 E.H.R.R. 56. For a general analysis see Sales, Philip, 'The Civil Limb of ECHR, Article 6' [2005] 10(1) *Judicial Review*, 52–65.

[20] See *Sovtransavto Holding v. Ukraine* [2002] E.C.H.R. 626, concerning property rights in shares.   [21] Wade and Forsyth, (as above n. 1), 377

[22] [1980] 4 E.H.R.R. 64. See also *X v. United Kingdom*, E.H.R.R, 25, CD 88; *A.P.B. Ltd A.P.P. E.A.B. v. United Kingdom*, E.H.R.R., 25, CD 141.

[23] There is no doubt that until the Secretary of State issued the notice of requirements, IGA (the company) was entitled by law to carry on insurance business within the limits imposed by its existing authorisations and the general law. In particular it was entitled to do so by entering into certain forms of insurance contract. Unless and until the Secretary of State removed that entitlement by exercising the appropriate powers under the Act, no one could lawfully prevent IGA from thus conducting its business. In the Commission's opinion, IGA thus had a 'right', within the ordinary meaning of the word, to conduct insurance business. It had initially been conferred by the Secretary of State when he authorised the company and he was entitled, under certain conditions, to interfere with it, or even effectively to remove it as he did here. However, these factors do not, in the Commission's opinion, alter its character as a 'right' for the purposes of Article 6(1) at least.

company to conduct insurance business was restricted in the manner set out in the notice under section 29 of the 1974 Act. As to whether the right to conduct insurance business was 'civil' in character, the Commission said that the fact that the right in question was exercised in the private sector, albeit subject to administrative authorization and supervision in the public interest, was sufficient to conclude that it was of a private nature and therefore a 'civil' right for the purposes of Article 6(1).

Similar reasoning is evident in the area of traffic licensing. In the *Pudas* case,[24] for example, the applicant alleged a violation of Article 6(1) as he had no possibility of having the revocation of his transport licence reviewed by a court. The Swedish Government first contended that the licence concerned did not constitute a 'right' for Mr. Pudas, since it was issued not for a fixed period of time but merely 'until further notice'. Secondly, they argued that even if it were accepted that an existing right of the applicant to carry out a public transport business was affected, the fact that he was developing a public-law activity precludes the existence of a 'civil' right for the purposes of Article 6(1). In particular, reference was made to the role of the authority in ensuring the availability of proper transport facilities and the access of the licence-holder to public funds to cover part of the costs of running the business. The court, however, accepted the view of the applicant that the licence did confer a 'civil right' in the form of an authorization to carry out a transport service in accordance with certain conditions. In the court's view, the features of public law attached to that business did not suffice to exclude applicant's rights from the category of civil rights under Article 6(1). It was held that the activity in question still takes the form of a commercial activity: 'It is carried out with the object of earning profits and is based on a contractual relationship between the licence-holder and the customers'. The dispute between Mr. Pudas and the Swedish authorities did therefore concern a 'civil right' and Article 6(1) was thus applicable to the case.

The Court's decision in *Tre Traktörer Aktiebolag*[25] also provides a good example of the applicability of Article 6(1) in the commercial context. In this case the Swedish Government had argued that there was no 'right' to obtain or retain a licence to serve alcoholic beverages, in view of the wide discretion enjoyed by the competent authorities. It also contended that there were specific public law elements which prevented the decision from coming within the scope of article 6(1), such as the non-transferable character of the licence and the fact that it constituted one of the means of implementing the social policy concerning alcoholic beverages. However, the court did not share this view. First, it explained that subject to the possibility of it being revoked, the licence conferred a 'right' on the applicant company in the form of an authorization to sell alcoholic beverages in accordance with the conditions set out in the licence and with the provisions of the respective Act. The court also accepted that the licence was directly 'decisive' for the existence and scope of such a right on the ground that it was one of the principal conditions for carrying on the commercial activity and that any withdrawal of the permission

---

[24] *Pudas v. Sweden* [1988] 10 E.H.R.R. 380. See also *Oerlemans v. Netherlands*, [1993] 15 E.H.R.R. 561.

[25] [1989] 15 E.H.H.R. See also *Benthem*, 1985, Series A, vol. 97, para 34.

may have had adverse effects on the goodwill and the value of the restaurant business run by the applicant. Thus, the licensing proceeding concerning the dispute at issue was clearly within the scope of Article 6(1). In second place, the court made clear that policy interests involved under the relevant statutory provisions do not preclude the existence of a civil right for the purpose of Article 6(1).[26]

The Strasbourg jurisprudence thus demonstrates a clear commitment to the idea of commercial licences as instruments conferring 'civil rights' for the purposes of Article 6(1) of the European Convention. It is worth mentioning that much of this reasoning is likely to be applied to other authorities which possess extensive licensing powers, regulating and controlling not only insurance business, public transport and liquor, but such activities as public utilities, financial services,[27] betting and gaming, cinemas, fireworks factories, and pawnbrokers.[28] Consequently, it is not surprising that the entire corpus of regulatory law may be developed in light of this provision, should the court come to the conclusion that administrative practice does not meet basic standards of procedural fairness.

3.2 Investigative proceedings

The discussion thus far has been concerned with the applicability of Article 6(1) where proceedings have been conducted by the authority empowered to 'determine' civil rights. It is time now to consider non-adjudicative procedures either in form or in substance. In particular, the discussion in the commercial context has focused on whether Article 6(1) applies to the investigations conducted under section 432 of the Companies Act 1985, which empowers the Secretary of State to appoint inspectors to investigate the affairs of a company and to report on them in such manner as he directs if it appears to him that there are circumstances suggesting wrongdoing. This issue arose in *Fayed v. United Kingdom*,[29] where the applicants argued that the inspectors' report, published to the world at large, had the force of a judgment convicting the applicants of dishonesty. The result of the inquiry was thus effectively 'determining' their civil right to honour and good reputation without any of the procedural guarantees of Article 6(1). However, the Strasbourg Court was of the opinion that such provision was not applicable to the

---

[26] It is true that in Sweden the wholesale distribution of alcohol is a State monopoly; however, the serving of alcoholic beverages in restaurants and bars is entrusted mainly to private persons and companies through the issuing of licenses (see paragraph 24 above). In such a case, the persons and companies concerned carry on a private commercial activity, which has the object of earning profits and is based on a contractual relationship between the license-holder and the customers. Taking into account these circumstances, the Court is of the view that the features of public law mentioned by the Government do not suffice to exclude from the category of 'civil rights' within the meaning of Article 6 para. 1 (art. 6–1) the rights conferred on TTA by virtue of the license…The dispute in question did therefore concern a 'civil right' of the applicant company and Article 6 para. 1 (art. 6–1) is thus applicable in the present case.

[27] See *Heather Moor & Edgecomb Ltd, R. (on the application of) v. Financial Ombudsman Service and another* [2008] E.W.C.A. Civ 642 at para 42.

[28] Engelman, Philip, *Commercial Judicial Review*, (London: Sweet & Maxwell, 2001) 147.

[29] 28/1993/423/502. See also *Saunders v. The United Kingdom* [1997] 23 E.H.R.R. 313.

proceedings conducted by the inspectors because they were, in practice as well as in theory, essentially investigative rather than determinative.[30]

Moreover, the court held that acceptance of the applicants' argument would entail that a body carrying out preparatory investigations at the instance of regulatory or other authorities should always be subject to the procedural guarantees set forth in Article 6(1), by reason of the fact that publication of its findings may have detrimental effects on the reputation of individuals whose conduct is being investigated. In its opinion, this stance is fundamentally unworkable because it runs directly counter to the spirit of flexibility that must characterize business regulation.[31]

Thus the ECtHR appears readily to reject any attempt to extend the scope of Article 6(1) to procedures whose main purpose is to set down factual information which would enable the various competent authorities to decide what action to take. This approach may therefore be of significance for investigative procedures contained in other statutes such as the Insolvency Act 2000 and the Financial Services and Markets Act 2000.

However, it must be emphasized that this is not to suggest that no court shall be competent to enquire into or give judgment on these findings. It is sufficient here to mention two matters which are indicative of this submission. First, it is plain from the Strasbourg reasoning that domestic courts remain capable of entering upon disputed questions of fact in proceedings for judicial review.[32] This assertion is bolstered when the acceptance of the 'wrong factual basis' doctrine by UK judges and scholars is considered. As seen above, it is already recognized that error of material fact has become a ground of review which allows the judges

---

[30] The Inspectors did not adjudicate, either in form or in substance. They themselves said in their report that their findings would not be dispositive of anything (see paragraph 21 above). They did not make a legal determination as to criminal or civil liability concerning the Fayed brothers, and in particular concerning the latter's civil right to honour and reputation. The purpose of their inquiry was to ascertain and record facts which might subsequently be used as the basis for action by other competent authorities – prosecuting, regulatory, disciplinary or even legislative.

[31] Such an interpretation of Article 6 para. 1 (art. 6–1) would in practice unduly hamper the effective regulation in the public interest of complex financial and commercial activities. In the Court's view, investigative proceedings of the kind in issue in the present case fall outside the ambit and intendment of Article 6.1. The Court accordingly concludes that the investigation by the Inspectors was not such as to attract the application of Article 6 para. 1 (art. 6–1).

[32] In *Fayed* the European Court of Human Rights said that,

judicial review would, for example, provide a remedy if Inspectors under the Companies Act were prejudiced or biased against the subjects of their report . . . ; or if the Inspectors reached conclusions which there were no facts to support, or took into account irrelevant considerations, or failed to take account of relevant considerations, or reached conclusions which no reasonable person in their position could have reached . . . ; or if their findings have not been properly based on material which has probative value . . . ; or if the Inspectors were dishonest or acted in bad faith . . . ; or if the Inspectors acted *ultra vires* or beyond their legal powers . . . ; or if the Inspectors acted against the legitimate expectations of those concerned . . . ; or if the Inspectors acted contrary to the rules of natural justice . . . ; or if the Inspectors acted unfairly. . . .', *Fayed v. United Kingdom* [1994] 18 E.H.R.R. 393.

to intervene where the executive action (e.g. decision, report, conclusion) rests on a misunderstanding or ignorance of an established and relevant fact.[33] Thus, it becomes apparent that the courts' scrutiny of findings of fact adopted pursuant to an investigative proceeding would take place by way of judicial review *in spite* of its non-adjudicative nature.

Secondly, and more significantly for the present purposes, even if Article 6(1) does not apply to pure investigative enquiries, this does not necessarily entail that findings of fact made in the course of such proceedings are exempt from full scrutiny at a further stage of the decision-making process. Where the same evidence is used as the basis for an action which effectively affects civil rights it must be subject to intensive review for the purposes of Article 6(1), since, logically, the ongoing proceeding would be essentially determinative rather than investigative. In the instant case, for example, the inspectors' report was referred to the Director of Public Prosecutions, the Director of the Serious Fraud Office, the Bank of England, the City Panel on Takeovers and Mergers, the Inland Revenue, the Office of Fair Trading, and the Monopolies and Mergers Commission. These commercial authorities have a range of decision-making powers which can be decisive for private rights. It is clear, therefore, that in such circumstances the courts should be willing to exercise 'full jurisdiction' over findings of fact supporting the decision even though they have originally been made by a privileged fact-finder.

3.3 'Full jurisdiction' in the commercial context

The ECtHR has recognized that the compatibility of commercial decisions with Article 6 may also depend upon whether there is adequate judicial review by a court that has 'full jurisdiction' and provides the guarantees of Article 6(1). This composite approach, which extends more widely to the whole decision-making process, is to be welcomed to the extent that it provides a heightened scrutiny of measures adopted by decision-makers which cannot be independent or impartial as they are appointed by the executive, or simply because they are empowered to make economic policy and apply that policy in particular cases. Alternatively, this requirement seems to be very convenient in the context of self-regulatory organizations, where there may be insufficient separation of the functions of prosecutor and judge. Consider, for example, proceedings which are instituted at the request of a person who is actually on the adjudicating body or cases where the adjudicator refers the matter to a subcommittee for hearing and report.

A more difficult question, however, concerns the meaning of the expression 'full jurisdiction' which is of crucial importance to assess the compatibility of decision-making processes with Article 6(1). In particular, European authority has said that, in determining the sufficiency of judicial review available, regard must be had to the specific nature, context, and circumstances of the case.[34] This approach

---

[33] See Section 3.1 in Chapter 3.
[34] *Bryan v. United Kingdom* [1996] 21 E.H.R.R. 342, para. 45.

has been exemplified in the domestic jurisprudence by Lord Hoffman's decision in *Alconbury*, a planning permission case.[35] His Lordship stated that 'full jurisdiction' means 'full jurisdiction to deal with the case as the nature of the decision requires'. The more recent decision in *SRM Global Master Fund LP and Ors v. HM Treasury*,[36] a case concerning the compensation to former shareholders in the nationalized bank Northern Rock, defined it as the court being amply equipped to receive all the material, fact or law, that might properly be required to mount a challenge against an administrative decision. It follows from this that the concept of 'full jurisdiction' may well be applied with varying degrees of intensity so as to accommodate the subject-matter of the contested decision. It is necessary, then, to go further in providing some guidance as to how the phrase should be understood in cases involving judicial review in the commercial context. Three points are considered.

First, the tendency appears to be to require a full review of the merits where the contested decision directly determines individual rights, particularly in cases concerning access to one's children,[37] employment[38] and professional discipline.[39] A decision of an agency will not satisfy this condition if, for example, it principally involves questions of policy or expediency. In such cases, where considerable public interest impinges upon individual rights, a mere review of the lawfulness of the decision appears to suffice.[40] This is especially so in the context of planning, where policy considerations suggest that it should be the executive rather than a court which takes the final decision on the merits even though the decision may affect an individual's rights.[41] In particular, the role of the decision-maker is to strike a delicate balance between individual rights of persons who wish to develop their land and the interests of the community in terms of provisions of an adequate supply of houses, retail facilities, and land for waste disposal.[42] As this function involves significant policy questions, the court should not substitute its own opinion for that of the administrative authorities.[43] Thus, the ECtHR has made clear that Article 6(1) does not guarantee a right to a full review by a court of the merits of planning decisions affecting private rights, but that there is compliance with the provision where there is a review concerned only with the question of lawfulness.

---

[35] As above, n. 18.

[36] [2009] E.W.C.A. Civ 788 at para 84.

[37] *W v. United Kingdom*, [1987] 10 E.H.R.R. 29.

[38] *Obermeier v. Austria*, [1990] 13 E.H.R.R. 290.

[39] *Le Compte, Van Leuven and De Meyere v. Belgium* [1981] 4 E.H.R.R. 1; *Albert and Le Compte* [2001] J.P.L. 920.

[40] See *Zumtobel v. Austria*, (as above n. 18).

[41] As above, n. 18.

[42] Poustie, Mark, 'The Rule of Law or The Rule of Lawyers? Alconbury, Article 6(1) and The Role of Courts in Administrative Decision-Making' [2001] 6 *European Human Rights Law Review*, 673.

[43] *Bryan v. United Kingdom*, (as above n. 34); *ISKCON v. UK* [1994] 76A DR 90. This principle is exemplified in the domestic jurisprudence by Mr. Justice Forbes's decision in *Friends Provident Life & Pensions Ltd. v. Secretary of State for Transport, Local Government and Regions* [1994] 1 W.L.R. 1450.

However, it would be mistaken to think that this approach will be confined to the planning sphere. The courts are likely to be called to apply it in similar areas, such as market regulation. After all, decisions in the commercial context also involve the balancing of individual and community interests and regulators are given discretionary powers to perform such function. Markets have to operate both in the interest of persons who wish to conduct a business but also in the interest of the society in terms of consumer protection, fair competition, and externalities. It follows from this that relevant decisions are taken within a framework of what is essentially political expediency. Consequently, as the Strasbourg Court has stressed, there should not necessarily be review on the full merits of regulatory decisions to ensure compatibility with Article 6(1).

Nevertheless, it is self-apparent from the foregoing analysis that the suggested approach does not provide any account of the intensity of review within the *legitimate* scope for the courts to 'cure' the failure of an initial decision to comply with Article 6(1). Its objective is only to ensure that the judicial review does not become an improper usurpation of powers which seriously undermines the principle of separation of powers. In other words, acknowledging that decisions cannot be reviewable on theirs merits does not effectively illuminate how sufficient or 'full' the supervisory jurisdiction of the court must be to provide the guarantees of Article 6 in the context of market regulation. Lawfulness is such a wide test that there is plenty of space between judicial review in the orthodox sense and substitution of judgement. It is therefore necessary to determine the specific point in the continuum from low-intensity and high-intensity modes of judicial intervention which allows dealing with commercial cases as the nature of the decision requires.

An answer to this question can be found in the doctrine of proportionality. It can be argued that, by applying this approach to regulatory decisions, it is possible to begin to deal with difficulties which may prevent individuals' civil rights from being determined by an independent and impartial tribunal. This argument is best substantiated by first considering the more limited form of review embodied in the *Wednesbury* approach. In general terms, this test suffers from the problem of being too deferential to the executive, given that it casts the decision-maker as the primary judge of where the balance lies between the different interests which are at stake in the market sphere. Such standard of review would not be sufficient to ensure that the decision-making process as a whole complies with Article 6, because it precludes the courts from reconsidering authorities' reliance upon their own policy and understanding of the public interest. The point is perhaps even more apparent when it is realized that Article 6 right to a fair trial is stated in terms which are unqualified or absolute, so that there is little scope for undue deference which may abrogate its nature.[44]

In contrast, the doctrine of proportionality expresses a rather different conception of the relation between judges and decision-makers, since it leaves it to

---

[44] See the judgment of Laws LJ in *International Transport Roth GmbH v. Secretary of State for the Home Department* [2002] E.W.C.A. Civ 158, (dissenting judgment), para 84: 'It is thus a context which militates against deference'.

the courts to determine how the balance between the litigants' interests and the competing public policy claims ought to be struck.[45] In this sense, it considerably widens the scope for effective scrutiny of commercial decisions by way of judicial review. These ideas are developed in greater detail in the following chapter; however, the contention presently being advanced is that only by engaging in relatively intrusive proportionality review, the courts will ensure that their jurisdiction over commercial authorities is sufficiently full in terms of Article 6 of the European Convention.

It is also important to note, for the present purposes, that review on the basis of proportionality does not touch the merits of the decision which the Strasbourg Court has left to the executive to determine. It is argued below that although this approach substantially narrows the range of lawful responses a decision-maker might make in a commercial case, it is widely accepted that it does not by any means demand that the court adopts an essentially appellate jurisdiction which permits judges to substitute their own judgment for that of the initial authority. Thus, the principle of proportionality simply allows the judiciary to place further limits on the political considerations of government decisions without permitting a court to determine the substantive outcome itself.[46]

Secondly, the sufficiency of review can be judged taking account of procedural safeguards at the initial stages of the decision-making process. The ECtHR has held that where such safeguards are present, then a limited form of judicial review will be sufficient to ensure compatibility with Article 6(1). In particular, it is said that such an approach can reasonably be expected in certain areas of law, where decisions have already been taken by expert bodies in the course of a quasi-judicial procedure governed by many of the safeguards required by Article 6(1).[47] Thus, for example, a full review of the facts may not be required in cases where the original decision-maker has fairly made the findings of evidence crucial to the dispute. In such cases, given the specialized nature of the subject-matter, it is sufficient that the court has power to overturn the decision if it has taken account of irrelevant considerations or if the evidence relied on has not been capable of supporting a finding in fact, or if the inference drawn from the facts is irrational.[48]

The application of this doctrine in the domestic sphere was vividly emphasized in *Runa Begum*,[49] a case concerning the availability of social housing for a homeless person. The House of Lords held that the absence of a full fact-finding jurisdiction in the court did not disqualify it for purposes of Article 6(1), since the

---

[45] See the dicta of Lord Steyn in *R v. Secretary of State for the Home Department, ex p Daly* [2001] U.K.H.L. 26. See also Elliott, Mark, 'The Human Rights Act 1998 and the Standard of Substantive Review' [2002] 8(2) *Judicial Review*, 302–315.

[46] Loveland, Ian, 'Does Homelessness Decision Making Engage Article 6(1) of The European Convention on Human Rights' [2003] 2 *European Human Rights Law Review*, 198.

[47] *Bryan v. United Kingdom* (as above n. 34).

[48] Ibid; *Chapman v. United Kingdom*, Application no. 27238/95, Judgment 18 January 2001.

[49] *Runa Begum v. Tower Hamlets* [2003] 1 All E.R. 731. See the commentary of this case in Forsyth, Christopher, 'Procedural Justice in Administrative Proceedings and Article 6(1) of the European Convention' [2003] 62(2) *Cambridge Law Journal*, 244.

administration of such a welfare scheme relates to an area of law in which rules provide safeguards that the decision-making process will be fairly and reasonably conducted. Consequently, there was no warrant for applying in this context notions of 'anxious scrutiny' or an approach which is more rigorous than that ordinarily and properly adopted by a careful and competent judge in judicial review proceedings.

Nevertheless, it is worth noting that domestic jurisprudence in specialised and quasi-commercial areas of law has made clear that not every kind of 'safeguard' attendant on the procedure is compatible with Article 6. For example, it has been held that a process in the planning sphere which includes the right to make representations and to submit evidence, and persons may be heard orally at a meeting of the relevant committee may still be inconsistent with Article 6 if there is nothing like public inquiry, no opportunity for cross-examination and no formal procedure for evaluating the evidence and making findings of fact.[50] In the Administrative Court's view, such a procedure would considerably reduce the scope for effective scrutiny of the decision on an application for judicial review. It would make it more difficult, if not impossible, to determine whether the decision has been based on a misunderstanding or ignorance of an established and relevant fact, or has been based on a view of the facts that was not reasonably open on the evidence.[51] In such circumstances, where procedural safeguards present in the initial stages of the decision-making process are insufficient to deal with the evaluation of facts, Article 6's 'full jurisdiction' test could only be met if the courts subject the evidential basis of the decision to a more to a rigorous analysis.

This national approach to Article 6, although it derives from a number of cases concerned with planning, is likely to be recognized in similar areas of specialized decision-making such as commercial regulation. In particular, there may be substantial arguments on its application in relation to public utilities, where procedures operated by regulators are even less legalistic than in the context of a planning decision. For example, it is argued that requirements of Article 6 could prove a problem for regulatory bodies which do not appear to have any published procedure for dealing with their various powers to determine certain disputes between companies and customers.[52]

Furthermore, to reduce the scope of 'full jurisdiction' by having regard to procedural 'safeguards' may be incompatible with Article 6 in cases where the initial decision is made by an authority which lacks the requisite independence from the executive. As Malcolm Grant observes, if the initial hearing was, by definition, conducted by a decision-maker that has no independent status, it would be impossible to understand how that shortcoming can be corrected by an application to a judicial body which does not possess the power to substitute its own findings of

---

[50] *R (on the application of Kathro and others) v. Rhondda Cynon Taff County Borough Council,* [2001] E.W.H.C. (Admin) 527.
[51] Ibid.   [52] Graham, Cosmo, *Regulating Public Utilities,* (Oxford: Hart Publishing, 2000), 139.

fact.[53] In particular, if the threat to the authority's independence stems from the government's power over his determinations or its direct connection to one of the parties to the dispute,[54] then judicial review on a point of law offers no escape from the violation.[55] Indeed, the limitation on review of facts to which courts are subject as a result of the existence of initial 'safeguards' may take effect as automatic constraint on its ability to bring independence and impartiality to bear on complex issues; one of the effects of this restriction is to deny that independence from the executive is necessary in the determination of 'civil rights and obligations'.[56]

It is therefore submitted that, in order to compensate for the lack of independence on the part of the primary decision-maker, the courts should be able to make fresh findings of fact. Within such a model, the authority continues to act under government influence, albeit subject to a system of review which effectively 'cures' the defects in the first instance process. Specifically, this approach may prove a successful means of obtaining a thorough review of facts supporting commercial decisions adopted by government departments such as Trade and Industry, Transport, Food and Rural Affairs, the Treasury, and Health.

Thirdly, and more specifically, the curative principle requires—in commercial matters at least—that the judicial review court has the power to quash the decision of a disqualified adjudicator, and that the case may then be remitted for a fresh decision by a different person to whom the objection does not apply. Thus, procedures where the courts are unable to transfer responsibility for deciding to another body because no one else is empowered to act would be incompatible with Article 6(1). According to the Strasbourg jurisprudence, such jurisdiction would not be sufficiently full to provide the guarantees of a fair trial. This point

---

[53] Grant, Malcolm, 'Human Rights and Due Process in Planning' [2000] *Journal of Planning and Environmental Law*, 1220–1221.

[54] See the judgment of the Strasbourg's Court in *Tsfayo v. United Kingdom*, [2007] E.C.H.R. 656. The court held that the old Housing Benefit and Council Tax Benefit Review Board (HBRB), was not merely lacking in independence from the executive, but was directly connected to one of the parties to the dispute, since it included five councillors from the local authority which would be required to pay the benefit if awarded.
For the application of this doctrine by domestic courts, see *Bewry (R. on the application of) v. Norwich City Council* [2001] E.W.H.C. (Admin) 657 and *Bono, R. (on the application of) v. Harlow District Council* [2002] E.W.H.C. (Admin) 423.

[55] In *Tsfayo* (as above, n. 54) the court said that:

> this connection of the councillors to the party resisting entitlement to housing benefit might infect the independence of judgment in relation to the finding of primary fact in a manner which could not be adequately scrutinised or rectified by judicial review. The safeguards built into the HBRB procedure (paragraphs 23–24 above) were not adequate to overcome this fundamental lack of objective impartiality.

> Nevertheless, the court considered that the decision-making process in the present case was significantly different from those which require a measure of professional knowledge or specialist expertise to determine the issue. It seems therefore that its judgement is not entirely apposite to the market regulation context, in which issues are generally to be determined by technical bodies. See the commentary of this case in Forsyth, C.F. 'Administrative decision-makers and compliance with Article 6(1): The limits of the Curative Principle' [2007] 66(3) *Cambridge Law Journal*, 487–490.

[56] Grant, (as above n. 53).

is well illustrated by the dicta of the ECtHR in *Kingsley v. United Kingdom*.[57] The applicant, a managing director of London Clubs International, challenged the decision of the Gaming Board for Great Britain which revoked his certificates for working in the gaming industry. He argued that the Board was biased. The Court of Appeal, however, found against the claimant.[58] Morritt LJ held that the allegation of bias could not prevail because even if the members of the Board were personally interested, apparent or real, their decision could not be delegated to an independent panel, then the decision would still have to be made by them.[59]

It appears that this argument relates to the classical model of judicial deference which remarks that it is only for the competent authority to take a conclusive decision in his field. The main difference may be that conceptualizing the matter in terms of 'necessity' reveals an intelligible legislative policy, according to which Parliament has ordained that no replacement is possible. Therefore, to substitute for the biased official an impartial body would be, indeed, a recognized type of *ultra vires*.[60] Nevertheless, the Strasbourg Court held that such a restriction on judicial powers violated Article 6(1) of the European Convention because the courts lacked 'full jurisdiction'. In particular, it explained that such notion necessarily encompasses, in the event of the impugned order being quashed, the power to remit the case for a fresh decision by the same or a different body.[61]

Regarding this case, Forsyth concludes that time has thus been called on the principle of necessity and the impact on the law of bias will be considerable.[62] Indeed, the ability to remit the case for a new decision by an impartial body is now inherent in the European concept of 'full jurisdiction'. Necessity then will have to give way to natural justice. In practice, however, the only remedy available to

---

[57] Application No. 35605/97 [2001] L.L.R. 7. Confirmed by the Grand Chamber, 28 May 2002.

[58] Court of Appeal, 4 July 1996, (unreported, Lexis).

[59] Therefore, on the doctrine of necessity, which is accepted, there could have been no meaningful independent panel and the decision would stand because the decision has to be made by the Board and could not be delegated to the independent tribunal. It seems to me that there is no arguable point, susceptible on this part of the case, which would justify giving leave to appeal.

[60] Wade and Forsyth, (as above n. 1), 392–393.

[61] [I]t is generally inherent in the notion of judicial review that, if a ground of challenge is upheld, the reviewing court has power to quash the impugned decision, and that either the decision will then be taken by the review court, or the case will be remitted for a fresh decision by the same or a different body. Thus where, as here, complaint is made of a lack of impartiality on the part of the decision-making body, the concept of 'full jurisdiction' involves that the reviewing court not only considers the complaint but has the ability to quash the impugned decision and to remit the case for a new decision by an impartial body. In the present case the domestic courts were unable to remit the case for a first decision by the Board or by another independent tribunal. The Court thus finds that, in the particular circumstances of the case, the High Court and the Court of Appeal did not have 'full jurisdiction' within the meaning of the case-law on Article 6 when they reviewed the Panel's decision. Consequently, there has been a breach of Art 6(1) of the Convention.
See also the judgment in *Tsfayo* (as above, n. 54).

[62] Forsyth, 'Article 6(1) of The European Convention and The Curative Powers of Judicial Review', (as above n. 55), 452.

circumvent the necessity exception would be to seek a declaration of incompatibility of legislation under section 4 of the HRA. It is also said that the power under the Civil Procedure Rules 54.19(3) for the courts to quash a flawed decision and 'take the decision itself' where 'there is no purpose to be served by remitting the matter to the decision-maker', may sometime enable judicial review to cure a lack of impartiality in the original decision-maker.[63]

The foregoing is not, and does not purport to be, a comprehensive analysis of the notion of 'full jurisdiction' in the commercial context *vis-à-vis* what quality of review is sufficient to meet the requirements of Article 6(1). This is reflected in the fact that the approach to decisions deriving from regulatory schemes may vary widely depending on numerous factors concerning questions of policy, procedural safeguards, legal context, and factual accuracy. It does, however, point towards one principal conclusion: the case law has developed and evolved towards a liberal position in favour of effective judicial scrutiny of economic decisions that determine 'civil rights'. Specifically, the High Court is now expected to be alert to any indication that these orders have been made by insufficiently independent or impartial regulators and to conduct a careful analysis of legal and factual considerations that secures compliance with European standards of procedural fairness. Such a model of review naturally calls into question the legitimacy of the deferential approach in the present area of law.

4. The Principle of Proportionality in the European Commercial Context

The second and most fundamental European influence that contributes to the application of an enhanced approach to decisions in the context of market regulation relates to the doctrine of proportionality. This is a well-established feature of the law of a number of European countries,[64] the European Community Treaty,[65] and the jurisprudence of the ECJ[66] and the ECtHR, which, in its basic form, ordains that administrative decisions must not be more severe than is *required* to attain the desired objectives; thus, only the measures really needed for achieving public goals may be used.[67] In this sense, the present principle certainly entails a stricter judicial scrutiny of measures which limit interests worthy of legal protection as it allows the courts to discuss whether such a qualification is strictly 'proportionate' to the competing policy aim being pursued. It follows from this that

---

[63] Leigh, Ian, 'Bias, Necessity and the Convention' [2002] *Public Law*, 412.

[64] See a comprehensive discussion in Ellis, Evelyn (ed.), *The Principle of Proportionality in the Laws of Europe*, (Oxford: Hart Publishing, 1999) 1–181.

[65] Article 3b of the Treaty of Rome 1957 provides that 'any action by the Community shall not go beyond what is necessary to achieve the objectives of this Treaty'.

[66] See eg Craig, Paul, *Administrative Law*, 6th edn. (London: Sweet & Maxwell, 2008), 655–715.

[67] Consider the simple definition provided by Lord Diplock in *R v. Goldstein* [1983] 1 W.L.R. 151 at 155: In plain English proportionality means that 'you must not use a steam hammer to crack a nut, if a nutcracker would do'.

the content and impact of the review process is ultimately determined by reference to, *inter alia*, the suitability and necessity of the impugned order, and the absence of disproportionate adverse effects on the individual.

5. Conclusion

When a judicial approach to regulatory decisions as strict as that suggested in Chapter 2 is taken, it inevitably raises some uncertainties as to the relationship between the courts and the executive. In particular, it may be argued that the movement from a largely deferential conception of review towards a regime embracing high-intensity control entails a fundamental alteration in the constitutional distribution of powers which is inappropriate for the judges unilaterally to bring about. Consequently, although they clearly wished to afford effective protection to market players by increasing the intrusiveness of their supervisory jurisdiction, they would be ultimately precluded from doing so by a concern to avoid undue interference with the executive's allotted constitutional province.[68] The purpose of this chapter has been to avoid any such an objection by explaining the existence of explicit constitutional and legislative warrants for the proposed rights-based, hard-edge approach.

Indeed, although the impetus which underpins the desire to articulate this standard of review is seen to be inconsistent with traditional notions of administrative autonomy, it undoubtedly stems in substantial part from the incorporation, by virtue of the Acts of Parliament, of European law into the English legal system. This legislation ordains that a rigorous scrutiny of executive measures is constitutionally legitimate within the specific context of business regulation, given the normative weight which is properly attached to commercial rights in open and competitive markets. Thus, it is possible to argue that the relatively intrusive doctrine advanced in the present work can ultimately be based on an intelligible legislative policy which reduces agency autonomy in light of the importance of securing adherence to liberal values and effective protection of economic freedoms against arbitrary regulatory decisions.

This ethos most commonly finds expression in the judgments of the ECtHR and the ECJ, which read regulatory powers as being subject to the 'full jurisdiction' of the courts and the application of the principle of proportionality. It is precisely this second notion which supplies the fundamental tool for articulating a more careful inquiry into the regulator's decision. By embracing the idea of fair balance between private interests and public policy objectives, it necessarily requires the courts to subject the impugned order to a higher level of scrutiny that focuses on the substantive nature of the values which are in play. Thus, it becomes apparent that, under the proportionality-based test, interference with commercial interests

---

[68] See Elliott, (as above n. 1), 207–233; and his 'The Human Rights Act 1998 and The Standard of Substantive Review', (as above n. 45), 310–311.

has to be justified objectively, and the primary judgement as to whether sufficient justification has been furnished falls to be made by the court.

The principal purpose of the following chapter is to consider the application of the doctrine of proportionality in the domestic context, in an attempt to supply a conceptual basis for the exercise of a more rigorous judicial approach to regulatory decisions which satisfies the requirements of a balanced assessment of the competing interests involved.

5

The Influence of the European Principle of Proportionality on UK Regulatory Law

There is little doubt that English courts, in cases decided under European law, will apply proportionality-based reasoning. This follows ineluctably both from the enactment of the HRA 1998 and the incorporation of the doctrine into Community law.[1]

As regards the first institution, it is necessary to say that, although the Act itself does not explicitly oblige the judiciary to apply a proportionality test, it implicitly does so by requiring, in section 2, a court or tribunal determining a question which has arisen in connection with a Convention right to take into account the jurisprudence of the ECtHR, in which the principle of proportionality is freely applied. Thus, English judges appear to be highly constrained by that case law to strike down disproportionate decisions which infringe fundamental rights. In addition, as Craig points out, it should be difficult for UK courts to depart from that doctrine, if this entailed giving a less protective reading to the Convention than that accorded by the Strasbourg's Court, since this might lead the disappointed applicant to pursue the claim directly through that body.[2]

A similar explanation can be given in respect to proportionality in European Community Law. It is suggested that English judges should give effect to this principle even in the absence of any legislative enjoinder, since it occupies a pivotal role in the jurisprudence of the ECJ to which the courts must necessarily conform.[3] As with human rights cases, national courts are therefore under a duty to apply a proportionality-based approach to all executive decisions involving a Community law dimension, in order to afford protection to the individual at least equal to that afforded by the ECJ.

Thus there exists a broad consensus that the principle of proportionality provides a significant normative basis for a more stringent form of judicial review of administrative decisions in the United Kingdom. In light of this—and, in particular, given the way in which it appears to offer a solution to the shortcomings of the deferential rationale offered by the orthodox approach—it is now necessary

[1] See Wade, W. and Forsyth, C.F., *Administrative Law*, 10th edn., (Oxford: Oxford University Press, 2009) 305.
[2] Craig, Paul, 'The Human Rights Act, Article 6 and Procedural Rights' [2001] *Public Law*, 2003, 760.
[3] See e.g. *R v. Intervention Board for Agricultural Produce, ex p E.D. and F. Man (Sugar) Ltd*. [1986] 2 All E.R. 115. Details below. This body was abolished in 2001 and its functions were taken over by the Rural Payments Agency.

to consider the specific implications of this approach in the economic context. In particular, it appears that proportionality entails a relatively high level of judicial intervention in the market regulation process which, for a series of theoretical and pragmatic reasons, it succeeds where the orthodox approach fails by providing a more substantive and effective protection of individual rights in the commercial arena. This exactly mirrors the position in the present book which advocates a regime embracing high-intensity review on substantive grounds.

Accordingly, this chapter will move on to consider, in section 1, the impact of the doctrine on the standard of substantive review, before addressing, in section 2, its potential implications for the interpretation of rules. Section 3 then briefly considers the consequences that proportionality may have on the courts' jurisdiction over factual matters, and section 4 addresses the extent to which incorporation of such an approach is likely to affect the exercise of the court's remedial discretion.

1. Substantive Review

It is relatively clear that the application of the principle of proportionality at a national level has resulted in an incremental reduction in administrative autonomy to exercise discretionary powers, as the courts have shifted from the low-intensity mode of protection like *Wednesbury* to a high-intensity device which certainly narrows the range of decisions and choices open to the executive body. This significant change in public law adjudication arises particularly as a response to the incorporation of the European Convention by the HRA 1998.

Indeed, prior to the enactment of the Act in the United Kingdom, there was a general reluctance of the courts to move beyond the *Wednesbury* principle as the basis of substantive intervention in fundamental right cases.[4] The judges recognized that a more intrusive review would have important implications for the relationship between judicial and other branches of government—reducing dramatically the agencies' autonomy—to the extent that it was inappropriate for them to institute it unilaterally.[5] In practice, however, this approach was of limited utility because, as Elliott remarks, the administration's decision was 'immune from review provided that it remained within the range of responses open to a reasonable decision-maker'.[6]

---

[4] See the judgment of Lord Ackner in *Brind and others v. Secretary of State for the Home Department*, [1991] 1 A.C. 696 at 763:

> Unless and until Parliament incorporates the convention into domestic law, a course which it is well known has a strong body of support, there appears to me to be at present no basis upon which the proportionality doctrine applied by the European Court can be followed by the courts of this country.

[5] Ibid. He cites *R v. Director of Public Prosecutions, ex p Kebilene* [2000] 2 A.C. 326 at 355.

[6] Elliott, Mark, *The Constitutional Foundations of Judicial Review*, (Oxford: Hart Publishing, 2001), 214. Nevertheless, it must be noted that, in certain fields, there was a pre-incorporation willingness to apply a more intensive form of review based on the judicial recognition of the right of access to the courts, yet this approach was certainly not applied consistently. Ibid., 214 at 218.

The HRA thus came to fulfil perhaps its most important role in administrative law by ordaining that a relatively intrusive form of review is constitutionally legitimate.[7] Specifically, this more rigorous approach is identified with the principle of proportionality. There is a common limitation for Convention rights which says that a public authority could interfere legitimately with an individual's right in circumstances where such interference is necessary and proportionate. The judiciary therefore has to ensure that executive bodies maintain a proper balance between any adverse effects which their decisions may have on the rights, liberties or interests of persons and the purpose which they pursue. In this manner, the proportionality principle creates a zone of discretion which is narrower than that permitted by the rationality test.

This point was recently illustrated by the House of Lords in the *A v. Secretary of State for Home Department* case,[8] a challenge to the Home Secretary's determination that some individuals should be certified and detained under the Anti-terrorism, Crime and Security Act 2001. It is noteworthy that, although the court endorsed the traditional deferential attitude towards national security measures on the basis of institutional competence and political expertise,[9] the majority judgment observed that, irrespective of the quality of such executive assessments, the judges may legitimate intervene in this area to ensure that actions taken are proportionate. In particular, Lord Nicholls of Birkenhead noted that Parliament has charged the courts with the duty of intervening when the decision-maker has given insufficient weight to the fundamental rights and freedoms of persons adversely affected.[10] Similarly, Lord Hope of Craighead and Lord Rodger of Earlsferry held that the final responsibility for determining whether measures taken to interfere with the right to liberty recognized in the Human Rights Act 1998 exceed those strictly required by the exigencies of the situation lie with the courts.[11] Thus a new, rights-based approach was adopted, which necessarily entails a more searching judicial scrutiny, for it also requires the courts to look critically at the justifications advanced by the political branch, and the practical effect of its measures on individual human rights. In this sense, the proportionality doctrine inherent in the HRA system clearly reduces the margin of discretionary judgement accorded to administrative decisions in the particular context at stake.

At first glance, it may be reasonable to think that such heightened scrutiny could draw the courts into an 'intrusion on the merits' of the dispute which would take them beyond their legitimate role. However, it must be pointed out that this fear is unwarranted. The role of the judiciary under the HRA is not to abrogate the separation of powers by second guessing the correctness of the policy choices made

[7] Elliott, Mark, 'The Human Rights Act 1998 and the Standard of Substantive Review' [2001] 60(2) *Cambridge Law Journal*, 311.
[8] [2004] U.K.H.L. 56, [2005] 2 W.L.R. 87. See also the passage of Lord Steyn in *R. v. Secretary of State for the Home Department ex p Daly* [2001] U.K.H.L. 26, [2001] 2 A.C. 532, at pp 547–8.
[9] See, *inter alia*, *Council of Civil Service Unions v. Minister for the Civil Service* [1985] A.C. 374 at 410; *R v. Secretary of State for the Home Department, ex p Doody* [1994] 1 A.C. 531, 560, *per* Lord Mustill; and *Secretary of State for the Home Department v. Rehman* [2001] U.K.H.L. 47, [2003] 1 A.C. 153. See also Ewing, Keith, 'The Futility of the Human Rights Act' [2004] *Public Law*, 829.
[10] (As above, n. 8), at para 80.   [11] Ibid., at paras 114, 116, and 177.

by the administrator but simply to determine whether they are in accordance with the Convention. Accordingly, the principle of proportionality does not necessarily entail the substitution of the court's own decision on the merits for that of the decision-maker.[12] This contention is evident in the contribution of advocates of proportionality to the debate on substantive review.

Thus, according to Richard Edwards, 'the courts are no more entitled under the HRA to substitute their views for those of the minister than they were before the Act was passed'.[13] The point is also stressed in some of Elliott's work. He says that this modern approach places potentially severe limits on the discretion of the executive, but it does not destroy that discretion.[14] Consequently, although the proportionality doctrine significantly attenuates the administration's capacity to make policy choices, this does not wholly collapse the distinction between appeal and review.[15] Similarly, Craig observes that there is nothing in the test which entails substitution of judgement on the merits by the courts for that of the agency.[16] In this sense, proportionality simply constitutes a legitimate judicial choice *within* the hinterland between traditional understandings of review on the one hand and full review of the merits on the other. In Ian Loveland's words, it does not demand that the decision be located only at L on the substantive review continuum, but that the permissible range is bounded by E and T or F and S.[17] A final reason in this account is advanced by Robert Thomas,[18] who remarks that it is precisely because the proportionality test seeks to further the chosen policy goal, rather than to frustrate it, that it avoids substitution of opinion.

It follows from this that proportionality and *Wednesbury* are not competing concepts but complementary.[19] They just represent different sections of the substantive review spectrum, the range of options which is open to a court in contexts within which substantive review is required.[20] Thus, their application will simply depend on the precise level of review which a given case calls for in light of numerous factors such as the substantive values which are at stake, the specific balance between

[12] See *R v. Minister of Agriculture, Fisheries and Food, ex p First City Trading*, [1997] 1 C.M.L.R. 250. See also *R v. Director of Public Prosecutions, ex p Kebilene*, (as above n. 5); *R v. Secretary of State for the Home Department ex p Daly*, (as above n. 8, Lord Steyn); *R (Farrakhan) v. Secretary of State for the Home Department* [2002] E.W.C.A. Civ. 606, [2002] 3 W.L.R. 481.

[13] Edwards, Richard, 'Judicial Deference under the Human Rights Act' [2002] 65 *The Modern Law Review*, 872.

[14] Elliott, Mark, 'Scrutiny of Executive Decisions under the Human Rights Act 1998: Exactly How 'Anxious'? [2001] 6(3) *Judicial Review*, 172.

[15] Elliott, Mark, 'The Human Rights Act 1998 and the Standard of Substantive Review' (as above n. 7), 313.

[16] Craig, Paul, *Administrative Law*, 6th edn. (London: Sweet & Maxwell, 2008) 638; see also his 'Regulation and Judicial Review: Perspectives from UK and EC Law', in *Regulation and Deregulation*, Christopher McCrudden (ed.), (Oxford: Clarendon Press, 1999) 104, 143.

[17] Loveland, Ian, 'The Compatibility of the Land Use Planning System with Article 6 of the European Convention on Human Rights' [2001] *Journal of Planning and Environment Law*, 541.

[18] Thomas, Robert, *Legitimate Expectations and Proportionality in Administrative Law*, (Oxford: Hart Publishing, 2000) 85.

[19] Elliott, 'The Human Rights Act 1998 and the Standard of Substantive Review', (as above n. 7), 311–315.

[20] Ibid. See also the idea of 'rainbow of review' explained by Taggart, Michael in 'Proportionality, Deference, Wednesbury' [2008] 3 *New Zealand Law Review*, 451–454.

agency autonomy and judicial control and the subject matter of the action.[21] For this reason, it would be an overreaction to suppose that proportionality should simply replace *Wednesbury* in every context.[22]

This last assertion raises the question whether commercial regulation is a context where *Wednesbury* approach should be replaced by proportionality. And it is worth emphasizing that relevant secondary sources and regulatory principles strongly support this alternative.

According to Engelman, for example, the concept of *Wednesbury* unreasonableness in the field of commercial judicial review 'may have to take on the mantles of proportionality and necessity where a European Convention point is raised under the HRA 1998'.[23] Similarly, Craig suggests that the proportionality inquiry requires an agency to furnish reasons for its regulatory choice in a manner which is not very different from hard look review in USA.[24] This approach has a beneficial effect in that it facilitates judicial oversight, more especially when compared with the less rigorous inquiry required by the *Wednesbury* approach.[25] In sum, as Smyth graphically illustrates, on any view the application of proportionality should lighten the mood of managing directors by now inured to receiving legal advice to the effect that an adverse decision cannot be successfully challenged in court unless shown to be unreasonable in *Wednesbury* terms. The Act must, on account of this closer inquiry into public law decisions, offer the prospect of relief for the corporate sector in this context.[26]

These views are echoed by Cosmo Graham in the field of public utilities regulation. He says that greater opportunities for challenge will arise under the HRA, and that 'these developments will make the case for a reformulation of our substantive rules for judicial review even more pressing'.[27] Similarly, Peter Vass, Director of the Centre for the study of Regulated Industries at the University of Bath has stated that developments like the HRA, higher public expectations of accountability, and the machinery of government improvements will necessarily lead the courts to adopt a more precise cost-benefit test which focuses on reasonableness rather than on irrationality.[28]

---

[21] See the dicta of Lord Cooke in *R v. Secretary of State for the Home Department, ex p Daly*, (as above n. 8). See also Elliott, Mark, 'The HRA 1998 and the Standard of Substantive Review' [2002] 7(2) *Judicial Review*, 99; Cooke, Robin, 'The Road Ahead for the Common Law', ICLQ, 2004, 282 and 284–285.

[22] Elliott, 'The Human Rights Act 1998 and the Standard of Substantive Review' (as above n. 7), 335–336. See also 322.

[23] Engelman, *Commercial Judicial Review*, (London: Sweet & Maxwell, 2001) 33. See also Black, Muchlinski and Walker, *Commercial Regulation and Judicial Review*, (Oxford: Hart Publishing, 1998) 16.

[24] Wade and Forsyth describe the modern version of the 'hard look' doctrine as 'an intensive technique of review where the *court* investigates relevance of motives, adequacy of evidence and preparatory studies, and other such factors', (as above n. 1), 324.

[25] Craig, Paul, 'Regulation and Judicial Review: Perspectives from UK and EC Law', (as above n. 16), 143.

[26] Smyth, Michael, *Business and the Human Rights Act 1998*, (Bristol: Jordan Publishing, 2000), 207.

[27] Graham, Cosmo, *Regulating Public Utilities*, (Oxford: Hart Publishing, 2000), 75.

[28] See his statement to the Select Committee on Constitution of the House of Lords, 6th Report of Session 2003–2004, *The Regulatory State: Ensuring its accountability*, Volume II, Wednesday 29 January 2003, question 46.

The same is true in relation to financial services regulation. Page holds that,

whether the Human Rights Act 1998 will lead to a change in the approach of the courts remains of course to be seen, but it is widely expected to lead to the subjection of regulatory action to more intense scrutiny where Convention rights are in issue.[29]

Concerning self-regulation in the company context, it is similarly argued that the principle of proportionality will become increasingly significant 'as the courts extend their supervisory powers over the exercise of *de facto* economic power'.[30]

The other source which falls for consideration is the principles of Good Regulation set out by the British Government, namely, the Better Regulation Task Force (BRTF) in 1997.[31] Proportionality is one of those principles. Specifically, it requires market regulators to only intervene when necessary. Policy solutions and enforcement regimes should therefore be proportionate to the perceived problem or risk posed, and costs identified and minimized. All the alternative means for achieving regulatory outcomes must be considered so that the most effective and cheapest measure is adopted. For example, where possible, decision-makers should adopt an educational rather than a punitive approach to non-compliance, or avoid knee-jerk reactions in the wake of the financial scandals which often lead to disproportionate regulation being introduced.

These principles were later put on a statutory footing by the Legislative and Regulatory Reform Act 2006, which sets proportionality as an explicit boundary of regulatory power. Specifically, section 2(3) of Part 1 provides that regulatory activities should be (a) carried out in a way which is proportionate and consistent; and (b) targeted only at cases in which action is needed. In addition, section 3(2) provides that the effect of regulatory provisions must be proportionate to the policy objective, and strike a fair balance between the public interest and the interests of any person adversely affected by it. Similarly, section 3(3)(a) of the Communications Act 2003 provides that in performing its duties under section 3(1), Ofcom must have regard, in all cases to, (a) 'the principles under which regulatory activity should be…proportionate, consistent and targeted only at cases in which action is needed'.

In the light of the foregoing, it seems undoubted that the principle of proportionality must have a particular impact on substantive review in the commercial context. It becomes clear that the human rights review—that is, the supervisory regime which exists since the activation of the HRA—and recently enacted regulatory principles require the court, in its evaluation of the regulatory decision and its effect, to form a primary judgement on the extent to which the infringement of the

---

[29] Page, Alan, 'Regulating the Regulator—A Lawyer's Perspective on Accountability and Control' in *Regulating Financial Services and Markets in the 21st Century*, E. Ferran and C.A.E. Goodhart (eds.), (Oxford: Hart Publishing, 2001), 144.

[30] Cane, Peter, 'Self-Regulation and Judicial Review' [1987] 6 *Civil Justice Quarterly*, 344.

[31] See the leaflet published in 1997 and revised in 2000 by the BRTF. In 2006, this body was replaced by the Better Regulation Commission which operated until 2008 under the oversight of the Department for Business, Enterprise and Regulatory Reform. The regulatory reform agenda is now led by the Better Regulation Executive, which is part of the Department for Business, Innovation and Skills.

right is proportionate and justifiable to the market policy being pursued. The ultimate freedom which the regulator enjoys under the *Wednesbury* approach, in terms of the range of reasonable options which are open to it, is thus greatly diminished. In this sense, the proportionality-style review is seen to express a rather different mode of relation between judges and economic regulators, according to which the control of impugned orders is relatively intrusive, bearing in mind the substantive nature of the values which are in play.

So far as these values are concerned, it can be suggested that the legitimacy of the principle derives, precisely, from the fact it gives legal expression to the political consensus concerning the liberal conception of judicial review which is felt appropriate in the commercial context, as seen in section 2 of Chapter 4. In particular, it expresses a general commitment to articulate normative orientations, separated from the purposes of governance, which 'replace the formal Diceyan conception of the rule of law with a more substantive conception in order to uphold individual freedom against the state', as Thomas puts it.[32] This ascription of the principle of proportionality to the status of normative content on the limits of executive power within a free society can therefore be echoed in commercial judicial review by shifting the focus from the desired regulatory objective to the competing interests at stake. Detailed evaluation of the philosophical aspects of this development lies beyond the scope of this book. Rather, for the purposes of the argument developed below, concerning the application of the principle in the market regulation area, it is necessary simply to identify the specific economic rights and freedoms against which regulatory intervention can be measured by using proportionality.

For instance, Article 1 of the First Protocol on the peaceful enjoyment of private possessions might be usefully employed in litigation as an argument for resisting unlawful regulation.[33] Two main reasons arise. First, as Smyth points out, by extending its protection to 'every natural or legal person', the provision, unlike other substantive features of the European Convention, explicitly includes within its reach commercial enterprises as well as majority shareholders.[34] Secondly, the word 'possessions' (or 'biens' in the French text of the Convention) has been interpreted to extend far beyond the pure corporeal to include, for example, contractual rights, patents, assests,[35] shares,[36] and established economic interests, such

---

[32] Thomas, Robert, *Legitimate Expectations and Proportionality in Administrative Law*, (Oxford: Hart Publishing, 2000), 86. See also Laws, Sir John, 'Wednesbury' in *The Golden Metwand and the Crooked Cord*, C.F. Forsyth and I. Hare (eds.), (Oxford: Oxford University Press, 1998) 185, 201; Laws, Sir John 'The Constitution: Morals and Rights' [1996] *Public Law*, 622.

[33] Black, Muchlinski and Walker, (as above n. 23), 16–17. They also argue that:

the extent to which an analogous provision in the US Constitution has been used to challenge regulatory decisions on the basis that they are unconstitutional 'taking' of property has been significant. Therefore, 'any parallel development could have a substantial impact on the operation both of judicial review and of commercial regulation if it were to be accepted. [Ibid.]

[34] Smyth, (as above n. 26), 298.

[35] See *Gasus dosier- und födertechnik GmbH v. the Netherlands* [1995] E.C.H.R. 7.

[36] See, for example, *Olczak v. Poland*, decision 7 November 2002 Reports 2002-X; and *Sovtransavto Holding v. Ukraine* [2002] E.C.H.R. 626.

as licences and the goodwill of a business.[37] Even claims can be possessions in European Convention terms, in respect of which the applicant can argue that he has at least a 'legitimate expectation' of obtaining effective enjoyment of a property right.[38] Thus, by being directed towards a wider category of individuals and interests, the right to property appears to form a helpful starting point for domestic protection of substantive values within the market sphere. Its broader scope of protection, in other words, allows the judiciary to police the boundaries of regulatory power in respect of various types of rights *in personam* and *in rem*, thereby making them enforceable.

These points are illuminated by the judgment of the Strasbourg's Court in *Tre Traktörer Aktiebolag*.[39] The Swedish Government had contended that Article 1 of the Protocol (P1-1) was not applicable to cases concerning licences to serve alcoholic beverages, because they could not be considered to be a 'possession' within the scope of the right to property. However, the Strasbourg Court took the view that most of the economic interests connected with the running of a business were indeed 'possessions' for such purposes, and therefore subject to the protection of the Convention.[40] It is also worthy of note that the judgment of the court interpreted the relevant provision as purporting the application of the proportionality test in the field of licensing powers.[41]

Consequently, it can be argued that cases of this type in the context of the HRA 1998 should generally involve, first, a determination that a commercial interest

---

[37] See the judgment of the court in *Nicholds and others v. Security Industry Authority* [2006] E.W.H.C. 1792 paras. 74–82). See also Williams, Susanah, 'The Human Rights Act 1998—Caveat Business?' [2000] 21 *Business Law Review*, 193; and Bratza, Nicolas, 'The Implications of the Human Rights Act 1998 for Commercial Practice' [2000] 1 *European Human Rights Law Review*, 6.

[38] See, *inter alia*, *Pine Valley Developments Ltd. and others v. Ireland*, [1992] 14 E.H.H.R. 319; *Pressos Compania Naviera S.A. v. Belgium* judgment of 20 November 1995, Series A no. 332, p. 21, 31; *Stretch v. United Kingdom*, Application no. 44277/98, Judgment of 24 June 2003 (unpublished, Justis).

[39] *Tre Traktörer Aktiebolag v. Sweden* [1989] 15 E.H.H.R.

[40] The Court has already found that the maintenance of the licence was one of the principal conditions for the carrying on of the applicant company's business, and that its withdrawal had adverse effects on the goodwill and value of the restaurant. Such withdrawal thus constitutes, in the circumstances of the case, an interference with TTA's right to the 'peaceful enjoyment of [its] possessions'. There was accordingly no deprivation of property in terms of Article 1 of the Protocol (P1-1). The Court finds, however, that the withdrawal of TTA's licence to serve alcoholic beverages in Le Cardinal constituted a measure of control of the use of property, which falls to be considered under the second paragraph of Article 1 of the Protocol (P1-1).

[41] [T]he second paragraph of Article 1 of the Protocol (P1-1) has to be construed in the light of the general principle set out in the first sentence of this Article (P1-1). This sentence has been interpreted by the court as including the requirement that a measure of interference should strike a 'fair balance' between the demands of the general interest of the community and the requirements of the protection of the individual's fundamental rights (see, inter alia, the above-mentioned *Sporrong and Lönnroth* judgment, Series A no. 52, p. 26, para. 69). The search for this balance is reflected in the structure of Article 1 (P1-1) as a whole (ibid.) and hence also in the second paragraph. There must be a reasonable relationship of proportionality between the means employed and the aim sought to be realised (see the above-mentioned *James and others* judgment, p. 34, para. 50).

falls within the scope of Article 1 of the Protocol (P1-1) and, secondly, examination of whether the regulatory infringement of it occurs in pursuit of a legitimate aim, and that the magnitude of restriction is proportionate to the objective being pursued. Indeed, it is this mode of enquiry which epitomizes Convention's rights review at a European level, and—given that it has to be taken into account by English courts in exercising supervision over market authorities—it is also expected to play a fundamental role in ensuring that domestic judicial review centres on the objective justification of rights infractions rather than on the mere rationality doctrine, which subordinates the assessment of regulatory policies and actions to the decision-maker's primary judgement.

Such an approach, it may be argued, is evident in *Interbrew v. the Competition Commission and the Secretary of State for Trade and Industry*[42] which concerned the respondents' decision to divest the claimant of the entire United Kingdom beer business of Bass Brewers in order to avoid the adverse effects foreseen as a result of a duopoly. Interestingly, the Administrative Court detected no real dispute as to the need to apply the proportionality test to the competition context on the basis both of Article 1 of the Protocol[43] and EC regulation on the control of concentrations between undertakings.[44]

Nevertheless, as Elliott demonstrates, the severity of limits placed by the principle of proportionality is not rigid, but it must be a function of the context. He remarks that,

the greater the degree of polycentricity inherent in the decision before the court, the less appropriate it will be to apply a version of the proportionality doctrine so strict that it tends towards substitution.[45]

Conversely, he explains,

in situations where the court is well-placed to balance the issues which are in play, or in cases concerning absolute rights where no balancing process is appropriate, the discretionary area of judgement will diminish substantially.[46]

This further distinction therefore implies that it is simply not sufficient to say to judges that, when exercising commercial judicial review, they must have recourse to the proportionality approach. This is only the starting point. The review will need to be focused on specific references related to the market regulation context. Perhaps, at the moment, the most compelling illustration of this specific standard of review is to be found in the instructive jurisprudence of the ECJ.

---

[42] [2001] E.W.H.C. (Admin) 367 (23rd May, 2001).

[43] See also the judgment of Kay LJ in *R (Clays Lanes Housing Co-operative) v. Housing Corporation* [2005] 1 W.L.R. 2229, concerning the regulation of registered social landlords. He concluded that the appropriate test of proportionality under Article 1 of the First Protocol requires 'a balancing exercise and a decision which is justified on the basis of a compelling case in the public interest and as being reasonably necessary but not obligatorily the least intrusive of Convention rights', at para. 25.

[44] Article 9(8) of the EEC Merger Regulation (Council Regulation (EEC) 4064/89) provides that 'the Member States concerned may take only measures *strictly necessary* to safeguard or restore effective competition on the market concerned'. Emphasis added.

[45] Elliott, 'Scrutiny of Executive Decisions under the Human Rights Act 1998: Exactly How "Anxious"?' (as above n.14), 173.   [46] Ibid.

1.1 European Court of Justice

In the commercial context, the principle of proportionality has been mainly applied in cases concerning measures designed to pursue Community objectives and penalties for breaching those decisions. The standard applied involves a structured weighing of interests to see whether action is proportionate or justified. Specifically, the ECJ appears to consider the interest of the applicant which is adversely affected on the one hand, as against the interest of the regulator in adopting the challenged decision, on the other. For example, it was held in *Germany v. Council*[47] that the common organization of the market could justify, in the context of a tariff quota regulation, restricting the exercise of the right to property and the freedom to pursue a trade or profession, provided that those restrictions in fact 'do not constitute a disproportionate and intolerable interference, impairing the very substance of the rights guaranteed'. The conclusion therefore has to be that the Court is able to strike down executive measures which affect private interests to an extent that goes beyond what is strictly required by the exigencies of the situation. In other words, as Gráinne de Búrca points out,

> if the right or interest of the complainant is seriously affected, or if the policy is enforced by a severe penalty or exceptionally harsh mean, then the Court is likely to question the necessity and proportionality of the measure and to find against it.[48]

In this sense, it might be useful to identify four particular trends in the Luxembourg jurisprudence.

First, the ECJ has ruled that severe commercial restrictions will be rigorously examined and deemed disproportionate if there were alternative and equally effective means of achieving those aims which interfere less with the individual's interest. In this sense, it seems to have relied on the notion of necessity or Pareto-optimality[49] in order to justify its findings of abuse of power: the law must insist that any failure or refusal to adopt the alternative decision which attains public interest objectives without unduly reducing the level of realization of private interests represents the displacement of reason by arbitrariness.

Thus, for example, in *Commission of the European Communities v. Federal Republic of Germany*,[50] the German government had prohibited the marketing of beers which, although lawfully manufactured and marketed in another Member State, contained any kind of additive. The ECJ said, however, that, in view of the principle of proportionality, such rule went beyond what was necessary in order to secure the protection of public health, since that possibility may have been ensured simply by the compulsory affixing of suitable labels giving the nature of the product sold. The court also declared the total ban on additives disproportionate on

---

[47] Case C-280/93, [1994] E.C.R. I-4973, para. 78.

[48] De Búrca, Gráinne, 'The Principle of Proportionality and its Application in EC Law', [1993] 13 *Yearbook of European Law*, 146.

[49] See Rivers, Julian, 'Proportionality and Variable Intensity of Review' [2006] 65(1) *Cambridge Law Journal*, 198.

[50] Case 178/84 [1987] E.C.R. 1227.

the ground that it was not properly justified under the findings of international scientific research.

Interestingly, this criterion concerning the effective addressing of legitimate goals by the imposition of the least restrictive burden has also been used in the field of price control, which is considered to be a paradigm of governmental intervention in the market. Thus, in *National Dried Fruit Trade Association*,[51] the ECJ invalidated a Community regulation introducing a countervailing charge at a fixed rate to enforce the minimum import price of dried grapes on the ground that it was levied at a higher level than is necessary to achieve its objective. In particular, it was observed that the exclusive aim of such measure was to equal the full minimum price equivalent in the case of shortfall so as to ensure community preference in the market for dried grapes produced by Member States; therefore, its aim was not to inflict an economic penalty on the trader who had imported them below the minimum price. On this view, the introduction of a single, fixed-rate countervailing charge, which is wholly unconnected to the difference between the import price and the minimum price, certainly amounted to an economic penalty which was disproportionate to the public aim in question. Indeed, in the Court's opinion, such an aim could have been equally achieved by just setting a rate equal to the difference between the import price and the minimum price.

A very similar approach was adopted by the court in *Werner Faus*[52] and *Winsche I*,[53] where it held a Commission Regulation levying the additional amount on imports of preserved mushrooms to be disproportionate on the ground that that quantity was fixed at a flat rate solely on the basis of the cost of one type of preserved mushrooms produced in the Community. In other words, the protective measure was being generally applied to the relevant products irrespective of their origin, quality, grade, or circumstances in which they were imported, thereby leading to a much greater burden being imposed on importers of mushrooms of a grade lower than that used for the calculation of the amount. Again, the court stated that the aim of the regulation was not to inflict an economic penalty on a trader who has imported in excess of the quantities allowed but to prevent disturbances on the Community market. Accordingly, a less restrictive alternative in this case would have been to fix additional amounts of different levels in the light of factors peculiar to the product.

In *Mignini*,[54] the court held that the obligation imposed by Community regulations on manufacturers of animal feeding stuffs based on soya beans to have storage facilities for those beans within the precincts of their production establishments, in order to properly control European aid for soya, was contrary to the principle

---

[51] *The Queen v. Customs and Excise, ex p National Dried Fruit Trade Association*, Case 77/86 [1988] E.C.R. 757.

[52] *Hauptzollant Hamburg-Jonas v. Werner Faust OHG*, Case C-24/90 [1991] E.C.R. I-4905.

[53] *Hauptzollant Hamburg-Jones v.Wünsche Handelsgesellschaft mbH and Co.*, Case C-25/90 KG, [1991] E.C.R. I-4939. See also *Hüpeden v. Hauptzollant Hamburg-Jonas*, Case C-295/94 [1996] E.C.R. I-3375, and *Pietsch v. Hauptzollant Hamburg-Waltershof*, Case C-296/94 [1996] E.C.R. I-3409.

[54] *Mignini SpA v Azienda di Stato per gli interventi sul mercato agricolo (AIMA)*, Case C-256/90 [1992] E.C.R. I-02651.

of proportionality. In particular, it declared that the objective of preventing fraud in that case could have been equally achieved by methods less restrictive than that adopted, such as the approval of external storage facilities, which makes it possible to avoid their construction thereby reducing costs for undertakings.

Support for this doctrine can also be found in *Bordesa*[55] and *Sanz de Lera*,[56] where the court reached the conclusion that a prior administrative authorization scheme for the export of coins, banknotes or bearer cheques of a certain value was disproportionate to the attainment of the legitimate object of the law, namely, to facilitate effective supervision of economic transactions in order to prevent criminal offences. It was argued that the same goal might have been attained by less restrictive measures than rendering the free movement of capital conditional upon executive consent, such as an adequate system of declarations indicating the nature of the planned operation and the identity of the declarant. Thus competent authorities would be allowed to proceed with a rapid examination of the declaration and, only if necessary, to carry out in due time the necessary investigations and to impose the requisite penalties.

It is worth noting that this particular approach, in turn, has even placed Parliamentary power under growing strain, given the common perception that legislative measures also attract the duty to adopt the least restrictive alternative to achieve the Member State's objective. Thus, in *Rau v. de Smedt*,[57] the court ruled disproportionate a Belgian law prohibiting the marketing of margarine where its external packaging does not have a particular shape, on the ground that the public objective in view—the protection of the consumer in order to prevent confusion between butter and margarine—may in fact have been attained just as effectively by other measures, for example, by rules on labelling, which hinder the free movement of goods to a lesser degree.

Similarly, in *Commission of the European Communities v. United Kingdom of Great Britain and Northern Ireland*,[58] the court declared that UK legislative provisions which introduced a licence system enabling consignments of imported milk to be identified, traced, and then repacked on premises within the country were disproportionate in relation to the objective pursued, namely the protection of human and animal health against foot-and-mouth disease arising from insufficient treatment of that product, on the ground that the same result may have been achieved by means of less restrictive measures. In the court's opinion, technical information on milk processing could have been obtained without creating further legal uncertainty for traders and without unduly imposing administrative or financial burdens, for example, by means of simple declarations signed by the importers, accompanied if necessary by the appropriate certificates. In addition, it held that the respondent could have ensured that the imported milk was free of any bacterial or virus infection simply by laying down certain requirements as to its

[55] *Criminal proceedings against Aldo Bordessa and Vicente Marí Mellado and Concepción Barbero Maestre*, Joined cases C-358/93 and C-416/93 [1995] E.C.R. I-00361.
[56] *Criminal proceedings against Lucas Emilio Sanz de Lera, Raimundo Díaz Jiménez and Figen Kapanoglu*, Joined cases C-163/94, C-165/94 and C-250/94, [1995] E.C.R. I-04821.
[57] Case 261/81 [1982] E.C.R. 3961.   [58] Case 124/81 [1983] E.C.R. 00203.

production cycle, rather than ordering it to be treated again within the UK, which amounted, owing to its economic effects, to the equivalent of a total and therefore unlawful prohibition on imports.

More recently, it is possible to see the same approach at work in *Commission v. Italy*.[59] The court decided that less restrictive measures exist for the prevention of such residual risks as misleading consumers of food products for sportsmen, such as,

notification of the marketing of the product in question to the competent authority by the manufacturer or distributor of that product together with transmission of a model of the labelling and the obligation requiring the manufacturer or the distributor of that product to furnish, if necessary, evidence of the accuracy of the factual data appearing on the label.[60]

In *Canal*,[61] the ECJ held that the legislative requirement imposed by Spanish law on operators of conditional-access services for digital television to register and indicate the characteristics of the technical equipment they use could be regarded as neither necessary nor proportionate to achieve the public aim pursued, namely informing and protecting consumers of those services, if it essentially duplicated controls which had already been carried out in the context of other procedures, either in the same state or in another Member State. In addition, it held that a prior administrative authorization scheme could be found to be disproportionate if the exercise of subsequent—and therefore less decisive—controls would have been equally effective to achieve the aim pursued; and if, on account of the duration and the costs to which the authorization system gives rise, it is such as to deter the operators concerned from pursuing their business plan.

One further example may be given of the areas in which the European Court of Justice is likely to apply the test of the least restrictive measure. Article 9(8) of the Council Regulation (EC) No 139/2004 of 20 January 2004 on the control of concentrations between undertakings[62] provides that the national bodies concerned may take 'only the measures strictly necessary to safeguard or restore effective competition on the market concerned'. It is relatively plain that this provision will fetter the court's freedom to decide the legality of those measures in order to ensure that competition authorities act in a proportionate manner.

Secondly, the ECJ has made clear that limitations in the commercial field cannot infringe the essence of property rights at stake and in no case may amount to an absolute prohibition of a legitimate business or a deprivation of the individual's right to carry on particular economic activities. For instance, it has been held that restrictive measures on the new planting of vines should in fact correspond to objectives of general interest pursued by the community and that, with regard

---

[59] Case 270/02, [2004], E.C.R. I-1559.   [60] Ibid. at para. 25.
[61] *Canal Satélite Digital SL v. Adminstración General del Estado, and Distribuidora de Televisión Digital SA (DTS)*, Case C-390/99 [2002] E.C.R. I-00607.
[62] (Official Journal No. L24, 29.01.04, p.1–22). It replaces Council Regulation (E.E.C.) No. 4064/89 on the control of concentrations between undertakings, as amended by Council Regulation (E.C.) No. 1310/97.

to the aim pursued, they should not 'constitute a disproportionate and intolerable interference with the rights of the owner, impinging upon the very substance of the right to property'.[63]

Thirdly, it has been held that the doctrine of proportionality can be applied even to measures which are justified by the regulator on grounds of national security, where much of the information and time available may be confidential and decisions might have to be made at short notice, or possibly involve complex judgements.[64] In other words, the nature of the State's interest of itself does not necessarily result in the court showing a considerable degree of deference to the State's decision. Even under these circumstances, the court is able to ensure that the restrictive measure is no more than is 'necessary' to achieve a legitimate aim.[65]

In the *Campus Oil* case,[66] for example, the court was asked to consider sensitive claims relating to national security in the context of restrictions on the free movement of goods. The Irish Minister for Industry and Energy made an order which required any person who imports petroleum products to purchase a certain proportion of their requirements of petroleum products from the Irish National Petroleum Corporation (INPC) at a price to be determined by the minister taking into account the costs incurred by the INPC. The applicant submitted that this order was contrary to Community law and in particular to the prohibition, as between Member States, of quantitative restrictions on imports and all measures having equivalent effect, laid down in Article 30 of the Treaty. The Irish Government contended that the measure was justified under Article 36 of the EEC Treaty, on grounds of public policy and public security since it was intended to guarantee the operation of Ireland's only refinery, which is necessary to maintain the country's supplies of petroleum products. The court accepted that the interest of the Irish State in ensuring the domestic supply of petroleum products can be protected by imposing specific purchasing obligation on importers. However, it imposed certain conditions to ensure that the purchasing requirement was not disproportionate in relation to the 'legitimate aim' of ensuring the survival of the domestic oil refinery. Thus, the court declared that the purchase would not exceed the minimum supply necessary to keep the refinery's production capacity available.[67]

---

[63] *Hauer v. Land Rheinland-Pfalz*, Case 44/79 [1979] E.C.R. 3727.
[64] De Búrca, (as above n. 48), 132–133.   [65] Ibid., 134.
[66] Case 72/83 [1984] E.C.R. 2727.

[67] [A]s regards, in the next place, the quantities of petroleum products which may, as the case may be, be covered by such a system of purchasing obligations, it should be stressed that they must in no case exceed the minimum supply requirements of the state concerned without which its public security, as defined above, and in particular the operation of its essential public services and the survival of its inhabitants, would be affected...Furthermore, the quantities of petroleum products whose marketing can be ensured under such a system must not exceed the quantities which are necessary, so far as production is concerned, on the one hand, for technical reasons in order that the refinery may operate currently at a sufficient level of its production capacity to ensure that its plant will be available in the event of a crisis and, on the other hand, in order that it may continue to refine at all times the crude oil covered by the long-term contracts which the state concerned has entered into so

Fourthly, as regards the agricultural sphere, it is necessary to note that, although the Luxembourg Court has reviewed regulatory decisions in a less intrusive way,[68] this attitude only constitutes an exception to the general application of the principle of proportionality in the commercial context. Craig points out that the phenomenon which occurs in the agricultural market may not be necessarily indicative of what the approach will be applied in other cases. In fact, there are other areas where the ECJ is willing to intervene with a more searching form of inquiry, particularly in the financial and economic field, where the administrative authorities posses a narrower discretionary power or one which is more clearly circumscribed.[69] The ECJ has thus recognized proportionality as a high level principle of European law, which must indeed be applied to the exercise of regulatory power over market activities.[70]

This exceptional character of the judicial approach in the agricultural context has also been confirmed in the domestic context by the clear judgment of Laws J in *First City Trading*.[71] The case concerned measures adopted by the British government to restore the operation of the beef market, after the blockage produced as a

that it may be assured of regular supplies . . . The proportion of the total needs of importers of petroleum products that may be made subject to a purchasing obligation must not, therefore, exceed the proportion which the quantities set out above represent of the current total consumption of petroleum products in the member state concerned.

[68] One of the earliest cases in this field is *Hans-Markus Stölting v. Hauptzollamt Hamburg-Jonas*, Case 138/78 [1979] E.C.R. 00713, concerning the imposition of a co-responsibility levy to stabilize a market characterized by structural surpluses. Here the court stated:

if a measure is patently unsuited to the objective which the competent institution seeks to pursue this may affect its legality, but on the other hand the council must be recognized as having a discretionary power in this area which corresponds to the political responsibilities which articles 40 and 43 impose upon it.

The court repeated this statement in a very similar case, *Hermann Schräder HS Kraftfutter GmbH & Co. KG v. Hauptzollamt Gronau*, Case 265/87 [1989] E.C.R. 2237, and complemented it by saying that,

Consequently, the legality of a measure adopted in that sphere can be affected only if the measure is manifestly inappropriate having regard to the objective which the competent institution intends to pursue.

See also *Bozzetti v. Invernizzi*, Case 179/84 [1985] E.C.R. 2301; *Jippes and others* (Agriculture) [2001] E.U.E.C.J. C-189/01; and *Spain v. Council (Agriculture)* C-310/04 [2006] E.U.E.C.J.

[69] Craig, (as above n. 16), 634–635.

[70] See, for example, the decision in *Hermann Schräder HS Kraftfutter GmbH & Co. KG v. Hauptzollamt Gronau*, (as above n. 68):

The Court has consistently held that the principle of proportionality is one of the general principles of Community law. By virtue of that principle, measures imposing financial charges on economic operators are lawful provided that the measures are appropriate and necessary for meeting the objectives legitimately pursued by the legislation in question. Of course, when there is a choice between several appropriate measures, the least onerous measure must be used and the charges imposed must not be disproportionate to the aims pursued. However . . . (exception for agriculture).

See also *R v. Minister of Agriculture, Fisheries and Food and Secretary of State for Health, ex p Fedesa and others*, Case 331/88 [1990] E.C.R. I-04023. The functions of the Ministry of Agriculture, Fisheries and Food have been taken over by the Department for Environment, Food and Rural Affairs.

[71] As above n. 12.

result of cattle affected by bovine spongiform encephalopathy (BSE). The measures favoured only one kind of exporters.[72] It is this exclusion of others which gave rise to the applicant's complaints of unjustifiable discrimination against them. In his contention, the respondent referred to *Roquette Freres*,[73] an agricultural policy case, to demonstrate that the court must take a less rigorous approach in reviewing economic decisions. However, the court held that this kind of approach, close to the *Wednesbury* test, was not applicable in all the cases. Commenting on the cited case, Laws J refused to apply such less rigorous scrutiny,[74] and instead opted for a solution based on the European principle of proportionality. Accordingly, he stressed a clear distinction between *Wednesbury* and this more intensive form of review. Importantly, it was confirmed that, in spite of the imperative of moving beyond the conventional approach to market regulation, there is nothing in the concept of proportionality which entails substitution of judgement on the merits by the court for that of the agency.[75]

Furthermore, it must be emphasised that in some cases in the agricultural sphere but involving forfeiture of deposits, when contractual or other undertakings are not fulfilled, the ECJ has been ready to declare such penalties disproportionate in spite of the greater discretion conferred on the Community institutions.[76] In the case

---

[72] Only those who also operate under licence a slaughterhouse or cutting plant.

[73] Case 138/79 [1980] E.R.C.R., 3333.

When the implementation by the Council of the agricultural policy involves the need to evaluate a complex economic situation, the discretion which it has does not apply exclusively to the nature and scope of the measures to be taken but also to some extent to the finding of the basic facts in as much as, in particular, it is open to the Council to rely on general findings. In reviewing the exercise of such a power the Court must confine itself to examining whether it contains a manifest error or constitutes a misuse of power or whether the authority in question did not clearly exceed the bounds of its discretion.

[74] Unsurprisingly Mr Parker [for the respondent] fixes on this passage to found a submission that in relation to the principle of equal treatment the Court of Justice accords the decision-maker – in the language of Strasbourg – a 'margin of appreciation', at least where the subject-matter is in economic terms complex and a decision had to be reached speedily. His argument, I think, amounted to a claim that in such circumstances (which, he would say, plainly apply to this case) the Court's jurisprudence in reality applies a test closely akin to *Wednesbury*. But *Wednesbury* is not the test.

[75] The difference between *Wednesbury* and European review is that in the former case the legal limits lie further back. I think there are two factors. First, the limits of domestic review are not, as the law presently stands, constrained by the doctrine of proportionality. Secondly, at least as regards a requirement such as that of objective justification in an equal treatment case, the European rule requires the decision-maker to provide a fully reasoned case. It is not enough merely to set out the problem, and assert that within his discretion the Minister chose this or that solution, constrained only by the requirement that his decision must have been one which a reasonable Minister might make. Rather the court will test the solution arrived at, and pass it only if substantial factual considerations are put forward in its justification: considerations which are relevant, reasonable, and proportionate to the aim in view. But as I understand the jurisprudence the court is not concerned to agree or disagree with the decision; that would be to travel beyond the boundaries of proper judicial authority and usurp the primary decision-maker's function. Thus *Wednesbury* and European review are different models—one looser, one tighter—of the same juridical concept, which is the imposition of compulsory standards on decision-makers so as to secure the repudiation of arbitrary power.

[76] De Búrca, (as above n. 48), 120.

of *SA Buitoni v. Fonds d'orientation et de regularisation des marches agricoles*,[77] for example, the Court was asked for a ruling on the validity of article 3 of Commission Regulation No 499/76 providing that where proof of importation of agricultural products has not been furnished within the six months following the expiry of the import licence, the security shall be forfeit save in case of *force majeure*. The applicant, which had imported a quantity of tomato concentrates within the period of validity of the licence, was refused release of the security on the ground that it had failed to submit proof of such fact within the period laid down in article 3. The company claimed that it is contrary to the principle of proportionality to apply the same penalty for failure to fulfil the obligation to import, which the security is intended to guarantee, and for mere delay in submission of the proofs of fulfilment of the obligation, which has been discharged correctly and within the prescribed period. The Court ruled that the fixed penalty, which was applied to an infringement which was considerably less serious than that of failure to fulfil the obligation which the security itself was intended to guarantee, must be held to be excessively severe in relation to the objectives of administrative efficiency in the context of the system of import and export licences.[78]

In the *Atalanta* case,[79] the ECJ applied the proportionality test to see whether the penalty imposed was justified in relation to the degree of failure to fulfil contractual obligations. The case concerned article 5(2) of Commission Regulation No. 1889/76, which provided that the deposit given for the fulfilment of obligations concerning the storage of pigmeat shall be wholly forfeit if these are not fulfilled or are only partially fulfilled. The Court observed that the absolute nature of the regulation was contrary to the principle of proportionality in that it did not permit the penalty for which it provided to be made commensurate with the degree of failure to implement the contractual obligations or with the seriousness of the breach of those obligations.

In the more recent case of *Man (Sugar)*,[80] the applicant, a British firm of sugar traders and brokers, was required to apply by a fixed date and time and to give a security deposit to the Intervention Board for Agricultural Produce when seeking a licence to export sugar to non-member countries. The deposit was to guarantee that the export would be done during the period of validity of the licence. The telex messages applying for the licences were sent with a slight delay. As a result of the delay the Board declared the entire deposit forfeit. The company thereupon

---

[77] Case 122/78 [1979] E.C.R. 667.

[78] (21) [A]lthough, in view of the inconvenience caused by the belated production of proofs, the commission was entitled to introduce the period laid down in article 3 of regulation no 499/76 for the furnishing of proof, it should have sanctioned failure to comply with that period only with a penalty considerably less onerous for those concerned than that prescribing the loss of the whole of the security and more closely allied to the practical effects of such an omission. (22) Indeed, even if administrative efficiency requires that files should not remain open indefinitely, it must, however, be noted that failure to comply with such a period will be exceptional in nature in that it is contrary to the very interests of the exporter or importer concerned, who will normally seek release of his security as soon as possible.

[79] *Atalanta v. Produktschap Loor Vee En Vlees*, Case 240/78 [1979] E.C.R. 2137.

[80] *R v. Intervention Board, ex p. Man (Sugar) Ltd.*, Case 181/84 [1985] E.C.R. 2889.

brought an action for repayment of the security, contending that its forfeiture was 'grossly unfair' and contrary to the principle of proportionality. The Court found for the applicant and held the penalty to be unduly severe relative to the gravity of the offence.[81]

The severity of the impact upon the applicant has also been taken into account in some agricultural cases not involving forfeiture but conditions attached to licences and the level of charges imposed by Community institutions. In the earlier case of *Bela-Muhle Josef Bergman v. Grows-Farm*,[82] for example, the applicant sought to quash a council regulation (EEC) No 563/76 which forced producers of animal feed to use skimmed-milk powder in their product, in order to curb the tendency towards over-production of milk. The purchase price for skimmed-milk powder was therefore fixed at a level three times higher than that of soya, the substance which it replaced. Here the Court built the notion of proportionality into specific rules which prohibits unjustified discrimination against economic agents and the enforcement of obligations which are unnecessary to achieve the aim pursued.[83]

These last cases thus demonstrate that the Luxembourg Court has been ready to intervene in agricultural cases, on the ground of proportionality, to avoid excessively severe effects in imposing penalties or heavy burdens on individuals. Thus, if the adverse impact upon the applicant's interest is particularly severe, then the Court will examine whether there are alternative less restrictive means to achieve the aim of the Community. The deferential test will not therefore automatically be applied in the sphere of agriculture, but will depend on the rigorousness of effect on the individual's rights and interests when weighed against the importance of the Community's interest.[84] Proportionality has thus made its way even into an area in which commercial regulators have specifically been given broad discretionary powers to control a varied and complex market.[85]

All this suggests that the premise behind the ECJ's case law is, therefore, that the principle of proportionality plays a fundamental role in substantive review of regulatory decisions in the business field. This doctrine allows the Court to infuse European administrative law with the sort of high-intensity, rigorous scrutiny of discretionary powers which narrows the range of feasible alternatives to

---

[81] [T]he entire security, in the event of an infringement significantly less serious than the failure to fulfil the primary obligation (to make the transaction within the period of validity of the licence), which the security itself is intended to guarantee, must be considered too drastic a penalty in relation to the export licence's function of ensuring the sound management of the market in question.

[82] Case 114/76 [1977] E.C.R. 1211.

[83] The obligation to purchase at such a disproportionate price constituted a discriminatory distribution of the burden of costs between the various agricultural sectors. Nor, moreover, was such an obligation necessary in order to attain the objective in view, namely, the disposal of stocks of skimmed-milk powder. It could not therefore be justified for the purposes of attaining the objectives of the common agricultural policy. In consequence, the answer must be that council regulation (EEC) no 563/76 of 15 March 1976 is null and void.

[84] De Búrca, (as above n. 48), 123.   [85] Ibid., 121.

a proposed regulatory action in support not only of the free movement of goods within EU but also, more broadly, the individual's freedom to perform legitimate economic activities. In particular, the importance which the present approach attaches to the interests of the regulatee finds expression in the requirement that market policies must be enforced by the less onerous option in terms of financial costs and interference with the right to property, even in more sensitive situations relating to national security and agricultural matters. It is submitted that these specific terms of reference used by the Luxembourg Court may serve as a useful guidance to design a methodology and reasoning for testing executive measures in the domestic context, in which proportionality is becoming especially prominent.

1.2 Departure from previous policies and legitimate expectations

Support for the notion that proportionality constitutes an adequate approach for the substantive review of market regulation can also be found in relation to the freedom of executive bodies to departure from their prior policies. The considerable zone of immunity that the *Wednesbury* test erects to protect policy reformulation from judicial scrutiny appears to be inconsistent with the principle of legal certainty, which embraces, in this context, the fundamental idea that those who have relied on a particular course of action may have a valid claim for some protection when it alters. Specifically, by requiring the individual to show that the policymaker's decision to act in an inconsistent manner was so unreasonable that no reasonable body would have done it, makes it almost impossible for him to succeed in protecting his legitimate expectations.

It follows that, in order to build a satisfactory approach for achieving consistency in this context, the alteration of existing schemes and guiding principles should normally be subjected to a more stringent judicial scrutiny which requires reasons to justify this in light of the interests of individuals who detrimentally relied on their implementation over time. The approach under this more intrusive, proportional standard of review is, in other words, grounded in the need to strike a fair and independent balance between the interests of the regulator and fairness to the individual. The idea of administrative autonomy to formulate regulatory programs thus becomes only *one* of the prominent factors that courts would examine in determining the validity of departing from current practices. Certainly, this mode of relation between judges and regulators is a good deal more satisfactory than that postulated by the *Wednesbury* rationale, in which the accommodation of competing interests concerning policy changes is primarily for the executive agency.

An early example of this doctrine can be seen in *R v. Liverpool Corporation, ex p Liverpool Taxi Fleet Operators Association*.[86] In that case, the taxi cab owners' association of Liverpool sought judicial review of the decision of the Liverpool

---

[86] [1972] 2 All E.R. 589.

Corporation which resolved to increase the number of licences for taxi cabs in the city. The applicants challenged this as being in breach, *inter alia*, of the undertaking given by the authority that no additional licences would be issued until proposed legislation to control private hire cars had come into force. In the Court of Appeal, Lord Denning remarked that a decision-maker cannot give an undertaking and break it as he pleases, but he has to be sufficiently satisfied that the public interest requires departing from the undertaking.[87]

This principle was also well considered by Sedley J in *R v. Ministry of Agriculture, Fisheries and Food, ex p Hamble Fisheries*.[88] Briefly, what had happened was that the Ministry of Agriculture, Fisheries and Food declined the applicant's request for its vessel, Nellie, to beam trawl for pressure stock[89] in the North Sea because of the changes in governmental policy prohibiting the aggregation of transferable licence entitlements. Hamble Fisheries applied for, *inter alia*, an order of certiorari to quash the decision of the respondent on the ground that it had in law a legitimate expectation that the said licence would be granted. Sedley J confirmed that expectations induced by government are also a crucial element which has to be considered by the courts in determining the validity of policy changes.[90]

Elliott observes that this approach clearly envisages a level of protection which goes beyond mere *Wednesbury* review, given that it casts the court as the primary judge of where the balance lies between the different interests which are at stake in such situations.[91]

It is worth noting that although this judgment was regarded as heretical and overruled by the Court of Appeal in *R v. Secretary of State for the Home Department, ex p Hargreaves*,[92] the criterion which it sets out is far from being demised. As

---

[87] So long as the performance of the undertaking is compatible with their public duty, they must honour it...At any rate they ought not to depart from it except after the most serious consideration and hearing what the other party has to say; and then *only if they are satisfied that the overriding public interest requires it*. The public interest may be better served by honouring their undertaking than by breaking it. This is just such a case. It is better to hold the corporation to their undertaking than to allow them to break it.

[88] [1995] 2 All E.R. 714.

[89] Species of fish incapable of sustaining unrestricted fishing within the limits of the applicable European Community quota.

[90] The balance must in the first instance be for the policy-maker to strike; but if the outcome is challenged by way of judicial review, I do not consider that the court's criterion is the bare rationality of the policy-maker's conclusion. While policy is for the policy-maker alone, the fairness of his or her decision not to accommodate reasonable expectations which the policy will thwart remains the court's concern (as of course does the lawfulness of the policy). To postulate this is not to place the judge in the seat of the minister. As the foregoing citations explain, it is the court's task to recognise the constitutional importance of ministerial freedom to formulate and to reformulate policy; but it is equally the court's duty to protect the interests of those individuals whose expectation of different treatment has a legitimacy which in fairness out tops the policy choice which threatens to frustrate it.

[91] Elliott, 'The Human Rights Act 1998 and the Standard of Substantive Review', (as above n. 7), 317.

[92] A case concerning eligibility of prisoners to apply for home leave [1997] 1 W.L.R. 906. The court concluded that it would intervene only if the proposed policy change was *Wednesbury* unreasonable.

Elliott explains, further developments in the case law on substantive expectation[93] recognize two central truths:

first, that the rationality and proportionality principles are simple different points on a single spectrum; and secondly, that the level of review which is appropriate in a given case is to be determined . . . by openly acknowledging and evaluating the various (and sometimes conflicting) factors which influence the rigour with which judges may properly scrutinise the decision in question.[94]

Thus, the adoption of a standard of review which is less intensive in a particular case may not necessarily be indicative of how the scrutiny will be undertaken in other cases which demands a more searching form of inquiry.

On the basis of this clarification, it is useful to point out that commercial regulation normally occurs within a legal framework in which the claimant is legitimately entitled to expect that he will receive a substantive benefit which flows from the implementation of a particular policy. Shaped by the notion that economic agents ought to be able to plan their business, secure in the knowledge of the legal consequences of their investments, the market-place is, in essence, a context for effective judicial protection of legitimate expectations. It therefore urges abandonment of the traditional deferential attitude of the courts towards sharp departure from regulatory policy choices, and advocates the adoption of a more rigorous approach which ensures that such power is not abused by unfairly denying an individual's expected benefits. Specifically, it is suggested that, in order to prevent defeat of reasonable reliance in this field, policy changes could only be approved if, in the court's opinion, there is an overriding public interest which justifies it. This stricter standard of review, which transcends rational supervision, certainly bears resemblance to the proportionality doctrine,[95] and is consistent with European law, which balances the protection of the general public interest against certainty in the market.

In this sense, it is worth emphasizing that the Luxembourg Court has sought to balance the needs of the Community to alter its economic policies for the future, with the impact that such alteration might have on traders who have based their commercial bargains on pre-existing norms.[96] This instructive criterion, which fairly recognizes private interest at stake without ossifying policies in the market area, significantly enhances the protection afforded to substantive benefits by

---

[93] In particular, see *R v. Secretary of State for Education and Employment, ex p Begbie* [2000] 1 W.L.R. 1115. In 2001 the employment functions of this body were transferred to the newly created Department for Work and Pensions, with it becoming the Department for Education and Skills.

[94] Elliott, 'The Human Rights Act 1998 and the Standard of Substantive Review', (as above n. 7), 321–322.

[95] Ibid., 318. See also the judgment of Laws LJ in *R (Abdi and Nadarajah) v. Home Secretary* [2005] E.W.C.A. Civ 1363 at 68. He openly acknowledged, probably for the first time in British legal history, that the proportionality test plays a role in legitimate expectation cases. See the commentary of this case by Elliott, Mark, 'Legitimate Expectations and the Search for Principle: Reflections on *Abdi and Nadarajah*' [2006] 11(4) *Judicial Review*, 281; Elliot, Mark, 'Legitimate expectations: procedure, substance, policy and proportionality' [2006] 65(2) *Cambridge Law Journal*, 254–256.

[96] Craig, Paul, 'Substantive Legitimate Expectations in Domestic and Community Law' [1996] 55(2) *Cambridge Law Journal*, 310.

judicial review. It may be helpful therefore to provide some examples of its application at a European level.

1.2.1 Legitimate expectations in Community law

The central idea that the necessary alteration of policy choices in the commercial field must be reconciled with the interests of those who have detrimentally relied on them has come to be regarded as a classic example of proportionality in European law. Indeed the Luxembourg Court's willingness to accommodate both values clearly illustrates judicial recognition that a balancing model of review must be adopted, under which the competing interests at stake are merely a factor to be weighed, rather than a trump card. It follows that the applicant in the instant context is entitled to claim some substantive benefit from a previous regulation, even if the new one is already in effect, when the economic authority has given rise to justified hopes that the former would be respected. Nevertheless, since the court's criteria on whether the economic agent's expectations are justified and, consequently, worthy of protection vary according to the particular course of conduct, it is clearly necessary to address in more detail the factors that are of relevance in this regard.[97] Three, in particular, stand out.

The first factor concerns the imposition of *ex post facto* restrictions or conditions which were not foreseeable by commercial operators at the time they entered into temporary undertakings. There are cases where the European Court has regarded expectations created under such specific circumstances as reasonable or legitimate and, therefore, sufficiently strong to entitle the applicant to be made subject to initial limitations only.

The *Mulder* case[98] is one of the leading decisions on this issue. In order to reduce the excess of milk and milk products in the common market, Regulation No. 1078/77 introduced a system of premiums for the non-marketing of these products and the conversion of dairy herds. The applicant was a Dutch farmer who entered into such undertaking in 1979 for five years. After this period, with a view to resume his production, he applied to the Minister for Agriculture and Fisheries for a reference quantity of milk which he would be allowed to produce without incurring the payment of an additional levy introduced by Regulation No. 856/84 during the non-marketing period. This application was rejected by the relevant authority on the ground that Mr. Mulder could not provide proof of milk production during 1983, the reference year adopted for the purpose of assigning reference quantities. As a consequence, he found himself refused such a quantity and thus totally excluded from the dairy market. The producer challenged that Regulation arguing, *inter alia*, that it infringed his legitimate expectations. In particular, he alleged that since he had been encouraged by a Community measure to suspend production and marketing for a certain period in return for a premium, he could

---

[97] For a detailed analysis of the European case law, see Sharpston, Eleanor, 'Legitimate Expectations and Economic Reality' [1990] 15 *European Law Review*, 103–160.

[98] *J. Mulder v. Minister van Landbouw en Visserij*, Case 120/86 [1988] E.C.R. 02321. See also *Von Deetzen v. H Hauptzollamt Hamburg-Jonas*, Case 170/86 [1988] E.C.R. 2355.

reasonably expect to be able to resume activities upon the expiry of that undertaking. The court found for him. It declared that the provision on the additional levy and reference quantities of milk was invalid on the ground that it frustrated his legitimate expectations to re-enter the market without being subject to particularly severe restrictions.[99]

This case demonstrates not only that the ECJ has no difficulty in recognizing legitimate expectations to what are commercial benefits, but also that the willingness to accept this species of expectation will not inevitably ossify policy within the relevant area. Indeed, for the court, there was no doubt that the modified rules on quotas were necessary, in the sense that they encapsulated public interest in the orderly operation of market. The simple legal issue remained that such provisions could not serve to justify the harsh effect upon those who had taken part in the earlier scheme. As Craig points out, relevant authorities in the instant situation 'were perfectly entitled to alter the rules on entitlement to milk quotas, but the new regime could not operate so as to prevent those who had taken the bargain in 1979 from re-entering the market'.[100] In this sense, the court's argument was entirely of a piece with the established principle of proportionality. Specifically, it consisted of two central propositions which underpin such standard of review in the instant context: that the public authority must have considerable room to manoeuvre in basic market management, in that it should be able to alter its policy choices for the future, but that there may, without contradiction, exist constraints on that liberty which prevent excessive uncertainty or risks in dealings involving private economic agents.

A similar plausible argument claiming consistency of treatment in this field was developed in *Firma Meiko-Konservenfabrik v. Germany*.[101] In this case, the court held that the retroactive establishment of an earlier date than that originally prescribed for forwarding concluded contracts made between the producers and the processors of sweet cherries to the appropriate agency (as a condition for state-aid) is invalid on the ground that it violates the principle of legal certainty and the legitimate expectations of those concerned. In particular, it stressed that processors were legally entitled to wait until the original time-limit to submit a copy of the documents, since they could not reasonably have anticipated the retroactive imposition of such measure.

---

[99] The fact remains that where such a producer, as in the present case, has been encouraged by a Community measure to suspend marketing for a limited period in the general interest and against payment of a premium, he may legitimately expect not to be subject, upon the expiry of his undertaking, to restrictions which specifically affect him precisely because he availed himself of the possibilities offered by the Community provisions.

There is nothing in the provisions of Regulation 1078/77 or in its Preamble to show that the non-marketing undertaking entered into under that Regulation might, upon its expiry, entail a bar to resumption of the activity in question. Such an effect therefore frustrates those producers' legitimate expectations that the effect of the system to which they had rendered themselves would be limited.

[100] Craig, Paul, 'Substantive Legitimate Expectations in Domestic and Community Law' (as above n. 96), 308.

[101] Case 224/82 [1983] E.C.R. 2539.

The second factor relates to the potential impact of consistent regulatory practice on the way in which economic operators plan their business and investment activities. The Luxembourg Court has recognized that reasonable hopes arise when a public authority deprives an individual of some benefit or advantage which he had in the past been permitted by a continuous, established pattern of governmental behaviour to enjoy and which he can legitimately expect to be allowed to continue to do until clear and timely evidence is given as to the modification of the previous practice.

This view was distilled with particular clarity in *Ferriere San Carlo SpA v. Commission*.[102] In this case, the applicant challenged the Commission's decision fining it for exceeding its production quota for 'reinforcing bars' to be delivered on the common market. It claimed, *inter alia*, that the sale was carried out in accordance with the general and continued regulatory practice of tolerating disposal of such stocks in addition to the delivery quota.

In the *Sofrimport* case,[103] a company incorporated under French law sought to quash two Commission Regulations suspending the issue of import licences for dessert apples originating in Chile, including those already in transit to the Community when the regulation was introduced. The applicant argued that the regulations breached Article 3(3) of Regulation No. 2707/72 which requires the Commission, in adopting protective measures, to take account of the special position of products in transit to the Community. The effect of that provision is to enable an importer whose goods are in transit to rely on a legitimate expectation that in the absence of an overriding public interest no restrictive measures will be applied against him. The Commission contended that a reasonably careful trader could have expected that it might at any time take protective measures once it had expressly reserved that possibility in Regulation No. 346/88, laying down the requirements for the importation of dessert apples from non member countries. However, the court ruled that simply to inform traders of the possibility of protective measures cannot be regarded as sufficient to prevent detrimental reliance on existing regulations.[104]

A similar readiness to protect legitimate expectations in the commercial context is evident in *CNTA*.[105] The case concerned a system of monetary compensation amounts (mcas) which provided payments to exporters for fluctuations in

---

[102] Case 344/85 [1987] E.C.R. 4435.

[103] *Sofrimport SARL v. Commission of the European Communities*, Case C-152/88, [1990] E.C.R. I-02477.

[104] In order to meet the requirements of the special protection provided for in Article 3(3) of Regulation No 2707/72, the measure should also have indicated the situations in which the public interest might justify the application of protective measures with regard to goods in transit...It must be held that the Commission has not in this case demonstrated the existence of any overriding public interest justifying the application of suspensory measures with regard to goods in transit. Consequently, the Commission has failed to fulfil its obligations under Article 3(3) of Regulation No 346/88. Regulations Nos 962/88, 984/88 and 1040/88 must therefore be declared void in so far as they concern products in transit towards the Community.

[105] *Comptoir national technique agricole (CNTA) SA v. Commission of the European Communities*, Case 74-74 [1975] E.C.R. 533.

exchange rates. The applicant was a company which had made export contracts with a view to take advantage of the fixed refunds. However, after these contracts had been made, but before they were to be performed, the Commission abolished mcas applicable to the exported products on the ground that the market situation was such that the application of those amounts no longer appeared indispensable in order to avoid disturbances to trade in that sector. The respondent, however, argued that the undertakings could not fail to be aware that that practice was no longer accepted with effect from the date on which a new regulation provided that the stocks in question no longer had to be reported.

The court found for the applicant. It held that such an exemption could not be regarded as a clear alteration of the previous practice, since its sole purpose was to improve monitoring of the system of production quotas. Besides, it became apparent from the statements that the Commission informed the plaintiff formally of the discontinuance of the practice in question after the period in regard to which the sanction was imposed. Consequently, in the court's opinion, it must be accepted that the affected company was entitled to consider that the regulator had not terminated its practice of tolerating deliveries in excess of quotas. It follows from this that the fine imposed on San Carlo was contrary to its legitimate expectation that the degree of tolerance that had been accepted until then would continue. The decision was therefore declared void and the respondent required to re-open the case and to verify that the excess complained of could not be attributed to the practice in question.

In light of this judgment, it is relatively clear that the second criterion described, like the first, concedes that the regulator is free to alter policy choices in the face of changing circumstances, but that such power must be exercised without unduly affecting the economic players' forward planning in respect of competitive advantages. Again, therefore, the very realization that governmental action has induced substantive expectations has led the court to weigh the public interest relied upon for the taking of a different course of action against the requirements of certainty, in order to ensure that such interference with private rights takes place only if it is absolutely necessary and proportionate in terms of its scope, impact and duration. In particular, it appears that the decision-maker is allowed to depart from consistent *de facto* regulation so long as it gives effect to such basic tenets of the morality of law as publicity, clarity, and prospectivity.

Finally, the recognizable likeness of a legitimate expectations argument succeeding in the commercial context has also been put by the European Court in relation to the modification of measures with effect to operations which have already started, but which have not yet been wholly concluded. There are cases where it has declared the application of the second policy choice in such circumstances to be unfair, on the ground that it substantially undermines the position of individuals who have been led by the earlier norm to expect something different while their particular transaction is in the process of completion. In particular, it has been argued that a significant, and therefore unfair, imbalance against the citizen's interests is caused when (a) the denial of legitimate expectations does not effectively serve any broader purpose; or (b) there are no transitional or 'pipeline' provisions between the two policies which would at least permit traders to avoid the loss resulting from a sharp change of course.

The *Deuka* case[106] provides a good example of the first situation. In the choice of means for the purpose of avoiding disturbances in the market of cereals, the Commission first decided to reduce and then to abolish the denaturing premium granted for common wheat. This measure was adopted even in respect of denaturing operations which had already been arranged and notified to the agency before the new regulation came into force, but which took place after that. The court, however, rejected the latter criterion. It first said that,

> protection of confidence requires that calculations of commercial operators based on the level of the premium in force at the time when the denaturing was begun, should not be upset without compelling reasons.

Crucially, it became apparent that no such strong rationale conceivably justified the particular decision in question. In reality, as the court pointed out, the payment of a reduced premium and the total abolition of the premium in respect of technical operations in progress would not in any event have been able to achieve the objective aimed at by the impugned regulation (to influence the evolution of the market), since all the arrangements and investments had already been made by the plaintiff for the purpose of the denaturing and the sale of the denatured wheat at the time the application was made to the intervention agency. Accordingly, the judges went on to conclude that, for the sake of legal certainty, the decision in question had to be applied in such a way that denaturing processes which were pending at the time it was published might still benefit from the system under the previous regulation.

The court took a very similar type of approach in a challenge to Council regulations, by way of Article 177 of the EEC Treaty, on a reference by the Pretore Circondariale (District Magistrate) of Perugia, Italy.[107] The reference put in issue the validity of measures which provided for reductions in the intervention prices and premiums granted to producers of tobacco of the 'Bright' variety after decisions on the size of the areas to be cultivated had already been made and put into effect. The Luxembourg Court declared those regulations to be invalid on the ground that the public purpose to be achieved—to curb any increase in the Community's tobacco production and at the same time to discourage the growing of varieties which are difficult to dispose of—could not be fulfilled in such circumstances: by then the planting out had already taken place and the harvest had begun long before the publication of one of the impugned measures. In the judges' opinion, therefore, the contested rules had infringed the legitimate expectations of the economic operators concerned, who 'were entitled to expect that they would be notified in good time of any measures having effects on their investments'.

---

[106] *Deuka v. Einfuhr-und Vorratsstelle für Getreide und Futtermittel*, Case 5/75 [1975] E.C.R. 759.
[107] *Crispoltoni v. Fattoria autonoma Tabacchi di Città di Castello*, Case 368/89 [1991] E.C.R. I-3695.

Another good illustration of challenge to community measures on the basis of legitimate expectations is evident in the *Sofrimport* case.[108] Here, a company incorporated under French law sought to quash two Commission Regulations suspending the issue of import licences for dessert apples originating Chile, including those already in transit to the Community when the regulation was introduced. The applicant argued that the regulations breached Article 3(3) of Regulation No 2707/72 which requires the Commission, in adopting protective measures, to take account of the special position of products in transit to the Community. The effect of that provision is to enable an importer in such circumstances to rely on a legitimate expectation that in the absence of an overriding public interest no restrictive measures will be applied against him. The Commission contended that a reasonably careful trader could have expected that it might at any time take protective measures once it had expressly reserved that possibility in Regulation No 346/88, laying down the requirements for the importation dessert apples from non member countries. However, the court ruled that simply to inform traders of the possibility of protective measures cannot be regarded as sufficient to prevent detrimental reliance on existing regulations. It is also necessary to indicate 'the situations in which the public interest might justify the application of protective measures with regard to goods in transit'. Since the Commission had not, in the instant case, demonstrated the existence of such an overriding public interest, the impugned measure was declared void with respect to products that were already being imported into the Community.

From a principled perspective, this judicial approach is also entirely consistent with the doctrine of proportionality, since it is clearly directed towards the question of means and the extent to which the infringement of commercial rights is necessary to the policy being pursued. Specifically, it recognises that the frustration of legitimate expectations must always ultimately be justified by reference, *inter alia*, to the effective achievement of social goals. Thus, any such governmental interference which is futile from a policy point of view—either because it was more extensive than necessary, or because no immediate deterrent effect could be produced; or simply because it contains no reference to an overriding reason of public interest—should be held to be unlawful on the ground that it is certainly unfounded, gratuitous, and unbalanced.

So far as the lack of transitional measures between the two policies is concerned, a good starting point is the approach adopted by the Court in *CNTA*.[109] The case concerned a system of monetary compensation amounts (mcas) which provided payments to exporters for fluctuations in exchange rates. The applicant was a company which had made export contracts with a view to take advantage of the fixed refunds. However, after these contracts had been made, but before they were to be performed, the Commission abolished mcas applicable to the exported products on the ground that the market situation was such that the application of those

[108] As above, n. 103.   [109] As above, n. 105.

amounts no longer appeared indispensable in order to avoid disturbances to trade in that sector. The company claimed that the withdrawal of the payments with immediate effect destroyed the expectation which he had of their maintenance when he entered into the contracts. The court held that although the system of compensatory amounts cannot be considered to be tantamount to a guarantee for traders against the risks of alteration of exchange rates, in practice it avoids the exchange risk, so that a trader, even a prudent one, might be induced to omit to cover himself against such risk.[110] The Commission was therefore held to have violated a superior rule of law in departing from its previous policy without adopting, in the absence of an overriding matter of public interest, transitional measures for the protection of the confidence which a trader might legitimately have had in the community rules.[111]

In light of the foregoing analysis, it seems fairly clear that the European Court of Justice has often adopted a proportionality-based approach towards decisions which purport to defeat the substantive legitimate expectations of economic agents. In doing it has also supplied some guidance *vis-à-vis* the extent to which the applicant is entitled to expect that the substance of the regulation would be adhered to. Thus, by being aware of the tension between the values of administrative freedom and legal certainty, and by acknowledging that neither of them should automatically outweigh the other in any particular case, the judges in Luxembourg's Court have been able to move beyond the idea that trust necessarily poses an unacceptable threat to regulatory improvement measures. Instead, it is argued that an optimal balance between these conflicting values must be reached which ensures both efficiency and fairness in public decision-making. In this sense, the present approach represents a very valuable point of reference for review on the ground of rationality in the domestic context. In particular, it countenances a form of substantive control which certainly rests on a broader conception of the problem and which, therefore, is not circumscribed by the undue deference to executive freedom which inheres in the *Wednesbury* test.

2. Interpretation of Wide Terms

It would be mistaken to think that the impact of the doctrine of proportionality should be strictly confined to the outcome of the decision-making process. It is the purpose of this section to demonstrate that the courts will also have to grapple with

---

[110] In these circumstances, a trader might legitimately expect that for transactions irrevocably undertaken by him because he has obtained, subject to a deposit, export licences fixing the amount of the refund in advance, no unforeseeable alteration will occur which could have the effect of causing him inevitable loss, by re-exposing him to the exchange risk.

[111] [T]he community is therefore liable if, in the absence of an overriding matter of public interest, the commission abolished with immediate effect and without warning the application of compensatory amounts in a specific sector without adopting transitional measures which would at least permit traders either to avoid the loss which would have been suffered in the performance of export contracts, the existence and irrevocability of which are established by the advance fixing of the refunds, or to be compensated for such loss.

it in the interpretation sphere. As seen above, the general approach of the judiciary has been to apply a *Wednesbury*-based reasoning to determine the validity of executive interpretation of terms which have a broad meaning. This approach has to be re-appraised in the light of the increasing incorporation of proportionality into British law.

2.1 The judicial control of regulatory discretion in the interpretative process

The central topic in this arena relates to the legal meaning of a term which has not been specifically intended by the rule-maker and is therefore unclear. Here the issue of exactly how the expression should be interpreted is open to question: should it be on the basis of purist literalism or, as is suggested here, should the court recognize a discretionary area of judgement where the regulator adopts specific meanings? In approaching this issue, it is crucial to take into account that rules which are less specific confer greater *discretion* on the interpreter of the rules as to how the rule should be construed than rules which are clear and precise. Accordingly, agency interpretations which fall under this category should be reviewed more by considerations of how much *discretion* a regulator should have in determining the specific meaning of the broad term rather than the exact meaning of the legal provision, which itself may be extremely broadly and vaguely framed.[112]

In that instance, the basis to determine the meaning of the term should switch from a 'hard-edge' question to a reasoning which is more sensible to the matter of judgement. By adopting this test, the court is still having primacy in determining the meaning of the term, but relying on a test which is particularly suited for vague rules. In other words, the court is not abdicating its constitutional function to say 'what the law is' by reading the broad term as conferring interpretive discretion on the regulator; it is simply applying the law as made by Parliament. This approach is exemplified by the decision of the House of Lords in *South Yorkshire Transport*,[113] where Lord Mustill suggested that, in the case of wide terms, the court still has to determine the right answer to a question of construction, but it should refrain from 'taking an inherently imprecise word, and by redefining it thrusting on it a spurious degree of precision'. A similar approach has been endorsed to the interpretation and application of primary legislation in the field of financial services. Although the courts will have primacy in interpreting regulatory objectives, section 2(1) of the Financial Services and Markets Act 2000 expressly identifies a discretionary area of judgement within which the Financial Services Authority can determine the most appropriate meaning for the purpose of meeting those regulatory objectives.[114]

---

[112] Black, Muchlinski and Walker, 'Reviewing Regulatory Rules: Responding to Hybridisation' (as above n. 23), 128.

[113] *R. v. Monopolies and Mergers Commission (MMC), ex p South Yorkshire Transport Ltd* [1993] 1 All E.R. 289, [1993] 1 W.L.R. 23, [1993] B.C.C. 111.

[114] Henderson, Andrew, 'Judicial Review and the Financial Services and Markets Act 2000' [2001] 6(4) *Judicial Review*, 258.

In light of the foregoing, the question then becomes what should be the specific standard of review which the interpretation of wide terms raises in the commercial context? Chapter 2 explains that, in order to determine whether the meaning adopted by the regulator was within a band of reasonableness, the courts have traditionally exhibited a deferential attitude which seems to underlie the logic of *Wednesbury*, that is to say, the notion that executive constructions of vague terms should be immune from judicial scrutiny insofar as they remain within the bounds of mere rationality.[115] However, as noted above, the doctrine of proportionality has replaced this less rigorous approach as the standard of substantive review in the relevant field. In my opinion, it is clear therefore that the exercise of *interpretive discretion* should also be controlled by reference to the weighing of interests approach which the principle of proportionality commends. Thus, it is suggested that this criterion is the better—and legally right—form of review to the interpretive problems which beset commercial rules. As with substantive review matters, the main normative foundations of this argument are to be found in the significant impact of the HRA 1998 on the interpretation of statutory terms, and the principle of consistency and legitimate expectations.

2.2 Vague rules and section 3(1) of the Human Rights Act

Section 3(1) of the Act reads 'so far as it is possible to do so, primary legislation and subordinate legislation must be read and given effect in a way which is compatible with the Convention rights'. This provision has traditionally been understood as requiring the courts to construe provisions in line with Convention norms.[116] The recent decision of the House of Lords in *Ghaidan v. Godin-Mendoza*[117] is now the leading decision on the matter. In this case, concerning the interpretation of terms for the purposes of succession to a statutory tenancy, Lord Nicholls of Birkenhead reaffirmed the generally accepted interpretation of section 3 that,

where the words under consideration fairly admit of more than one meaning the convention-compliant meaning is to prevail. Words should be given the meaning which best accords with the convention rights.

---

[115] See Irvine of Lairg, Lord A.A.M., 'Judges and Decision-Makers: The Theory and Practice of *Wednesbury* Review' [1996] *Public Law*, 73.

[116] See the interesting analyses by Alison Young in 'Judicial Sovereignty and the Human Rights Act 1998' [2001] 61(1) *Cambridge Law Journal*, 53 at 65; and '*Ghaidan v Godin-Mendoza*: avoiding the deference trap' [2005] *Public Law*, 23–34. For a detailed analysis of the role of legislative intent in statutory interpretation post-HRA 1998, see Kavanagh, Aileen, 'The role of parliamentary intention under the Human Rights Act 1998' [2006] 26(1) *Oxford Journal of Legal Studies*, 179–206. A similar interpretive obligation is relevant for the EC Court. To this effect, see *Von Colson and another v. Land Nordrhein-Westfalen*, Case C-14/83 [1984] E.C.R. 1891; *Marleasing SA v. La Comercial Internacional de Alimentacion SA,* Case C-106/89 [1990] E.C.R. I-04135. For the application of this criterion in the UK, see *Garland v. British Rail* [1983] 2 A.C. 751; *Pickstone v. Freemans* [1988] U.K.H.L. 2; *Litster v. Forth Dry Dock and Engineering Co. Ltd.* [1988] U.K.H.L. 10.

[117] [2004] 3 All E.R. 411. For post-*Ghaidan* case law in other contexts, see Craig, (as above n. 16), 561–562.

Thus, as Elliott explains, the Convention rights must be rationalized as interpretive constructs which shape the internal contours of enabling provisions, thereby ensuring that the courts enforce the limits of discretionary powers which enabling legislation—properly interpreted—sets.[118] In other words, these rights 'constitute limits which, by virtue of section 3 of the HRA, must be implied into every statutory provision which creates decision-making competence'.[119]

In practice, this means that when the courts are confronted with a statutory provision which creates a power, they must understand that the decision-maker may infringe the Convention rights only if its action serves a legitimate public purpose and is proportionate to that objective.[120] In this sense, the scope of the interests which the Convention recognizes can be understood only when they are taken with their limits as a whole. It follows that a section 3 analysis requires the courts to have recourse to proportionality in order to understand the extent and reach of these rights themselves.[121] The notion of proportionality is therefore central to the interpretation of statutory provisions in line with the Convention norms. The implications of this analysis for the interpretation of vague rules are significant.

First, if the interpretation of an ambiguous term leads the regulator to interfere with one of the interests which the Convention recognizes, it is only possible to determine whether that specific construction breaches one of the Convention rights by means of applying the proportionality-based test. Thus, it is simply not conceivable that the language of *Wednesbury* may be applied to interpretation of broad terms in commercial cases decided under the HRA. Such an application might strongly frustrate the intention of Parliament, which since the enactment of the HRA 1998 has probably assumed that the courts will adopt a more rigorous approach concerning the construction of enabling legislation.[122] In this sense, it might also disappoint deeply-held expectations of individuals that they can rely on proportionality to protect them from regulatory interpretations.

Where necessary, the court should therefore determine whether the meaning chosen is proportionate to the competing policy and aim being pursued. Consequently, an interpretation which proportionately qualifies the right which

[118] Elliott, Mark, *The Constitutional Foundations of Judicial Review*, (Oxford: Hart Publishing, 2001) 238.

[119] Elliott, 'The Human Rights Act 1998 and the Standard of Substantive Review', (as above n. 7), 329.

[120] Ibid., 331.

[121] Ibid., 330.

[122] In this sense, Lord Nicholls of Birkenhead held in *Ghaidan* that:

[e]ven if, construed according to the ordinary principles of interpretation, the meaning of the legislation admits of no doubt, s 3 may none the less require the legislation to be given a different meaning... From this it follows that the interpretative obligation decreed by s 3 is of an unusual and far-reaching character. Section 3 may require a court to depart from the unambiguous meaning the legislation would otherwise bear. In the ordinary course the interpretation of legislation involves seeking the intention reasonably to be attributed to Parliament in using the language in question. Section 3 may require the court to depart from this legislative intention, that is, depart from the intention of the Parliament which enacted the legislation. In other words, the intention of Parliament in enacting s 3 was that, to an extent bounded only by what is 'possible', a court can modify the meaning, and hence the effect, of primary and secondary legislation' (as above n. 117).

the Convention protects raises no breach of the Convention. A 'disproportionate' choice of meaning, in contrast, would be unlawful because the HRA 1998 precludes interpretations which are inconsistent with Convention interests. It follows that this approach significantly narrows the range of options which are available to the regulator at the interpretive level because it requires the judiciary to prefer a possible interpretation of legislation that is consistent with Convention rights to any alternative construction that is inconsistent with them.[123]

In this reformulated approach, the court plays its oversight role not so much by seeking to ensure the mere rationality of the executive interpretation, but by aligning the chosen meaning with the right-based structure implicated by the decision. For example, if a statute merely provided that a regulator has power to control the price of utility services to protect the consumer interest, the provision would be read down to ensure that the decision-maker did not have statutory authority to reduce it in a manner that would be contrary to the right to property. The court would then be called upon to decide whether the agency's interpretation of the statutory provision strikes a 'fair balance' between the demands of the general interest of the community and the requirements of the protection of the company's peaceful enjoyment of property rights.

It is worth noting that this proportionality-based test has also been used by the European Court of Justice to determine whether executive interpretation of a Community regulation is lawful: if, on balance, a particular meaning adopted in the pursuit of a public interest is insufficient to outweigh the detriment thereby occasioned to the claimant, it will be unlawful. This formulation achieved particular prominence, for example, in the *Wachauf* case.[124] The question for the court was, *inter alia*, whether Article 5(3) of Regulation No. 1371/84—relating to the transmission of reference quantities exempt from an additional levy on milk in the case of change of ownership or occupancy of a holding—could be interpreted as exclusively benefiting a lessor who retakes possession of the property upon the expiry of the lease, at the expense of the departing lessee who actually built-up the system of milk production on the holding. The court held that such construction, imposed by the regulatory agency, was unacceptable, provided that it constituted, with regard to the public aim pursued (the common organization of a market), a disproportionate and intolerable interference, depriving the lessee, without compensation, of the fruits of his labour in the tenanted property. Indeed, the particular meaning applied was more than necessary to achieve that objective, since significantly less intrusive and equally effective interpretations of the provision could have been adopted:

either by giving the lessee the opportunity of keeping all or part of the reference quantity if he intends to continue milk production, or by compensating him if he undertakes to abandon such production definitively.

---

[123] Lester of Herne Hill, Lord Anthony 'The Art of Possible: Interpreting Statutes under the Human Rights Act' [1998] 6 *European Human Rights Law Review*, 669.

[124] *Hubert Wachauf v. Bundesamt für Ernährung und Forstwirtschaft*, Case 5/88 [1989] E.C.R. 02609.

Secondly, it is important, however, to recognize that the foregoing approach is doomed to fail if vagueness permeates not the means (powers) but the ends (objectives) of regulatory intervention. Where a public objective is formulated in wide terms, it is very difficult for the court to determine whether specific restrictions to rights are proportional or not to it since any measure is necessary to go further in securing that aim. In particular, as Mark Elliott explains, largely open-ended objectives, such as merely protecting people from a certain risk, make it relatively easy for the decision-maker to establish that more severe restrictions are proportionate in the sense that they all seem to be necessary to achieve the desired outcome.[125] In such cases, however, Elliott says that rather than allowing decision-makers to define or secure a general objective, the court should apply the doctrine of proper purposes to identify a more specific objective which may be concealed 'behind the smokescreen' of the vague one. Nevertheless, if the objective is finally found to be legitimate and very wide, and the measure necessary, there is still a chance to apply the proportionality test by having recourse to its narrow version, which requires the court to determine whether the losses inflicted by the measure are justified or outweighed by the specific gains which it entails.[126]

Thirdly, as regards the scope of section 3 of the HRA, it is clear that this general provision enables the courts to adopt an intensive review (proportionality-based) of the interpretation of any statutory power. As Elliott explains,

the Convention rights constitute limits which, by virtue of section 3 of the Human Rights Act, must be implied into *every* statutory provision which creates decision-making competence.[127]

Indeed, he continues,

as what is arguably the foundational provision of the Human Rights Act, it is imperative that section 3 is the broadest possible application: it represents the central mechanism by which the Convention rights are made effective in domestic law.[128]

In particular, given that section 3 operates irrespective of whether the situation with which the court is faced is horizontal or vertical, statutory duties are to be interpreted in line with the Convention even in situations where they are imposed upon private bodies which do not constitute 'public authorities' for section 6 purposes.[129] Accordingly, the interpretive duty contained in section 3(1) should also extend to the interpretation of rules made by private self-regulatory bodies acting under statutory powers.[130] In this manner the logical effects of section 3(1) may

---

[125] Elliott, Mark, 'Proportionality and Deference: The importance of a Structured Approach' in C.F. Forsyth, M. Elliott, S. Jhaveri, A. Scully-Hill and M. Ramsden (eds.), *Effective Judicial Review: A Cornerstone of Good Governance*, (Oxford: Oxford University Press, 2010) 275.

[126] Ibid., 276.

[127] Elliott, 'The Human Rights Act 1998 and the Standard of Substantive Review', (as above n. 7), 329.

[128] Ibid., 331.   [129] Ibid., 333–334.

[130] See Wade, William, 'The United Kingdom's Bill of Rights', in *Constitutional Reform in the United Kingdom: Practice and Principles*, Cambridge Centre for Public Law, (Oxford: Hart Publishing, 1998) 63.

indeed seem to contribute to build a unitary standard of interpretation based on the principle of proportionality.

Two further points should be made in relation to this analysis, concerning the application of section 3 to the interpretation of regulatory rules. First, it may be suggested that the analysis about section 3 is wholly inapplicable to regulatory powers which do not derive from statute. Probably this is so. Nevertheless, this does not mean that applicants cannot challenge breaches of the Convention by agencies purporting to act under non-statutory powers. As Elliott points out, claimants who wish to challenge, on Convention grounds, exercises of such powers must rely instead on the arguments concerning the application of section 6(1), which provides that 'it is unlawful for a public authority to act in a way which is incompatible with a Convention right'. Moreover, section 6(2) renders unlawful any use of the discretionary power (including interpretive power) which is 'incompatible with a Convention right'. Thus, the objective of securing compliance with human rights standards by regulators remains constant, while the juridical basis of enforcement differs in order to accommodate the constitutional distinction between the two forms of power.[131]

In second place, it may also be argued that this interpretive test cannot be applied to regulatory decisions that do not involve an alleged breach of rights protected under the HRA 1998. It is undeniable that section 3 applies only to cases that fall within the scope of the Act. However, it is suggested that reliance should also be placed on arguments concerning the indirect influence of the HRA and Community law on administrative law.[132] As noted in the following chapter, it is immediately apparent that the proportionality-based test will play a broader role in the domestic jurisprudence as principles of English administrative law evolve in light of the Convention. Approaching the matter in this way reveals that the interpretive doctrine based on proportionality may also be extended into general administrative law.

2.3 Departure from previous meanings and legitimate expectations

The importance of the principle of proportionality for executive interpretation of market legal rules can also be brought out in relation to the departure from the actual meaning of words, and hence the effect, of primary and secondary legislation. It can be argued that the relatively generous zone of regulatory autonomy to modify earlier meanings supplied by the rationality approach might clearly breach the legitimate expectations and understandings that those subject to the rules have that they will be adhered to. Indeed, the doctrine that the court could only preclude deprivation of reasonable reliance interests if the decision to reinterpret was manifestly unreasonable reflects the underlying notion that they should

---

[131] Elliott, Mark, 'Fundamental Rights as Interpretive Constructs: The Constitutional Logic of the Human Rights Act 1998' in *Judicial Review and the Constitution*, Christopher Forsyth (ed.), (Oxford: Hart Publishing, 2000) 280.

[132] Elliott, 'The Human Rights Act 1998 and the Standard of Substantive Review' (as above n. 7), 333.

be protected only in rather extreme circumstances. Thus, a basic tenet of the rule of law, concerning the individual's ability to plan his business on the basis of one interpretive choice made by the regulator, is violated by the application of interpretations which were not in force at the time that the individual's commercial decision is taken.

In light of this, it is necessary to accept that, in order to provide a more balanced and satisfactory protection of the interests involved in commercial judicial review, the value of legal certainty should necessarily be of relevance to the initial evaluation of the problem, and that the interpretive approach which follows from this acceptance should be markedly different from that which exists if the only value was rationality in the *Wednesbury* sense. Specifically, the very realization that there are competing values at stake should lead the courts to adopt a more intrusive, proportionality-based test, which facilitates review and forces the authority to give a reasoned justification for its change of meaning.

This kind of reasoning is particularly strong in circumstances where there is a longstanding and ratified interpretation of a term. Thus, Thomas Merrill has suggested that stricter scrutiny of departure from long-established meanings is desirable because,

it promotes equality of treatment between similarly situated parties, protects reliance interests, and renders administrative action more predictable, thereby allowing private parties to engage in meaningful planning.[133]

Besides, as Craig points out, this view is reinforced by rule of law considerations in the light of the work of Professor Joseph Raz.[134] This author stresses the 'principled faithful application of the law' in which the courts are seen as guardians of longer-term tradition to protect citizens from legislative or administrative decisions influenced by the urgencies of short-term exigencies.[135] It is for these reasons that Sunstein suggests that new departures should be accorded somewhat less judicial deference than longstanding interpretations, thereby securing a consistent executive position over time as an effect that seems closely analogous to that of *stare decisis* in the judicial context.[136]

The application of the proposed interpretive approach in the market field is well illustrated by the decision of the Court of Appeal in the *H.T.V. Ltd. v. Price Commission* case.[137] In a letter dated June 26, 1973, the Price Commission notified to the plaintiffs, who were television programme contractors, that sums payable by them, commonly known as 'the Exchequer levy', should be treated as a cost for the purpose of determining the net profit margin under the Counter-Inflation

---

[133] Merrill, Thomas, 'Judicial deference to Executive Precedent' [1991–1992] 101 *Yale Law Journal*, 1029.

[134] Cited by Craig, (as above n. 16), 652.

[135] Raz, Joseph, *Ethics in the Public Domain* (Oxford: Oxford University Press, 1996) Chapter 17.

[136] Sunstein, Cass, 'Law and Administration after Chevron' [1990] 90 *Columbia Law Review*, 2104. Cf. the 'Executive Precedent Model' proposed by Merril, (as above n. 133), 1003–1033. See also Woodward and Levin, 'In Defense of Deference: Judicial Review of Agency Action' [1979] 31 *Administrative Law Review*, 333.

[137] *H.T.V. Ltd. v. Price Commission* [1976] I.C.R. 170.

Act 1973. This statement was repeatedly acknowledged by the agency in several respects in the subsequent years. However, in 1975, the Price Commission held that these payments did not fall within the words 'total costs per unit of output' when determining whether a price increase was permitted by paragraph 39 of the revised Price Code of 1974.[138] H.T.V. sought a declaration that the levy was certainly a cost for the purpose of calculating the amount of permissible price increase, for it retained the same characteristics both before and after the change of the Code. Consequently, it was not permissible for the Price Commission to turn round now and treat the payments differently.

Lord Denning found the action well justified. It was plain to him that the Exchequer levy retained the same character both before July 1974 and after it. It was still a payment by H.T.V. to the authority in return for a licence to produce the programmes. Therefore, he saw no warrant whatever for treating it differently after 1974 from before. In particular, his Lordship stressed that the Price Commission was not permitted to make the distinction on the ground of fairness and consistency.[139] Interestingly, he reached his judgment without even deciding whether the words 'total costs' were wide enough to include the 'Exchequer levy'. The judgment was exclusively based on the executive precedent.[140]

Furthermore, Lord Denning said that departure from a longstanding interpretation in the absence of an overriding public interest constitutes a serious misuse of power which has no basis in law.[141] It is worth emphasizing that this reference, in a judgment of 1976, to the existence of prevailing public considerations as an important requisite for policy change is remarkably in tune with the language of proportionality, which allows public authorities to interfere with private rights insofar as it protects a 'pressing social need'.

---

[138] In this case, it was said, the levy was to be treated as a 'compulsory transfer to the state of a share of the proceeds of a monopoly'.

[139] It is, in my opinion, the duty of the Price Commission to act with fairness and consistency in their dealings with manufacturers and traders. Allowing that it is primarily for them to interpret and apply the code, nevertheless if they regularly interpret the words of the code in a particular sense—or regularly apply the code in a particular way—they should continue to interpret it and apply it in the same way thereafter unless there is a good cause for departing from it. At any rate they should not depart from it in any case where they have, by their conduct, led the manufacturer or trader to believe that he can safely act on that interpretation of the code or on that method of applying it, and he does so act on it. It is not permissible for them to depart from their previous interpretation and application where it would not be fair or just do so.

[140] In these circumstances I do not think it necessary to decide whether or not the 'Exchequer levy' is properly included in 'total costs'. All I need to say is that the Price Commission in the past has regularly treated it as proper to be included: and it would not be fair or just for it now to be treated differently.

[141] It has been often said, I know, that a public body, which is entrusted by Parliament with the exercise of powers for the public good, cannot fetter itself in the exercise of them. It cannot be estopped from doing its public duty. But that is subject to the qualification that it must not misuse its powers; and it is a misuse of power for it to act unfairly or unjustly towards a private citizen when there is no overriding public interest to warrant it.

The need to control and constrain a sharp departure from long-standing and consistent executive interpretation of regulatory rules was also expressed by the House of Lords in *Re Energy Conversion Devices Incorporated*.[142] An American Corporation had appealed against a decision of the UK Patent Office that two international applications for patents made under section 89 of the Patents Act 1977 should be taken to be withdrawn on the ground that the filing fee was not paid on time. In particular, it was argued that the Patents Act 1977 and the Patents Rules 1978 should be construed to allow for delays in complying with the provisions of Article 22 of the Patent Co-operation Treaty, which lays down a period of twenty months for payment of national fees in designated countries. In deciding the interpretive issue, Lord Diplock suggested that, so long as relevant provisions remain unaltered by the rule-maker itself, it is not open to other bodies to modify their meaning *secundum eventus litis*.[143]

The foregoing cases thus conceptualize the particular problem in a manner that provides a more accurate account of the interests which are at play in this area: that of the regulator, which needs to develop its policy by departing from interpretations made at one particular moment in time, and that of the individual, who has relied on the earlier meaning and seeks the substantive benefit that would be forthcoming if this still represented the regulator's chosen interpretive option. It therefore becomes apparent that the potential breach of substantive legitimate expectations, as resulted from the application of the *Wednesbury* approach in the given area, is no longer plausible. Rather, it is for the courts, by imposing rule of law requirements of consistency and proportionality, to undertake a closer inspection of executive interpretations of terms in order to strike a better balance between change and stability.

For present purposes it is of particular significance that this doctrine, according to which the mere rationality of the regulator's choice is not enough to justify a change of interpretation, has been advocated even in the area of self-regulation, where the administrative construction of the law is made by the rule-maker itself. As Wade and Forsyth correctly observe,

> after all, even if the regulator had the power to make a rule in the terms desired, those affected are surely entitled to the application of the rule as it stands. If the regulator's interpretation were only reviewable on the ground of irrationality, the temptation to interpret the rule in a way that the regulator favours rather than in the actual sense of the words would be irresistible. The regulator is invested with legislative power and his rules should be interpreted accordingly.[144]

---

[142] [1983] R.P.C. 231.

[143] [N]o tribunal and no court of law has any discretion to vary the meaning of the words of primary or secondary legislation from case to case in order to meet what the tribunal or the court happens to think is the justice of the particular case. Tempting though it may sound, to do so is the negation of the rule of law. If there are cases in which the application of the Patents Rules leads to injustice, the cure is for the Secretary of State to amend the Rules. If what is thought to be the injustice results from the terms of the Act itself, the remedy is for Parliament to amend the Act.

[144] Wade and Forsyth, (as above n. 1), 134.

The writing of Professor John Manning also furnishes a helpful point in this regard.[145] The core of his argument is that stringent judicial check upon the agency's interpretation of its own rules promotes the rule of law by giving these bodies incentives both to adopt clear regulations and to apply them faithfully. He explains that if a court just enforced a 'permissible' regulatory self-interpretation that diverged significantly from what a first-time reader of the rule might conclude was the 'best' interpretation of their language, it would surely supply the agency with incentives to promulgate rules that are imprecise, vague, or even misleading; and the text of the regulation would fail to serve as a reliable guide to one's rights and duties.

Manning argues that a solution to these potential difficulties lies ready to hand in the adoption of a more intensive form of judicial review of 'reasonable' self-interpretations that explicitly focuses on its intrinsic persuasiveness. Specifically, the court should accord to it the weight indicated by 'the thoroughness evident in its consideration, the validity of its reasoning, and its consistency with earlier and later pronouncements',[146] rather than simply treat it as binding. Thus, the court would succeed in promoting heightened deliberation, clear and straightforward lawmaking, fair notice of the agency's understanding of its own rule, and limited official discretion.

The foregoing approach, says Manning, would also be consistent with the traditional principle of interpretation that indulges strict assumptions against the drafter of ambiguous or doubtful provisions on the basis that it was his affair to word the instrument well: *verba ambigua fortius accipiuntur contra proferentem*.[147]

This approach is to be welcomed, as it embodies the basic idea that regulatory interpretations should be capable of providing effective guidance to market actors in planning their affairs and investments. In this sense, it is entirely of a piece with the argument advanced in this section that high-intensity tools of review such as proportionality leave decision-makers with a smaller margin of interpretive freedom than the mere rationality model of review, thereby effectively avoiding the introduction of uncertainty or unpredictability in regulatory texts.

3. Questions of Fact

It is necessary to mention briefly that the application of the principle of proportionality may also increase pressure for a wider ground of factual review in the commercial area. Questions which occur under the Convention or EU law will often involve the issue whether, on the facts, the action complained of is justified and proportionate to its aim.[148] Thus, a regulatory decision may well give rise to disproportionate interferences with Convention or Community rights if, in the

---

[145] Manning, John, 'Constitutional Structure and Judicial Deference to Agency Interpretations of Agency Rules' [1996] 96 *Columbia Law Review*, 612–696.

[146] Ibid., 687.

[147] Ibid., p. 656: 'Ambiguous words are more harshly understood against the one speaking them'.

[148] See Kent, Michael, 'Widening the Scope of Review for Error of Fact' [1999] 4(4) *Judicial Review*, 242.

court's opinion, another more fact-sensitive law could realistically have been used to achieve the policy objective at issue.[149] This strong reliance on the detailed factual context in which the decision is adopted should necessarily be accompanied by a broader approach to review of regulatory fact-finding.

The point is expressed well by Supperstone and Coppel in relation to the application of the Human Rights Act 1998.[150] They observe that, in counterpoint to the *Wednesbury*-based system—where respondents merely identify the facts which they considered 'without going into detail as to why they chose to give one matter greater weight than another'[151]—the principle of proportionality involves a genuine and more searching review which requires the decision-makers to adduce evidence not only of the facts underlying their decision, but also of the thought processes and complementary information which made them adopt the relevant measure.

In practice, this means that the High Court may be led to exercise its discretion to permit discovery and interrogatories, and to order cross-examination on the contents of affidavit and witness statements more frequently than at present. It is also these writers' view that the greater scope for argument about the facts underpinning applications for judicial review under the HRA may require the court to engage in the process of ascertaining 'legislative facts', that is to say, evidential material which contains,

not merely the facts of the dispute between the parties (adjudicative facts) but the facts which underpin and gave rise to a particular policy or piece of legislation which is then applied as between the parties.[152]

Specifically, it is argued that this special reliance on empirical data informing legislative judgement, which transcends the pure legal theory to argue a case, can be canvassed by way of a 'Brandeis brief'.

This term was coined after Louis Brandeis (later to become a judge of the United States Supreme Court), acting as a litigator, persuaded the Supreme Court to make effective, as a matter of judicial cognizance, the use of written legal argument which contains extensive sociological, economic, medical, and other scientific information.[153] Importantly, therefore, it encompasses the procedural necessity to rely on wide-ranging statistics or extra-legal data to prove arguments in complex cases. The potential use of this technical information in Britain has already been underscored by the judgment of Henry LJ in *ex p Smith*:

if the Convention were to be made... part of our domestic law, then in the exercise of the primary jurisdiction the court in, for it, a relatively novel constitutional position, might

---

[149] Sales and Hopper, 'Proportionality and the Form of Law' [2003] *Law Quarterly Review*, 426–454.

[150] Supperstone and Coppel, 'Judicial Review after the Human Rights Act' [1999] 3 *European Human Rights Law Review*, 301–329.

[151] Ibid., 326.

[152] Ibid. See also David, Kenneth, 'An approach to problems of evidence in the administrative process' [1942] 55 *Harvard Law Review*, 364–402.

[153] See *Muller v. Oregon*, 208 U.S. 412 [1908]. See also *Brown v. Board of Education of Topeka*, 347 U.S. 483 [1954].

well ask for more material than the adversarial system normally provides, such as a Brandeis brief.[154]

The implications of this practice for judicial review in the business field become apparent once the balance between regulatory autonomy and judicial control which the proportionality doctrine institutionalizes is taken into account. Given that, under this principle, the regulator is required to justify its market policy as a necessary or minimally impairing restriction upon commercial rights, and that the evaluation of the relative importance of the competing interests at stake is primarily for the courts, it follows that judges should take notice of legislative facts submitted by means of the Brandeis brief or otherwise[155] in order to appreciate the precise purpose and effect of the impugned regulations.

It is also helpful to approach this matter by reference to the judicial control of the agency's findings of fact, its interpretation of evidence, and its factual inferences in EC law. To this effect, Michael Kent remarks that the ECJ has seemed to go further in supporting a wider role of national judicatures in reviewing question of facts within that province.[156] In particular, he says that,

> it is at least arguable that, under the EC Treaty and, by extension, in relation to the vindication of Community rights by the courts of member states, the Luxemburg approach does permit a wider review for error of fact than the English authorities apparently allow.[157]

Actually, as the ECJ does not need to have regard to the doctrine of Parliamentary sovereignty, the approach 'forbidden' in domestic judicial review, namely the review of facts, should be more permissible in Community law.[158]

The adoption of such more intensive form of review of facts in the field of market regulation received explicit support from the Luxembourg Court in *Upjohn Ltd. v. The Licensing Authority established by the Medicines Act 1968 and Others*.[159] It was held that any national procedure for judicial review of decisions of domestic bodies revoking marketing authorizations must enable the court or tribunal seised of an application for annulment of such a decision effectively to apply the relevant principles and rules of Community law when reviewing its legality. This means that, in the case of decisions revoking authorizations to market proprietary medicinal products, competent national courts and tribunals are empowered to substitute their assessment of the facts and, in particular, of the scientific evidence relied

---

[154] *R v. Ministry of Defence, ex p Smith* [1996] Q.B. 517. See Henderson, Andrew, 'Brandeis Briefs and the Proof of Legislative Facts in Proceedings under the Human Rights Act 1998' [1998] *Public Law*, 1998, 563–571.

[155] Ibid., 566. Henderson explains that the reception of legislative facts is also possible by reference to Parliamentary proceedings utilizing the rule in *Pepper v. Hart* [1993] A.C. 593. In this case the House of Lords held that the well-settled rule which excludes reference to Parliamentary material and history as an aid to statutory construction should be relaxed so as to permit such reference in some circumstances.

[156] Kent, Michael, 'Widening the Scope of Review for Error of Fact', (as above n. 198), 241.

[157] Ibid., 242.

[158] Engelman, Philip, *Commercial Judicial Review*, (London: Sweet & Maxwell, 2001), 277–278.

[159] Case C-120/97. Reference for a preliminary ruling: Court of Appeal (England), United Kingdom [1999] ECR I-223.

on in support of the revocation decision for the assessment made by the national bodies competent to revoke such authorizations.

A similar approach can be seen in *Commission v. Tetra Laval*.[160] This case dealt with the discretion to be enjoyed by the European Commission in assessing market concentration matters. The court held that such margin does not mean that the Community Courts must refrain from reviewing the Commission's interpretation of information of an economic nature:

Not only must the Community Courts, *inter alia*, establish whether the evidence relied on is factually accurate, reliable and consistent but also whether that evidence contains all the information which must be taken into account in order to assess a complex situation and whether it is capable of substantiating the conclusions drawn from it. Such a review is all the more necessary in the case of a prospective analysis required when examining a planned merger with conglomerate effect [para. 39].[161]

It is worth noting that, in the domestic context, there have already been some seminal judgments concerning the application of this criterion based on European norms. In *R v. Minister of Agriculture, Fisheries and Food, ex p Bell lines*,[162] for example, the High Court recognized that Community law may well entitle and require UK courts to draw into the business of fact-finding in order to decide whether and to what extent national regulations restricting the import of milk to specified ports of entry constitute an impermissible restriction on intra-Community trade. In rejecting a judicial approach to regulatory fact-finding closely associated to the *Wednesbury* test Forbes J stated:

It is plain that this court is, some may think unfortunately but nevertheless ineluctably, being drawn into the business of fact-finding. Indeed, there are pronouncements in the House of Lords which make it clear that the provisions for cross-examination of deponents on affidavits and so on and so forth mean that in certain cases this court can be required to find facts at least if it is necessary to find certain facts in order to define its jurisdiction. I do not believe that this country should be left in a situation where, if it were plain that a decision of a Minister was one which was contrary to Community law, or that part of Community law which becomes part of this country's domestic law, those persons with rights arising under Community law should be denied any means of enforcing them. In my view, that would be wrong....

In relation to market investigation, the judgment of the Competition Appeal Tribunal in *UniChem*[163] is also relevant, for it indicates that the above mentioned

---

[160] C-12/03 [2005] E.C.R. I-1113. See Prete, L. and Nucara, A., 'Standard of proof and scope of judicial review in EC merger cases: everything clear after Tetra Laval' [2005] 26(12) *European Competition Law Review*, 692; and Vesterdorf, Bo, 'Standard of Proof in Merger Cases: Reflections in the Light of Recent Case Law of the Community Courts' [2005] 1 *European Competition Journal*, 3; see also Craig, Paul, *EU Administrative Law*, (Oxford: Oxford University Press, 2006), 464–474.

[161] See also para. 40 to 45. A similar approach was adopted in *Microsoft v. Commission* (Competition), T-201/04 [2007] E.U.E.C.J., at para. 89.

[162] [1984] 2 C.M.L.R. 502. See also *R v. Secretary of State for Social Security, ex p Schering Chemicals Ltd.* [1987] 1 C.M.L.R. 277; and *R v. Minister of Agriculture, Fisheries and Food, ex p Roberts* [1991] 1 C.M.L.R. 555.

[163] *UniChem v. OFT* [2005] CAT 8, paras. 168 and 169.

doctrine of the ECJ in *Tetra Laval*[164] is, in any event, of interest as to the approach to be adopted by a Court exercising a similar jurisdiction to that of the Tribunal.

In light of the foregoing, it transpires that there is, in relation to the principle of proportionality and European norms, a spectrum of relevance of judicial review over facts. In particular, this relevance is highly conspicuous in situations where the magnitude of the qualification placed on the applicant's rights appears to be based on a misunderstanding of fact which renders it out of proportion in light of regulatory objectives. Any exercise of discretionary power which engaged a Convention right or EU law would therefore have to be based upon correct factual findings, and it would be a matter for the court's primary judgement whether sufficient evidence has been presented. This emphasis on questions of fact clearly enables the judicial review jurisdiction to furnish a fully comprehensive system of individuals' protection against disproportionate interference with their commercial rights.

4. Discretionary Remedies

Finally, it is readily apparent that the application of the principle of proportionality might also produce a more satisfactory result in relation to the exercise of remedial discretion in the context of volatile markets. It was explained above that the problem with the present, cautious approach—according to which the courts should withhold relief against unlawful decisions in order to protect the interests of the administration and third parties—is that it absolutely fails to safeguard the rights of innocent and successful applicants. For this reason it was contended that, in order to overcome the problem of competing interests in the remedial sphere, the courts should not be merely sacrificing one interest for the other. Instead, it may be argued that, while each interest is relevant, their endeavour must be confined to the application of a more moderated approach that also purports to pay due regard to the interests of the plaintiff. The following sub-sections seek to demonstrate that such solution is forthcoming once the principle of proportionality is taken into account.

4.1 The proportional approach to remedies

As seen above, it is not at all clear that it is correct to assert that the interest of the individual in getting relief from unlawful orders should be subordinated to the demands of the executive and third parties. Rather, there exist a series of normative and pragmatic reasons for maintaining that they should be afforded a relatively similar protection by the courts. It therefore follows that any judgement that simply refuses a remedy in the interest of the latter parties represents an unfair balance between the needs of subjects who are likewise entitled to the protection of the law. In other words, since the substantial hardship caused to the applicant in this situation is by no means less important—in rule of law terms—than the damage

---

[164] (As above, n. 160).

that the refusal is designed to prevent, it is clear that such limitation of rights is too extreme to the legitimate aim being pursued.

Thus, in view of the question, under the proportionality test, whether the absolute denial of effective relief in commercial judicial review is proportional *sensu stricto* to achieve the aim of the court (which is to provide protection to the position of third parties and the interests of the administration), it can be argued that it is not because it entails excessive burdens and disadvantages, in particular considerable financial losses on the part of the innocent applicant and individuals concerned, in relation to the alleged benefits such measure may bring. It would also seem that the court's decision that no protection should be provided against unlawful orders which are advantageous to some parties cannot be regarded as reasonable, because, as explained below, it does not appear to be the more suitable and necessary mean to achieve the desired end.

In light of this, it becomes apparent that the application of the principle of proportionality at a remedial level would allow the court to exercise its discretion in a manner which is much more consistent with the requirements of fairness in public law adjudication. Thus, whereas adopting an approach exclusively founded on administrative convenience or third party reliance merely shifts the potential loss from those who took the benefit of the flawed decision to the applicant and the public affected by it, a proportional approach which also rests upon the interests of the latter clears the way for a judgement that serves to avoid such an unreasonable interference with private rights. This kind of judicial intervention is both convincing, in the sense that it provides a satisfactory account of the principles that safeguard the countervailing interests of the individuals, and workable in terms of individual justice, in that it accurately captures the idea that the court's primary role is to protect citizens against executive abuse.

Having thus contended that the suitability of the current approach to remedies needs to be reappraised in light of the doctrine of proportionality, the remaining sub-sections will embark upon the task of identifying and articulating a specific method which the court ought to use in protecting the different interests at stake. Two options fall to be considered.

4.2 The proportional spread of loss among interested parties

First, it appears that a solution to this problem lies ready to hand in the case of decisions which affect private activities constantly and over a long period of time. Indeed this type of decision has the advantage of allowing the court to spread the loss caused by administrative wrongdoing more equitably over different individuals who are exposed to it, thereby affording a similar protection to all the potential victims. Specifically, a fair compromise might be a declaration which invalidates the *ultra vires* decision only from the date the legal action against the decision is known and governs future exercises of the same discretion. In this manner, the effects of the same decision prior to that date are left unaffected, notwithstanding that the court has come to the conclusion that they are legally flawed. This formula clearly reflects a proportional choice regarding the weight which ought to be attached to the position of competing parties on the issue of remedies. Indeed, it ensures that the interests of innocent parties who relied on the validity of the decision are protected until the very moment when reliance is no longer reasonable or legitimate. Yet it also succeeds in allowing the court to grant effective relief to parties presently affected by the misapplication of the legal rule. Thus, long term decisions clearly provide a suitable framework to ensure a more equitable burden-sharing among interested parties.

This point is best illustrated by example. Assume that, in the *Imperial Chemical Industries* case (ICI),[165] the oil companies were not cognizant of the judicial review proceedings against the administrative decision until the date of the judgment. This fact implies that their investment prior to that date was effectively made on the legitimate expectation that the tax amount they were paying would remain unchanged. Reasonableness of reliance would, therefore, seem to be a good reason for the court to withhold relief. However, the adoption of such choice would be detrimental to the interests of ICI which succeeded in demonstrating that the approach of the Inland Revenue to the taxation of oil companies was unlawful. The harm would be in the form of having to compete with companies that pay lower taxes due to a misapplication of the statutory rule. The question therefore arises whether, and if so how, there is a possibility to protect the interest of third parties without unduly affecting the rights of the successful applicant. Viewed in this manner, it may be argued that the decision of the Inland Revenue, which could potentially cover a period of up to 15 years, specifically permits the court to satisfy this dual imperative. Indeed, as Lewis points out, a solution to this difficulty lies ready to hand in the form of a 'modified prospective declaration'.[166] The particular decision in question would be declared void from the date of the judgment but not to invalidate acts done on the basis of the acceptance prior to that date. In practice, this approach would ensure that the oil companies were not prejudiced in the period before the outcome of the case was known, and would provide an effective remedy to the applicant in regard to the contemporary decision. In this sense, the existence of a temporal basis for dividing the loss among different individuals provides a suitable framework for dealing with the clash between the principle of legality and the principle of legal certainty in the context of remedial discretion.

Although it is submitted that this is a more satisfactory solution to the problem of competing interests in the remedial context, that is not an end of the matter. Given that the approach can only be applied to long term decisions, it is self-evident that it would not be helpful to the resolution of conflicts related to other types of decisions. For example, it provides no guidance on how to deal with a case in which the effects of the *ultra vires* decision are limited to a single activity and third parties know the existence of the conflict only from the date of the judgment. In this situation, there is neither temporal basis for dividing the loss among competing

---

[165] *R v. Attorney General ex p Imperial Chemical Industries (ICI) Plc.* [1987] 1 C.M.L.R. 72.
[166] Lewis, Clive, 'Retrospective and Prospective Rulings in Administrative Law' [1988] *Public Law*, 91.

individuals nor possibilities to grant relief on the basis that third parties could have foreseen that the decision was likely to be altered. The question therefore arises as to how the court should exercise its discretion where there are no contextual criteria which favours the application of a proportional approach to the present problem. The answer to this question, which provides the second option to be considered, will be developed in the following paragraphs, where it will be argued that, for a series of conceptual and pragmatic reasons, the exercise of remedial discretion must necessarily be accompanied by the provision of alternative remedies, namely, the provision of compensation.

4.3 The monetary remedy

Indeed it is the contention of the present work that, in such circumstances, it would be much better to allow compensation to the individual who has been harmed as a result of the exercise of court's decision on whether to grant or withhold relief. Thus, if the court decides to refuse a remedy for the sake of administrative expediency or legal certainty, the party who established the nullity should be entitled to compensation for the loss suffered as a result of allowing such order to be effective. Otherwise, if the judge decides to quash the executive decision in order to give effect to the principle of legality and to safeguard the position of the plaintiff, those who have been reasonably misled by it might obtain redress for harm they suffered as a consequence of the decision-maker's wrongful action. Assuming that regulatory efficiency is also affected by the granting of relief, the administration, however, is not entitled to redress because of the principle that no subject may profit from its own wrong. This doctrine is to be welcomed to the extent that it offers an alternative to the unconvincing approach which leaves the loss with one of the parties when the court has determined to give precedence to the interests of the other.

As regards the subject liable to make the payment, the present thesis argues that it is the regulatory body which should bear responsibility for the loss suffered either by the applicant or third parties as a consequence of the outcome of the case. Ultimately, it should be obliged to compensate because it is precisely its unlawful action that caused the harmful effect on the party against whom the remedial discretion is exercised. In particular, the principle of liability raises special consideration which requires the regulator to be answerable for its *ultra vires* decision in order to eliminate the burden being placed on one innocent party to prevent undue hardship to the others. Understood thus, it becomes clear that this approach complements the exercise of remedial discretion because it rightly imposes the burden on the public body which made the offending order, thereby avoiding any undue loss to the individuals. In this sense, the system of compensation has the advantage of facilitating the reconciliation of the competing values and interests at stake without unduly interfering with private rights.

It is with these considerations in mind that we turn to state the main reasons which justify the provision of compensation to the different parties interested in the outcome of commercial judicial review proceedings.

4.4 Compensation to the applicant

The first point which must be made in this regard relates to the position of the applicant. It may be argued that only by holding the decision-maker liable for the damages caused to the person seeking relief, is it possible to justify the misapplication of rules in order to safeguard the interests of the administration and the position of third parties; a legal regime which does not allow subsequent compensation in that case would necessarily cause an unacceptable loss to the party who is refused the remedy. Compensation should therefore be seen as a necessary consequence flowing from such denial, precisely because it relieves the innocent applicant from bearing the burden of protecting the competing interests at stake.

It is worth noting that this suggestion draws particular inspiration from the contribution of some judges and commentators to the debate on the law relating to invalidity. It has already been argued that if the court decides to qualify the concept of retrospective nullity, because its effect on some parties is regarded as unacceptable,[167] respect for the person who has established the legal flaw in the particular decision can be secured only if it is given adequate redress in the form of monetary compensation. This argument is illuminated by Lord Wilberforce's dissenting speech in *Hoffmann-La Roche*.[168] Approaching the issue in the context of voidable decisions he regards the compensation to be given to the aggrieved applicant as a necessary condition to allow the impugned administrative decision to take effect. The core of his Lordship's argument can be resolved into two components. He begins by revealing the rationale which, he maintains, underlies the use of the term voidable:

In truth when the court says that an act of administration is voidable or void but not *ab initio* this is simply a reflection of a conclusion, already reached on unexpressed grounds, that the court is not willing *in casu* to give compensation or other redress to the person who establishes the nullity. Underlying the use of the phrase in the present case, and I suspect underlying most of the reasoning in the Court of Appeal, is an unwillingness to accept that a subject should be indemnified for loss sustained by invalid administrative action.

Having thus contended that the employment of this term reflects a reluctance of the courts to compensate the aggrieved applicant for damages suffered from the date the challenged decision was first made, Lord Wilberforce then goes on to praise the approach available in 'more developed legal systems' which avoids this particular difficulty by giving indemnity to persons injured by illegal acts of the administration. In particular, he asserts that one of the virtues of this system of compensation is that it allows the decision to be effective without necessarily affecting the interests of the person who establishes the nullity:

Consequently, where the prospective loss which may be caused by an order is pecuniary, there is no need to suspend the impugned administrative act; it can take effect (in our language an injunction can be given) and at the end of the day the subject can, if necessary, be compensated.

---

[167] See Craig, (as above n. 16), 771.
[168] *Hoffmann-La Roche v. Secretary of State for Trade and Industry* [1974] 2 All E.R. 1128.

Thus, for his Lordship, so long as the harm to the successful applicant can be avoided by way of monetary remedy, the court is legitimately entitled to qualify the concept of retrospective nullity, thereby allowing the contested order to stand. It follows that it would be very difficult, on this view, for the judge to compromise the principle of legality if no subsequent compensation is available to the affected party by the public body who has made a mistake.

This is precisely the approach which some writers have suggested in order to vindicate the interests that might clash with the rights of the applicant. Thus, Craig says that a system of damages could be particularly useful in cases where the individual asserts the invalidity of an administrative act, and the public body raises the argument that there is a real prospect of administrative upheaval or chaos. In this case, he says,

a court could say that the action was void, but that the only remedy was compensation, and not an order to quash the act or declare it to be null. This could be well the most equitable solution.[169]

A relatively similar approach is apparent in the views expressed by writers such as Wade and Forsyth as regards detrimental reliance on unlawful decisions. In particular, they argue that one way of avoiding the difficulties raised by the problem of reliance on decisions later held to be void is to apply the doctrine of relativity which postulates that the particular decision could be valid in favour of *bona fide* parties and invalid against the decision-maker.[170] In this manner, justice for the applicant can still be done by allowing a claim for redress against the relevant authority, which ought to answer for its wrongdoing. For example, in a case concerning arrest which was later found to have been unlawful, Schiemann LJ said that a sensible answer might be that no remedy should be given which may affect the party who acted in good faith but that a remedy should be granted against the authority who made the invalid decision.[171]

In light of the foregoing analysis, it seems appropriate to suggest, by way of analogy, that the doctrine contained in the preceding paragraphs should also be applied in the remedial context. As is apparent from the cases mentioned in Chapter 2, when remedies are refused in order to avoid substantial prejudice to administrative effectiveness or the position of third parties, the person who establishes the nullity of the *ultra vires* decision is not able to obtain any compensation or other type or redress. There is, therefore, an unwillingness to accept that this subject should be indemnified for loss sustained by the void decision that could have been quashed. However, a more balanced approach would certainly require the interests of the applicants to be taken into account and protected; in Lord Wilberforce's terms, this would demand that they be given some form of compensation for such loss. Thus, if the monetary remedy is finally granted, appropriate weight may be attached to the arguments of administrative convenience and legal certainty without necessarily causing hardship to the individual who impugned the validity of the particular

---

[169] Craig, (as above n.16), 776.   [170] Wade and Forsyth, (as above n. 1), 252–253.
[171] *Percy v. Hall* [1997] Q.B. 924 at 951.

decision in question. In this sense, the redress system would operate to fashion an outcome that will do justice to all the parties involved.

4.5 Compensation to third parties

The other subject, whose position must be considered in determining remedies for harm suffered as a result of administrative mistake, is the party who detrimentally relied on the validity of the *ultra vires* decision. As seen above, if the court decides to quash the offending order and render it retrospectively null, this person will suffer a loss of substantial investment made on the legitimate expectation that the impugned decision would remain valid. During the period between the doing of the act and the moment in which the action brought against the decision is known the party will have done some deals and carried out commercial activities on the basis that the decision is lawful. The subsequent recognition of the invalidity of the decision with *ex tunc* effect will therefore render all the matters done in the meantime worthless, thereby causing a significant loss of money and resources to the *bona fide* investor. In such circumstances, legal instincts may rebel against imposing that burden on the people who legitimately conducted their business as the law then prescribed. Indeed, it is hard not to feel that the decision-maker should take some responsibility for the outcome of the case as the mistake in question was ultimately committed by him. In light of this, it may be argued that it would be much fairer to accept that third parties are entitled to some form of compensation than simply to admit the undesirable consequences that will follow if effective relief is granted to the applicant.

This analysis can be usefully related to the discussion of the possible responses to the problem of reasonable reliance in the context of *ultra vires* representations. Indeed there exists a high degree of symmetry between the positions of *bona fide* parties in regard to the exercise of remedial discretion and the assurance that turns out to be outside the power of the public body, or the officer who made it. In each case, the rigid application of the retrospective doctrine may cause substantial hardship to their interests. Moreover, the concern to give effect to the principle of legal certainty and to ensure that the courts respect the legitimate expectations created by executive action is substantially similar in both dimensions. In this way, it would be readily comprehensible to hold that these approaches could be complemented by an analogous mechanism which secures a measure of protection to the aggrieved person, because the kinds of considerations that will weigh with those applying the principle of legality in the specific contexts are seen to share one common normative foundation. In particular, it may be argued that the system of compensation suggested in the law concerning *ultra vires* representations could be developed in a similar way in the context of remedies. This matter can be best addressed by providing a brief description of the discourse on legitimate expectations which justifies the adoption of this form of relief in the context where it has already been suggested, and considering its relevance to the comparable area of law.

The jurisdictional principle, as it has been traditionally applied in the law relating to *ultra vires* representations, embodies the idea that the assurance which is beyond the powers of the representor cannot be binding. Accordingly, it is said that estoppel or legitimate expectations can have no role in this area.[172] In Craig's words, a moment's reflection will, however, make evident the hardship that this approach causes to the individual.[173] Indeed, if this principle is taken to its logical extreme, the person who reasonably relied upon such representation will be left without any remedy for the loss suffered as a result of the subsequent invalidation of the decision. Thus, the 'burden' of preventing extension of power falls exclusively on the innocent representee. In light of such difficulty, it is submitted that a more satisfactory response to the problem might be to prefer an approach that invalidates the misrepresentation without going so far as to deny any redress to the aggrieved party. In this sense, it is suggested that it would be much more sensible to develop a system of compensation for wrongful administrative action based on the principle of legal certainty.[174]

The dicta of the national courts in *Matrix Securities*[175] and *Rowland v. Environment Agency*[176] provide at least some indication that the award of damages may be helpful in this respect. Although these cases are not concerned principally with commercial activities, the doctrine applies equally to cases which are, since the general wording in which the relevant observations are made suggests that the monetary remedy should be available for any breach of the right to property. Thus, in the first case, Lord Griffiths suggested, *obiter*, that in a case where the applicant has been entitled to rely upon an *ultra vires* representation made by the inspector of taxes and has spent money accordingly before the decision made is revoked, then 'it seems to me that fairness demands that the applicant should be reimbursed for this out-of-pocket expense and it could be regarded as an abuse of power for the Revenue to refuse to do so'.

The second case concerns the purchase by Mr. Rowland of the Hedsor Wharf Estate, a property whose grounds include the riverbed of a loop in the River Thames, in the belief that that loop was private. In particular, he had reasonably relied on the signs and weirs erected by the navigation authorities which indicated that there was no thoroughfare through Hedsor Water and that it was private. In addition, he was told by the owners of the estate, who had lived there for nearly 20 years, that the various navigation authorities had for many years treated that part of the river as private water. After Mr. Rowland's death, his widow, the claimant, complained to the Environment Agency about trespass by boats into the loop.

---

[172] See Craig, (as above n.16), 675, 682–684.   [173] Ibid., 671.

[174] See Wade and Forsyth, (as above n. 1), 340–342; Schonberg, Soren, *Legitimate Expectations in Administrative Law*, (Oxford: Oxford University Press, 2000) 167–236; Fordham, Michael, 'Reparation for Maladministration: Public Law's Final Frontier' [2003] 8(2) *Judicial Review*, 107; Steele, Iain, 'Substantive Legitimate Expectations: Striking the Right Balance' [2005] 121 *Law Quarterly Review*, 322–327.

[175] *R v. Inland Revenue Commissioners, ex p Matrix Securities Ltd* [1994] 1 W.L.R. 334. For the general use of compensation as a remedy for breach of legitimate expectations, see also *R v. North and East Devon HA, ex p. Coughlan* [2001] Q.B. 213 at [82]; *R (on the application of Bibi) v. Newham LBC* [2002] 1 W.L.R. 237 at [56]; *R v. Commissioners of Customs and Excise, ex p F & I Services* [2001] E.W.C.A. Civ. 762 at [72].

[176] [2003] 1 All E.R. 625.

As a result of that complaint, the authority asserted that the ancient navigable status of the Thames at Hedsor had never been extinguished by statute or by any other competent authority, and accordingly advised the widow that she would need to remove all signage prohibiting, or appearing to prohibit, public navigation over the loop. In response, Mrs. Rowland brought proceedings against the authority, contending, *inter alia*, that the acknowledgment by the navigation authorities that Hedsor Water was not subject to public rights of navigation (PRN) and the reliance by Mr. Rowland on that acknowledgment when he purchased the estate had created legitimate expectations which entitle the riparian owner to the extinguishment of PRN or other relief in respect of the exercise of such rights.

The Court of Appeal, however, found for the defendant. It stated that Mrs. Rowland's claim to a legitimate expectation that she would continue to be entitled to enjoy Hedsor Water as private was bound to fail under the jurisdictional principle because it was based on unlawful representation. The authorities have never had the power to extinguish or permanently preclude exercise of PRN over the loop, therefore any misleading act or statement made in the past can only be considered as an *ultra vires* assurance which should not be binding on the public body. In this sense, Gibson LJ held that courts should be slow to fix a public authority permanently with the consequences of a mistake, particularly when it would deprive the public of their rights.

Nevertheless, the court made clear that this position does not preclude the application of protection measures to the aggrieved party which would mitigate the occasion for injustice. In particular, it was held that an expectation encouraged by a public body, although the product of an *ultra vires* practice, can be regarded as a 'possession'[177] within the meaning of Article 1 of the First Protocol to the HRA which may entitle the party to some form of relief which is *within* the powers of the decision-maker to afford, such as the benevolent exercise of a discretion available to alleviate the unfairness or *payment of compensation*. Thus, the *Rowland* decision clearly suggests that, by acknowledging that the economic loss suffered by *bona fide* parties amounts to an unjustified interference with the right to property under the HRA, they are perfectly entitled to damages against the responsible body.

The foregoing analysis is particularly based on the jurisprudence of the ECtHR. In *Stretch v. United Kingdom*,[178] for example, the court said that there are some circumstances in which the individual affected by the application of the *ultra vires* doctrine should obtain some kind of compensation in order to satisfy his legitimate expectations. In this case, the applicant had entered into a lease agreement with a local authority which contained an option for renewal for a further 21 years. Subsequently, on the basis of this possibility, he proceeded to build on the land and entered into sub-leases with other persons who conducted business in the premises which he constructed. Thus, the building obligations were undertaken not only

---

[177] See also *R (on the application of Quark) v. Secretary of State for Foreign and Commonwealth Affairs (No 2)* [2003] E.W.H.C. (Admin) 1743, affirmed [2004] 3 W.L.R. 1.

[178] (As above n. 38), re *Stretch* and *Pine*.

with the purpose of recouping the expenditure in the initial term of the lease, but with the reasonable expectation of deriving future return from the investment if the option was renewed. However, when the lessee gave notice to exercise the option, the contracting party determined that its predecessor had unknowingly acted *ultra vires* in granting the option, which was therefore invalid. This decision was upheld by the domestic courts. The applicant contended before the Strasbourg Court that the authority's refusal to grant the option constituted an interference with the peaceful enjoyment of his possessions which was wholly disproportionate as he did not received any compensation for the loss caused to his contractual and property rights under the lease. In light of this, he claimed an award for damage in accordance with Article 41 of the Convention which provides that the court shall, if necessary, afford 'just satisfaction' to the victim of violation of human rights where 'the internal law of the High Contracting Party concerned allows only partial reparation to be made'.

The court found for the applicant. It first held that, notwithstanding the *ultra vires* nature of the council's act, the lessee must be regarded as having at least a legitimate expectation of exercising the option to renew, and this may be considered as a 'possession' for the purposes of Article 1 of the First Protocol. In light of this reasoning, the application of the *ultra vires* doctrine was regarded as interference with the peaceful enjoyment of the applicant's possessions which required to be justified by the authority in accordance with the principle of proportionality. The court said however that, in the present case, the interference was unjustified due to the disproportionate consequences of the invalidity of the option to renew the lease. In particular, the fact that the innocent applicant did not have any possibility to obtain some redress for the application of the principle of legality caused him a great loss of benefits which he reasonably expected to obtain had the option remained valid. Deciding therefore on an equitable basis, the court provided a monetary remedy for pecuniary and non-pecuniary damage that had been shown to flow from the breach. In the judges' opinion, this alternative offers a convincing response to the problem of *ultra vires* representations, in order that the general interest in applying the jurisdictional principle may be reconciled with the interests of the innocent representee:

The position under domestic law was that the option was unenforceable and incapable of giving rise to that further lease. The Court would also note that the domestic system could arguably have reconciled the doctrine of incapacity with the individual interests at stake without necessarily enforcing the option in its original form, for example, by providing an alternative benefit or form of compensation or return of his consideration...this may be regarded as the element which would most appropriately reflect the loss suffered by the applicant when he entered into the lease agreement containing an unenforceable option clause.

It follows that the approach adopted in these cases to protect the aggrieved representee possesses two elements. The former holds that the fact that the misleading action is in excess of power should not debar an expectation relating to property from constituting a possession, the peaceful enjoyment of which is entitled to protection under Article 1. If this view is accepted, the focus then shifts to the relief that might be available. Given that the legitimate expectation cannot entitle a party to realization of the expectation which is beyond the powers of the public body to realize, it is clear that the court cannot give positive relief by allowing the *ultra vires* decision to bind. Nevertheless, this does not mean that there are no alternative remedies to prevent injustice in this area of law. Specifically, it is suggested that one possible relief may be by way of a claim for damages. The idea is to afford 'just compensation' in monetary form to a person who has detrimentally relied upon a misrepresentation, taking into account the past injustice and the potential loss which would result to him if the relevant expectation were to be undermined even in relation to future activities.

In light of this, it is readily apparent that the need to apply the jurisdictional doctrine is not *per se* a sufficient condition for causing hardship to private interests. In some cases, an effective remedy must be provided in order to ensure that public duties are performed in a way which is justified and proportionate to the loss suffered by the party who benefited from the flawed assurance. The award for damage has thus the advantage of allowing the authority to resile from its previous stance without prejudicing the representee. In this manner, it is a helpful tool which permits the principle of legality—which prevents the court from holding the agency to be bound by unlawful practice or promise—to be reconciled with the principle of legal certainty, which maintains that the innocent individual should not suffer the consequences of the agency's initial failure to observe the law.

Although the discussion in the foregoing paragraphs regarding the position of *bona fide* parties is particularly focused on the problem of *ultra vires* representations, it is clear that the approach suggested is, at root, concerned with the fundamental issue which arises when the application of the principle of legality has potential adverse effects on legitimate expectations fostered by the public body. In this sense, it is submitted that it could usefully be deployed in the law relating to remedies, where the invalidation of decisions already taken might equally undermine certainty for interested parties who acted in good faith.

In particular, the thrust of the argument in favour of the analogy drawn from the context of representations is that, if the court decides to quash the particular decision in question, and if it was practically impossible for third parties to be aware of the legal challenges against it, then they will find themselves in the same position as if the executive authority had decided not to be bound by the *ultra vires* action. That is to say, they will have suffered a loss of the investment made on the belief that the decision would remain to be valid. As is evident from the cases cited above, such kind of expectation, although founded on a legal flaw, can be afforded a measure of protection as a 'possession' within the meaning of Article 1 of the First Protocol. This is especially so in the commercial context, where expectations encouraged by decision-makers can normally be attached to property right.

In this sense, Iain Steele points out that although the courts are likely to take a narrow view of the circumstances in which a legitimate expectation qualifies as a 'possession', this is not ordinarily the case where more traditional property rights are in play. Thus, for example, there is little doubt that legitimate expectations related to substantive economic or commercial benefits which are quantifiable fall inside the protection of Article 1 of the First Protocol:

> where the loss is quantifiable—as where the individual's complaint is that he has spent an ascertainable amount of money in reliance upon the representation—compensation to the value of that loss may adequately address the individual's grievance without forcing the body to fulfil its promise.[179]

Moreover, and more promisingly, both he and Michael Fordham envisage that English law may in the future acknowledge an independent public law notion of compensation beyond the human rights context, so that the courts could generally reconcile the need to vindicate the claimant's expectation and the 'overriding public interest' in the state defeating it, by ensuring reparation as the 'price' for upholding the state action.[180]

It would follow from this that the payment of compensation may well be a good solution to the problem of competing interests at a remedial level, because it ensures that interference with third parties' possessions—which inevitably arises as a result of the quashing of a wrongful administrative action—strikes a 'fair balance' between the demands of the *ultra vires* doctrine and the requirements of legal certainty. In other words, it is possible to suggest that recognition of the rationale underlying the award for loss may assist the public law system to resolve disputes in a more principled manner, since it serves to establish a reasonable relationship of proportionality between the means employed, namely, the frustration of legitimate expectations, and the aim sought to be realized, namely, the protection of those who benefit from the correct application of legal rules.

4.6 Objections to compensating third parties

There are at least two objections that might be made to the proposed approach to the problem of third parties. The purpose of this sub-section is to defend it from these criticisms and to reinforce the position that it provides a convincing alternative to full substantive protection of legitimate expectations at a remedial level.

In the first place, it might be argued that the implementation of the compensation system in the context of *ultra vires* representations is possible because there is a direct relationship between the public body and the representee, and that such an approach is therefore justified on the basis that there has been a sort of breach of 'contract' which renders the decision-maker liable for damages. The monetary remedy cannot, it might be observed, be applied in the same way in the remedial context, because the authority has not entered into any direct relationship with third parties who have been misled by the offending order. Where there is no promise, there is no breach of any kind, and no damage could thereby be claimed.

This objection is unconvincing. It is relatively clear from the cases identified above that the liability to give redress in respect of economic loss arises from the frustration of legitimate expectations relating to property ('possesions' for the

[179] Steele, (as above n. 174), 325.   [180] Ibid. See also Fordham, (as above n. 174), 104–107.

purposes of Article 1 of the First Protocol) rather than from the contravention of any type of assurance given to the individuals. It is also apparent that direct promises or assurances are not the only forms of public action which can be used as the basis for such reliance. For example, it is possible that an expectation for this purpose may be founded on a representation made to a person other than the claimant. Indeed, this is precisely what we find in the *Rowland* case, where the applicant's expectations were based on the assurance given to the previous owners of the estate.[181] Moreover, the courts' willingness to refuse relief in order to protect commercial deals done in reliance on the validity of *ultra vires* decisions, which is particularly evident in cases such as *Argyll, Datafin and Guinness*, clearly illustrates judicial recognition that third parties have at least a legitimate expectation of being able to continue to trade on that assumption. It is undeniable that this can be regarded as a component part of the right to property entitled to protection under Article 1 of the First Protocol. Consequently, there may well be cases in which compensation for damages must be awarded notwithstanding the fact that there is no direct relationship between the claimant and the public body.

A second objection to this proposal might be cast as follows. In the case of *ultra vires* representations, there is a clear causal connection between the damage claimed by the applicant and the governmental action. In particular, the loss of investment suffered by the party who benefited from the mistaken assurance arises as a direct result of the authority's decision not to be bound by it. This causal relationship is not, it might be argued, present in the remedial context, where interference with the peaceful enjoyment of the individual's possessions is directly caused by the court's decision to quash the contested order rather than by the decision-maker. Indeed, it is for the judges and not to the executive to decide which of the parties shall suffer harm from the granting or refusal of the remedy. Consequently, it would be self-apparent that, in such case, the executive authority should not make reparation for the loss suffered by the applicant. In particular, it would be unfair and even dangerous to establish a precedent that allows commercial regulators to be held liable for acts committed by other subjects, namely, the courts. This prompts two responses.

In the first place, it is perhaps somewhat simplistic to suggest that the defendant is of no relevance to the issue here. It is clear that, in these situations, the *ultra vires* nature of the decision is the predominant cause of the loss, to the extent that the position of third parties would not be undermined if the public body acted within its powers. Naturally, once the judge comes to invalidate the offending order, the interference with the innocent party's possessions, described above, arises. However, it is undeniable that the intervention of the court is, in turn, a direct consequence of the defendant's action. As seen earlier, the mere existence of a legal flaw in the decision which creates legitimate expectations inevitably makes

---

[181] Mance LJ stressed that,

> the defendant was never asked to, and did not, issue any formal statement or enter into any direct commercial relationship with the claimant. Still less did it purport to convey to the Rowlands any right for which the Rowlands paid anything. The agency and the Rowlands were never in direct contact before the purchase in 1968 [as above n. 176].

the remedial system to trump either the interests of the applicant or those of third parties. In this sense, any determination of the court in regard to the relief claimed can be seen as a logical effect of the administrative mistake rather than as an independent and isolated event which causes harm to one of the parties in conflict. Specifically, the judge's decision to quash the contested measure appears to be just a link in the causal chain between the defendant's conduct and the party's injury; a necessary product of the *ultra vires* act which contains in itself both the origin of the individual's legitimate expectations and the seed of their future and necessary frustration. Hence, even if the court subsequently interferes with the possessions of third parties in order to give effect to the principle of legality, it is plain from the foregoing analysis that the agency remains to be obliged to pay, particularly because it has given rise to legitimate expectations doomed to be defeated.

There is, however, a second—and more fundamental—response to this objection. Even if the liability for the violation of the Convention right cannot be assigned with clarity, it does not establish that the analogy drawn from the context of *ultra vires* representations is incorrect. Ultimately, it may be argued that, from a theoretical perspective, the award of compensation to the victim should be based on a causal relationship between the unjustified interference with her rights and the conduct of the State as a whole. In particular, it may well be assumed that it is the State which has decided, through its judicial organ, not to be bound by its own administrative decision which gave rise to legitimate expectations, thereby interfering with the possession of *bona fide* parties. It follows from this that the State is objectively liable for the mistake committed by its organs irrespective of whether the specific liability for loss is attached to the court and/or the agency.

Within this view, therefore, the fact that the interference with third-party possessions is caused by a subject other than the decision-maker presents no obstacle to the implementation of the compensation system. The monetary remedy could still be justified by reference to the conduct of one single entity, the State, to which the acts of all public authorities can ultimately be attributed. This is not to say, however, that the definition of the scope of the liability of the agency and the court, if any, in relation to the loss caused to third parties is unimportant and should be neglected. Actually, it may be crucial to securing public accountability and to identifying the appropriate budget from which the funds for compensation will be derived. But it is to say that the court must, in the final analysis of whether the damages should be awarded, base its conclusion solely on the existence of an unjustified interference with private possessions by the State.

It is interesting to note that this approach is fully consistent with the language and spirit of Community law[182] and the European Convention.[183] Indeed it is relatively clear that the award of compensation under these institutions is based, above all, on the alleged breach of their provisions and the protocols thereto by the State. Consequently, in determining whether to award damages to compensate injured parties, the respective courts must focus on the general liability of the State

---

[182] See *R v. Secretary of State for Transport, ex p Factortame Ltd.* [1996] E.C.R. I-1029, para. 34.
[183] See Article 41 (the 'High Contracting Part').

rather than on the specific liability of public organs whose conduct has contributed to cause the loss. For the present purpose, this point is well illustrated by the judgment of the Strasbourg's Court in *Pine Valley*.[184] In this case, the Supreme Court of Ireland had held that an outline planning permission for industrial warehouse and office development on a site in Dublin was a nullity *ab initio*. The ECtHR held that such judgment, which frustrated the applicants' legitimate expectations of being able to carry out their proposed development, had to be regarded as an interference with the right to the peaceful enjoyment of their possessions. It is therefore clear that, in the court's view, the interference in question arose as a result of the judicial decision holding the permission to be invalid rather than as a consequence of the administrative misrepresentation. However, in deciding whether compensation should be provided, the Court did not base its analysis solely on the judiciary's decision but on the State's general failure to validate retrospectively the permission or to provide compensation or other remedy for the reduction in value of the property. Thus, it implicitly recognized that, as far as the position of private individuals is concerned, a fair application of the compensation approach necessarily requires the court to regard the combined effect of the *ultra vires* decision and the subsequent judgment of the court as a single cause of the damage which can ultimately be attributed to the State.

Nevertheless, it may be counter-argued that this approach could not be adopted under domestic law in a similar case, because section 8 of the HRA 1998 expressly provides that damages must be awarded against specific public authorities. Perhaps this is so. However, it is submitted that this requirement does not necessarily preclude the application of a similar 'unitary' approach at a national level. If it appears that many acts are involved in the violation, the victim may well bring an action against all the public bodies which would be liable in respect of the same damage.[185] In practical terms this means that a single compensation would be paid by the different organs which have, in fact, contributed or may have contributed to cause the loss. Thus, it becomes clear that even if the loss is caused by a series of successive decisions adopted by several authorities, the court may, in fact, consider the effect of a State's conduct as a whole by apportioning responsibility between the concurrent decision-makers.

However, it may be further claimed that this approach is difficult to apply in the present context, because the courts—whose decision to invalidate the unlawful administrative order may be regarded as contributing to the loss suffered by *bona fide* parties—enjoy immunity under section 9(3) the HRA for damages in respect of acts done in good faith. Presumably, therefore, only that part of the loss attributable to the executive body would attract damages. This is correct and should be taken into account in the apportionment formula. The strength of this argument is, however, diminished because, as seen above, it appears that the administrative

---

[184] (As above n. 38). For the application of this approach in other areas see *H v. United Kingdom*, A 143-A [1988] 13 E.H.R.R. 435; *EDC v. United Kingdom* [1998] B.C.C. 370.

[185] In this sense section 8(5) of the Human Rights Act enables a public authority which has been held liable to the victim in tort to claim contribution from any other individual or body who has also been involved in the violation.

authority is principally responsible for the frustration of legitimate expectations on the part of third parties. Consequently, it seems likely that it will be required to pay all the damages.[186]

4.7 Statutory immunity of the FSA and the Takeover Panel

Having set out the importance of giving compensation either to aggrieved applicants or third parties in the context of discretionary remedies, it is appropriate at this point to note that there may be some practical difficulties in trying to impose such obligation on the FSA and the Takeover Panel, as the Financial Services and Markets Act 2000[187] and the Companies Act 2006[188] respectively provide that they are almost completely immune from liability in damages. Prima facie, this situation would fundamentally undermine the effectiveness of the proposed system of compensation, since, in practice, most of the cases in which it would be needed relate to unlawful orders regulating financial services markets, exchanges and firms. Because of this serious restriction in the scope for legal redress, it is probable that few liability cases against these authorities would arise and therefore few affected parties would receive payment. Nevertheless, it is also worth pointing out that this statutory immunity, while undeniable and in need of reform, might become an increasingly relative phenomenon. Two main points arise.

First, as the relevant legislation expressly provides, it cannot be pleaded,

so as to prevent an award of damages made in respect of an act or omission on the ground that the act or omission was unlawful as a result of section 6(1) of the Human Rights Act 1998.[189]

Thus, it would be correct to say, *a contrario sensu*, that where the FSA or the Takeover Panel act in breach of Convention rights will the question of liability in damages arise. This provision may certainly have a very substantial and positive impact on the courts' ability to award monetary remedies in the case at hand; particularly in light of the right to property, which entitles market actors to be indemnified by public bodies in respect of unlawful decisions that interfere with the peaceful enjoyment of their possession. Consequently, the position is reached that, so long as these authorities remain liable for infringement of a Convention right, the proposed award of damages can be founded on nothing other than Article 1 of the First Protocol.

---

[186] See para. 4.84 of the Law Commission's report on *Damages under the Human Rights Act 1998* (Law Com No. 266). Report on a Reference under section 3(1)(e) of the Law Commission Act 1965 presented to the Parliament of the United Kingdom by the Lord High Chancellor by Command of Her Majesty, October 2000.

[187] Schedule 1, paragraph 19(1): Neither the Authority nor any person who is, or is acting as, a member, officer or member of staff of the Authority is to be liable in damages for anything done or omitted in the discharge, or purported discharge, of the Authority's functions.

[188] Part 28, Chapter 1, section 961, Exemption from liability in damages. (1) Neither the Panel, nor any person within subsection (2), is to be liable in damages for anything done (or omitted to be done) in, or in connection with, the discharge or purported discharge of the Panel's functions.

[189] Financial Services and Market Act 2000, Schedule 1, paragraph 19(3)(b); Companies Act 2006, s 961(3).

Secondly, it is possible to argue that the rule that no general liability should attach to the FSA and the Takeover Panel may be called into question on procedural rights grounds. In particular, there are good reasons to maintain that it constitutes a disproportionate interference with the applicants' right of access to a court under Article 6(1) of the European Convention.[190] This point becomes apparent upon consideration of the arguments of the Strasbourg's Court in *Osman v. United Kingdom*,[191] a case concerning a claim in negligence arising out of the activities of the police in the investigation and suppression of crimes. It was first held that limitations to the 'right to a court' cannot 'restrict or reduce the access left to the individual in such a way or to such an extent that the very essence of the right is impaired'. Consequently, the particular attempt of the court to refuse to grant damages 'on the basis that the rule provided a watertight defence to the police and that it was impossible to prise open an immunity which the police enjoy from civil suit' only serves to confer a 'blanket immunity' on the offending body which amounts to a 'disproportionate' and 'unjustifiable' restriction on an applicant's right enshrined in Article 6(1) of the Convention.

In light of this judgment, it may well be the case that legislation such as that described above, which lays down an almost absolute exclusionary rule to protect the FSA and the Takeover Panel from liability actions, fails to strike a fair balance between the public interest (in avoiding threats of legal actions that undermine the effectiveness and quality of supervision) and the individuals' right of access to court. There may accordingly be a disproportionate interference with their procedural rights, contrary to Article 6(1) of the Convention, which needs to be remedied. Nevertheless, if this idea is accepted, the situation arises in which the court cannot simply order compensation to be paid on due process grounds. Since the immunity in question is statutory, in contrast to the common law immunity successfully challenged in the *Osman* case, such an action would be inconsistent with the principle of parliamentary sovereignty.

It therefore becomes apparent that the only way in which the competing objectives mentioned above can be reconciled is by recourse to the methodology of statutory interpretation, in accordance with section 3(1) of the HRA. Thus, a rule of construction might be applied which is based on the presumption that Parliament would not wish to abrogate citizens' basic right to access to a court. In particular, the exclusionary rule might be interpreted as simply underscoring the existence of a kernel of effective control which cannot be jeopardized by the constant risk of exposure to tortious liability. The practical effect of this may be to allow the court to provide a system of compensation in respect of certain degrees of negligence or of harm suffered which complies with the basic standards of regulatory efficiency in the financial field. In this manner, an open account of the court's reaction to statutory immunity might certainly be provided which avoids the charge of constitutional impropriety in the form of judicial disobedience to Parliament.

---

[190] This breach has been noted, with some doubts, by Page, Alan, 'Self-regulation: The Constitutional Dimension' [1986] 49(2) *The Modern Law Review*, 145–147.

[191] [2000] 29 E.H.R.R. 245. See also *Z v. United Kingdom* [2002] 34 E.H.R.R. 97 and *TP and KM v. United Kingdom* Application No. 28945/95, judgment 10 May 2001.

Finally, it is worth pointing out that, in any event, voluntary payments may also be an appropriate way to award compensation to businesses or individuals damaged by maladministration. To this effect, the FSA maintains a complaints scheme in accordance with its obligations under paragraphs 7 and 8 of Schedule 1 to the Financial Services and Markets Act which includes 'the offer of a compensatory payment on an *ex-gratia* basis' as a remedy for 'any expression of dissatisfaction' about the manner in which it has carried out, or failed to carry out its functions.[192] Applicants who are dissatisfied with the outcome of this procedure, can also refer the matter to the Complaints Commissioner, who may, if he thinks it appropriate, recommend that the FSA remedy the matter complained of by offering a monetary remedy.

4.8 Limited societal funds and public needs

Another potential difficulty with the proposed system of compensation is that it may be unrealistic, in the sense that it overlooks the fact that societal funds set aside for compensation are far from being sufficient to afford just satisfaction to parties who 'may be numbered in thousands'.[193] This situation was described with particular clarity by Lord Woolf when he said extra-judicially that the 'days when public bodies could be regarded as having purses of bottomless depth are now past'.[194] Thus it appears that it is extremely implausible to assert that the courts should award damages to numerous victims of commercial rights infringements, precisely because public funds would not be sufficient to cover such great loss. In practical terms, such system of payments would raise the prospect of the courts imposing significant restrictions on the allocation of scarce public resources. As a consequence, enormous amounts of money would be diverted from their legitimate use in the satisfaction of pressing social needs.[195]

Moreover, in the case of damages under the HRA 1998, it may be argued that to provide compensation to numerous parties is inconsistent with section 8(3)(b), which entitles the courts to take into account general policy issues, such as the need to avoid floods of claims for damages. Crucially, it provides that 'No award of damages is to be made unless, taking account ... the consequences of any decision (of that or any other court) in respect of that act'. It should therefore not be open to judges to award damages in cases where the consequences of providing such remedy may be too severe for the defendant to bear.[196] In light of this, it becomes apparent that no monetary relief should be available in respect of loss suffered at a

---

[192] See the part of the FSA Handbook in Redress entitled 'Complaints against the FSA' (COAF) <http://fsahandbook.info/FSA/html/handbook/> accessed 5 October 2010.

[193] Expression used by Lord Donaldson in *Datafin*.

[194] Woolf, Lord Harry, 'The Human Rights Act 1998 and Remedies', in *Judicial Review in International Perspective: Volume II*, M. Andenas and D. Fairgrieve (eds.), (Leiden: Kluwer Law International, 2000) 433.

[195] See a similar line of reasoning in the dicta of the House of Lords in *Stovin v. Wise*, [1996] A.C. 923; see also the judgment of the Court of Appeal in *Anufrijeva v. London Borough of Southwark* [2003] E.W.C.A. Civ 1406, [2004] 2 W.L.R. 603 at [75].

[196] See Amos, Merris, 'Damages for Breach of the Human Rights Act 1998' [1999] 178 *European Human Rights Law Review*, 186–187.

remedial level, since the consequence of that judicial decision may be that a large number of potential victims will have a similar claim imposing a significant burden on the public purse. The foregoing analysis prompts three responses.

First, it is worth noting that this view, according to which a system of compensation to numerous parties would pose a threat to the expenditure of public resources, involves a degree of generalization which may fail to capture the real range of *bona fide* persons who might be harmed and the scale of their losses. In particular, it tends to overlook the fact that judicial recognition of third-party rights does not necessarily entail the existence of countless individuals entitled to protection by the public system. In the *Air Europe* case,[197] for example, the court allowed an *ultra vires* report to stand for the sole purpose of avoiding the prejudice which British Airways, a single third party, would suffer by being put out of the competition after much activity since the decision-maker allowed it back into the commercial arena. In light of this, it is perfectly plausible that the number of individuals potentially affected by the invalidation of the executive decision might be even less than that of applicants. Moreover, it is worthy of mention that such recognition does not either necessarily imply the imposition of large indemnity payments. Indeed there may be cases in which numerous parties are entitled to just a small amount of money in accordance with the little loss sustained. Once these possibilities are acknowledged, it becomes apparent that the objection based on massive claims for compensation is unduly simplistic. To the extent that it denies the possibility of payment to innocent parties on the mere assumption that their claims would be *per se* numerous and expensive, it is indeed incapable of accommodating the different situations that may arise as a result of the court's decision to grant or withhold relief.

Thus it transpires that only by relating the availability of monetary remedies to the *extent* of the damage that may arise in respect of the contended decision is it possible to provide a realistic response to the claims involved. Indeed this factor supplies a much more sensitive basis for the judges to decide whether to award damages or not which avoids the artificiality of the numeric approach. The crucial point for the present purpose is that it allows the judicial balancing test to be applied in terms of the precise sums necessary to make reparation in respect of the pecuniary losses. Within this framework, therefore, so long as the court remains capable of assessing the real implications of the *ultra vires* decision, it is able to provide a level of protection that is necessary to afford just satisfaction to all the subjects involved.

Secondly, as regards the obligation to take into account policy factors under s. 8(3)(b)—which has been construed as a precluding the courts from awarding damages to numerous victims—it must be argued that such interpretation is fundamentally inconsistent with the section's legal framework, given that it fails to accord with the fundamental principles which can be deployed to provide citizens with appropriate remedies for breaches of human rights. This is a point which the Law Commission clearly recognizes in its report on damages under the HRA

---

[197]   *R v. Monopolies and Mergers Commission, ex p Air Europe Limited* [1988] 4 B.C.C. 182.

1998.[198] In particular, it suggests that the basic requirement for 'just satisfaction' to the injured party clearly demarcates a level of administrative justice from which no legal interpretation can justify a refusal to provide compensation. Thus,

where the victim has suffered an identifiable and readily measurable loss, and is otherwise held to be deserving of a monetary remedy, there seems to be little scope for the consideration of other wider interests, such as those of potential defendants.

It also argues that to have regard to such considerations would be difficult to reconcile with the general principle of *restitutio in integrum* adopted by the Strasbourg Court.

Moreover, the Public Law Team of the Law Commission has argued in its recent discussion paper on monetary remedies in public law[199] that it is illogical to assert that because a breach has caused widespread loss, that loss should not be compensated. Such reasoning in effect means that 'the more damage respondent bodies could point to, the more likely they were to avoid liability'. Consequently, the possibility of a large number of claimants should not, in itself, rule out liability actions against public bodies.

Nevertheless, as Duncan Fairgrieve points out, this does not mean that it is inappropriate to consider wider considerations in deciding whether to award damages under the HRA. But in doing so, the public policy concerns must not systematically trump the rights of the individual, and should rather complement the search for a just and appropriate remedy to ensure the securing of civil liberties.[200]

It is important to note that this approach to damages, according to which policy considerations should not pose a serious obstacle to liability claims, has been clearly recognized by the House of Lords in relation to damage to property. Thus, in *Junior Books Ltd v. Veitchi Ltd*,[201] a case concerning pure economic loss suffered by a company as a result of construction defects, it was held that although it cannot be denied that 'floodgates' arguments have from time to time been allowed to play their part in the tort of negligence, today its scope is best determined by considerations of principle rather than of policy. Consequently:

if principle suggests that the law should develop along a particular route and if the adoption of that particular route will accord a remedy where that remedy has hitherto been denied, I see no reason why, if it be just that the law should henceforth accord that remedy, that remedy should be denied simply because it will, in consequence of this particular development, become available to many rather than to few.

Thirdly, the present thesis argues that one useful way in which these competing objectives may be reconciled is by recourse to an exercise of remedial discretion which is sensitive to the prospect of liability claims. Given that the decision-maker

---

[198] The Law Commission, (as above n. 186), Part IV, para. 4.41.

[199] The Law Commission, Public Law Team, Discussion Paper entitled *Monetary Remedies in Public Law*, 11 October 2004, paragraph 4.29. Published on the Law Commission's website: <http://www.lawcom.gov.uk> accessed 5 October 2010.

[200] Fairgrieve, Duncan, 'The Human Rights Act 1998, Damages and Tort Law' [2001] *Public Law*, 702.

[201] [1983] 1 A.C. 520 at 539.

will be required to make reparation for the pecuniary loss caused to the party against whom the court's decision is adopted, it is suggested that, in order to protect the public purse so far as possible, the court should always exercise its discretion in favour of the party who otherwise would suffer the greatest economic loss. In this manner, it will ensure that the public authority is only liable to pay the lower amount of damages in comparative terms. Thus, for example, if by balancing the different interests at stake the court reaches the conclusion that the financial loss which the applicant would suffer as a result of relief being withheld is outweighed by that of third parties as a consequence of the same remedy being granted, it would be much simpler for it to withhold relief in order to ensure that the future possible compensation is the lower. Contrariwise, if the court is satisfied that the plaintiff is going to suffer more than third parties, then the court should logically quash the decision in order to avoid the greater evil and cause the public body to pay just the smaller amount for the hardship suffered by the latter.

On this approach, therefore, the potential economic loss to each party becomes the principal factor upon which the courts are to determine what limits should be imposed on discretionary powers to grant or withhold relief. Importantly, it reflects the best choice concerning the extent to which public authorities should be subsequently liable for any unlawful decision in the commercial context. In particular, by exercising its discretion to allow the lowest possible amount of damages, the court would be able to achieve a fair balance between the need to protect the individual's rights and the demands of the general interest of the community in protecting societal resources. A reasonable relationship of proportionality would therefore be established between the means employed and the aims pursued. Interestingly, it would be a case in which the principle of proportionality is conversely applied in order to avoid the imposition of severe restrictions to public interest which go well beyond what is strictly necessary to achieve the desired outcome of doing justice to all private parties. Within this framework, it would be very difficult for the courts, when protecting the rights of applicants or third parties, to award huge amounts of compensatory damage, because, if such protection was required, it may well be afforded instead by granting the remedy sought by the party who will suffer the greater loss.

4.9 Relating compensation to the exercise of remedial discretion

It is readily apparent from the discussion above that, under the orthodox doctrine, the exercise of remedial discretion in respect of an *ultra vires* decision which gives rise to legitimate expectations necessarily causes hardship either to the applicant or to third parties who detrimentally relied upon it. The present thesis argues that this situation is inconsistent with the very notion of rule of law, which provides that a relatively similar degree of consideration should be given to the competing interests at stake. In light of this, any attempt of the courts to protect one party at the expense of the other constitutes a disproportionate and unjustified interference with the rights of the latter which needs to be remedied. The purpose of the foregoing sub-sections has been to begin exploring the provision of compensation as a potentially significant solution to this problem. It appears that this remedy is capable of securing the reconciliation of the various legitimate interests involved by simply requiring the decision-maker to make a payment of money in lieu of the benefit lost by the party against whom the remedial discretion is exercised. Thus, the proposed approach certainly answers the well-founded criticisms which can be levelled at the current model of adjudication while safeguarding both the proportionate restriction of rights and its compatibility with the constitutional framework.

5. Conclusion

The present chapter has used the conceptual framework of proportionality set out in Chapter 4 to support the adoption of a more intensive form of review that extends to all the aspects of the contended order. On this view, it must be the case that any exercise of regulatory power that infringes private rights must be proportionate to the objective being pursued. Consequently, it seems that judges must recognize the substantial implications of such criteria not only in relation to the standard of reasonableness, but also in regard to the interpretation of wide terms, questions of fact, and discretionary remedies.

As regards substantive review in the specific context of commercial regulation, it is important to note that Article 1 of the First Protocol of the HRA—on the peaceful enjoyment of private possessions—and the Legislative and Regulatory Reform Act 2006 form a crucial part of the juridical foundation upon which proportionality rests. It must also be borne in mind that, due to the broad range of issues and polycentricism involved in market affairs, the test could take several forms. A good illustration of this variety is supplied by the judgments of the ECJ. The Court has been ready to strike down regulatory decisions which are disproportionate on different grounds: failure to consider equally effective but less burdensome alternative means to achieve public aims, impingement upon the very substance of economic rights, and causation of excessively severe effects in imposing penalties or altering previous policies. In all these cases, the application of the proportionality principle has provided a more balanced and impartial approach to measures than that postulated by the *Wednesbury* rationale, in which the accommodation of competing interests is primarily for one of the parties: the executive agency.

The proportionality approach could also aid the construction of wide terms. Relatively unclear expressions undoubtedly leave a margin of interpretive discretion to the regulator as to which precise meaning can be ascribed to the text. In these cases, rather than automatically upholding any meaning which remains within the bounds of mere rationality, the judiciary should, it is argued, approve the meaning which is most proportionate to the regulatory aim being pursued. In this manner the courts' interpretive endeavour is of a piece with Parliament's intention that so far as it is possible to do so, legislative provisions must be read and given effect in a way which is compatible with the content of rights.

Additionally, this doctrine may also prompt a wider ground of factual review in the commercial area. The HRA requires the courts to form a primary judgement on the extent to which the regulatory encroachment on rights is proportionate to the policy being pursued. In order to do so, they need to engage in the process of ascertaining all the evidence related to the case, so that the factual preconditions for the balance of interests that proportionality embodies are taken into account. In practice, this means that the courts' attention should also be directed towards the 'legislative facts' which underpin the particular policy that is being implemented through the impugned decision, not merely the 'adjudicative facts' which are in dispute.

Finally, the proportionality principle also provides a satisfactory solution to the problem faced by remedial discretion when the granting of relief against an unlawful decision would affect the interests of the administration and third parties. In these cases, rather than simply allowing the court to withhold such relief—as the orthodox approach seems to suggest —the doctrine of proportionality requires it to strike a fairer balance between the needs of the successful applicant and the interests of the executive and third parties. In particular, this compromise might be achieved either by spreading the loss caused by the flawed decision among the parties equitably over a long period of time or by providing compensation to the individual who has been harmed by the court's decision on whether to grant or withhold relief. Thus proportionality has the advantage of facilitating the reconciliation of the interests at stake without unduly interfering with private rights.

Based on the foregoing set of reasons, it is strongly arguable that proportionality in fact clears the way for a general approach which is substantially more robust, and therefore fairer, than that which the English courts have adopted thus far. Furthermore, when these advantages are taken into account, then it is difficult to persist with the idea that the test must be confined to the areas where it currently already applies. This issue will be addressed in the following chapter, where it will be argued that there are good reasons to extend the acceptance of the proportionality test from the EC law and HRA to purely domestic law challenges.

6

The Broader Effect of the Principle of Proportionality

1. Proportionality as the General Standard of Review

A final point concerning the recognition of proportionality as an independent ground of review within domestic law needs to be made. The previous chapter demonstrates that this principle, which allows the court to build a satisfactory approach to commercial judicial review, has been particularly applied in human rights and EU cases. Accordingly, it may be argued that the proposed test could not be applied in those contexts in which administrative law has not already embraced. Thus, a bright-line distinction may be postulated between a proportionality-based standard for Convention and Community rights infringement and a less rigorous system of substantive review for purely domestic law cases.[1] Such reasoning, however, overlooks some crucial points. Even if there are areas in which claimants who wish to challenge regulatory decisions cannot directly invoke European institutions, and must instead rely on national law principles, this does not mean that proportionality is to be precluded from operating. Rather, there are justified reasons to think that this approach will have a broader influence on English law, thereby imposing upon the courts a wider obligation to adopt a more intensive form of review even where there are no fundamental rights or Community matters at stake. Three principal arguments can be advanced in support if this contention.

First, there is little doubt that the incorporation of the European Convention and Community law may exert indirect effects on domestic administrative law, for it, like the common law, has a capacity to evolve over time in response to relevant changes in the juridical system. Consequently, it is entirely possible that, as the context within which public law adjudication occurs, changes under the indirect influence of European legal sources, the English judiciary will become acclimatized to the concept of proportionality on a wider scale. This view has been expressed with particular clarity by Wong. He observes that the current mandatory application of a control of proportionality to cases involving a Community

---

[1] See the approach of the House of Lords in *R v. Chief Constable of Sussex, ex p International Trader's Ferry Ltd.* [1999] 2 A.C. 418; and the judgment of the Court of Appeals in *Association of British Civilian Internees (Far East Region) v. Secretary of State for Defence* [2003] E.W.C.A. Civ. 473 [2003] Q.B. 1397, which assumes that it is only for the House of Lords to decide whether proportionality must completely replace the *Wednesbury* test.

dimension and those that fall under the HRA will in time attune and accustom English judges to the concept itself: 'this may make a practical reception of this principle into general administrative law easier and less fraught with difficulties'.[2]

In particular, it is important to realize that the provisions of the HRA 1998 will have a pervasive effect on the whole legal system, but in no area more than in administrative law. Thus, it is hoped that constant practice in the field of human rights will develop the existing corpus of administrative law so as to extend the scope of intensive review to others matters.[3] This philosophy is evident in Lord Irvine's contribution to the debate on the indirect effect of the HRA. Actually, he posed the question 'how long the courts will restrict their review to a narrow *Wednesbury* approach in non-Convention cases, if used to inquiring more deeply in Convention cases?'[4] This question is the same thing as asking whether the differences between both approaches will be eliminated by 'spill-over effect' from human rights.[5] His Lordship's answer was that 'the Convention rights must pervade all law and all court systems. Our courts will therefore learn these techniques and inevitable will consider their utility in deciding other non-Convention cases.'[6] This is precisely the kind of convergence which European influences are likely to bring about, and 'it is evident already in the numerous references to proportionality which judges are making freely, and which are paving the way for its general acceptance'.[7]

This outcome is plainly justified by the text of the HRA itself and other textual indicators such as the White Paper which accompanied the Bill and the reports in *Hansard* of the parliamentary debates on the Bill.[8] Particular attention must be paid to the express inclusion of ordinary courts and tribunals within the definition of public authorities obliged by section 6(1) to act compatibly with the Convention. As Elliott explains, the governmental proposal that the Convention should be applied by courts at every level reflects the idea that 'the Convention is not to be viewed as something separate from ordinary law but, rather, as forming the normative basis upon which domestic law is now to be understood and developed'.[9] It therefore follows that English administrative

---

[2] Wong, Garreth, 'Towards the Nutcracker Principle: Reconsidering the Objections to Proportionality' [2000] *Public Law*, 107. See also Craig, Paul, 'The Impact of Community Law on Domestic Public Law', in *Administrative Law Facing the Future: Old Constraints and New Horizons*, P. Leyland and T. Woods (eds.), (Oxford: Oxford University Press, 1997) 277.

[3] Elliott, Mark, 'The Human Rights Act 1998 and the Standard of Substantive Review' [2001] 60(2) *Cambridge Law Journal*, 327.

[4] Irvine of Lairg, Lord A.A.M., 'The Development of Human Rights in Britain under an Incorporated Convention on Human Rights' [1998] *Public Law*, 234.

[5] Wade, W. and Forsyth, C.F., *Administrative Law*, 10th edn., (Oxford: Oxford University Press, 2009), 372.

[6] Irvine of Lairg, 'The Development of Human Rights in Britain under an Incorporated Convention on Human Rights', (as above n. 4), 232.   [7] Ibid.

[8] Murray Hunt demonstrates that these texts contain a number of indications which, taken together, strongly suggests that the proper reading of the legislation will be that it makes the Convention apply to all law. See Hunt, Murray, 'The "Horizontal Effect" of the Human Rights Act' [1998] *Public Law*, 438.

[9] Elliott, 'The Human Rights Act 1998 and the Standard of Substantive Review', (as above n. 3), 328. See also Bamforth, Nicholas, 'The Application of the Human Rights Act 1998 to Public Authorities and Private Bodies' [1999] 58(1) *Cambridge Law Journal*, 163.

law, like other branches of domestic law, must coalesce in one system with the Convention.

Secondly, there are some pragmatic reasons which militate in favour of proportionality as a general standard of review. Craig points out that this approach provides a more structured and reasoned form of inquiry which focuses the attention of both the public body being reviewed and the court undertaking the review.[10] Specifically, the decision-maker has to explain why its decision really was necessary and suitable to reach the desired end, and why it did not impose an excessive burden on the applicant. Thus, if the reviewing court is minded to overturn the agency choice, it too will have to give reasons that are consonant with the proportionality inquiry. In this view, as Jowell says, proportionality will certainly act as a standard of good administration. By requiring means to have reasonable relation to ends, this principle will enhance the sensitivity of decision-makers to the impact of their actions and heighten their awareness of balance and proportion: 'This can be only for good. Public administration is about means as well as ends. So is democracy. One of the hallmarks of tyranny has been the priority of ends over means'.[11]

Thirdly, as Wong points out, the rejection of proportionality as an independent and general criterion of review may be tantamount to a lack of consistency which 'smacks of artificially induced distinction unfounded on any principled consideration'.[12] He illustrates this argument by outlining two hypothetical cases relating to the judgment of the ECJ in the cited German beer case.[13] Here the court used a control of proportionality to strike down a rule which propagated a nationwide ban on all additives in beer sold domestically. Accordingly, if the UK government were to prohibit the importation of beers containing any additive it is beyond doubt that national courts could apply the principle of proportionality to declare such rule invalid. However, if the English government were to preclude the use of such substances in the *production* of domestic beer rather than its importation, courts would be unable to invoke this doctrine, since that case would no longer fall under the rubric of Community law. Prospective applicants in the second example would therefore be excluded from the strict scrutiny review which EU law offers to foreign importers into England for the mere fact that they are local producers.[14] Given the absurdity and inequality inherent in such reasoning, it would be unsurprising if the courts explored a more satisfactory approach which at least provides that like demands of justice can be treated alike.

The idea is thus expressed that the extent of legal protection available to individuals should not vary depending on whether the particular facts of the instant case may be interpreted as involving a European Community dimension, or whether there is an alleged breach of rights protected under the HRA 1998.[15] Consequently,

---

[10] Craig, Paul, *Administrative Law*, 6th edn., (London: Sweet & Maxwell, 2008) 637–638.
[11] Jowell, Jeffrey, 'Is proportionality an Alien Concept?' [1996] 2(3) *European Public Law*, 410. See also, De Smith, S., Woolf, Sir H., Jowell, J. and Le Sueur, A., *De Smith, Woolf and Jowell's Principles of Judicial Review*, (London: Sweet & Maxwell, 1999) 517.
[12] Wong, (as above n. 2), 96.
[13] *Commission v. Federal Republic of Germany*, Case 178/84 [1987] E.C.R. 1227.
[14] Wong, (as above n. 2), 95.
[15] Ibid., 96.

it seems that English courts should be empowered to review administrative decisions on the grounds of proportionality irrespective of which side of the borderline a case is said to fall. As Wong points out,

if we agree with the fundamental axiom of justice that like should be treated alike, then as a matter of principle we must also concede that a control of proportionality should be available in English judicial review to all deserving cases.[16]

It is particularly instructive to consider the development of this notion in relation to the doctrine of substantive legitimate expectations given that this is one context in which the European principle of proportionality is likely to have the most major influence upon domestic administrative law.[17] In short, there is no reason why domestic legitimate expectations should be less well protected than European expectations. As Forsyth envisaged some years ago, it cannot be the law that the courts will balance the broader public interest against the protection of legitimate expectations in cases arising under EU law, but in similar domestic cases they will only be able to intervene on a *Wednesbury* basis.[18] Rather, the extent of legal protection should be equally available to the same category of legitimate expectation irrespective of whether the particular facts of the instant case may be interpreted as involving some aspect of Community law. Moreover, support for this conclusion can be found, at present, in the acceptance that different standards of review may co-exist, since this allows the judiciary to treat like cases on substantive expectation alike without fearing that they are imposing a monolithic, more rigorous form of review unfounded on any context consideration.

In light of this, we could predict that a tighter model of substantive review, developed under the influence of the HRA and Community law, will be the general approach for judicial supervision over administrative action. This is a point which Lord Slynn of Hadley clearly recognises in the *Alconbury* case:[19]

I consider that even without reference to the 1998 Act the time has come to recognise that this principle (proportionality) is part of English administrative law, not only when judges are dealing with community acts but also when they are dealing with acts subject to domestic law. Trying to keep the *Wednesbury* principle and proportionality in separate compartments seems to me to be unnecessary and confusing.

Actually the British government has already accepted that the requirement that decisions be 'proportionate' and not excessively onerous or harsh when less restrictive measures are available is part of the general requirement for 'reasonableness' in decision-making.[20] Moreover, the concept of proportionality has been enshrined

---

[16]   Ibid.

[17]   Craig, 'The Impact of Community Law on Domestic Public Law', (as above n. 2), 284.

[18]   Forsyth, Christopher, 'Wednesbury Protection of Substantive Legitimate Expectations' [1997] *Public Law*, 381.

[19]   *R v. Secretary of State for the Environment, Transport and the Regions, ex p Alconbury Developments Ltd.* [2001] 2 W.L.R. 1389. Lord Cooke expressed a similar view in the *Daly* case: *R v. Secretary of State for the Home Department, ex p Daly* [2001] U.K.H.L. 26, [2001] 2 A.C. 532.

[20]   The Treasury Solicitor's Department, *The Judge Over Your Shoulder*, 3rd edn., (Government Legal Service, 2000), 20.

in the new Rules of Civil Procedure. According to the new rules, the overriding objective of the scheme is to enable all courts to deal with cases justly when it exercises any power given to it by the Rules or interprets any rule. This includes, so far as practicable, dealing with the case in ways which are proportionate (i) to the amount of money involved; (ii) to the importance of the case; (iii) to the complexity of the issues; and (iv) to the financial position of each party.

This is also the approach that can be envisaged as regards market regulation, since this is a context in which the notion of proportionality has been explicitly embraced by the legislator in terms not necessarily related to the HRA or EU law. As seen above, in section 1 of Chapter 5, the Legislative and Regulatory Reform Act 2006 has required regulatory functions to be exercised so as to comply with the principle of proportionality. Importantly, therefore, it is possible to acknowledge the legislative necessity of this approach even in areas insulated from human rights and European considerations.

2. The Problem: The Absence of Parameters to Define Proportionality

At this point, however, an objection might be made that the practical application of the proposed approach to purely domestic law cases is difficult, because there are normally no clearly defined rights at stake against which the proportionality of the regulatory decision can be measured. Specifically, the possible protection of interests whose content and limits are not expressly set out in any text would preclude the court from exercising a more intensive review, since the range of responses open to the decision-maker in such situations naturally allows a zone of discretion which is wider than that permitted by the much sharper tools of objective justification and proportionality. In practice, this may mean that the distinction between the different modes of review becomes substantially less marked, to the extent that they may shade into one another. Thus, it is probable that decisions regarded as 'disproportionate' in this context will ultimately reflect the underlying notion of irrationality in a '*Wednesbury* sense'.

For example, it appears that the expression 'far more serious penalty than anything the justices could inflict', which is used by the Court of Appeal in *ex p Hook* (below) to describe a disproportionate punishment, is substantially similar to the model of review founded on the *Wednesbury* principle. This assertion is notably supported by Wade and Forsyth;[21] and extra-curially by Lord Hoffman, who said that it is not possible to see daylight between them.[22] In light of this, it might well be argued that attempts to replace the deferential doctrine with proportionality as the criterion of substantive review in the domestic field are unnecessary or, perhaps, relevant only for academic purposes.

[21] Wade and Forsyth, (as above n. 5), 312.
[22] Hoffmann, Lord L.H., 'A Sense of Proportion' [1997] 32 *Irish Jurist*, 58; see also his '*The Influence of the European Principle of Proportionality upon UK Law*', in *The Principle of Proportionality in the Laws of Europe*, (Oxford: Hart Publishing, 1999) 107–11. See also the judgment of Lord Slynn in *R v. Chief Constable of Sussex, ex p International Trader's Ferry Ltd.* [1999] 2 A.C. 418 at 439F).

Approaching the issue from this perspective, Michael Taggart, for example, holds that proportionality should not be applied to cases where fundamental rights are not directly engaged because, *inter alia*, it loses much of its analytical and structuring qualities. Rather, he says, the case should be situated on the 'non-rights' or 'public wrongs' side of the rainbow of review, where scrutiny operates according to the usual grounds of review and *Wednesbury* unreasonableness as a residual 'safety net'.[23]

The present thesis holds that it is right to acknowledge such difficulty, but it should not be allowed to obscure the rationale which ultimately underpins the application of proportionality. It must be recalled that the impetus which underlies the whole of the test is, essentially, a desire to avoid the achievement of a legitimate end by means which are excessive to a person's interests. It follows that it can be applied to protect any legal right even though its imprecise formulation requires the court to weigh many administrative choices. In this sense, as Craig points out, the fact that the decision-maker has a wider discretion to qualify domestic rights does not mean that proportionality has no role to play in this context. What it does mean is that the judge must decide, *inter alia*, on the intensity with which proportionality will be applied.[24]

This is well captured by the Luxembourg's Court jurisprudence, in which the proportionality test can be applied with varying degrees of intensity according to the nature and context of the different interests at stake.[25] Thus, those areas in which the regulator has a broad discretion might be subject to a less rigorous form of proportionality review, while those in which the discretion was more narrowly confined would be subject to a more searching inquiry.[26] For example, there is a series of cases in which the court has said that the lawfulness of EC agricultural legislation—where the rule-maker enjoys a wider discretion—can be affected only if the measure is 'manifestly' inappropriate in terms of the public aim being pursued.[27] It follows therefore that the variability in the intensity with which proportionality is applied will itself be of assistance in this regard.

A similar point is underscored by the experience of those jurisdictions—notably the United States—in which Congress has explicitly required agencies to adopt the proportional approach when making policy. In a number of contexts, such model of statutory rationality recognizes that the precise content and impact of proportionality must always ultimately be determined by reference to

---

[23] Taggart, Michael, 'Proportionality, Deference, Wednesbury', [2008] 3 *New Zealand Law Review*, 477–481.

[24] Craig, (as above n.10), 630. For example, the above cited variant of proportionality in the agricultural legislative context was applied by the High Court in *Telefonica O2 Europe Plc and others, R (on the application of) v. Secretary of State for Business, Enterprise and Regulatory Reform* [2007] E.W.H.C. (Admin) 3018, a case concerning the validity of the Mobile Roaming European Communities Regulations 2007, SI 2007/1933.

[25] De Búrca, Gráinne, 'The Principle of Proportionality and its Application in EC Law', [1993] 13 *Yearbook of European Law*, 105.

[26] Craig, 'The Impact of Community Law on Domestic Public Law', (as above n. 2), 284.

[27] See, for example, *Jippes & Ors* (Agriculture), Case 189/01 [2001] E.U.E.C.J. and *Spain v. Council* (Agriculture), Case 310/04 [2006] E.U.E.C.J.

the adverse effects on the regulatees rather than to clearly defined rights which give rise to a remedy. Thus, in America, section 9 of the Consumer Product Safety Act requires the Commission to make appropriate findings for inclusion in its rules with respect to 'any means of achieving the objective of the order while minimizing adverse effects on...commercial practices'.[28] Similarly, the Toxic Substances Control Act 1976 requires the Environmental Protection Agency to choose, as part of its rulemaking function, 'the least burdensome requirement' that provides adequate protection against the risk of injury to health and the environment presented by the commercial distribution of hazardous chemicals.[29] The Environmental Protection Act 1990 in the UK provides in the same vein that the objectives of the enforcing authority are, *inter alia*, 'ensuring that, in carrying on a prescribed process, the best available techniques *not entailing excessive cost* will be used'.[30]

Moreover, it must be argued that the debate surrounding the recognition of a new, more expansive ground of judicial review under the heading 'proportionality' cannot be, by any means, a waste of breath. As seen above, the *Wednesbury* review has traditionally expressed a conception of the separation of powers within which the balance between private interests and competing public policy claims is primarily for the decision-maker. It follows that the use of the orthodox and generous rationality standard cannot be reasonably employed to justify a more intensive review of substantive issues which leaves it to the courts to determine how such balance ought to be struck. In Loveland's words, such attempt 'seems to amount to a case not so much of pouring new wine into old bottles as simply changing the labels on an existing vintage'.[31] Laws LJ had captured the same point in *Mahmood*,[32] an immigration case, when he remarked that the application of so exiguous a standard of review to administrative interference with domestic human rights would involve a failure to recognize what has become a 'settled principle' of the common law, one which is entirely independent of the incorporation of the Convention by the Human Rights Act 1998: any such action will require a substantial objective justification from the executive and a more 'muscular' court than has been its habit. It therefore becomes apparent that the adoption of a more rigorous scrutiny necessarily requires recognition of something akin to proportionality which goes beyond the scope of control mandated by the *Wednesbury* principle as currently understood in the commercial context.

---

[28] Codified at 15 U.S.C. 2051–2084. (Public Law 92–573; 86 Stat. 1207, Oct. 27, 1972). See also Diver, Colin, 'Policymaking paradigms in Administrative Law' [1981] 95(2) *Harvard Law Review*, 415–421.

[29] Codified at 15 U.S.C. Title 15, Chapter 53, Subchapter I, § 2605.

[30] Section 7(2).

[31] Loveland, 'Does Homelessness Decision Making Engage Article 6(1) of The European Convention on Human Rights' [2003] 2 *European Human Rights Law Review*, 196.

[32] *R v. Secretary of State for the Home Department, ex p Amjad Mahmood* [2001] H.R.L.R. See also the judgment of Charles J in *R (Suleiman) v. Secretary of State for the Home Department* [2006] E.W.H.C. (Admin) 2431 at paras 16–18.

3. Proportionality and Market Regulation in Domestic Law

The implications of the foregoing analysis are highly significant to the present discussion concerning the application of a proportionality test in the commercial context. First, it implies that even if the claimant who wishes to challenge a regulatory decision cannot establish the infringement of Community law or a fundamental right (i.e. protection of property) in order to trigger a more intensive form of review, he will still be entitled to challenge the decision on the sole basis that it breaches the principle of proportionality, provided that domestic principles of administrative law developed in light of those legal sources support such an approach. This criterion may be applied even to judicial review of the provisions of self-regulatory bodies. As Cane says, it is arguable that the court should not restrict itself to ensuring fidelity to the positive aims of the regulatory regime, but that it should also test self regulatory codes against independent principles requiring, *inter alia*, proportionality.[33] Thus, for example, a regulatee may rely on the proportionality doctrine to complain about a decision which just fails to balance conflicting interests.

A good illustration of the application of proportionality as an independent ground of commercial judicial review in a case which does not concern Convention rights or EU law can be seen in *R. v. Barnsley Metropolitan Borough Council, ex p Hook*.[34] Here the Court of Appeal quashed a regulatory decision to revoke a market trader's licence on the ground that the penalty was disproportionate to the offence. Briefly, what had happened was that a street trader in the Barnsley Market was banned from trading in the market for life because he had urinated in the street after the market and all its toilets had closed. It is worth noting that this case does not fall under either the rubric of Community law or the HRA 1998. Rather, the case involves an alleged breach of the common law right to hold a market, which says that every member of the public is entitled to come into the market-place to bring things there for sale. However, the common law nature of the right involved did not prevent the judiciary from applying the test of proportionality to decide whether the corporation, in exercise of its powers of administering the market, could thus directly deprive Mr Hook of his right to trade in the market and thereby indirectly deprive him of his livelihood. Lord Denning stated,

But there is one further matter; and that is that the punishment was too severe...there are old cases which show that the court can interfere by certiorari if a punishment is altogether excessive and out of proportion to the occasion...So in this case if Mr Hook did misbehave, I should have thought the right thing would have been to take him before the justices under the byelaws, when some small fine might have been inflicted. It is quite wrong that the corporation should inflict on him the grave penalty of depriving him of his livelihood. That is a far more serious penalty than anything the justices could inflict. He is a man of good character, and ought not to be penalised thus. On that ground alone, apart from the others, the decision of the corporation cannot stand.

---

[33] Cane, Peter, 'Self-Regulation and Judicial Review' [1987] 6 *Civil Justice Quarterly*, 344.
[34] [1976] 3 All E.R. 452; [1976] 1 W.L.R. 1052, 140 JP 638, 74 L.G.R. 493. For an earlier application of the principle of proportionality to penalties, see *Commins v. Massam* [1643] March NR 196, 202.

Similarly Sir John Pennycuick said,

It seems to me that the isolated and trivial incident at the end of a working day is manifestly not a good cause justifying the disproportionately drastic step of depriving Mr Hook
of his licence, and indirectly of his livelihood. I would base my judgment in part on that
ground.

It is interesting to note that the proportionality doctrine has also been expressly
applied in domestic regulatory law as an aspect of rationality. Thus, in *R. v.*
Secretary of State for Transport, ex p Pegasus Holidays (London) Ltd and another,[35]
the Queen Bench's Division said that in testing the validity of the government's
suspension of the permits of Romanian pilots, regard should be had to the 'lack of
proportionality or lack of reasonableness'. In particular, Schiemann J held that the
general adoption of this approach can be viewed against a legal backdrop of which
certain recommendations of the Council of Europe form an important part,

It would perhaps be difficult for anyone appearing for the Government to take issue on
the principle of proportionality being applied by administrative authorities, bearing in
mind recommendation R(80)2 of the committee of ministers concerning the exercise of
discretionary powers by administrative authorities which was adopted by the Committee
of Ministers of the Council of Europe on 11 March 1980 and which recommends gov-
ernments of member states to be guided in their law and administrative practice by the
principles annexed to this recommendation, one of which basic principles is that an administrative authority when exercising a discretionary power should maintain a proper balance
between any adverse effects which its decision may have on the rights, liberties or interests
of persons and the purpose which it pursues.

In the more recent case of *ex p Else Ltd*[36] Popplewell J also took into account proportionality as 'an aspect of rationality' and held that the decision of the Committee
on Quotations of the International Stock Exchange to cancel the listing of a company's shares 'was not disproportionate to the damage which it was designed to
prevent within the doctrine of proportionality either at common law or under
Community law'. A similar approach can be seen in *National Grid Plc v. Gas &*
Electricity Markets Authority and Ors,[37] in which proportionality was included in
the assessment of the 'seriousness of the infringement'. In this case, however, the
decision to impose a penalty of £30 million on the applicant for abusing its domin-
ant position in the gas meters market was said by the court to be excessive in light
of the authority's involvement in the process that led to the making of the agree-
ments which gave rise to the fine.

 However, in the recent case of *ICO Satellite Ltd, R. (on the application of) v. The*
Office of Communications[38] the court clearly considered proportionality as a different standard of review. The claimant, a satellite operator, sought judicial review of
Ofcom's decision to write to the International Telecommunications Union (ITU)
to request the cancellation of the radio spectrum assigned to it due to failure to

---

[35] [1989] 2 All E.R. 481 [1988] 1 W.L.R. 990.
[36] *R v. International Stock Exchange, ex p Else Ltd.* [1993] Q.B. 534.
[37] [2010] E.W.C.A. Civ. 114.   [38] [2010] E.W.H.C. (Admin) 2010.

bring its satellite network into commercial operation. It was argued that such measure was disproportionate on the ground that it was not the least onerous option to
accomplish the public objective that radio frequencies must be used rationally, efficiently, and economically. The modification or retention of the basic characteristics of the entry was advocated as a much more suitable course of action. Although
the court finally dismissed these alternatives and found for the respondent, it is
interesting to note that proportionality was embraced as a completely different
ground of judicial review.

A clear criterion can thus be perceived in relation to punitive actions. The particular sanction chosen among the range of enforcement tools must be a proportionate response to non-compliance. The regulator is therefore required to achieve
effectively its desired outcome of compliance, deterrence or retribution by adopting
the least intrusive measure on that continuum of disciplinary actions if its action
is not to be condemned as disproportionate. Consequently severe decisions such as
licence revocation or suspension must be reserved for weightier matters, whereas
softer approaches such as civil penalties and warning letters should be applied to
less serious offences. This view is also consistent with the notion of 'responsive
regulation' which demands that enforcement techniques to correct market failure
be dependent on the gravity of the violation.[39]

Secondly, in this general context, the principle of proportionality provides that
when a vague term is interpreted, the regulator should adopt that specific meaning
which does least harm to individual rights or interests. This approach is remarkably in tune with the common law principle that legislation restricting freedom is
to be interpreted in the way that least restricts freedom. Moreover, William Bishop
identifies similar doctrines in different legal systems in Europe. He observes, for
example, that in analogous circumstances the principle of proportionality is used
by German and French law, but the latter designates it as part of the general principle of law that the liberty of the individual is to be respected by the state and
its organs. Thus, a more intense control of statutory interpretation is involved in
the sense that the decision-maker must show real benefits to offset the presumed
disadvantages of interfering with individual freedom.[40] In this manner, the proportionality approach draws on an understanding of likely legislative purpose and
perceptions about regulatory failure. As Sunstein points out, the fact that statutes
often fail because of excessive controls and overregulation should lead the judiciary
to generally assume that Parliament wants to avoid these problems and therefore
intends agencies to impose decisions after a balancing process.[41]

In practice, this view calls for consideration to be given to alternative meanings
of the term which are less restrictive or oppressive than others. This requirement
certainly narrows down the range of situations in which a court would uphold

---

[39] See Ayres, I. and Braithwaite, J., *Responsive Regulation: Transcending the deregulation debate*,
(Oxford: Oxford University Press, 1992); and Harlow, C. and Rawlings, R., *Law and Administration*,
3rd edn., Law in Context, (Cambridge: Cambridge University Press, 2009) 242–243. See also
Hawkins, Keith, *Law as Last Resort*, (Oxford: Oxford University Press, 2002) 41–47.
[40] Bishop, William, 'A Theory of Administrative Law' [1990] 19 *The Journal of Legal Studies*, 508.
[41] Sunstein, 'Interpreting Statutes in the Regulatory State' [1989] 103 *Harvard Law Review*, 487.

the regulator's interpretation of vague words because it involves a lower margin of appreciation to the decision-maker. If it is possible to interpret a rule in many ways the courts will choose the interpretation which is most proportionate to the legitimate aim pursued. In some cases, the application of this doctrine may also involve cost-benefit analysis. From this point of view, the essence of interpretive discretion would be to conceive the regulator, not as being told by the statute what to do, but rather as being told, first, to asses the costs and benefits of the available meanings and, second, to follow the course of action offering the highest net benefit.[42]

The analysis of the cited *South Yorkshire*[43] case will serve as an illustration. As seen above, this concerned the meaning of the statutory phrase 'a substantial part of the United Kingdom' for the purpose of section 64(3) of the Fair Trading Act 1973. In particular, the issue was whether some districts in the counties of South Yorkshire, Derby, and Nottingham may be described as a substantial part of the United Kingdom to the extent of at least one-quarter so as to trigger the jurisdiction of the Mergers and Monopolies Commission to investigate and report upon possible merger situations.

It is important to note that the statutory provisions governing mergers have traditionally been concerned with significant mergers. Since the Monopolies and Mergers Act 1965 this has been ensured, for example, by an assets test under sub-paragraph (b)(ii) which provided that the value of the assets taken over must exceed £5 million (now £30 million). Another example of this policy can be seen in the Fair Trading Act 1973, which abandoned and deleted the 'substantial part' test for the investigation of monopolies (it was substituted by the 'any part of the United Kingdom' test to improve investigations) but kept it for the purposes of a merger reference. Therefore, it is suggested that Parliament must have intended to empower the Commission only to investigate relevant merger situations in the context of its comparison with the United Kingdom as a whole, so as 'to ensure that the expensive, laborious and time-consuming mechanism of a merger reference is not set in motion if the effort is not worthwhile'.[44]

In the instant case, the area specified in the reference was roughly 1.65 per cent of the total area, and had a population of some 1.8 million, or 3.2 per cent of the total population of the United Kingdom. Moreover, the extent of the economic activity being investigated (i.e. the provision of local passenger bus services) within the reference area as a proportion of the same business within the United Kingdom as a whole was just 4.04 per cent. Based on the foregoing data it is plain that the reference area was something little by comparison with the whole so it could not qualify for the description of a 'substantial part of the United Kingdom'. However, the Commission concluded that the specified area may be within the scope of the provision by merely identifying and cataloguing its particular attributes. In particular, it was argued that the area includes Sheffield, the third largest metropolitan district in England on the basis of population, and has 'traditional industries

---

[42] Bishop, (as above n. 40), 509.
[43] *R v. Monopolies and Mergers Commission, ex p South Yorkshire Transport Ltd.* [1993] 1 All E.R. 289.
[44] See the judgment of Lord Mustill at the House of Lords.

based on mining and steel, a range of other manufacturing and service activities, significant academic and sports facilities, and parts of the Peak District favoured for recreation'. The authority therefore opted for an abstract meaning which, in practice, enabled it to investigate a merger in a small part of the United Kingdom as regards surface area, population and volume of the economic activity with which the reference is concerned. Consequently, there was clear disproportion between the language of the provision and the decision of the authority, a lack of consistency between the less restrictive purpose of the Fair Trading Act and the more interventionist approach adopted by the Commission.

However, the House of Lords upheld the decision of the commissioners on the ground that the court was entitled to substitute its own interpretation of vague terms for that of the regulator only if the construction was 'so aberrant that it cannot be classed as rational'. It seems fair to submit that the application of the principle of proportionality would have led the court to a different decision. The judiciary would have been obliged to take into account the relative proportions of the area by comparison with the United Kingdom as a whole. By applying this test to the present case, the court would have possibly concluded that section 64(3) does not empower the Commission to intervene in so small an area.

4. Conclusion

This chapter has argued that there are good reasons to hold that the proportionality-based test will have a broader influence on UK regulatory law, thereby requiring the judiciary to engage in a more intensive form of review even where European law does not apply.

In the first place, the general application of this approach can be rationalized properly against the background of the malleability of English law and its capacity to adapt to legal trends. So far as the balance of power between judges and regulators is concerned, it was noted that the incorporation of continental legal sources supplies the former with a clear signal that intensive review of the latter is necessary to uphold substantive values which are in play even in non-European contexts.

Secondly, a more pragmatic reason can be considered. The principle of proportionality prescribes a much more structured approach to regulatory decisions than the Wednesbury doctrine. In particular, it requires the court to examine the precise extent to which executive interference with rights is proportionate to the public aim being pursued, not merely the general reasonableness of the decision. The review is thus oriented towards ensuring a basic standard of good administration—the adequate choice of means—in a manner which enjoys greater clarity and rigour. Such formulation should therefore be preferred to the vagueness of the previous test.

The third argument relates to the commitment to equality before the law which lies at the core of the rule of law. The very idea that proportionality better captures the role of regulators and the scope of their powers to interfere with rights urges its adoption as a general standard of review in order to subject the content and impact of their decisions to the same level of scrutiny. Any attempt to apply a different approach to purely domestic cases on the mere ground that they are not ruled by European law would necessarily entail an arbitrary distinction which infringes the principle of justice that like cases should be treated alike.

Nevertheless, the application of the proportionality test to the domestic context may still be open to criticism on the ground that it is difficult to find expressly defined rights against which the proportionality of the regulatory decision could be measured. Although it is right to acknowledge this problem, it must be noted that the broader margin of discretion afforded to the decision-maker in such situations should not deter the court from applying the proportionality approach. Rather, what the judge should do here is to vary the degree of intensity with which the proportionality test must be applied.

7

Conclusion

1. Introduction

Although the debate regarding the intensity of judicial review in the commercial context engages a broad range of issues, it is, at root, concerned with one central question: *viz.* whether the courts should defer to regulatory determinations of law or fact. As is apparent from the discussion in the foregoing chapters, judges have traditionally operated under what can be referred to as the deferential model of supervision. In particular, this means that a high degree of finality should be accorded to the contested action in order to pay due regard to the decision-maker's special skills, experience and powers, which in turn facilitate the efficient resolution of complex issues within the specific area of practice. Thus, if it is found that the regulator has jurisdiction to act, his original determination is often given conclusive effect and is upheld.

Against this background, it has been the purpose of this work to provide a critical view of the orthodox approach in legal and practical terms, and to propose an alternative form of review which avoids its main shortcomings. Such evaluation stems in a substantial part from a wish to abandon the wide level of immunity which the lack of effective judicial control creates, and to acknowledge and give credit to the fundamental role which the rule of law should play in fashioning the important safeguards which ensure that market regulation is duly justified, and subject to adequate oversight.

Thus, the foregoing chapters have addressed the question of judicial deference towards economic authorities in relation to its conceptual and supposed normative foundations, as well as developing the most compelling arguments for the adoption of a more neutral and thorough form of inquiry which succeeds where the traditional approach fails by effectively requiring the regulator to legitimate interference with commercial interests in light of the principles of legality, legal certainty, and equality under the law. No attempt will be made here to summarize the specific conclusions reached in relation to those points. Instead, some of the broader themes which arise from this analysis will be addressed as a way of conclusion. The first important point which emerges concerns the need to remark on the existence of contextual factors which support the application of a stricter judicial scrutiny in the specific area of law.

2. General and Context-Sensitive Considerations

When reading the criticism of the orthodox doctrine and the rationales behind the approach proposed in this book, it becomes apparent that they are justified not only by reference to prevailing constitutional values but also to the specific context within which review is sought. While the former facilitate a rather general argument, that administrative reasoning and decisions must be subject to effective and impartial scrutiny, or at the very least that the courts should not accord great deference to decision-makers, the latter relates to the factual circumstances under which the regulatory power is exercised, and which therefore provides a series of further, specific, reasons for preferring a more searching model of judicial review.

In this sense, it is perhaps somewhat simplistic to suggest that abstract and general considerations of law are able to reflect and reinforce *all* those dynamics of judiciary-regulators relations which the proportional approach to market regulation presently describes. Rather, their function is to vouchsafe the legitimacy of the courts' neutral and effective intervention by exposing in especially clear terms the shortcomings of the deferential doctrine. What sort of statement is it to say, for example, that a great level of judicial cautiousness entails a partial and biased view of the matter in question which deprives the individual of his right to equal justice under the law and proper access to a court; or that such an approach amounts to a serious abdication of the judge's primary responsibility to protect private rights in particular and the legal order as a whole, thereby undermining incentives for good administration? They are, surely, principled means for requiring a fair and efficient review but which, unlike other kinds of arguments, cannot be regarded as specifically related to the area of commercial regulation.

In light of this, it becomes apparent that, in order to assert that a stricter form of judicial review is appropriate within the specific context at stake, some further rationales must be provided which rely on the principles and institutional constraints which are raised by the factual matrix in question. It is precisely this imperative of legitimating the standard of review by reference to issues of market regulation which dictates the necessity of identifying the context-sensitive arguments within the book. Six, in particular, stand out.

First, it is submitted that the proposed approach serves to reduce the evil effects of regulatory capture, as it ensures that the decision-maker is not simply using its discretion in the interest of the regulated. Secondly, by effectively assessing the decision in light of the regulatee's claims, it gives due recognition to its often high level of expertise and capacities to supply 'technical' alternative views to those of the agency. Thirdly, it achieves a good fit with Parliament's specific intention not to accept a high level of judicial deference in the business field. Fourthly, it serves to counteract the progressive diminution in the authority and efficacy of ministerial and parliamentary control over market regulators, thereby maintaining the constitutional balance of powers within the particular area of law. Fifthly, the stricter scrutiny is entirely consistent with the ongoing processes of liberalization and juridification in the economic sectors, which require meaningful judicial oversight of related decisions in order to protect the legal content of market relations and freedoms. Sixthly, it contributes to fair competition in the relevant field, as it prevents *ultra vires* decisions which favour certain undertakings to stand.

In consequence, it seems fair to conclude that there exist several specifically-related reasons for characterizing commercial regulation as a context which requires the exercise of a more intensive form of judicial review. They all look beyond the generalized tenets of the rule of law doctrine, either at the substantive or the procedural level, to justify an increased level of supervision in a range of particular situations where it would be neither satisfactory nor convincing for the courts to simply rely on the criteria and findings of the regulator. In this manner, the policy of control is effectuated in a way which combines both principles and fine-tuned, fact-bound analysis.

3. Less Damaging Solutions to the Problem of Judicial Intervention

Another important contention of this work is that acknowledgement of the need to avoid some of the shortcomings of the court's intervention *vis-à-vis* regulatory decisions should not lead inevitably to the denial of effective supervision or remedies. In most of the cases, such an approach would be wholly inappropriate and out of proportion, since it would fail to consider alternative means to deal with this issue without seriously affecting the applicant's interest in seeking review and protection. This book draws attention to five such possible responses, in a spirit of reconciliation between the competing values and principles at stake.

First, it appears that attempts to reduce the risk of regulatory ossification or fettering need not occur at the expense of simply discarding judicial review of policy changes, which in turn frustrates the legitimate expectations of those who relied on the prior norm. Considerations of legal certainty point towards a more satisfactory response which facilitates the implementation of policy choices *in actum* by providing transitional protection for the affected parties or the payment of compensation. Secondly, and relatedly, the introduction of these mechanisms would allow the court to exercise its remedial discretion in a manner which safeguards *all*, rather than just some, of the interests involved. Thirdly, it can be argued that proper consideration of the leave filter regulated in the Civil Procedure Rules, Part 54 provides a better solution to the problem of tactical litigation in the business field than the deferential approach, since it is a previous stage for the review process itself, and therefore incapable of precluding the subsequent assessment of meritorious claims. Fourthly, by replacing the agency's criteria with its own judgement against a backdrop of reports provided by independent experts, the court is able to overcome its technical knowledge deficit without undermining its quality control function. Fifthly, the proportional approach has the advantage of avoiding impermissible intrusion on the merits with no need to unduly reduce the intensity of judicial supervision, as it represents an intermediate position in the review spectrum which is exclusively concerned with the legality of the contested action.

Against the background of such developments, it becomes clear that it is possible to circumvent relevant difficulties that beset commercial judicial review in a manner which accords with, rather than ignores, the applicant's legitimate right to obtain a meaningful assessment of the legality of the impugned order. This precisely captures the view of the present book about the competing considerations involved in judicial review proceedings, in that it represents a valuable attempt to reconcile them in light of the relatively similar degree of importance that can be ascribed to the specific interests they seek to protect.

4. Time Factor and the Allegory of the Cave

Finally, it is necessary to bear in mind that free market regulation through technical rules is a relatively new phenomenon in the United Kingdom. As seen above, this process can be linked to the liberalization of trade regimes and the privatization of leading public utilities in the eighties, which have necessitated the creation of sophisticated regulatory structures headed by experts and especially skilled decision-makers. In the face of this phenomenon, it becomes readily apparent that the current reluctance of the judiciary over complex decisions is, to some extent, understandable: it may be conceived as a natural human reaction to something relatively new rather than a substantive and well justified principle of public law adjudication.

Thus, in the commercial context, the adoption of a more intensive form of review seems likely to be a function of the court's familiarity with the technical background of the disputes. Consequently, it appears that, so long as the judges are able to grasp the realities and complexities of the matter in question, the difficulties in controlling related orders will disappear. Evidence of this adjustment can already be seen in relation to decisions made in the context of disciplinary proceedings. Andrew Lidbetter, for instance, observes that in such cases, where the applicant may be regarded as being in a position akin to that of a defendant, the courts appear less reluctant to defer to the regulators on the basis, *inter alia*, that it is 'is a matter upon which the courts are particularly well qualified to rule and there is less need to consider the nature and abilities of the regulator conducting the proceedings'.[1]

Approaching the issue from this perspective, this author therefore envisages that,

as the body of case law increases the Courts will have the opportunity to refine both the principles governing judicial review in the specific company and commercial context and the application in that context of the general principles of judicial review.[2]

[1] Lidbetter, Andrew, 'Judicial Review in the Company and Commercial Context' [1995] 10 *Butterworths Journal of International Banking and Financial Law*, 68.
[2] Ibid.

Richard Gordon captures the same point when he remarks that as Lord Justice Bingham's 'uncharted minefield' becomes more familiar territory, 'the courts' reluctance to intervene too boldly in the affairs of the financial regulators will inevitably diminish'.[3]

In light of this, and taking into account recent attempts in English administrative law to translate important notions and concepts into vivid metaphors,[4] it may be said, with great respect, that the gradual process of knowledge experienced by the judges in the present field is comparable to that of the prisoner in the cave whose bonds are loosened and starts ascending to sunlight in Plato's famous allegory.[5] In particular, it appears that although the process may at first be frightening, so long as the learner acquires familiarity with the reality of things, he will eventually be able to handle them better. Thus, by way of conclusion, a helpful analogy may be drawn which illustrates what such judicial improvement is like in platonic, metaphorical terms.

First, judges will have pain in their eyes which will make them turn away to take in the objects of vision which they can see (reluctance), and which they will conceive to be in reality clearer than the things which are now being shown to them (intensive review).[6] But then the virtue of knowledge will be implanted by habit, exercise,[7] and effort.[8] Willingness is also necessary because,

just as the eye was unable to turn from darkness to light without the whole body, so too the instrument of knowledge can only by the movement of the whole soul be turned from the world of becoming into that of being, and learn by degrees to endure the sight of being, and of the brightest and best of being, or in other words, of the good.[9]

---

[3] Gordon, Richard, *Judicial Review: Law and Procedure*, 2nd ed., (London: Sweet & Maxwell, (1996) 254.

[4] The use of expressions such as 'fig leaves', 'fairy tale', 'golden metwand' and 'crooked cord' in the field of judicial review is particularly illuminating. See Forsyth, Christopher, 'Of Fig Leaves and Fairy Tales: The *Ultra Vires* Doctrine, the Sovereignty of Parliament and Judicial Review', in *Judicial Review and the Constitution*, Christopher Forsyth (ed.), (Oxford: Hart Publishing, 2000) 29–46; see also the book jacket explanation and the preface of *The Golden Metwand and the Crooked Cord*, Forsyth and Hare (eds.), (Oxford: Oxford University Press, 1998.

[5] Plato, one of the most inspired and influential philosophers in the Ancient Greece, wrote this dialogue about 360 B.C.E between Socrates and Glaucon, in which the former shows in a figure how far the human nature is enlightened or unenlightened. In particular, he illustrates the situation of people who ignore the reality of things through the image of prisoners living in an underground den from their childhood. These people have their legs and necks chained so that they cannot move, and can only see on the wall the shadow of different objects passed behind them. Thus, what they observe is only a poor image of 'real' things and events outside the cave. In these circumstances, if a prisoner were dragged out into the sunlight, there is little doubt that he would at first be overcome and hurt by its splendour, to the extent that he would try to escape and turn back to things which he could see distinctively. Soon afterwards, however, he would certainly come to have a genuine knowledge of those objects and see how far removed from reality he previously had been. The present image thus seems to represent Plato's idea that the ascent of the mind to the realm of reality, although difficult and arduous at the time, is the only way to act with wisdom, either in our own life or in matters of state. For general analysis see, for example, Melling, David, *Understanding Plato*, (Oxford: Oxford University Press, 1987) 109–111; and Rice, Daryl, *A Guide to Plato's Republic*, (Oxford: Oxford University Press, 1998) 79.

[6] Cf. Plato, *The Republic*, Book VII, 515e (Stephanus Numbers). Benjamin Jowett's translation in *The Republic*, (New York: Vintage Classics, 1991) 253–261.

[7] 518 e.   [8] 517 b.   [9] 518c–518d.

At the end, an intensive approach will be taken, and then, when they remembered their old habitation, do you not suppose that they would felicitate themselves on the change? Certainly, they would.[10]

However, in order to ensure this stance, some help from Parliament is also required. In practice, the legislator should turn to the difficulties of the adjudicatory process in order to improve methods and techniques of judicial review so that it is more capable of dealing with the complex and empirical problems surrounding decisions in the context of market regulation. Following Plato's allegory,

then, I said, the business of us who are the founders of the State will be to compel the best minds to attain that knowledge which we have already shown to be the greatest of all—they must continue to ascend until they arrive at the good; but when they have ascended and seen enough we must not allow them to do as they do now.[11]

---

[10] 516 c.   [11] 519c–519d.

Bibliography

1. BOOKS

Allan, T.R.S., *Constitutional Justice*, Oxford: Oxford University Press, 2001.

Allison, John, *A Continental Distinction in the Common Law*, Oxford: Oxford University Press, 1996.

Andenas, Mads and Fairgrieve, Duncan (eds.), *Judicial Review in International Perspective: Volume II*, Leiden: Kluwer Law International, 2000.

Anthony, Robert, *Unlegislated Compulsion: How Federal Agency Guidelines Threaten Your Liberty*, Cato Policy Analysis No. 312, Washington, D.C.: The Cato Institute, 1998.

Ayres, I. and Braithwaite, J., *Responsive Regulation: Transcending the deregulation debate*, Oxford: Oxford University Press, 1992.

Baldwin, Robert and Cave, Martin, *Understanding Regulation*, Oxford: Oxford University Press, 1999.

—— and McCrudden, Christopher, *Regulation and Public Law*, Law in Context, London: Weidenfeld & Nicholson, 1987.

Birks, P.H.B. (ed.), *The Frontiers of Liability, Vol. 1*, Oxford: Oxford University Press, 1994.

Black, Julia, Muchlinski, Peter and Walker, Paul (eds.), *Commercial Regulation and Judicial Review*, Oxford: Hart Publishing, 1998.

Blom-Cooper, Sir Louis QC (ed.), *Experts in the Civil Courts*, Oxford: Oxford University Press, 2006.

Bolick, Clint, *David's Hammer: the Case for an Activist Judiciary*, Washington D.C.: Cato Institute, 2007.

Bondy, Varda and Sunkin, Maurice, *The Dynamics of Judicial Review Litigation: The resolution of public law challenges before final hearing*, The Public Law Project, London, 2009.

Breyer, Stephen, *Economic Reasoning and Judicial Review*, AEI-Brookings Joint Center 2003 Distinguished Lecture, Washington D.C.: The AEI Press, 2004.

Cambridge Centre for Public Law, *Constitutional Reform in the United Kingdom: Practice and Principles*, Oxford: Hart Publishing, 1998.

Cane, Peter, *Administrative Law*, 4th edn., Oxford: Clarendon Law Series, 2004.

Cheffins, Brian R., *Company Law*, Oxford: Oxford University Press, 1997.

Collins, Laurence, *European Community Law in the United Kingdom*, 4th edn., London: Butterworths, 1990.

Craig, Paul, *EU Administrative Law*, Oxford: Oxford University Press, 2006.

——, *Administrative Law*, 6th edn., London: Sweet & Maxwell, 2008.

—— and Rawlings, Richard, *Law and Administration in Europe*, Oxford: Oxford University Press, 2003.

Department of Trade and Industry, London: *DTI*, 2005. *Company Law Implementation of the European Directive on Takeovers Bids. A consultative document*.

De Smith, Stanley A., Woolf, Sir Harry, Jowell, Jeffrey L. and Le Sueur, Andrew P., *De Smith, Woolf and Jowell's, Principles of Judicial Review*, London: Sweet & Maxwell, 1999.

Dicey, Albert V., *An Introduction to the Study of the Law of the Constitution*, London: Macmillan, 1885.

Dyzenhaus, David (ed.), *The Unity of Public Law*, Oxford: Hart Publishing, 2004.

Edley, Christopher, *Administrative Law: Rethinking Judicial Control of Bureaucracy*, New Haven: Yale University Press, 1990.

Elliott, Mark, *The Constitutional Foundations of Judicial Review*, Oxford: Hart Publishing, 2001.

Ellis, Evelyn (ed.), *The Principle of Proportionality in the Laws of Europe*, Oxford: Hart Publishing, 1999.

Emberland, Marius, *The Human Rights of Companies*, Oxford: Oxford University Press, 2006.

Engelman, Philip, *Commercial Judicial Review*, London: Sweet & Maxwell, 2001.

Feldman, David (ed.), *English Public Law*, Oxford: Oxford University Press, 2004.

Ferran, Eilís and Goodhart, C.A.E. (eds.), *Regulating Financial Services and Markets in the 21st Century*, Oxford: Hart Publishing, 2001.

Fordham, Michael, *Judicial Review Handbook*, 3rd edn., Oxford: Hart Publishing, 2001.

Forsyth, Christopher (ed.), *Judicial Review and the Constitution*, Oxford: Hart Publishing, 2000.

—— and Hare, I. (eds.), *The Golden Metwand and the Crooked Cord*, Oxford: Oxford University Press, 1998.

——, Elliott, M., Jhaveri, S., Scully-Hill, A. and Ramsden, M. (eds.), *Effective Judicial Review: A Cornerstone of Good Governance*, Oxford: Oxford University Press, 2010.

Foster, C.D., *Privatization, Public Ownership and the Regulation of Natural Monopoly*, Oxford: Blackwell, 1992.

Gordon, Richard, *Judicial Review: Law and Procedure*, 2nd edn., London: Sweet & Maxwell, 1996.

Goyder, Joanna and Albors-Llorens, Albertina, *Goyder's EC Competition Law*, 5th edn., Oxford: Oxford University Press, 2003.

Graham, Cosmo, *Is there a Crisis in Regulatory Accountability?*, Discussion paper, London: Chartered Institute of Public Finance and Accountancy, 1995.

——, *Regulating Public Utilities*, Oxford: Hart Publishing, 2000.

Jowell, Jeffrey and Oliver, Dawn, *The Changing Constitution*, Oxford: Oxford University Press, 1994.

Hadfield, Brigid (ed.), *Judicial Review: A thematic approach*, Dublin: Gill & Macmillan, 1995.

Hague, D.C., Mackenzie, W.J.M and Barker, Anthony P. (eds.), *Public Policy and Private Interests: The Institutions of Compromise*, London: Macmillan Press, 1975.

Hand, G.J. and McBride, Jeremy (eds.), *Droit Sans Frontières: Essay in Honour of L. Neville Brown*, Holdsworth Club, Birmingham, 1991.

Harlow, Carol and Rawlings, Richard, *Law and Administration*, 3rd edn., Law in Context, Cambridge: Cambridge University Press, 2009.

Hawkins, Keith, *Law as Last Resort*, Oxford: Oxford University Press, 2002.

Leyland, Peter and Woods, Terry (eds.), *Administrative Law Facing the Future: Old Constraints and New Horizons*, Oxford: Oxford University Press, 1997.

McCrudden, Christopher (ed.), *Regulation and Deregulation*, Oxford: Clarendon Press, 1999.

Melnick, R. Shep, *Regulation and the Courts: The Case of the Clean Air Act*, Washington: The Brookings Institution, 1983.

Melling, David, *Understanding Plato*, Oxford: Oxford University Press, 1987.

Ogus, A., *Regulation: Legal Form and Economic Theory*, Oxford: Clarendon Press, 1994.

Plato, *The Republic*, Benjamin Jowett (trans.); New York: Vintage Classics, 1991.

Prosser, Tony, *Law and Regulators*, Oxford: Clarendon Press, 1997.

Rabkin, Jeremy, *Judicial Compulsions: How Public Law Distorts Public Policy*, New York: Basic Books, 1989.

Raz, Joseph, *The Authority of Law*, Oxford: Oxford University Press, 1979.

Rice, Daryl, *A Guide to Plato's Republic*, Oxford: Oxford University Press, 1998.

Richardson, Genevra and Genn, Hazel (eds.), *Administrative Law and Government Action*, Oxford: Clarendon Press, 1994.

Schønberg, Soren, *Legitimate Expectations in Administrative Law*, Oxford: Oxford University Press, 2000.

Select Committee on Constitution of the House of Lords, *The Regulatory State: Ensuring its Accountability*, 6th Report of Session 2003–2004, 2004, available at <http://www.publications.parliament.uk/pa/ld200304/ldselect/ldconst/68/68.pdf>.

Smyth, Michael, *Business and the Human Rights Act 1998*, Bristol: Jordan Publishing, 2000.

Supperstone, Michael and Goudie, James, *Judicial Review*, 2nd edn., London: Butterworth & Co, 1997.

Taggart, Michael (ed.), *Judicial Review of Administrative Action in the 1980s*, New York: Oxford University Press, 1986.

Treasury Solicitor's Department, *The Judge Over Your Shoulder. A Guide to Judicial Review for UK Government Administrators*, Government Legal Service, 3rd edn., 2000.

Thomas, Robert, *Legitimate Expectations and Proportionality in Administrative Law*, Oxford: Hart Publishing, 2000.

——, *Administrative Law*, 10th edn., Oxford: Oxford University Press, 2009.

Turner, Lord Adair, *The Turner Review: A Regulatory Response to the Global Banking Crisis*, March 2009, available at <http://www.fsa.gov.uk/pubs/other/turner_review.pdf>.

Wade, William and Forsyth, Christopher, *Administrative Law*, 10th edn., Oxford: Oxford University Press, 2009.

Walden, Ian and Angel, John (eds.), *Telecommunications Law*, 1st edn., London: Blackstone Press, 2001.

Ward, Angela, *Individual Rights and Private Party Judicial Review in the EU*, Oxford European Community Law Library Series, Oxford: Oxford University Press, 2007.

Wilson, Geoffrey P. (ed.), *Frontiers of Legal Scholarship*, Chichester: Chancery Law Publishing, 1995.

Wood, Robert (ed.), *Remedial Law: When Courts Become Administrators*, Boston: University of Massachusetts Press, 1990.

2 ARTICLES

Alexander of Weedon, Lord Robert, 'Judicial Review and City Regulators' [1989] 52 *The Modern Law Review*, 640–648.

——, 'Takeovers: The Regulatory Scene' [1990] *Journal of Business Law*, 203–216.

Allan, Trevor, 'Doctrine and Theory in Administrative Law: An Elusive Quest for the Limits of Jurisdiction' [2003] *Public Law*, 429–454.

——, 'Legislative Supremacy and Legislative Intention: Interpretation, Meaning and Authority' [2004] 63 *Cambridge Law Journal*, 85.

——, 'Human Rights and Judicial Review: A Critique of Due Deference' [2006] 65(3) *Cambridge Law Journal*, 671–695.

Allison, John, 'The Procedural Reason for Judicial Restraint' [1994] *Public Law*, 452–473.

Amos, Merris, 'Damages for breach of the Human Rights Act 1998' [1999] 178 *European Human Rights Law Review*, 178–194.

Andenas, Mads, 'European Take-over Regulation and the City Code' [1996] 17(5) *Company Lawyer*, 150–152.

Anthony, Robert, 'Which Agency Interpretations should get Judicial Deference: A Preliminary Inquiry' [1998] 40(1) *Administrative Law Review*, 121–137.

Austin, John, 'Varieties of Overruling and Judicial Law-Making; Prospective Overruling in a Comparative Perspective' [1978] 23 *The Judicial Review*, 33–64.

Bamforth, Nicholas, 'The scope of judicial review: still uncertain' [1993] *Public Law*, 239–248.

——, 'Significant Articles on the Scope of Judicial Review' [1996] 1(3) *Judicial Review*, 167–169.

——, 'The Application of the Human Rights Act 1998 to Public Authorities and Private Bodies' [1999] 58(1) *Cambridge Law Journal*, 159–170.

——, 'The True Horizontal Effect of the Human Rights Act 1998' [2001] 117 *The Law Quarterly Review*, 34–41.

Barendt, Eric, 'Grievances, Remedies and the State' [1987] 7(1) *Oxford Journal of Legal Studies*, 125–135.

Beatson, Jack, 'The Scope of Judicial Review for Error of Law' [1984] 4(1) *Oxford Journal of Legal Studies*, 22–45.

Beloff, Michael, 'Judicial Review–2001: A Prophetic Odyssey' [1995] 58(2) *Modern Law Review*, 143.

Bingham, Sir Thomas, 'The Rule of Law' [2007] 66(1) *Cambridge Law Journal*, 67–85.

——, 'Should public law remedies be discretionary?' [1991] *Public Law*, 64–75.

Bishop, William, 'A Theory of Administrative Law' [1990] 19 *Journal of Legal Studies*, 489–530.

Black, Julia, 'Which Arrow?: Rule Type and Regulatory Policy' [1995] *Public Law*, 94–117.

——, 'Constitutionalising Self-regulation' [1996] 59(1) *Modern Law Review*, 24–55.

——, 'Tensions in the regulatory state' [2007] *Public Law*, 58–73.

Blom-Cooper, Louis, 'Lawyers and Public Administrators: Separate and Unequal' [1984] *Public Law*, 215–235.

Boyron, Sophie, 'Proportionality in English Administrative Law: A Faulty Translation?' [1992] 12(2) *Oxford Journal of Legal Studies*, 237–264.

Boynton, Sir John, 'Judicial Review of Administrative Decisions—A Background Paper' [1986] 64 *Public Administration*, 147–161.

Bradley, A.W., 'The Judge Over Your Shoulder' [1987] *Public Law*, 485–488.

——, 'Protecting Government Decisions from Legal Challenges' [1998] *Public Law*, 1–4.

Bratza, Nicolas, 'The Implications of the Human Rights Act 1998 for Commercial Practice' [2000] 1 *European Human Rights Law Review*, 1–13.

Breyer, Stephen, 'Judicial Review of Questions of Law and Policy' [1986] 38 *Administrative Law Review*, 363–398.

Brewer, Scott, 'Scientific Expert Testimony and Intellectual Due Process' (1997–1998) 107 *Yale Law Journal*, 1535–1681.

Bruff, Harold H., 'Legislative Formality, Administrative Rationality' [1984] 63(2) *Texas Law Review*, 207–250.

Cane, Peter, 'Self-Regulation and Judicial Review' [1987] 6 *Civil Justice Quarterly*, 324–347.

Chayes, Abram, 'The Role of the Judge in Public Law Litigation' [1976] 89(7) *Harvard Law Review*, 1281–1316.

Clayton, Richard, 'Judicial deference and "democratic dialogue": the legitimacy of judicial intervention under the Human Rights Act 1998' [2004] *Public Law*, 33–47.

——, 'The Limits of What's "Possible": Statutory Construction under the Human Rights Act' [2005] 5 *European Human Rights Law Review*, 559–566.

——, 'Principles for Judicial Deference' [2006] 11(2) *Judicial Review*, 109–135.

Cohn, Margit, 'Judicial review of non-statutory executive powers after Bancoult: a unified anxious model' [2009] *Public Law*, 260–286.

Cooke, Robin, 'The Road Ahead for the Common Law' [2004] 53(2) *International and Comparative Law Quarterly*, 273–284.

Craig, Paul, 'Compensation in Public Law' [1980] 96 *The Law Quarterly Review*, 413–455.

——, 'Constitution, Property and Regulation' [1991] *Public Law*, 538–554.

——, 'Formal and substantive conceptions of the Rule of Law: An analytical framework' [1997] *Public Law*, 467–487.

——, 'Substantive Legitimate Expectations in Domestic and Community Law' [1996] 55(2) *Cambridge Law Journal*, 289–312.

——, 'The Courts, The Human Rights Act and Judicial Review' [2001] 117 *Law Quarterly Review*, 589–603.

——, 'The Human Rights Act, Article 6 and Procedural Rights' [2003] *Public Law*, 753–773.

Cross, Frank, 'The Judiciary and Public Choice' [1999] 50(2) *Hastings Law Journal*, 355–382.

Cross, Thomas, 'When "To Star" is "To Continue": Statutory Interpretation in the *Brian Haw* Case' [2007] 12(2) *Judicial Review*, 126–133.

David, Kenneth, 'An Approach to Problems of Evidence in the Administrative Process' [1942] 55 *Harvard Law Review*, 364–402.

De Búrca, Gráinne, 'The Principle of Proportionality and its Application in EC Law' [1993] 13 *Yearbook of European Law*, 105–150.

DeLeon, Linda, 'Accountability in a Reinvented Government' [1998] 76 *Public Administration*, 539–558.

DeLong, James V., 'The New Wine for a New Bottle: Judicial Review in the Regulatory State' [1986] 72 *Virginia Law Review*, 339–445.

Demetriou, Marie and Houseman, Stephen, 'Review for Error of Fact – A Brief Guide' [1997] 2(1) *Judicial Review*, 27–32.

Diver, Colin, 'Policymaking Paradigms in Administrative Law' [1981] 95(2) *Harvard Law Review*, 393–435.

Drewry, Gavin, 'Public Lawyers and Public Administrators: Prospects for an Alliance' [1986] 64 *Public Administration*, 173–188.

Dyzenhaus, David, 'Formalism's Hollow Victory' [2002] 4 *New Zealand Law Review*, 525–556.

Easterbrook, Frank, 'Foreword: The Court and the Economic System' [1984] 98 *Harvard Law Review*, 4–60.

——, 'Legal Interpretation and the Power of the Judiciary' [1984] 7 *Harvard Journal of Law and Public Policy*, 87–99.

Edwards, Richard, 'Judicial Deference under the Human Rights Act' [2002] 65 *The Modern Law Review*, 859–883.

Elliott, Mark, 'Scrutiny of Executive Decisions under the Human Rights Act 1998: Exactly How 'Anxious'?' [2001] 6(3) *Judicial Review*, 166–176.

——, 'The Human Rights Act 1998 and the Standard of Substantive Review' [2001] 60(2) *Cambridge Law Journal*, 301–336.

——, 'The HRA 1998 and the Standard of Substantive Review' [2002] 7(2) *Judicial Review*, 97–109.

——, 'Unlawful Representations, Legitimate Expectations and Estoppel in Public Law' [2003] 8(2) *Judicial Review*, 71–80.

——, 'Legitimate Expectations and Unlawful Representations' [2004] 63(2) *Cambridge Law Journal*, 261–264.

——, 'Legitimate Expectations and the Search for Principle: Reflections on *Abdi & Nadarajah*' [2006] 11(4) *Judicial Review*, 281–288.

——, 'Legitimate Expectations: Procedure, Substance, Policy and Proportionality' [2006] 65(2) *Cambridge Law Journal*, 254–256.

Epstein, Richard A., 'The Pitfalls of Interpretation' [1984] 7 *Harvard Journal of Law and Public Policy*, 101–108.

Errera, Roger, 'Changes in Judicial Review: An Outsider's Reflections' [1986] 64 *Public Administration*, 189–195.

Ewing, Keith, 'The Futility of the Human Rights Act' [2004] *Public Law*, 829–852.

—— and Gearty, Conor, 'Rocky Foundations for Labour's New Rights' [1997] 2 *European Human Rights Law Review*, 146–151.

Fairgrieve, Duncan, 'The Human Rights Act 1998, Damages and Tort Law' [2001] *Public Law*, 695–716.

Farina, Cynthia, 'Statutory Interpretation and the Balance of Power in the Administrative State' [1989] 89 *Columbia Law Review*, 452–528.

Fiss, Owen, 'Foreword: The Forms of Justice' [1979] 93 *Harvard Law Review*, 1–58.

Fordham, Michael, 'Reparation for Maladministration: Public Law's Final Frontier' [2003] 8(2) *Judicial Review*, 104–108.

—— and De la Mare, Thomas, 'Anxious Scrutiny, The Principle of Legality and the Human Rights Act' [2000] 5(1) *Judicial Review*, 40–51.

Forsyth, Christopher, 'The Scope of Judicial Review: Public Duty not Source of Power' [1987] *Public Law*, 356–367.

——, 'Wednesbury protection of Substantive Legitimate Expectations' [1997] *Public Law*, 375–384.

——, 'Article 6(1) of The European Convention and The Curative Powers of Judicial Review' [2001] 60(3) *Cambridge Law Journal*, 449–452.

——, 'Procedural Justice in Administrative Proceedings and Article 6(1) of the European Convention' [2003] 62(2) *Cambridge Law Journal*, 244–247.

——, 'Administrative Decision-Makers and Compliance with Article 6(1): The limits of the Curative Principle' [2007] 66(3) *Cambridge Law Journal*, 487–490.

Freeman, M.D.A., 'Standards of Adjudication, Judicial Law-Making and Prospective Overruling' [1973] *Current Legal Problems*, 166–207.

Freedman, James, 'Expertise and the Administrative Process' [1976] 28(3) *Administrative Law Review*, 363–378.

Friedmann, Wolfgang, 'Limits of Judicial Lawmaking and Prospective Overruling' [1966] 29(6) *Modern Law Review*, 593–607.

Fuller, Lon L., 'The Forms and Limits of Adjudication' [1978] 92 *Harvard Law Review*, 553–409.

Garland, Merrick B., 'Deregulation and Judicial Review' [1985] 98(3) *Harvard Law Review*, 505–591.

Gerwin, Leslie, 'The Deference Dilemma: Judicial Responses to the Great Legislative Power Giveaway' [1987] 14 *Hastings Constitutional Law Quarterly*, 289–393.

Gieve, John, 'The Financial Cycle and the UK Economy', speech given at the London Stock Exchange, 18 July 2008, available at: <http://www.bankofengland.co.uk/publications/speeches/2008/speech353.pdf>.

Graham, Cosmo, 'Judicial Review and The Regulators' [1997] 8(4) *Utilities Law Review*, 107–108.

Grant, Malcolm, 'Human Rights and Due Process in Planning' [2000] *Journal of Planning & Environmental Law*, 1215–1225.

Henderson, Andrew, 'Brandeis Briefs and the Proof of Legislative Facts in Proceedings under the Human Rights Act 1998' [1998] *Public Law*, 563–571.

——, 'Judicial Review and the Financial Services and Markets Act 2000' [2001] 6(4) *Judicial Review*, 255–261.

Hilson, Chris, 'Judicial Review, Policies and the Fettering of Discretion' [2002] *Public Law*, 111–129.

Hoffmann, Lord L.H., 'A sense of proportion' [1997] 32 *Irish Jurist*, 58.

Hopper, Martyn, 'Financial Services Regulation—Illegality' [1998] 3(1) *Judicial Review*, 40–44.

Hunt, Murray, 'The "Horizontal Effect" of the Human Rights Act' [1998] 3(1) *Public Law*, 423–443.

Irvine of Lairg, Lord Alexander Andrew Mackay, 'Judges and Decision-Makers: The Theory and Practice of *Wednesbury* Review' [1996] *Public Law*, 59–78.

——, 'The Development of Human Rights in Britain under an Incorporated Convention on Human Rights' [1998] *Public Law*, 221–236.

——, 'The Impact of the Human Rights Act: Parliament, the Courts and the Executive' [2003] *Public Law*, 308–325.

Jones, Timothy H., 'Mistake of Fact in Administrative Law' [1990] *Public Law*, 507–526.

Jowell, Jeffrey, 'The Takeover Panel: Autonomy, Flexibility and Legality' [1991] *Public Law*, 149–156.

——, 'Is Proportionality an Alien Concept?' [1996] 2(3) *European Public Law*, 401–411.

——, 'Beyond the Rule of Law: Towards Constitutional Judicial Review' [2000] *Public Law*, 671–683.

——, 'Judicial deference: servility, civility or institutional capacity?' [2003] *Public Law*, 592–601.

Kavanagh, Aileen, 'The Role of Parliamentary Intention under the Human Rights Act 1998' [2006] 26(1) *Oxford Journal of Legal Studies*, 179–206.

Kennelly, Brian, 'Judicial Review and the Competition Appeal Tribunal' [2006] 11(2) *Judicial Review*, 160–170.

Kent, Michael, 'Widening the Scope of Review for Error of Fact' [1999] 4(4) *Judicial Review*, 239–243.

Kerry, Sir Michael, 'Administrative Law and Judicial Review—The Practical Effects of Developments over the Last 25 Years on Administration in Central Government' [1986] 64 *Public Administration*, 163–172.

Klug, Francesca, 'Judicial Deference Under the Human Rights Act 1998' [2003] 2 *European Human Rights Law Review*, 125–133.

Knight, Christopher, 'Proportionality, the Decision-Maker and the House of Lords' [2007] 12(4) *Judicial Review*, 221–227.

Laws, Sir John, 'The Constitution: Morals and Rights' [1996] *Public Law*, 622.

Lee, Simon, 'Judicial discretion in controlling administrative discretion' [1987] 104 *Law Quarterly Review*, 166–168.

Legere, Edite, '*Locus Standi* and the Public Interest: A Hotchpotch of Legal Principles' [2005] 10(2) *Judicial Review*, 128–134.

Leigh, Ian, 'Bias, necessity and the Convention' [2002] *Public Law*, 407–414.

——, 'Taking Rights Proportionately: Judicial Review, the Human Rights Act and Strasbourg' [2002] *Public Law*, 265–287.

Lester of Herne Hill, Lord Anthony, 'The Art of possible: interpreting statutes under the Human Rights Act' [1998] 6 *European Human Rights Law Review*.

Levin, Ronald, 'Administrative Discretion, Judicial Review, and the Gloomy World of Judge Smith' [1986] 2 *Duke Law Journal*, 258–275.

——, 'Understanding Unreviewability in Administrative Law' [1990] 74 *Minnesota Law Review*, 689–781.

Lewis, Clive, 'Retrospective and Prospective Rulings in Administrative Law' [1988] *Public Law*, 78–105.

Lidbetter, Andrew, 'Judicial Control of Financial Services Legislation' [1995] *Journal of Business Law*, 590–596.

——, 'Judicial Review in the Company and Commercial Context' [1995] 10 *Butterworths Journal of International Banking and Financial Law*, 62–70.

——, 'Privatised Utilities and Judicial Review' [1996] 1(4) *Judicial Review*, 249–251.

——, 'Delay in Commercial JR' [1996] 1(4) *Judicial Review*, 51–53.

——, 'Commercial Judicial Review: Essential Cases' [1999] 4(4) *Judicial Review*, 275–281.

Loughlin, Martin, 'Innovation Financing in Local Government: The limits of Legal Instrumentalism—Part 2' [1991] *Public Law,* 590.

Loveland, Ian, 'The compatibility of the land use planning system with Article 6 of the European Convention on Human Rights' [2001], *Journal of Planning & Environment Law*, 535–547.

——, 'Does homelessness decision making engage Article 6(1) of The European Convention on Human Rights' [2003], 2 *European Human Rights Law Review*, 176–204.

Majone, G., 'The rise of the Regulatory State in Europe' [1994] 17 *West European Politics*, 77–101.

Manning, John, 'Constitutional Structure and Judicial Deference to Agency Interpretations of Agency Rules' [1996] 96 *Columbia Law Review*, 612–696.

Marsden, Christopher, 'Judicial Review of Channel 5 TV Licence Award: ITC Exercises Model Care' [1996] *Nottingham Law Journal*, 86–91.

Marston, Geoffrey, 'The United Kingdom's Part in the Preparation of the European Convention on Human Rights' [1993] 42 *International and Comparative Law Quarterly*, 796–826.

Mason, Keith, 'Prospective Overruling' [1989] 67 *The Australian Law Journal*, 526–529.

McGarity, Thomas, 'Some Thoughts on "Deossifying" the Rulemaking Process' [1992] 41 *Duke Law Journal*, 1385–1462.

McGowan, Carl, 'A Reply to Judicialization' [1986] 2 *Duke Law Journal*, 217–257.

McHarg, Aileen, 'Regulation as a private law function?' [1995] *Public Law*, 539–550.

——, 'A Duty to be Consistent? *R. v. Director General of Electricity Supply, ex p. ScottishPower plc*' [1998] 61 *The Modern Law Review*, 93–101.

McKnight, Elizabeth, 'R. v. The Director General of Electricity Supply ex. p. Scottish Power Plc' [1997] 8(4) *Utilities Law Review*, 126–132.

Merrill, Thomas, 'Judicial deference to Executive Precedent' (1991–1992) 101 *Yale Law Journal*, 969–1041.

Mikba, The Honorable Abner J., 'Speech: How Should the Courts Treat Administrative Agencies?' (1986–1987) 36 *The American University Law Review*, 1–9.

Miller, Geoffrey, 'Independent Agencies' [1986] *The Supreme Court Review*, 41–97.

Morse, G.K., 'The City Code on Take-overs and Mergers—Self-regulation or Self-protection?' [1991] *Journal of Business Law*, 509–524.

Mullen, David, 'Judicial Deference to Executive Decision–Making: Evolving Concepts of Responsibility' [1993–1994] 19 *Queen's Law Journal*, 137–178.

Nash, M. and Furse, S., 'Companies Human Rights' [1995] *Business Law Review*, 248–250.

Nicol, Andrew G. L., 'Prospective Overruling: A New Device for English Courts?' [1976] 39 *The Modern Law Review*, 542–560.

O'Brien, David, 'Marbury, the APA and Science Policy Disputes: the Alluring and Elusive Judicial/Administrative Partnership' [1984] 7(2) *Harvard Journal of Law and Public Policy*, 443–481.

Oliver, Dawn, 'Law and Politics and Public Accountability. The Search for a New Equilibrium' [1994] *Public Law*, 238–253.

——, 'The Judge Over Your Shoulder—Mark II' [1994] *Public Law*, 514–515.

Page, Alan, 'Self–regulation: The Constitutional Dimension' [1986] 49(2) *The Modern Law Review*, 141–167.

Pannick, David, 'Principles of Interpretation of Convention Rights and the Human Rights Act and the Discretionary Area of Judgement' [1998] *Public Law*, 545–551.

——, 'Commercial Judicial Review and the Human Rights Act 1998' [1999] *Judicial Review*, 177–181.

Perry, Michael J., 'Judicial Activism' [1984] 7 *Harvard Journal of Law and Public Policy*, 69–75.

Peters, Aulana, 'Independent Agencies: Government's Scourage or Salvation?' [1988] 2(3) *Duke Law Journal*, 286–296.

Phillips, Stephen, 'The Courts v. the Executive: Old Battles on New Battlegrounds' [1996] 1 *European Human Rights Law Review*, 45–51.

Pierce, Richard, 'Chevron and its Aftermath: Judicial Review of Agency Interpretations of Statutory Provisions' [1988] 41 *Vanderbilt Law Review*, 301–314.

——, 'Seven Ways to Deossify Agency Rulemaking' [1995] 47 *Administrative Law Review*, 59–98.

——, 'The Choice between Adjudicating and Rulemaking for Formulating and Implementing Energy Policy' (1979–1980) 31 *The Hastings Law Journal*, 1–102.

—— and Shapiro, Sidney, 'Political and Judicial Review of Agency Action' [1981] 59(7) *Texas Law Review*, 1175–1222.

Poustie, Mark, 'The Rule of Law or The Rule of Lawyers? Alconbury, Article 6(1) and The Role of Courts in Administrative Decision–Making' [2001] 6 *European Human Rights Law Review*, 657–676.

Prete, Luca and Nucara, Alessandro, 'Standard of Proof and Scope of Judicial Review in EC Merger Cases: Everything clear after Tetra Laval' [2005] 26(12) *European Competition Law Review*, 692.

Rawlings, Harlow, 'Judicial Review and the Control of Government' [1986] 64 *Public Administration*, 135–145.

Richardson, Genevra and Sunkin, Maurice, 'Judicial Review: Questions of Impact' [1996] *Public Law*, 79–103.

Rivers, Julian, 'Proportionality and Variable Intensity of Review' [2006] 65(1) *Cambridge Law Journal*, 174–207.

Romero, Alejandro, 'La Fundamentación de la Sentencia como elemento del debido proceso' [2006] in A.F. Vöhringer, *Sentenceias destacadas 2005: una mirada desde la perspectiva de las políticas públicas*, Santiago: Instiuto Liberatad Desarrollo.

Sales, Philip, 'The Civil Limb of ECHR, Article 6' [2005] 10(1) *Judicial Review*, 52–65.

—— and Hopper, Martyn, 'Proportionality and the form of law' [2003] *Law Quarterly Review*, 426–454.

Saunders, Kevin, 'Agency Interpretations and Judicial Review: A search for limitations on the controlling effect given agency statutory constructions' [1988] 30 *Arizona Law Review*, 769–800.

Scalia, Antonin, 'Judicial Deference to Administrative Interpretations of Law' [1989] 3 *Duke Law Journal*, 511–521.

Scatena, Patrice C., 'Deference to Discretion: Scalia's Impact on Judicial Review of Agency Action in An Era of Deregulation' [1987] 38 *The Hastings Law Journal*, 1223–1260.

Schuck, Peter H. and Elliott, E. Donald, 'To the Chevron Station: An Empirical Study of Federal Administrative Law' [1990] 5 *Duke Law Journal*, 984–1061.

Schwartz, Louis B., 'Legal Restriction of Competition in the Regulated Industries: An Application of Judicial Responsibility' [1954] 67 *Harvard Law Review*, 436–475.

Scott, Colin, 'Anti-Competitive Conduct, Licence Modification and Judicial Review in the Telecommunications Sector' [1997] 8(4) *Utilities Law Review*, 120–122.

——, 'Regulatory Discretion in the Licence Modifications: The Scottish Power Case' [1997] *Public Law*, 400–409.

Shapiro, Sidney A. and Levy, Richard E., 'Heightened Scrutiny and the Fourth Branch: Separation of Powers and the Requirement of Adequate Reasons for Agency Decisions' [1987] 3 *Duke Law Journal*, 387–440.

Sharpston, Eleanor, 'Legitimate Expectations and Economic Reality' [1990] 15 *European Law Review*, 103–160.

Smith, Loren A., 'Judicial Review of Administrative Decisions' [1984] 7(1) *Harvard Journal of Law and Public Policy*, 61–67.

——, 'Judicialization: The Twilight of Administrative Law' [1985] 2 *Duke Law Journal*, 427–466.

Solove, Daniel, 'The Darkest Domain: Deference, Judicial Review, and the Bill of Rights' [1999] 84 *Iowa Law Review*, 941–392.

Starr, Sunstein, Willard and Morrison, 'Judicial Review of Administrative Action in a Conservative Era' [1987] 39(3) *Administrative Law Review*, 353–398.

Steele, Iain, 'Public Law Liability—The Human Rights Act and Beyond' [2005] 64(3) *Cambridge Law Journal*, 8–11.

——, 'Substantive Legitimate Expectations: Striking the Right Balance' [2005] 121 *Law Quarterly Review*, 300–328.

Stewart, R.B., 'The Reformation of Administrative Law' [1975] 88 *Harvard Law Review*, 1667–1813.

Steyn, Karen, 'Consistency—A Principle of Public Law?' [1997] 2(1) *Judicial Review*, 22–26.

Steyn, Lord Johan, 'Deference: A Tangled Story' [2005] *Public Law*, 346–359.

Strauss, Peter L., 'The Place of Agencies in Government: Separation of Powers and the Fourth Branch' [1984] 84(3) *Columbia Law Review*, 573–669.

Sunstein, Cass, 'Deregulation and the Hard-Look Doctrine' [1983] *The Supreme Court Review*, 177–213.

——, 'In Defense of the Hard Look: Judicial Activism and Administrative Law' [1984] 7(1) *Harvard Journal of Law and Public Policy*, 51–59.

——, 'Factions, Self-Interest, and the APA: Four Lessons since 1946' [1986] 72 *Virginia Law Review*, 271–296.

——, 'Constitutionalism after the New Deal' [1987] 101 *Harvard Law Review*, 421–510.

——, 'Interpreting Statutes in the Regulatory State' [1989] 103 *Harvard Law Review*, 405–508.

——, 'Law and Administration after Chevron' [1990] 90 *Columbia Law Review*, 2071–2120.

Supperstone, Michael and Coppel, Jason, 'Judicial Review after the Human Rights Act' [1999] 3 *European Human Rights Law Review*, 301–329.

Swift, John, 'Judicial Control of Competition Decisions in the UK and EU', Competition Commission Autumn Lecture, September 2004, available at <http://www.competition -commission.org.uk/our_role/cc_lectures/judicial_control_210904_swift.pdf>.

Taggart, Michael, 'Corporatisation, Privatisation and Public Law' [1991] 2 *Public Law Review*, 77–108.

——, 'Corporatisation, Contracting and the Courts' [1994] 3 *Public Law*, 351–358.

——, 'Proportionality, Deference, Wednesbury' [2008] 3 *New Zealand Law Review*, 423–481.

Tolley, Michael C., 'Judicial Review of Agency Interpretation of Statutes: Deference Doctrines in Comparative Perspective' [2003] 31(3) *The Policy Studies Journal*, 421–439.

Tridimas, Takis, 'Self-regulation and Investor Protection in the United Kingdom: The Take-over Panel and the Market for Corporate Control' [1991] 10 *Civil Justice Quarterly*, 24–43.

Vesterdorf, Bo, 'Standard of Proof in Merger Cases: Reflections in the Light of Recent Case Law of the Community Courts' [2005] 1 *European Competition Journal*, 3.

Vining, Joseph, 'Authority and Responsibility: The Jurisprudence of Deference' [1991] 43 *Administrative Law Review*, 135–146.

Vocino, Thomas, 'American Regulatory Policy: Factors Affecting Trends Over the Past Century' [2003] 31(3) *The Policy Studies Journal*, 441–450.

Wade, William, 'Horizons of Horizontality' [2002] 116 *The Law Quarterly Review*, 217–224.

Wald, Patricia, 'Judicial Review of Economic Analyses' (1983–1984) 1 *Yale Journal on Regulation*, 43–62.

——, 'Regulation at Risk: Are Courts Part of the Solution of Most of the Problems?' [1994] 67 *Southern California Law Review*, 621–657.

Werhan, Keith, 'The Neoclassical Revival in Administrative Law' [1992] *Administrative Law Review*, 567–627.

Williams, Susanah, 'The Human Rights Act 1998—Caveat Business?' [2000] 21 *Business Law Review*, 190–193.

Woehrling, Jean-Marie, 'Judicial Control of Public Authorities in Europe: Progressive Construction of a Common Model' [2005] 10(4) *Judicial Review*, 311–325.

Woolf, Harry, 'Judicial Review—The Tensions Between the Executive and the Judiciary' [1998] 114 *The Law Quarterly Review*, 579–593.

Wong, Garreth, 'Towards the Nutcracker Principle: Reconsidering the Objections to Proportionality' [2000] *Public Law*, 92–109.

Woodward, David R. and Levin, Ronald M., 'In Defense of Deference: Judicial Review of Agency Action' [1979] 31 *Administrative Law Review*, 329–344.

Woolf, Lord Harry, 'Droit Public—English Style' [1995] *Public Law*, 57–71.

——, 'Judicial Review—The Tensions between the Executive and the Judiciary' [1998] 114 *Law Quarterly Review*, 579–593.

——, 'The Rule of Law and a Change in the Constitution' [2004] 63(2) *Cambridge Law Journal*, 317–329.

Woolhandler, Ann, 'Judicial Deference to Administrative Action—A Revisionist History' [1991] 43 *Administrative Law Review*, 197–251.

Young, Alison, 'Judicial sovereignty and the Human Rights Act 1998' [2002] 61(1) *Cambridge Law Journal*, 53–65.

——, 'Ghaidan v Godin-Mendoza: avoiding the deference trap' [2005] 23 *Public Law*, 23–34.

——, 'In Defence of Due Deference' [2009] 72(4) *The Modern Law Review*, 554–580.

Index